THE FAMILY AND PUBLIC POLICY

Frank F. Furstenberg, Jr., and Andrew J. Cherlin

General Editors

The Two Sexes

GROWING UP APART, COMING TOGETHER

Eleanor E. Maccoby

The Belknap Press of
Harvard University Press
Cambridge, Massachusetts
London, England

First Harvard University Press paperback edition, 1999

Library of Congress Cataloging-in-Publication Data

Maccoby, Eleanor E., 1917–
The two sexes : growing up apart, coming together / Eleanor E. Maccoby.
p.   cm. — (Family and public policy)
Includes bibliographical references and index.
ISBN 0-674-91481-3 (cloth)
ISBN 0-674-91482-1 (pbk.)
1. Sex differences (Psychology).   2. Gender identity.
3. Man-woman relationships.   I. Title.   II. Series.
BF692.2.M33   1998
155.3′3—DC21   97-30594

Contents

Preface

This book has had a long gestation period. Two earlier books (*The Development of Sex Differences*, 1966, and *The Psychology of Sex Differences*, 1974) have provided a foundation of a kind, but the point of view in this book diverges considerably from that of those earlier writings. The focus is no longer on sex differences, in the sense of comparisons between males as a group and females as a group on a list of attributes. Rather, this book is concerned with the way people interact with people of their own sex and people of the other sex at different points of the life cycle and in different contexts.

In the process of writing, I have had helpful comments on early drafts of chapters, suggestions for useful source materials, and provocative conversations about gender issues with more people than I can possibly acknowledge. I have given talks on gender differentiation at a number of universities, and at each one have had searching discussions with faculty and graduate students that have called for rethinking some of the issues discussed in this book. My especial thanks go to Andrew Cherlin, one of the series editors for Harvard University Press, who has given me feedback on successive versions of each chapter and valuable advice on how to organize major segments of material. Laura Carstensen has been a valued consultant on the book throughout, and helped in the initial drafting of the chapter on heterosexual relationships. Frank Furstenberg, the other series editor, has given me consistent encouragement and many valuable suggestions concerning source materials and interpretations of data. Campbell Leaper also provided detailed feedback on the manuscript. The following people have provided me with reference materials and helped me to clarify specific points: Katherine Barnard, Jay Belsky, David Buss, Linda Carli, Leda Cosmides, Martin Daly, Kay Deaux, Beverly Fagot, Shirley Feldman, Anne Fernald, Kate Funder, Jean Berko Gleason, John Gottman, Megan Gunnar, Susan Hanson, Elizabeth Hansot, Jerry Jacobs, Grazyna Kochanska, Seymour Levine, Zella Luria, Howard Markman, Hazel Markus, Kim Powlishta, Harriet Presser, Martha Putallaz, Lisa Serbin, Roger Shepard, Myra Strober, Steven Suomi, Deborah Tannen, John Tooby, David Tyack, Kim Wallen, Margot Wilson, and Robert Zajonc. My thanks also go to Donna Mumme for her expert help in reviewing the literature.

At several points in the book, I have used materials—some previously published, some not—taken from the longitudinal study I conducted jointly with Carol Jacklin during the seventies and early eighties. My warm thanks go to Jacklin for the good, long collaboration which provided the foundation from which much of the thinking in this book has grown.

A grant from the Carnegie Corporation supported the modest costs for secondary data analysis and secretarial help needed to produce the book.

I cannot sufficiently acknowledge the indispensable contributions of Patricia Weaver to bringing this book into being. Not only has she prepared the manuscript and cheerfully dealt with a continually revised list of references, but she has been consistently vigilant in the pursuit of accuracy in matters large and small.

There have been times when I thought that this book would never be finished. During its writing, a flood of new materials was being published, some of it calling urgently for inclusion and rewriting, but even so, it was evident that my coverage could not be as complete as I would wish. Furthermore, the social context for gender issues, and the ideologies concerning them, has been changing before my very eyes. I finally realized that any writing on this subject must be thought of as a work in progress. I hope readers will take the book in this light.

Eleanor E. Maccoby
Stanford University

Introduction

This book is about sex (or gender) in the broadest sense: about how an individual's development from infancy into adulthood is affected by being either a male or a female. Although some individuals are hermaphrodites, the vast majority of human beings are biologically clearly either male or female. And, again in the vast majority of cases, the sex identity assigned to an individual by society, as well as the sex identity adopted by the individual, corresponds to the person's biological sex. This book will be concerned with the development of people who are unambiguously members of one gender category or the other.

In many respects, males and females take quite similar developmental paths. But in some important respects, their paths diverge. In this book I begin by showing that when boys and girls are engaged in social play, they congregate primarily with others of their own sex during the preschool and middle-childhood years, and that different childhood "cultures" prevail in these gender-segregated playgroups. I will consider the set of possible reasons why this divergence occurs, and discuss the implications of childhood divergence for the ways in which males and females interact when the two sexes converge in adolescence and adulthood. In particular, I will consider how the different social histories of the two sexes affect the relationships of heterosexual couples, the way men and women relate to each other as co-parents, and the nature of same-sex and cross-sex interactions that occur in the workplace. Most of the information we have on these matters comes from modern Western societies, but I will try to take a cross-culturally broader perspective whenever possible.

Every known human society has rules and customs concerning gender. Members of every society have expectations and beliefs—sometimes explicit, sometimes unspoken—concerning what boys and girls, or men and women, are supposed to do or not do. Some of these expectations are clearly grounded in the different roles of the two sexes in human reproduction, and relate to their different physical characteristics. The fact that females give birth and lactate and males don't has always imposed certain constraints on the roles of men and women, but there is great variation among societies with respect to how broadly the constraints are conceived. It is reasonable to assume that the constraints imposed by the different functions of the two sexes in reproduction become less pervasive as cultures move away from a hunter-gatherer form of socioeconomic life toward modern forms of social organization.

In a similar vein, the greater upper-body strength of males may once have led fairly directly to a sexual division of labor. (We should be aware, though, that in the surviving simple, preliterate societies that have been available for study, women have been found to do much of the heavy manual labor and much of the carrying of heavy burdens.) But in most modern societies there are few jobs that call for the spurts of physical strength that males on the average are more capable of than females.

Much has been made of the roles of the two sexes in sexual behavior: the intrusiveness of the male, the receptiveness of the female. By analogy, these roles in sexual intercourse have been extended into concepts of the essential personalities of the two sexes: of activity or "agency" as being the essential element in masculinity, and passivity or compliance the essential element in femininity. These ideas were elaborated in Freud's early writings, and have since been extensively challenged by feminist theorists, including those with a more modern psychodynamic orientation.[1]

Among modern societies, there is an astonishing variety of prescriptions and proscriptions concerning how people of the two sexes should behave, and these sex-role requirements are currently undergoing rapid change. The cross-cultural variety is enough to make it obvious that biology is not destiny, even though the differentiated reproductive biology of the two sexes is something that every society weaves into its gender definitions in some way. Not only do societies differ in what kinds of requirements they set up for men and women, but they differ in how pervasive such requirements are. In some societies, every sphere of life is different for the two sexes: not only domestic roles, but also access to education and occupations, political entitlements, and ownership and inheritance of property. In other societies, there are large spheres of life in which people function primarily as human beings—in which the two sexes have more nearly equal social entitlements, and in which gender is less pertinent. It may be that the most rapid social change now occurring in the roles of the two sexes has to do with the declining importance of gender in determining how individuals will live whole segments of their lives. These changes, in their turn, probably stem in large part from the fact that women have so many fewer children, and live so much longer, than they formerly did. The child-rearing role in particular, important though it continues to be, now takes up a much smaller portion of the life-span than it once did.

The Traditional View: Socialization as the Wellspring of Gender Differentiation

Nevertheless, the differentiation of the two sexes with respect to behavior, interests, and social roles remains pervasive even in modern societies. Social science has long taken it as an important objective to understand how gender differentiation comes about. In the last several decades, the dominant perspective has been that gender is socially constructed, and that gender differentiation is best understood as a product of *socialization*.[2] Sociologists have noted that societies and groups could not function without "an extraordinary degree of conformity by group members to commonly held expectations regarding what constitutes appropriate behaviors, attitudes and values in a wide range of situations" (Goslin, 1969, p. 2). In any society children must learn what these needed behaviors, attitudes, and values are, and must somehow be motivated to conform to them (in the sense of either outward compliance or internalized acceptance). In many respects, children of the two sexes must learn the same things: for example, both boys and girls are held to similar standards when it comes to eating rituals (table manners), safety precautions, and deference to elders. But boys and girls usually are expected to learn some different things too, including in most societies rather complex customs concerning how members of the two sexes should behave toward each other, and what their obligations to each other are.

Socialization, then, has traditionally been seen as the set of processes whereby each generation of adults passes along to the upcoming generation of children the fund of knowledge, beliefs, and skills which constitutes the culture of the social group. The socialization processes occurring in child-hood have been seen as largely anticipatory: as a matter of preparing children for the roles they will need to play as adults. From this point of view, when socialization proceeds successfully, the needed cultural elements become incorporated into each individual's personality.

These ideas have been applied to gender differentiation in the following way: Since societies prescribe somewhat different social roles for adults of the two sexes, boys and girls need different preparatory socialization. In traditional societies, girls are trained in domestic skills and the care of children, while boys are given apprenticeship training in doing heavy agricultural work such as caring for large animals and clearing fields, or are trained as hunters or skilled artisans. Through a range of socialization pressures, children of the two sexes are also thought to be gradually inducted into more subtle, diffuse personality characteristics concordant with their future roles: for girls, this means being "ladylike" (modest, behaviorally restrained), compliant, and nurturant to others; for boys, being independent, adventurous, willing to take initiative and risks. Since many of the relevant personality characteristics are thought to be inculcated early in life, parents have been seen as playing a major role in gender socialization. But other socialization agents, such as teachers, religious leaders, coaches, and cultural heroes contribute too, as do TV, literature, and other channels of mass culture when available.

By what means are socialization agents thought to bring about the gradual differentiation of boys and girls? Within psychology, the behaviorist zeitgeist of the mid twentieth century led researchers to focus first of all on direct teaching. Adults were seen as establishing the agenda of what children were to learn, and providing regimes of reward and punishments that would instill the desired habits. The assumption was that children of the two sexes learned different things because different tasks were set for them to learn, and because they were reinforced or punished differentially. Boys became "boisterous" because they were allowed or encouraged to be so. Girls became "dainty" because they were given pretty dresses and because their mothers spent more time arranging their hair and both parents praised them for keeping clean and looking pretty.

Some theorists viewed socialization almost entirely as a top-down process whereby adults managed and controlled the conditions for children's learning, but others emphasized the active role of children in utilizing inputs from the adult culture as they began to understand (and sought to adopt) the characteristics they needed to have. Freud had stressed the importance of the process of *identification* with a child's same-sex parent. A child identifying with the same-sex parent would adopt a wide range of that parent's values and attributes, including those that were sex-typed. Freud thought that the identification process normally occurred at about the age of 4 or 5, in the service of resolving the Oedipus complex. Identification was reformulated by social-learning theorists as a process of imitation or "modeling." Although they recognized that children would learn a great deal by imitating models of either sex, their claim was that children would come more and more to imitate same-sex models, including the same-sex parent, rather than other-sex models, because they would have discovered that they were more likely to experience positive outcomes by doing so.[3] Social influence via teaching and reinforcement has sometimes been called *direct* socialization, while the learning that children do via observation and imitation is sometimes referred to as the result of *indirect* socialization or self-socialization. In social-learning theory, both direct reinforcement and imitation were thought to be important in the transmission of the gender-related aspects of culture to new generations of children.

It has been customary in psychological writings to treat gender differentiation under the heading "Individual Differences," along with analyses of how psychological characteristics differ (if at all) by race and social class. Usually, distributions are shown of males' and females' scores on a measure of some psychological characteristic, such as IQ, aptitude or achievement in an intellectual domain, or a personality dimension. Such comparisons usually reveal little or no sex differentiation, and even with respect to characteristics where there is a significant difference in the mean scores of the two sexes, the overlap between the two distributions is great, and there is great variation among the children of a given sex (see Figure 6 in Chapter 4).[4] Even on measures of "masculinity" or "femininity," however these are defined, scores for the two sexes are never greatly distinct. Within each sex children vary greatly with respect to how closely they conform to stereotypes or social prescriptions for their gender. Some boys are more "masculine" than others, some girls more "feminine" than others. From the standpoint of social-learning theory, this is to be expected, since some children have been subjected to more intensive gender socialization than others. It has been a central objective of developmental research to discover what the socialization conditions are that lead to these within-sex variations.

The Various Meanings of "Masculinity" and "Femininity"

Of course, writers have not always meant the same thing when they talk about "masculinity" and "femininity." We can distinguish at least three meanings:

1. A masculine or feminine person is one who embodies the characteristics prescribed by the male or female sex roles in the person's society. Thus a "feminine" woman would be nurturant (consistent with her mothering role) and a masculine man would be able to hold his own in the competitive world of work and earning.

2. A masculine or feminine person is one who exemplifies the characteristics that have been shown to differentiate the sexes. A measure of how masculine or feminine an individual is can be constructed, made up of items on which there is a consistent mean difference between the sexes. Among children, liking to play with dolls would raise an individual's score on femininity. Among adults, preference for showers rather than tub baths was included under masculinity at one time. It is doubtful whether it would survive as a significant differentiator of the sexes today, since women have adopted more informal hairdos and are willing to get their hair wet. Still reliable as a masculine item, however, is a preference for watching football on TV.

3. A feminine woman is one who is, and strives to be, attractive to men, and a masculine man is one who is attractive to women. Thus a feminine woman in modern societies is sexy and good-looking. A woman who strives to be feminine in this sense takes pains to make her appearance as attractive as possible, and knows how to flirt gracefully, perhaps how to be a "good listener"; in short, she knows how to look and behave in such a way that the men she meets—or at least, the ones she wants to attract—will be interested in her. What it takes for a man to be attractive to women is less easy to define. Is it being tall, and having a rugged, muscular body? or having an assertive, self-assured manner? Perhaps feminine women and masculine men share certain characteristics under this definition: presumably they would

both be more attractive to a partner of the other sex if they displayed sensitivity to the partner's needs and interests. We don't know a great deal about how men and women signal their sexual interest in each other, or about the variations in what potential partners find attractive, but it is a good assumption that the variations in both signals and responses must be very great within and between cultures. There are many more ways to be masculine or feminine under the third meaning of these terms than under the first two.[5]

Individuals who can be considered quite "masculine" or "feminine" under one of these definitions may not be so under another. Thus a man who has exceptionally strong ability in math or spatial tasks would be considered masculine under Definition 2, but not necessarily so under Definitions 1 or 3. And a woman who is skillful and nurturant with children, and therefore "feminine" under Definition 1, is not necessarily feminine under the third criterion.

The Socialization Research Agenda

Developmental psychologists have focused a great deal of research energy on identifying variations among children in how "masculine" or "feminine" they are, and in attempting to discover what the conditions are in children's lives that lead them to be more or less sex-typed. Presumably, the reasoning goes, there are certain socialization pressures that make boys more masculine than girls, and girls more feminine than boys, and these same socialization pressures vary within a sex as well. That is, some boys are subject to more intense masculinizing pressures, and hence become more masculine, than other boys. The implicit assumption is that whatever conditions make some boys more masculine than other boys will be the same conditions that make boys more masculine than girls. Thus studies of the antecedents of "M" and "F" scores should contribute directly to our understanding of sex differences.

The research agenda dictated by socialization theory has been tackled in several ways. In sociology (and to some extent in anthropology as well) a favorite strategy has been to start with Definition 1: to identify the different role requirements for the two sexes in a given culture, and then to see how these are reflected in differential rearing conditions provided for male and female children. Developmental psychologists have usually adopted a different strategy. They usually begin by identifying any psychological characteristics wherein the sexes differ, and then look for links between these and any differential socialization practices that might have set the two sexes moving along different trajectories. In pursuing this strategy, psychologists have generally adopted Definition 2 above. A major part of their research agenda has involved cataloguing any sex differences in skills, interests, and personality characteristics that proved to be significant and replicable. A given child's degree of sex-typing could then be assessed in terms of whether (or to what degree) the child displayed those characteristics most commonly found among children of the child's own sex, and did *not* display the characteristics of the other sex.

Once measures of sex-typing were available for a set of individual children, it was possible to analyze the relation of their scores to the socialization conditions to which individual children had been exposed. One could then examine the impact of gender socialization in two ways: One could compare the mean scores for boys with the means for girls on some psychological variable of interest (such as aggressiveness or affiliation); and one could then compare the means for the two groups on a parental socialization variable presumed to be relevant, such as permissiveness for aggression or rewards given for positive social approaches to others. If the socialization means differed in a direction consistent with the sex difference in the outcome variable, this was taken as evidence that one had led to the other.

A second approach was to correlate the sex-typing scores for children of a given sex with their parents' scores on some aspect of socialization. For example, if parents who consistently offered masculine toys to their sons, and never gave them dolls, had sons who were more "masculine" than other boys on a measure of sex-typing, this would be seen as evidence that the children's sex-typing had been "shaped" by the parental management of the children's play environments.

In the 1960s and 1970s, an accumulating body of research began to indicate that direct socialization alone did not provide an adequate account of children's acquisition of sex-typed characteristics. In the 1980s, research attention was focused more and more heavily on *indirect* socialization: on the question of whether children began to socialize themselves (by patterning themselves on same-sex models) once their own gender identity was established and they began to understand the nature of the social expectations that applied to members of their own sex. At this time, gender cognitions—knowledge of social stereotypes and the formation of gender "schemas" as the central cognitions guiding gendered behavior—became popular topics of study. Gender schemas were thought to have two functions: to guide selective attention, so that children would pay more attention to, and learn more from, same-sex models; and to ensure that whatever gender knowledge was acquired would be employed differently by children of the two sexes, depending on what rules and customs were seen to apply specifically to their own sex.

Limitations of the Socialization Account

One central theme of this book is that the socialization account has not proved adequate to the task of explaining gender differentiation. The socialization account is not *wrong*—just too narrow, too limited. We now know that there are powerful gender-linked phenomena that do not fit into the traditional framework. They cannot be understood in terms of sex-typed personality traits or dispositions inculcated in each individual child through the process of socialization. Rather, they require us to shift our focus from the individual to the dyad or larger social group. Sex-linked behavior turns out to be a pervasive function of the social context in which it occurs. This may seem like a truism. We know that all behavior is a function of context; relevant conditions for the performance of a given behavior must be present. And to say that behavior is contextual suggests that we are talking about behavior that is chameleonlike and easily modified, or about behavior that is quite variable across cultures and subcultures. But when it comes to the differentiation of male and female behavior, we can move beyond simple contextual relativism. We can point to a specific aspect of context which has broad relevance and which indeed is cross-culturally universal. It turns out that the relevant condition is the gender composition of the social pair or group within which the individual is functioning at any given time. The gendered aspect of an individual's behavior is brought into play by the gender of others.

The need for this new focus began to be apparent in the late 1970s. A longitudinal study that Carol Jacklin and I conducted at the Stanford laboratory will serve to illustrate the point. In this study (Jacklin and Maccoby, 1978), 46 pairs of previously unacquainted children—all of whom were very close to 33 months of age—were brought by their mothers to a laboratory playroom. Mothers were asked to bring the children in gender-neutral clothes (pants and T-shirts), and not to use the children's names, so that there would be few cues as to whether a given child was a girl or boy.[6] The experimenter came in several times during the play session, bringing a new toy or toys. Observers (viewing the children through a one-way window) noted the nature of any social behavior that the children directed toward one another in the course of their play. Social behaviors included offering a toy to the partner, accepting a toy from a partner, or grabbing a toy from a partner; hitting or pushing, patting or hugging, smiling or frowning at the partner; issuing a vocal invitation, command, threat or prohibition to the partner. In short, both positive and negative social behaviors were included. As may be seen in Figure 1, both boys and girls directed approximately twice as much social behavior toward same-sex partners as they did toward other-sex partners in mixed-sex pairs.

These findings were replicated by Lloyd and Smith (1986) in their work with 60 pairs of young British children. A wider age range (from 19 to 42 months) was included in this study, and the children were drawn from

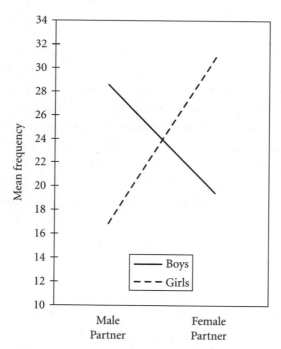

Figure 1. Mean frequency of social behavior at age 33 months, by sex of subject and sex of partner. (Source: Jacklin and Maccoby, 1978, pp. 557–569.)

playgroups, and thus had been previously acquainted. Observers, working from video tapes of play sessions, coded the frequency of social-behavioral events or episodes. In spite of the differences in time, place, age range, previous acquaintance, and observational method, the results are strikingly similar to those of the earlier Jacklin and Maccoby study (Figure 2).

It is important to note that the higher levels of social interaction among same-sex pairs or groups of children are also found outside the laboratory. In their year-long study of the free play behavior of three-year-olds in five preschool classrooms, Serbin and colleagues (Serbin, Moller, Gulko, Powlishta, and Colburne, 1994) report that when pairs of children were playing together, there was more genuine interaction in same-sex pairs. In mixed-sex groupings, there was more "parallel" (noninteractive) play, and there were more instances in which a child stood passively watching the other child or children play.

The importance of these studies lies as much in what they did *not* find as in what they did find. No difference was found between the average

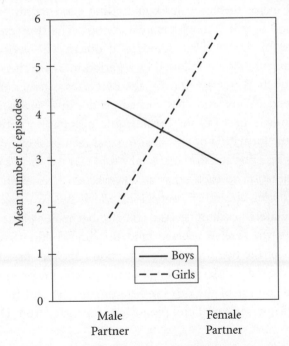

Figure 2. Mean number of episodes of total social behavior at ages 19 to 39 months, by sex of subject and sex of partner. (Source: Lloyd and Smith, 1986, pp. 33–41.)

"social behavior" scores of boys and girls if the sex of the partner is disregarded and scores for the behavior of children of a given sex are simply averaged across partner conditions. Thus we are not seeing a sex difference in a personality trait such as "sociability" acquired more strongly by one sex or the other. It is only when one compares same-sex with mixed-sex *dyads* that the importance of gender springs into bold relief.

This book deals with social behavior in social contexts. It is the thesis of the book that many of the robust behavioral distinctions between human males and females are of the group-contextual kind. Vast amounts of research on sex differences in personality traits have found only very modest differentiation between the sexes.[7] I invite the reader to consider the possibility that much of the work that has been done on individual sex-typing—for example, on the acquisition of "masculine" versus "feminine" traits—will turn out to be essentially irrelevant to the gender differentiation that depends on social context.[8] This differentiation is a powerful phenomenon in need of explanation.

A second major theme of this book is that gender differentiation can be understood only in a developmental context. The two sexes diverge at certain stages of development, converge at others. The period of gender separation in childhood is followed by a period in which the strong forces of sexual attraction emerge, drawing the two sexes together. But the prior period of gender segregation has created gender divergences in modes of relating to others that call for considerable negotiation between people engaged in the formation of new heterosexual relationships. When people of the two sexes enter the workplace, they find themselves in a context that calls for adaptation to each other as coworkers—a situation that differs considerably from the other contexts in which the two sexes have previously encountered each other. And still another major phase of relationships between the sexes is ushered in at the time children are born. The distinct roles of the two sexes in reproduction engender pressures toward new forms of gender differentiation, but the parental roles must be negotiated in the context of the existing heterosexual tie and the continuing pull toward same-sex social groupings that is a legacy from childhood.

I

Divergence in Childhood

1

Gender Segregation in Childhood

In this chapter, I trace the development of preferences for same-sex, and avoidance of opposite-sex, social partners. Such preferences or avoidances, when they are strong and consistent, take the form of de facto segregation of the two sexes in situations where children have a choice as to whom their social partners will be. Conceivably, same-sex choices could manifest themselves across generations, taking the form of especially close bonds between mother-daughter pairs and father-son pairs. In this chapter, however, I will be primarily concerned with the development of sex-based social groupings among age-mates.

Changes in Playmate Preferences with Age

Infants and Toddlers

In the first two years of life, children do not spend much time with other children of their own age (unless they are twins, of course). Their social context is largely determined for them by their parents, and consists mainly of adults who are taking care of them, playing with them, and teaching them. If there are older siblings present in the family, they, too, form part of the child's social environment. For some infants and toddlers, a certain amount of time each day may be spent in group care—in a family daycare home or a daycare center—and in such settings there are opportunities for play with age-mates. Is there any evidence that at this early age children show any special compatibility with others of their own sex? Any special attraction to, or avoidance of, someone of the other sex?

When it comes to interactions with parents, same-sex preferences or avoidances do not emerge. Children are inclined to go to their mothers more readily than to their fathers when they are in need of comfort (when tired, upset, ill), or to their fathers when they are looking for fun and games, but children of the two sexes show these preferences equally. Boys and girls have not been found to differ in the quality of their attachment to either of the parents. Boys do not appear to be more interested in their fathers than girls are, nor are girls more likely than boys to seek closeness to their mothers rather than their fathers.

There is reason to believe that infants and toddlers may be somewhat more compatible with same-sex older siblings, though the evidence is sparse. Dunn and Kendrick (1982) made home observations of pairs of siblings in which the younger child was 14 months of age and the older child about two years older. There was considerably more friendly inter-action (and less hostility) in same-sex pairs, and this same-sex compatibility could be seen developing even earlier, when the younger child was still an infant of 8 months. Both younger and older siblings imitated same-sex siblings more frequently than opposite-sex siblings. This greater same-sex rapport may, however, have been instigated by the older child, so this study does not give us clear evidence that children show same-sex preferences in their first two years. Ideally, we would like to have a comparison between same-sex pairs of fraternal twins and pairs of opposite-sex twins, to see whether there is more conflict, or more sustained bouts of harmonious play, in one kind of pair than the other at this early age. So far, such evidence is lacking.

In recent years, increasing numbers of mothers have been returning to work while their children are still quite young. Many of their infants are cared for by relatives or in family daycare homes in which there may be few or no other children of the same age. But some are in group settings where a choice of playmates is possible, and several researchers have repeatedly observed the play of individual children in a group to see whether playmate preferences emerge during the first two years of life, and if so, whether children appear to be choosing playmates on the basis of gender.

LaFrenier and colleagues (LaFrenier, Strayer, and Gauthier, 1984) observed children in a large daycare center in Montreal. The center enrolled children of a wide range of ages (1 to 6 years), with the children being grouped in different areas according to age. There were 26 children (in three groups) between the ages of 12 months and 24 months. Each child was repeatedly observed, and all "affiliative" acts (positive approaches to another child) were recorded, along with the sex of the other child whom the target child approached. The study found that these toddlers were indiscriminate as to the sex of the other child: their affiliative behavior was as often directed toward a child of the other sex as to a same-sex child.

The social skills of toddlers in their second year are, of course, quite rudimentary. They have too little command of language to achieve sustained communication through talk, and much of their play with other children is merely parallel: two children engage in the same activity side by side, appearing contented but not seeming to pay much attention to each other. But certain forms of play are more interactive. They may involve differentiation of roles, as in run-and-chase games, or reciprocal turn-taking, as when rolling a ball back and forth; and mutual imitation occurs.

Through repeated observations of 34 children between the ages of 12 and 24 months in group daycare settings, Howes (1988a) has shown that toddlers are selective when it comes to their interactive partners.[1] Even at this young age, children do have "friends." There are certain pairs of children who are frequently seen close to each other, showing pleasure in each other's company, and interacting with each other in the simple ways available to toddlers: exchanging smiles or glances, offering objects, and so forth. An individual child may have more than one friend, but there is a clear distinction between friends and occasional playmates. Among the toddlers studied by Howes, toddler friendships were maintained over a considerable span of time, and having such friendships was associated with more rapid development of social skills. But among children of this age, there was no tendency to prefer same-sex other children as friends (Howes, 1988b).

The study by LaFreniere and colleagues, and that by Howes, involved small numbers of children, and the number of different settings in which young toddlers have been observed is limited so far. Still, these two studies do indicate that a preference for same-sex playmates has not yet developed in the second year of life.

The Third Year

Earlier we saw evidence that before their third birthday, children played more comfortably with an unfamiliar partner if that partner was of their own sex. It would not be surprising, then, if children of this age, when they have a choice of playmates, show preferences for playmates of their own sex. How early do such preferences start? We saw that among children in group-care settings where a choice of playmates is possible, toddlers in their second year appear to make friendly social approaches with fairly equal frequency to other children of the same or the other sex, and that "friendships" are as likely to be formed between mixed-sex as between same-sex pairs. This picture changes in the third year.

In the study of toddler friendships conducted by Howes, children in their third year had begun to choose their friends mainly from among same-sex peers (Howes, 1988, table 5). When children had formed cross-sex friendships earlier (in the second year), they tended to maintain these friendships into the preschool years if their early friends were still available, despite the fact that there was increasing gender segregation among their peers. The basis for maintaining these friendships appeared to be a compatibility of playstyles and social skills between a boy-girl pair who had become friends as young toddlers. In the third year and later, however, new friendships were usually with same-sex partners (Howes and Phillipsen, 1992). There was some indication in the Howes's work that girls' same-sex preference was somewhat stronger than boys' in the third year, but the sample sizes were not great enough to establish the point. Girl-girl friendships formed early were more likely to be maintained from one age to the next than were boy-boy friendships.

Further evidence on the drift toward same-sex playmate preference comes from a longitudinal study of 100 children conducted by Fagot and colleagues (Fagot, 1991). The children were observed as they interacted with peers in play groups from age 18 to about 30 months. Fagot reports: "Gender segregation evolved slowly over the time period from 18 months to three years, so that by 30 months of age, most children spent the majority of their time with same-sex peers" (1991, p. 6). In the large daycare center in Montreal studied by LaFrenier and colleagues, girls began in their third year to direct more of their affiliative behavior to other girls, rather than to boys. Boys began to show a similar same-sex preference approximately a year later, usually after they had passed their third birthday (see Figure 3).

Pitcher and Schultz (1983) found similar trends in their study of a large number of children (255) ranging in age from 2 through 5. They observed the children during periods of free play, and report that by the age of 3, the girls were already initiating positive social behavior toward other girls considerably more often than toward boys. Boys, by contrast, were fairly gender-neutral in their social initiations at age 3, but changed quickly thereafter, so that by age 4 their same-sex preferences were strong, and by age 5, stronger than those of the girls. Serbin and colleagues (1994) also find three-year-old girls showing stronger same-sex playmate preferences than boys.

Research evidence converges, then, in showing that by the third year of life, the tendency to prefer same-sex playmates is clearly established in girls, and is established in boys soon thereafter. But play in mixed-sex groups continues to occur quite often in the early years.

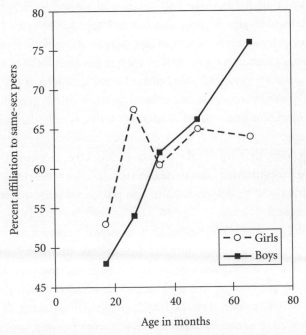

Figure 3. Mean affiliative activity directed to same-sex peers, by age and sex. (Source: LaFreniere, Strayer, and Gauthier, 1984, pp. 1958–1965.)

Preschoolers

The age period of roughly 3 through 5 is a time when, in many societies, children have increasing opportunities to interact with other children near their own age. In societies where children are confined to a compound of some sort—as in parts of India, where sisters-in-law live with their children in an enclosure, or parts of Africa, where co-wives with their children share a compound—they have access mainly to siblings, half-siblings, or cousins. In modern industrial societies they spend time with other children (usually unrelated children) in daycare settings or preschools, such as the French *écoles maternelles*.

It is primarily in settings where children encounter a number of other children near in age to themselves that gender differentiation emerges. In these settings, children become progressively more sophisticated in their playful interactions with each other. As noted above, a toddler in a daycare center may simply stay close to a preferred other child, playing "in parallel" with an occasional exchange of glances or play materials, or a one-word demand. With increasing age and social experience, exchanges become elaborated, until by age 5, most children are capable of extended "bouts" or chains of interaction in which each reacts to the other's just-preceding action or statement in a succession of exchanges all related to a joint play theme or goal. At the most sophisticated level, children learn to take up reciprocal "pretend" roles (doctor-patient, teacher-pupil, parent-child) and act out a mutually understood sequential script which they elaborate as they go along.

We have seen that in the third year of life children begin to show a preference for same-sex playmates. Consider now whether, and how strongly, this trend manifests itself in the preschool period—among children aged 3 to 5.

The adults in charge of preschools and daycare centers set up routines for the day, including periods of adult-prescribed, structured activity such as brief concept-teaching sessions, story reading, naptime, snack-time. But there are also periods of free play in which children may choose their activities and playmates. And in less formal settings, such as the compounds referred to above, children ages 3 to 5 are often left to play together on their own except when adult intervention is needed. Here, I will be primarily interested in the social play of children during times when there is a minimum of adult-imposed structure.

Observers who repeatedly watch the free-play activities of the same group of preschoolers over a span of time soon notice certain regularities in the children's social relationships. There are some children who engage in solitary activity more than others, either because they are shy or because they disrupt the play of other children and are avoided or rejected. Most children, however, are sociable, and among these, certain children choose each other especially often as playmates. These are stable pairs of "best friends." Also, there are small social groupings or networks of three or four children who play together frequently. Strayer (1977) identified such groups in a number of French-Canadian nursery schools where he observed children at play. He found that these small groups had what he called a strong focal pair: a pair (almost always a same-sex pair) of children who related reciprocally to each other. In addition, each group had one or two other children who related to one of the children in the focal pair, but not reciprocally. Usually, these more marginal group members were of the same sex as the focal pair, but not always. When a boy spent time with a girls' group, he was always a kind of hanger-on, never a member of the focal pair, and the same was true of a girl who spent time with boys—she was never a central member of the group, always peripheral.

Strayer's observations give us a detailed picture of the form gender segregation took among the preschoolers he studied. Researchers working at a wide variety of times and places have studied the social networks of preschool children,[2] and the results have been remarkably consistent: there is a substantial degree of sex segregation among children of preschool age, and this trend has been found in many different cultural settings.[3] The anthropologists Whiting and Edwards (1988) report observations from ten small societies in widely scattered places (including villages or neighborhoods in Africa, India, the Philippines, Mexico, and the United States). They find that children aged 4–5 in these cultures consistently spent most of their play time with other children of their own sex. When only the interaction with non-siblings was considered, same-sex playmates were chosen approximately two thirds of the time by children aged 3–6; by age 6 to 10, the proportion had increased to more than three-fourths time spent in same-sex play.[4] Omark, Omark, and Edelman (1973) made playground observations in three countries: the United States, Switzerland, and Ethiopia, and they too reported substantial segregation in each of these cultural settings. Similar findings are reported by Dunn and Morgan (1987), who observed nursery and "infant" (ages 5–6) classrooms in northern Ireland, and by Lloyd and Duveen (1992) in their observations of children in the "reception classes" of British schools, at approximately 5 years of age.

In the longitudinal study I conducted with Carol Jacklin (Maccoby and Jacklin, 1987) of children living in the peninsular region of the San Francisco Bay, nearly 100 children (attending many different preschools and elementary schools) were observed during free play at two successive ages: 4½ years and 6½ years (first grade). At preschool age, the children were spending nearly three times as much time playing with same-sex others as with opposite-sex others, although there was also a considerable amount of play in mixed-sex groups. By age 6½, the ratio of same- to other-sex play partners had increased to 11 to 1 (Figure 4).

When children prefer members of their own sex as playmates, or avoid members of the other sex, are these choices based on experiences with individual children? Have children had initial exploratory contacts with a number of other children of both sexes, in which they have had more positive experiences with the children who are of their own sex, so that these more compatible others become their friends? Or do children form categorical judgments, based on the sex of other children, such that they approach or avoid others before they have any individual knowledge of whether a particular child would be fun to play with? By preschool age, there is reason to believe that the latter is the case. Wasserman and Stern

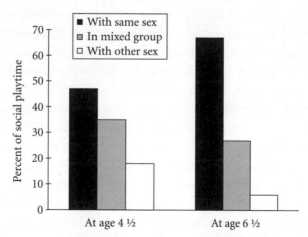

Figure 4. Percent of social play time children spent with children of their own or the other gender, on preschool and first-grade playgrounds. (Source: Maccoby and Jacklin, 1987, p. 259.)

(1978) did experiments which they described to preschoolers as studies of "how children walk." They would ask one preschooler to stand at the end of a long strip of carpet; another preschooler—the "approacher"—would then start off from the other end of the rug, being asked simply to "walk up to" the other child. Children systematically stopped farther away from an opposite-sex child than from a same-sex child, and this was true whether the other child was known to the "approacher" or not. Furthermore, "approachers" angled their bodies more slant-wise, turning somewhat away from an other-sex stationary child; same-sex children were approached more directly, face to face. We see, then, that preschoolers appear to be displaying categorical reactions, based on their coding of other children's gender. Maccoby and Jacklin's study of 33-month-olders (reported in the Introduction) tells the same story: children made more social overtures to same-sex others with whom they were previously unacquainted.

Middle Childhood

The anthropologists John and Beatrice Whiting, with their colleagues, have carried out extensive observations of children's social behavior in a number of non-Western, nonindustrialized societies.[5] They report that children of different sexes are often assigned different tasks, which automatically place them in the company of same-sex peers. In middle childhood, boys, more often than girls, are assigned the task of herding large animals, which takes them away from the household and into the company of boys and men, while girls are more often assigned child-care duties, which keep them closer to home and more often in the company of girls and women. Even when children are not carrying out tasks but are simply playing together in situations where children of both sexes are present, children are usually found in closer proximity to other children of the same sex, and relatively few of their social acts are directed toward children of the other sex.[6] The same-sex preferences are especially pronounced when the other children present are of similar age. Whiting and Edwards, reporting on their own cross-cultural studies and those of others, say: "In sum, our findings, together with those from the other studies, suggest that the emergence of same-sex preferences in childhood is a cross-culturally universal and robust phenomenon" (1988, p. 81).

Research in Western societies suggests that when children enter school, patterns of gender segregation become more firmly entrenched than they were at younger ages, but only in certain settings. It depends on how much choice the children have as to their social partners. In coeducational schools many teachers make seating assignments without regard to sex. In modern Western societies, it is rare for teachers to pit the boys against the girls in spelling bees, or instruct the boys and girls to line up separately to go out to a boys' playground or a girls' playground. Teachers often try to include both boys and girls when composing small work groups. In most schools, then, children have a great deal of experience as members of mixed-sex groupings within their classrooms. Same-sex social preferences are seen mainly in the corridors, on the playgrounds, in lunchrooms, or during extracurricular activities in which adults have not established gender-integrated structures.[7]

During the grade school years, children almost exclusively nominate same-sex children as "best friends" or "close friends." If one takes repeated observational "snapshots" of the way children are grouped on playgrounds or in corridors—who is standing near whom, interacting with whom— children are overwhelmingly more likely to be near, and interacting with, children of their own sex.[8] In school lunchrooms, the children usually have a shared understanding that certain tables are "girls' tables" and other tables are for boys. Very few instances are seen in which a child sits down next to a child of the other sex after emerging from the cafeteria line. Racial segregation is also seen in the cafeteria seating patterns in "integrated" schools, but the lines of separation by gender are stronger, so that if most of the seats are taken, and a child must choose between sitting next to a child of either the other sex or the other race, cross-gender avoidance prevails (Schofield, 1981).

Thorne notes that segregation at the lunchroom tables is less pronounced among first-graders, and almost complete among sixth-graders. Illustrating the processes whereby the separation comes about, I draw on Thorne's field notes:

> In the lunchroom, when the two second-grade tables were filling, a high-status boy walked by the inside table, which had a scattering of both boys and girls, and said loudly, "Oooo, too many girls," as he headed for a seat at the far table. The boys at the inside table picked up their trays and moved, and no other boys sat at the inside table, which the pronouncement had effectively made taboo. (Thorne, 1986, p. 171)

The fact that these patterns represent the children's own choices, rather than the dictates of adults, is illustrated by an observation from an early-morning sports program that was designed for grade school children whose parents needed to drop them off at school before the beginning of classes. The school provided an adult coach, who saw to it that the group games—baseball, mainly—were equally open to boys and girls. Children of the two sexes had equivalent turns at bat. But the coach did not tell the children where to sit while waiting their turn at bat, and the children quickly established a girls' bench and a boys' bench, where they spent their (segregated) waiting time.

On school playgrounds, most games are segregated, and there are certain spaces where each sex customarily plays. Boys usually claim the larger, more central spaces, while girls have more peripheral spaces for jump-rope or hopscotch, or sometimes claim their own jungle gym. There are a few games in which both boys and girls participate. Dodge-ball is one of these, and Thorne suggests that this can be integrated because there is no choosing-up of sides, so that in most cases a child can simply take a place in a circle without there being any issue about being allowed by other children to join in.

In classrooms where teachers rather than students have the major role in establishing structure, there is much less segregation than on the playgrounds. In instances in which teachers allow a free choice of seats, segregation does emerge:

> The chairs in Mr. Socker's room are arranged in the shape of a wide shallow U. As the first few kids come into the room, Harry says to John, who is starting to sit down in an empty section of the room along one side of the U, "Don't sit there, that's where all the girls sit." Harry and John sit elsewhere. (Schofield, 1981, p. 62)

In classrooms where children have assigned seats, their preferential orientation to their own sex is less explicit but appears to be lurking beneath the surface. When children are asked to nominate classmates whom they would be willing to work with on a classroom project, same-sex nominations strongly outweigh other-sex nominations, although a substantial minority of third- and fourth-grade children express a willingness to work in mixed-gender groups when given a choice between such groups and sex-segregated groups (Lockheed, 1984).[9]

In many classrooms, it is common for children to offer to help each other with classroom assignments, but almost all such helping occurs between children of the same sex; instances of a grade school child spontaneously helping a child of the other sex with schoolwork are extremely rare (Damico, 1975). Grant (1985), after making repeated observations through most of a school year in six ethnically mixed first-grade classrooms in a working-class community, says: "Peer interaction . . . constituted a quasi-autonomous component of classroom life not directly regulated (and sometimes not even fully observable) by teachers" (p. 70), and she found that this peer component of classroom life was substantially different for boys and girls.

Sometimes teachers make explicit efforts to increase the amount of cross-sex interaction, but such efforts have not usually been effective. Lockheed and colleagues (Lockheed and Harris, 1984) have found that giving grade school children year-long experience in working on school projects in small mixed-sex groups did slightly increase the amount of cross-sex interaction seen in the classroom outside the structured small-group settings. But the year-long experience did not increase children's willingness to work with the other sex if new groups were to be formed; same-sex preferences remained strong, and girls exhibited even stronger negative stereotypes about boys after extensive experience working with them. Among preschool and kindergarten children, it has been found that children's tendency to segregate—especially that of girls—weakens over the summer vacation, so that at the beginning of the new school year girls show less avoidance of boys than they did at the end of the previous year; but a drift toward resegregation is soon seen during the new year.[10] Thus experience in working or playing together does not appear to weaken the underlying forces that bring about the separation of the sexes.

Indeed, when teachers make efforts to bring about more gender integration, their efforts can meet resistance. In an interview, an 11-year-old girl described teachers who tried to get boys and girls to play more together as "geeky ughs." She talked about one teacher who on occasion had asked the children in her class to sit in a circle, arranged boy-girl-boy-girl, and hold hands; she said this teacher was especially unpopular (Maccoby and Jacklin, 1987). Another example of unwelcome teacher pressure is reported by Schofield:

Mr. Little instructs the students to form groups of *three* for a science experiment. None of the groups formed are sexually integrated. Mr.

Little notices a group of four boys, and instructs one of its members, Juan, "Go over and work with Diane" . . . Shaking his head, Juan says: "No, I don't want to." Mr. Little says quietly, but with an obvious edge in his voice, "Then take off your lab apron and go back to the regular class." Juan stands absolutely still and doesn't reply. After a long heavy silence, Mr. Little says "Okay, I'll do it for you." He unties Juan's apron and sends him out of the room. (Schofield, 1981, p. 63)

The power of the tendency for the sexes to separate in middle childhood is further underscored by Gray and Feldman (1997) in their observations of the informal social groupings in an ungraded school. In this school, there were many more opportunities than in the usual school for children to interact with others older or younger than themselves. In this situation, cross-age mixing was much more common than cross-sex mixing. Indeed, between the ages of 8 and 11, the median percent of social time spent with children of the other sex was zero.

Variation in the Prevalence of Segregation

Clearly, we can say with some confidence that the preference for same-sex playmates that began to appear in the third year of life becomes stronger during the preschool years, so that substantial segregation of the sexes is taking place at this age in settings where the children have freedom to choose their play partners. And the pull toward same-gender social association becomes even stronger in middle childhood, probably reaching its peak at about ages 8–11. The phenomenon is seen in many different cultural settings—in advanced industrial societies as well as in traditional preliterate ones. It is also fairly resistant to change. Consider this example: a short-term intervention designed to increase cross-sex play through reinforcing children for such play produced a shift in the desired direction, but these effects faded when the intervention ended, and the children quickly returned to their baseline pattern of same-sex preference (Serbin, Tonick, and Sternglanz, 1977).

It would be a mistake to conclude, however, that children's tendency to segregate themselves by sex is not subject to influence from cultural and subcultural conditions. There is considerable variability among different settings in the degree to which segregation occurs. For example, it has been reported that children are more likely to play with a child of the other sex in their residential neighborhood than at school.[11] And there is evidence that children feel freer to engage in cross-sex play in private settings than in public situations (Gottman and Parker, 1987). Of course, in some cultures the structures adults set up for children's daily lives automatically produce segregation, as in those where only boys are sent to school, or when boys and girls attend separate schools, or when boys are allowed more freedom to go away from the home yard or compound. But even in situations where children of both sexes are present and subject to the same requirements, there is variation in how strong a "pull" there is for or against segregation. Bianchi and Bakeman (1983) contrasted classrooms in two preschools: one "traditional," the other designed to provide a more "open," individuated classroom experience based on the British infant school model. Teachers in the "open" school deliberately tried to avoid sex stereotypes in the way they dealt with children, and there were both male and female teachers. The children were aged 4–6. During the free-play periods, children in both schools spent 80 percent of their time playing with other children, so they did not differ in sociability. But in the traditional school the children spent nearly 70 percent of their social-play time playing with same-sex others, while in the open school this percentage was substantially less (41 percent), and boys and girls were often seen playing in mixed groups. With grade school children, similar differences between a traditional and a "progressive" school were reported by Thorne and Luria (1986).

It is possible to set up a play environment which will entice children of both sexes to participate in and construct joint games. Theokas, Ramsey, and Sweeney (1993) provided a preschool classroom with a novel set of materials for pretend space travel, including a space capsule large enough for several children to occupy at one time. The amount of mixed-sex play increased substantially while these materials were available. When the materials were withdrawn, mixed-sex play declined quickly, but when the children were observed five weeks after the intervention had ended, mixed-sex play remained somewhat more frequent than it had been before the intervention began. It remains to be seen, of course, how long such effects would last.

Whiting and Edwards (1988), in their cross-cultural comparisons, note that boys make especially strong efforts to disassociate themselves from women in societies where men have considerably higher status than women. We may assume that this gender-status factor would also bring about a stronger avoidance of girls of their own age among boys in strongly male-dominant societies.

Thus we see that although there is a powerful trend toward same-sex playmate preference among children aged 4–11, and although so far as we know this trend is cross-culturally universal, sex segregation is nevertheless not a monolithic thing that is impervious to cultural conditions and local variations in settings. Perhaps it would be most accurate to say that there is a strong bias in every society for children to be drawn toward playmates of their own sex, but that societies and subcultures differ in terms of whether this bias is supported and extended through social attitudes and arrangements, or counteracted by conditions that support gender-free interactions among children.

Which Sex Is Most Responsible for Segregation?

After about the age of 4, boys appear to play a more active role in establishing and maintaining the separation of the sexes. We saw earlier that girls seem to start the process, in that they begin to show affiliative preference for their own sex in the third year of life, while boys begin to show same-sex preferences approximately a year later. But boys soon surpass girls in this respect, and by age 5 their same-sex preferences are clearly stronger than girls'.

When it comes to friendship choices, girls as well as the boys overwhelmingly make same-sex choices. And there are certain things about male interaction that girls actively avoid. (More will be said about this in Chapter 3.) But boys appear to be more strongly oriented than girls do to age-mates of their own sex; they seem more bent on excluding girls from their social circle, and more likely than girls to tease or derogate each other for associating with the opposite sex (see Chapters 2 and 3).

Summary and Comment

There is a powerful tendency for children to segregate themselves by gender in childhood and to play more compatibly with same-sex partners. The drift into same-sex groups is found in small, nonindustrialized societies as well as in modern industrial ones. It first begins to show itself in the third year of life—with same-sex preference being shown somewhat earlier by girls—and progressively strengthens until it is strong indeed by middle childhood. After the first few years of childhood, the ratios of same-sex over other-sex choices have been found to vary from 3 or 4 to 1 to more than 10 to 1. The tendency of dyads or groups to be gender-homogeneous is much more robust than average sex differences on measures of the usual dimensions of individual difference (see Chapter 4).

After the first few years, boys appear to be more active than girls in bringing about, and maintaining, the social separation of the sexes. The two sexes are able to get along together and interact competently in situations structured by adults to be gender neutral, such as classroom settings where the boys and girls are all equivalently in the role of student. But even in these situations there are subtle peer-oriented interactions which reflect gender differentiation. The separation of the two sexes is seen most strongly in situations where adult-imposed structure is absent, such as school corridors, lunchrooms, and playgrounds.

Despite the ubiquity and power of sex segregation in childhood, and the fact that adult efforts to change this situation are usually ineffective and may backfire, there is indeed variation in how deep the gender divide becomes. Simply bringing children of the two sexes together, or putting them in joint small groups for school projects, doesn't seem to produce much change in children's social preferences and avoidances. But experimental treatments aimed at changing the status relations of boys and girls do bring about more equity in their social exchanges (Lockheed and Hall, 1976), and, by inference, might diminish cross-sex avoidance. And the fact that gender segregation is less pronounced in some "progressive" schools than in "traditional" schools suggests that the effects of a school's ideological climate may extend even onto playgrounds and into other relatively unstructured settings.

The fact that children do congregate spontaneously in same-sex pairs or groups opens up the possibility that the acquisition of interactional styles takes a somewhat different developmental course for boys and girls. Male groups and female groups *may* provide a different context for social development, by virtue of pursuing different agendas or adopting different modes or scripts for their interaction with each other. Whether the kind of social interactions that occur, and the scripts that are elaborated, are different among female playmates than in groups of male children is the subject of the next chapter.

It is important to note, too, that even among children who very seldom play with children of the other sex, there is considerable variation in how much they are involved with children of their own sex. Some children do not have a best friend of either sex; some may have a best friend but avoid taking part in larger-group activities. The reasons for these variations are many: some children are rejected by other children because of the way they behave or look; others are simply shy; still others have solitary interests—books, computers—and are not particularly drawn toward the activities of their same-sex playgroups, joining in such activities only rarely. Still, they typically do not violate the implicit rules of childhood concerning the separation of the sexes.

2

The Two Cultures of Childhood

As we have seen, the third year of life is the time when children who have access to other children near their own age begin to focus their social lives within same-sex groups or dyads. Between the ages of 3 and 6, same-sex groups more and more constitute the context within which children's social experience occurs. How similar, and how different, are the contexts that male groups and female groups provide for their members?

Gender Divergence in Playstyles

Play is a major enterprise of childhood. It is an activity which strongly distinguishes children from adults. It marks the early phases of development in other mammalian species as well as in humans. Playful behavior is not something directly taught by the older generation to the younger. Nor is it something young creatures learn by watching the behavior of their parents. We have only to imagine the playful antics of a kitten or puppy to realize how different this activity is from the more sober behavior that adult animals display most of the time. Play is an emergent kind of activity, something that waxes and then wanes during childhood.

Some play is solitary, but in most mammalian species, when two or more young animals are together, special social patterns emerge, such as chasing and mock biting. In humans, the playful behaviors of the young are enormously varied, and they change greatly with age, so that by the ages of 4 and 5, human children are sometimes seen engaging in rather complicated reciprocal role play where they act out mutually understood scripts—scripts that are often invented as they go along. Much of their social play, however, is simpler, and is made up of fairly short bouts of interaction. As Corsaro and Eder (1990) note, generating shared meanings and coordinating play with social partners is a difficult task for young children; the "culture" of childhood groups is something that must be co-constructed by the participants. Perhaps the most important thing about play is its emotional tone: it is clearly *fun*. Although children do sometimes get hurt or angry while playing, and may cry, most of the time they are either calm or pleasantly aroused, smiling or laughing frequently.

Boys' groups and girls' groups are similar in an important respect: in the preschool years play is the major social enterprise for both sexes. In groups of any gender composition, children derive great pleasure from play. But the two sexes occupy somewhat different play spaces: from the ages of 4 or 5, boys congregate in larger groups,[1] and more often play outdoors, while girls more often play in twos and threes in indoor settings.[2] When the two sexes are both present on a playground, the boys take up more space for their games. And the nature of the interaction that goes on among boys is qualitatively different in some respects from what goes on in all-girl dyads or groups.

Roughness

Boys are more "physical" in their play than girls. Charlesworth and Dzur (1987) provide an example in their research: they brought quartets of preschool-aged boys into a situation where they had to compete for access to a movie-viewer that had only one eyepiece. One boy usually emerged as dominant and got a greater share of access than the others; he usually did so simply by shouldering the other boys out of the way. When quartets of girls competed in this situation, a dominant girl would also usually emerge, just as in the boys' groups, but she usually got greater access by verbal bargaining and persuasion rather than by pushing.

On playgrounds in northern Ireland, Dunn and Morgan (1987) observed differences in the way boys and girls 5 to 7 years old used the same toys. They noted, for example, that when riding wheeled vehicles, boys played "ramming" games, deliberately running into each other, while girls (on the rare occasions when they could get access to the wheeled toys) rode around carefully, avoiding hitting other children's vehicles.

Boys engage in a good deal of roughhousing such as play wrestling and mock fighting. In my work with Jacklin and DiPietro, this difference became very apparent when we brought trios of preschool boys or trios of girls to a playroom.[3] The room was thickly carpeted, and equipped with a child-sized trampoline, an inflated Bobo doll, and a beachball. The boys engaged in rough-and-tumble play with these items over four times as often as did the girls.[4] These higher male levels did not seem to reflect a generally higher activity level, as evidenced by the fact that the girls (in three cohorts of children) did considerably more jumping on the trampoline than did the boys.[5] But in this very active form of play, girls almost always jumped one at a time and took turns. Only in the male triads was one child seen to throw himself onto another child who was jumping on the trampoline. When this happened, the boys would fall to the floor in a mock wrestling match. Observations in other cultures confirm that this kind of rough play occurs much more frequently among boys than among girls in a wide variety of cultural settings.[6]

Most rough-and-tumble play occurs in high good humor. Pitcher and Schulz (1983), drawing on their observations of a large sample of preschoolers, describe the male playstyle as follows:

> Among 4-year-olds, boys have a boisterous heyday in their numerous same-sex contacts in rough-and-tumble play, positive teasing, and foolish word play. They wrestle, bump into and fall on one another. One child pushes another back and forth in playful tussles, shouting "You're my brother." They make machine-gun sounds, and chase one another around with space guns and spray bottles. They are convulsed with laughter as they pretend to make toy horses sneeze and fall down. Boys put clay in one another's hair, play puppet fighting, tickle and pretend to shoot one another, fall dead and roll on the floor. They slide from piles of blocks, fall over chairs, pretend to drink and eat fire. (Pitcher and Schultz, 1983, p. 59)

Enjoyable play of these kinds occurs far more frequently than aggression among boys. They seem to be trying out each other's strength and toughness, without letting the situation escalate into serious confrontation. Occasionally, however, this kind of play does become angry and turns into fighting. A field observation made by the Romneys in a village in Mexico (Juxtlahuaca) illustrates how this happens:

> Juvenal and several boys are running around the school playground engaging each other in wrestling. There is much laughter in the wrestling match with the first boy. In spite of the fact that they are

both showing strength, it is easy to see that they are not trying to harm each other . . . In one of the movements, they fall to the ground intertwined. They go rolling around the ground until Juvenal remains on top and stops. While he looks at his opponent, laughing and breathing heavily, he pulls up his pants, which have fallen down, and adjusts his belt with both hands, which seems to signal that he hopes that the other boy will stop wrestling also. The other boy stands up and begins to run, looking at Juvenal (a chase and capture sequence follows) . . . Another boy comes running from the courtyard and grabs Juvenal from behind as if he wants to fight. Juvenal loosens himself, and with a push almost throws him to the ground. He laughs. The two again lock in a struggle, trying to intertwine their legs so that they will both fall to the ground . . . The other takes Juvenal's leg and throws him to the ground. Juvenal gets up. The other boy remains laughing in an expectant attitude. They grab each other again. This time Juvenal throws the other to the ground. The boy hits quite hard upon falling. He gets up, no longer laughing. He grabs Juvenal by the arms and twists them. Juvenal laughs but immediately begins to try to free himself, becoming rather serious. He seems to realize that the other boy is no longer "playing" but is now angry. (Whiting and Edwards, 1988, pp. 254–255)

This episode illustrates the fact that boys' play more frequently puts them on the edge of aggression, in a state of greater likelihood that provocations to fighting will occur, than is the case for girls (see also Smith and Boulton, 1990). And, indeed, direct aggression—both verbal and physical—is more common among boys than among girls. The sex difference in the frequency of aggression may be seen as early as the third year of life. In their observations of the social behavior of children toward each other in the large Montreal daycare center mentioned in Chapter 1, Legault and Strayer (1990) were interested in what they called agonistic behavior: aggression or competitive struggles over toys or control of space. Among children under 2, no sex differences were seen in the frequency of such behavior. In the third and fourth years, however, girls dropped off notably in the frequency with which they displayed agonistic behavior, while in boys the frequency was not only maintained but somewhat increased (see Figure 5), so that in the third and fourth years the frequencies were twice as high for boys as for girls.

The greater frequency of conflictual behavior among boys in the third year has been noted in a number of other studies.[7] Howes (1988), in reporting her observations of interaction among toddlers, noted that male toddlers had more difficulty with their peers: they were more likely to become upset if a peer interfered with their play or bossed or attempted to dominate them; they were more often involved in episodes of hitting or pushing, and had more difficulty sharing toys. Girls, by contrast, were more sociable, and showed more concern over others' distress.

From this early age into adulthood, a robust sex difference in rates of direct (overt) aggression is reliably seen.[8] We are accustomed to thinking of boys' aggressiveness as a personality trait (as when we say "boys are more aggressive than girls"), but we must keep two facts in mind: first, most boys are *not* aggressive, in the sense of possessing a consistent personality disposition that involves frequent fighting and getting into trouble with adults and peers through fighting; and second, boys almost

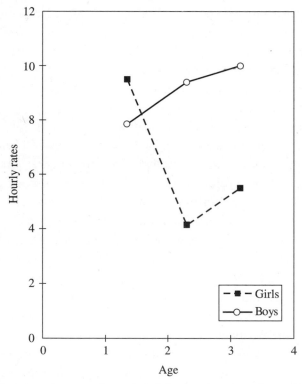

Figure 5. Mean hourly rates of agonistic behavior, by sex and age. (Source: Legault and Strayer, 1990, p. 75.)

always choose other boys as their targets for aggression. And as Fagot and colleagues (1985) have shown, boys are more responsive to aggressive (assertive) actions directed toward them by other boys than they are when the instigator of such actions is a girl. Thus fighting is a characteristic of male-male play—better seen as a property of male dyads or groups than of individuals. Part of the male aggressive pattern is a greater readiness to be aroused to anger by displays of anger in others (Cummings, Vogel, Cummings, and El-Sheikh, 1989), and boys are more likely than girls to attribute hostile intent to a playmate's assertive behavior (Feldman and Dodge, 1987). I must reiterate, however, that among most groups of boys, fighting does not occur frequently, and most of their rough play occurs more in the spirit of fun than of anger.

Indeed, it is worth emphasizing how much fun boys have together. Several studies have documented that during their play boys show more positive affect, more high spirits, than girls do during their play.[9] This difference is foreshadowed early in life: in the longitudinal study Carol Jacklin and I conducted, we asked mothers to fill out 24-hour "mood" diaries (in which they recorded a child's predominant mood for every 15-minute waking interval) on several occasions during the first 18 months of their children's lives. They reported that their infant sons were more often in a happy or excited mood, while their daughters were more often quiet and calm.[10]

We do not have a very reliable mapping of the frequency with which rough play and fighting occur at the successive age periods of childhood, but what evidence we do have suggests that it declines through middle childhood. Indeed, for most boys, the peak frequency may be reached at about the age of 4 (see Pitcher and Schultz, 1983). There is a subgroup of boys, however, for whom aggression (including bullying) and rough, confrontational behavior are sustained and become a dominant mode of behavior. Such behavior is consolidated in their male peer groups: deviant boys seek and find other deviant boys with whom they congregate, providing for each other conditions that maintain deviant behavior.

Dominance and Toughness

One of the things boys appear to be doing in their rough-and-tumble encounters is establishing a dominance hierarchy. The concept of such a hierarchy first came from the work of ethologists studying the behavior of a number of different animal species, including nonhuman primates. It became clear that when two animals compete with each other on a number of occasions for a scarce and desirable resource—a bit of food, access to a mate—one of the two is more likely to emerge a winner from the encounter than the other. Usually, such encounters do not involve combat; instead, threat gestures displayed by the dominant animal are enough to make the other animal back away. Although among young animals one member of a pair may win on some occasions and the other on other occasions, a hierarchy soon emerges in which Animal A usually dominates Animal B, Animal B usually dominates Animal C, and so on, in a transitive series through a social group.

Ethological methods of observation and scoring have been applied to groups of human children. Strayer and colleagues (Strayer, 1980a, 1980b), for example, identified a clear dominance hierarchy in several nursery schools. They reported that there were more boys than girls in the top echelons of the dominance hierarchy when one considered all the children in a class. As we have seen, however, children in preschools spend a majority of their social time with same-sex others, so we need to ask about the nature of dominance hierarchies among girls and among boys separately. Omark and colleagues (Omark, Omark, and Edelman, 1973) reported that male hierarchies are more well defined than those of girls, in the sense that all the boys agree about the ranking, and that the rankings are more stable over time than girls' hierarchies.

How quickly do boys form stable hierarchies? Petit, Bakshi, Dodge, and Coie (1990) investigated this question by forming groups of unacquainted boys—six boys in each group of first- or third-graders—who met and played together several times. The observers noted any asymmetries between pairs of boys in the giving and receiving of aggression, and in attempts to influence a partner. It was apparent that dominance hierarchies had begun to form even during the first play session, and after several sessions the hierarchies had become quite stable and transitive, with certain boys clearly being more influential and less often aggressed against, while others were consistently on the receiving end of both influence attempts and aggression. The hierarchies emerged more quickly, and became more stable, among third-graders than among first-graders.

The question of who is tougher than whom seems to be much more salient to boys than to girls, and more efforts to establish or maintain dominance may be seen among boys than among girls.[11] In preschool and kindergarten, then, we see the beginning of boys' concern not to appear weak in the eyes of their male peers.

As we saw in the work of Charlesworth and Dzur (1987), one dominant girl often emerged in a quartet of girls—one who got more than her share of a scarce resource. Among groups of girls who congregate together spontaneously, there are girls who are especially likely to take a leadership position. But their rank appears to depend less on toughness or unwillingness to back down when confronted—the basis for dominance among young boys—than it does on other leadership qualities.

Competition

The physical and verbal jousting among boys that occurs in establishing dominance relations often takes a more generalized form, namely competition. Even when with a good friend, boys take pleasure in competing to see who can do a task best or quickest, who can lift the heaviest weight, who can run faster or farther. Boys' games are more competitive than girls' games.[12] In middle childhood, male competitiveness undergoes a structural change: boys in their larger groups tend to organize their competitive play in the form of structured games.

Observing the free play activities of fourth- and sixth-graders, Crombie and Desjardins (1993) found that boys spent the majority of their play time in games, while girls spent much less time playing games. Girls' games involved turn-taking 21 percent of the time, while less than 1 percent of the boys' games had this element. When in their large same-sex playgroups, boys were engaged in direct competition with other boys 50 percent of the time, while for girls in their smaller same-sex groups, direct competition occurred only 1 percent of the time. Much of the competition among boys took the form of competitive activity between *groups*. This competition among groups of boys can be informal and temporary, but it can also evolve into competition between formally recognized sports teams or gangs. Once again, it is worth emphasizing that most of the male intergroup competition is not aggressive. Indeed, it has been shown that among groups of inner-city first- and third-grade boys, group members act to *discourage* any individual's aggressive behavior when they are engaged in a competitive game.[13] Thus the very need to win a competition between groups carries with it the requirement to cooperate within the in-group: for example, to subordinate individual egos for the sake of a group effort.

So, among boys, cooperation and competition are by no means antithetical, but are woven into the same web of social relationships. Despite girls' generally more cooperative playstyles, identification with a team or gang is probably stronger among boys.

So far, I have depicted males as the aggressive sex, and females as though their interactions were free from conflict or meanness. This is far from the reality. Although conflict does arise more frequently among boys, the interaction among girls is by no means free of conflict, and recent studies have pointed to a distinctively female element in conflictual behavior—*relational aggression*[14]—that greatly modifies any idea we might have about girls being made of "sugar and spice and everything nice." Cairns and colleagues conducted a longitudinal study, enrolling 220 children in the fourth grade and interviewing them each year through the ninth grade.[15] At each interview, they asked the children to describe recent conflicts they had had with same-sex and other-sex peers. Girls, far more often than boys, reported using what the Cairns group called "social alienation": when conflicts occurred, girls sometimes retaliated against other girls by attempting to manipulate another girl's friendship or affiliation status, by saying "I won't be your friend anymore," by excluding another girl from their social group, or by spreading negative gossip about another girl so as to alienate the girl's friends. The frequency of alienating tactics among girls increased sharply with age, from about one tenth of conflict themes in the fourth grade to over a third in the seventh grade. These tactics were almost never mentioned by boys in their interviews.

Similar findings are reported by Crick and Grotpeter (1995), who studied children in grades 3–6, and assessed relational aggression by having children identify which classmates exemplified certain characteristics. Included were such traits as: "When mad, gets even by keeping the person from being in their group of friends." Girls, more often than boys, were described by their classmates as using relational forms of aggression, while boys were the ones most often said to use direct, overt forms of aggression (starts fights, yells, calls others mean names). In a review article, Bjorkquist (1994) found considerable consistency across several cultures in females' greater use of relational aggression in conflict situations.

It is worth noting that the sex difference in direct aggression is greater than that for relational aggression in studies where the comparison can be made.[16] In the Cairns study, boys reported that physical aggression was involved in nearly 50 percent of their conflicts with other boys (compared to about 15 percent among girls), regardless of age; relational aggression among girls did not reach this high a level even among the older children, and occurred much less often than did the boys' direct aggression among the younger children.

Different Themes for Pretend Play

Pretend play does not occupy a major portion of children's time in nursery school, but when it does occur, interesting sex differences are apparent.

Boys' Themes

Boys' pretend play often involves assuming the role of a heroic character (Ninja Turtle, Superman, or Batman are recent favorites), and carrying out fantasy actions involves themes of danger and righteous combat. Historically, favorite roles for boys' fantasy play have included soldier, cowboy, policeman, and Robin Hood. Boys' fantasy play is sometimes stimulated by the presence of appropriate costumes or props—for example, a bow-and-arrow set—but when such props are not available, children improvise, using other objects as surrogates. Many nursery school teachers report how ingenious boys are in devising make-believe guns or swords in situations where more realistic toy armaments are not allowed.[17]

Flannery and Watson (1993) noted that at age 4, boys' pretend aggression occurred at twice the girls' rate, and at ages 5 and 6–8 the discrepancy was much greater: over six to one. Boys' pretend play often involves high levels of physical activity, and tends to occur outdoors. Often, such play occurs in conjunction with other boys who are playing similar or complementary roles, but a boy playing alone will also enact heroic or warlike themes by himself.

Girls' Themes

Girls' pretend play is less often solitary, more likely to involve cooperative role-taking. It frequently invokes domestic or school themes such as "I'll be the teacher, you be the child."[18] McLoyd (1983) suggests a reason why girls' pretend play is more often a cooperative matter with two or more girls taking reciprocal roles: that the scenarios girls prefer to enact—family interactions, teacher-child interactions—have several roles that are familiar to all children. Boys' favorite roles, by contrast, are often learned from TV characters who are portrayed as lone superheroes, and it is difficult for another boy to know what a reciprocal role might call for. Obviously, reciprocal role-taking is facilitated if two or more children already know similar scripts having more than one clearly delineated role. And this is more likely to be the case for the scripts that girls prefer than for those that boys prefer.

Girls' fantasy play frequently involves enacting family roles. Girls seem comfortable in assuming the role of father as well as mother, though the mother role is more central. (It is worth noting that boys seldom take on the pretend roles of either mother or father when playing with each other.) When girls enact family-based pretend scenarios, the preparation and serving of food looms large, as do other aspects of domestic life: managing households, entertaining guests, caring for children.[19] When one girl takes the role of mother and another girl takes the role of child or baby, the "mother" enacts a number of nurturant activities: feeding the "baby," putting on a Band-Aid, engaging in soothing talk when the "child" is hurt, and rocking a "child" to sleep.

Girls, of course, often use dolls as props for their domestic play, and doll play has often been seen as the prototype of female nurturance. We should, however, be aware that in modern American society, nurturant play with baby dolls quickly gives way to doll play with entirely different themes. Girls become interested in Barbie dolls and paper dolls at least by age 5, and the play themes enacted with these dolls have much more to do with adornment than nurturance. Play with Barbie dolls can be seen as expressing fantasies of becoming attractive, glamorous young women. The emphasis is on clothes, hairdos, jewelry, cosmetics. (One can see a commercial side to all this: the elaborate kits provided with Barbie dolls prepare girls for their future as consumers of a myriad products designed to enhance female attractiveness.)

In acting out their pretend scripts of glamour and romance, girls often make use of dress-up props. In preschool dress-up corners, bridal dresses and veils are popular with girls, as are ballet costumes and ball gowns. When dressing up, girls may be seen arranging one another's hair, adorning one another with beads, trying on hats for each other's approval. Their choices of dress-up props stand in sharp contrast to boys' choices of Batman capes or space or police helmets, though we should note that many girls try out male dress-up items as well as female ones.

The Growth of Same-Sex Coherence in Fantasy Themes

Not only is it true that boys and girls differ in their fantasy themes for pretend play. It is also true that children become more similar to their same-sex peers over a year's preschool experience, and more different from other-sex peers. Nicolopoulou (1997) collected 495 stories, told by 18 members of a preschool class during an academic year. The procedure was as follows:

> Every day, any child in the class can choose to dictate a story to a designated teacher, who records the story as the child tells it. At the end of each day, at "circle time," the same teacher reads aloud to the entire class all the stories dictated during that day; while each story is being read, the child/author, and other children whom he or she chooses, act out the story. Note that under this arrangement, children tell their stories not only to adults, but primarily to each other. (Nicolopoulou, 1997, pp. 162-163)

The stories told by children of the two sexes diverged sharply. Girls' stories were focused on social relationships, and frequently dealt with the maintenance and restoration of order in these relationships. "Home" was an anchoring locale, and characters were shown moving away from home and returning home. The boys, by contrast, did not portray their characters as members of stable social groups, but rather as individual characters linked to each other through their actions. Their stories focused on struggle, conflict, and destruction, with the resolution depending on physical size and power. The gender differentiation in story themes was very large indeed: during the fall, 76 percent of the girls' stories dealt with family relationships, while only 18 percent of the boys' stories did so. Aggressive-violent themes emerged in 87 percent of the boys' stories, and in only 17 percent of the stories told by girls. The heroic-agonistic themes of boys' stories, and the social-relationship (domestic, familial) themes of girls' stories, are clearly isomorphic with the themes, described above, that are enacted by boys and girls in their spontaneous pretend play. Child story-tellers also overwhelmingly chose to enact same-sex roles. The composition of the play-acting castes is worth noting, too: children who acted in another child's story much more often participated in a story told by a child of their own sex. Boys almost never enacted a female role. Girls somewhat more often enacted male roles, especially when called upon by a male storyteller to do so (usually, a boy called upon a younger girl to be the "bad guy").

There was evidence that over the school year, children of the two sexes were becoming increasingly polarized. Among boys, the excess of aggressive-violent story themes over family themes became greater as the year went on. And girls were less often called upon—or less often volunteered—to enact a part in a story told by a boy. The children seemed to become aware that certain kinds of stories were "for boys," others "for girls," and their preference for own-gender roles relative to gender-neutral roles increased during the year. The authors suggest that the children were using their narratives to mark themselves off from the other gender symbolically, as part of the formation of a group identity based on gender. They note, too, that the boys seemed consistently more preoccupied with distinguishing themselves sharply from girls than girls were with distinguishing themselves from boys.

Although these findings are based on a very small number of children, they are consistent with a study done previously by the same author and colleagues in a different preschool (Nicolopoulou, Scales, and Weintraub, 1994), and with the work on pretend play themes summarized above. For present purposes, the important point is that the gender divergence in story themes occurred in a setting where the school staff were making deliberate efforts to achieve a nonsexist atmosphere. Furthermore, the children came mainly from families professing egalitarian values. And the boys and girls were being exposed to similar themes in the stories read to them by adults. The strongest interpretation is that boys and girls were being exposed to the same array of possible themes, but were selecting and utilizing quite different elements from the array. I will return to this issue when I discuss self-socialization in Chapter 7.

Different Activities and Interests

In view of the above-noted differences in playstyles and in the themes of stories and dramatic play, it is not surprising that the nature of the preferred play activities in boys' groups and girls' groups should differ. Indeed, Huston has claimed that it is their divergent interests and activities, rather than their dispositions or "traits," that most distinguish boys and girls.[20] In middle childhood, boys' heroic fantasies are continued in the form of preference for adventure stories on TV and in books. And boys' interest in the heroics of fantasy combat are metamorphosed into more organized, less fantasized, activities. Preeminent among these is organized sports, in which boys consistently take a much greater interest than girls. Their interests are expressed not only through participation in sports, but in a preference for watching sports programs on TV, trading baseball or football cards, talking about sports among themselves, and wearing caps or T-shirts that declare partisanship for certain teams. And, of course, there are certain games, such as marbles, which are not organized as team sports but are understood to be "boys' games."

Boys' social contacts with each other tend to occur as by-products of their joint activities. Indeed, boys tend to choose friends on the basis of similarity in activity interests (such as a love of baseball), while girls choose more on the basis of personality compatibilities (Erwin, 1985). Girls more often seem to arrange social occasions simply for the sake of getting together. When they are old enough and can arrange transportation, they like to go shopping together. They watch TV or movies together, and their interest in romantic themes expresses itself in their choice of programs: soap operas and romances are popular, although some girls are also interested in sports and adventure programs. In recent years, schools have offered much more in the way of active sports programs for girls, and although sports have not become as pervasive and absorbing an activity for girls as for boys, they now do provide a major focus of interest for a substantial subgroup of girls. (It is notable, however, that after the first few years of grade school, participant sports activities are almost entirely sex-segregated.)

Girls' tastes and interests are broader, more eclectic, than boys'. It has long been evident that from an early age, girls are more interested in boys' toys and games than boys are in toys and games stereotyped as feminine.[21] It is common doctrine among producers of children's television fare that girls will watch not only girl-type romantic or family-oriented programs but also action-adventure programs with a boy as the lead character. Boys, by contrast, seldom watch girl-type programs with a girl as the leading character. (These beliefs among media program managers are presumably based on private rating data not available for citation.) Clearly, the way to maximize viewership among children is to offer male-type programs. At the time of this writing, children's programs being produced and broadcast on American networks that have a girl as the leading character are rare indeed.

Discourse in Boys' Groups and Girls' Groups

In Preschool

The amount of talking that children do during their play increases greatly during the age range from 3 to 6. Researchers have recorded children's talk as it occurs either in structured situations where two or three children are working or playing together in a laboratory room, or in more unstructured free-play situations. At preschool age, children of the two sexes talk to their same-sex playmates in quite similar ways, on the whole. Nevertheless, their styles of talking to each other do begin to diverge at this age, in ways that foreshadow the greater differences that appear when they reach middle childhood.[22]

A predominant theme is that girls' speech to each other is more coop-erative, more reciprocal. Leaper (1991) uses the apt term *collaborative*. Although "conversations" are somewhat brief and fragmented at preschool age, girls more often than boys sustain longer sequences of exchanges with each other in which they take turns speaking and maintain a joint theme. Girls achieve this in a number of ways. They use more "extending state-ments" or "relevant turns"—their responses build on something the part-ner has just said. More often than boys, they express agreement with a partner's suggestions. When they make suggestions of their own, they are likely to put them in the form of a question, or add a tag question in a way that softens the suggestion and keeps it from seeming coercive or dominating: "I'll be the doctor, OK?" They refer to themselves jointly: "*We'll* do . . ." or "Let's" or "Why don't we."

Boys, by contrast, are more likely to use direct imperatives ("give me"; "put it there") or prohibitions ("don't touch that"; "stop it!") when talking to each other. They are more likely to reject a suggestion made by a partner, and more likely to "grandstand" by talking about their own activities without reference to what a partner is doing. And there are more "domi-neering" exchanges between boys, in which one boy issues orders or prohibitions and the other either simply remains silent or tries to withdraw (Leaper, 1991).

These speech styles are particularly apparent when conflicts arise. Here are two examples of conflict episodes among boys. The first comes from a study by Jaqueline Sachs (1987, p. 185):

Two boys are playing doctor. S.U. (the one who was playing the patient role) has walked off with the toy stethoscope.

CH: No. You're not the doctor. Now take that off.
SU: No. Stop that. You pinched me on the eye.
CH: I didn't mean to.
SU: Then be my friend.
CH: Then don't talk like that.
SU: And you too.
CH: And you too, cause I didn't mean to do that.
SU: Not me either.
CH: Can you take that off? Just one person can be doctor.

Sachs (1987) notes that C.H. finally uses a mitigating utterance, softening his demand by transforming it into a polite question. She uses this example to illustrate what she believes is the case: that boys have such strategies in their repertoire, and know how to use them, but simply employ them less frequently than girls.

Another example of conflict between two four-year-old boys comes from the work of Amy Sheldon (1992b). The boys are in a playroom; Tony is sitting on a small foam chair/couch, pushing the buttons on the base of a touch-tone phone on his lap:

Tony: I pushed two squares (giggles), two squares like this.
Charlie: (comes closer, puts his fist up to his ear and talks into an imaginary phone): Hello!
Tony: (puts his fist to his ear and talks back): Hello.
Charlie: (picks up the receiver that is on Tony's couch) No, that's my phone!
Tony: (grabs the telephone cord and tries to pull the receiver away from Charlie) No, tha-ah, it's on *my* couch. It's on *my* couch, Charlie, it's on *my* couch.
Charlie: (ignoring Tony, holding onto the receiver and talking into it:) Hi.
Tony: (gets off couch, sets phone base on floor). I'll rock the couch like

this. (turns the chair over on top of the base and leans on it as Char-
lie tries to reach for it under the chair) Don't! That's my phone!
Charlie: (pushes the chair off the phone and pulls it closer to himself).
I needa use it.
Tony: (sits back on his heels and watches Charlie playing with the
phone).

Sheldon gives this as an example of what she calls single-voiced discourse, found more commonly in interaction among boys than among
girls, in which the children do not negotiate or try to persuade, and do
not try to adapt themselves to their partners' wishes. Each simply persists,
pursuing his own objective, and their conflict escalates. Girls, Sheldon
finds, more often use double-voiced discourse. An example of this kind of
discourse is seen in a conflict between two four-year-old girls playing with
a doctor's kit:

Arlene: Can I have that—that thing? (referring to the blood-pressure
gauge in Eileen's lap). I'm going to take my baby's temperature.
Elaine: (who is talking on the toy telephone) You can use it—you can
use my temperature. Just make sure you can't use anything else unless you can ask. (turns back to telephone)
Arlene: (picks up thermometer from table and takes her baby's temperature) Eighty three! She isn't sick. Yahoo! May I? (She asks Elaine, who
is still on the phone, if she can use the hypodermic syringe.)
Elaine: No, I'm gonna need the shot in a couple of minutes.
Arlene: But I—I need this though.
Elaine: (firmly) Okay, just use it once.

Although it appears that Elaine is dominating a compliant partner, later
in this considerably extended discourse Arlene demands and gets some
reciprocal compliance:

Arlene has given her doll a shot, and picks up the earscope to check
her ears.
Elaine: (picks up the syringe) Now I'll give her—I'll have to give her—a
shot.
Arlene: There can only be *one* thing that you—that—*no,* she only needs
one shot.
Elaine: Well, let's pretend that it's another day, that we have to look in
her ears together.

Sheldon argues that girls' discourse has been misunderstood. Girls have been described as compliant, polite, considerate of their partners' wishes—as though they seldom had conflicts and willingly subordinated their own interests for the sake of social harmony. Sheldon points out that girls do have disputes and do confront each other. She describes their conflict talk as double-voiced discourse because, while each pursues her own objective vigorously, each also negotiates with the partner and takes the other's wishes into account.

Several researchers have noted girls' use of "conflict mitigating" strategies (which include trying to find out what their partners' objectives are, and showing opposition indirectly rather than directly).[23] It appears that girls tend to talk to each other in ways that keep interaction going. The things that boys more commonly do, however, such as issuing commands and prohibitions, can stop interaction in its tracks and alienate partners.

In Middle Childhood

The themes apparent in preschool discourse are continued and elaborated in the school-aged years. Since the early influential review by Maltz and Borker (1982), the distinctive patterns of discourse in boys' and girls' groups has been described and reviewed by a number of scholars, and the results are well known, so I will simply summarize the main themes here.[24]

Conflict occurs less often among girls than among boys; when it does occur, the two sexes have somewhat different strategies for resolving it. Among girls, the double-voiced discourse is evident, in that while expressing their own point of view they also use conflict-mitigating strategies. These strategies include: displaying anger indirectly, proposing a compromise, and attempting to clarify the feelings or intent of the partner (Miller, Danaher, and Forbes, 1986), as well as simply softening one's claims by using more polite forms of speech and avoiding the power-assertive strategy of yelling or shouting (Crick and Ladd, 1990). Girls, too, more often avoid conflict by simply yielding to what a partner wants done, even when it is not in accord with their own preferences. Challenges to a partner are more often issued by boys, and this is often done in direct, power-assertive ways. In discussing a disagreement, boys are also less likely than girls to give a rationale for their position, simply asserting (or reasserting) their position (Hartup et al., 1993).

Boys' speech to each other is more "egoistic" than girls', in the sense that it is more likely to include bragging, threatening, overriding a partner's attempt to speak, or ignoring a partner's suggestion or demand. Boys' speech to each other more often includes direct commands and the giving of information. Girls, by contrast, more often acknowledge or agree with what a partner has said, and willingly give up the floor to a partner, so that there is an easier flow of turn-taking in the talk among girls.

Boys' talk fairly often includes the giving and receiving of "dares." Boys taunt each other with jibes of "scaredy-cat" and "stupid" and "sissy" or "faggot," challenging each other to do risky, limit-testing things, to prove their toughness. "Dirty" talk is much more common among boys than girls, and boys sometimes generate considerable excitement by trying to outdo each other in seeing who can say the most outrageously dirty thing (Thorne and Luria, 1986).[25] Homophobic remarks increase during middle childhood, as do references to female bodies and explicit talk about sexuality.

In view of the different styles of discourse summarized above, it is not surprising that boys and girls employ somewhat different tactics when attempting to join the play of pairs (or larger groups) of other children already engaged in play. Some children watch to see what activity is going on in the existing playgroup, and try to fit into the framework already established, by making comments or offering suggestions related to the ongoing activity. This is usually a successful tactic. Other children, however, will do what is called redirecting, trying to change the focus of the existing group and direct attention toward themselves—a tactic which is usually unsuccessful. Boys use "redirect" more commonly than do girls, and when girls do use it, they are less successful in getting group entry by this means than are boys using the same tactic.[26] There is also a sex difference in the receptiveness of the "host" children, who are already engaged in play when an outsider attempts to join. Borja-Alvarez and colleagues (1991), observing second- and third-grade children, report that a pair of "host" girls are more socially attentive to a would-be playmate, on the average, than a pair of "host" boys; the girls less often ignore the efforts of another child to join in.[27] And girl "guests" are more responsive to the readiness signals from potential "hosts," with the result that girls entering girl groups have the highest rate of entry success.

When one compares the frequency of the various kinds of discourse in boys' groups and girls' groups, the differences are quite apparent and consistent across studies. Still, it is easy to overemphasize the differences.

By no means all of what children say to each other in their segregated playgroups conforms to the gendered patterns described above. In fact, most utterances fall into neutral territory. For example, Miller, Danaher, and Forbes (1986), analyzing conflict-resolution strategies, identified a form of influence attempt called moderate persuasion. This consisted of a range of processes including appeals to a social norm, appeals to a situational constraint, expressions of pleasure or displeasure, and entreaties. While girls were using twice as many conflict mitigations as boys (22 percent of influence attempts by girls were of this sort, as compared to 10 percent for boys), the two sexes did not differ in their use of moderate persuasion techniques; more important, these moderate techniques constituted the *majority* of strategies used by both sexes. In sum, the conversations occurring in boys' and girls' groups are much alike in many respects.

What is the essence of the divergence, then? I suggest that what is distinctive about the discourse within all-male and all-female pairs or groups of children is directly linked to the playstyle differences noted earlier. When boys issue dares, shout at each other, boast, and refuse to listen or yield the floor, they are doing the same thing they are doing in their rough play and physical confrontations: they are defending their turf, and vying for dominance—for recognition of status from other boys. This is the element in the male agenda that most distinguishes their interactions from those of girls. But boys are not engaged in dominance encounters all the time. When they are not, their style of talk can be quite similar to that of girls.

The Greater Strength of Boys' Groups

A number of studies have shown that when boys and girls are asked to name their friends, or say which children in the class they would most prefer to sit next to or participate in a project with, the same-sex preference is equally strong in boys and girls. And behavioral measures usually show similar rates of staying close to, or playing with, a same-sex peer (for example, Turner and Gerai, 1995), although there are a few girls who consistently join boys' games while boys very seldom join girls' games.

Monitoring Gender Boundaries

Despite the fact that children of both sexes are powerfully oriented toward others of their own sex, however, the forces drawing boys together, and involving the exclusion of girls, appear to be stronger than the own-gender forces binding groups of girls.[28] This asymmetry shows itself first of all in the degree of rejection of the other sex. Girls are more open to association with boys, more willing to listen to and interact with them, than boys are in relation to girls. Girls tend to be interested in masculine—as well as feminine—activities.

Boys, however, seem to play mainly to a male audience. In their toy and activity choices, preschool boys are concerned with not appearing to be girl-like. They tease or reject other boys who do girl-like things (Feiring and Lewis, 1987) or play with girls, and reinforce their male playmates for male-typical behavior; girls, by contrast, are usually unconcerned about tomboy behavior in another girl. In order to prove his toughness to other boys, a boy must avoid any activities that might earn the label "sissy." Clearly, an essential element in becoming masculine is becoming *not-feminine*, while girls can be feminine without having to prove that they are not masculine.[29]

Separation from Adults

A second major asymmetry is that boys' groups are more separated from, less oriented toward, the world of adults. This greater separation from adults has its beginning within the family. Clarke-Stewart and Hevey (1981) reported that between the ages of 24 and 36 months, boys showed a drop-off in the rate at which they initiated contact with their mothers, while for girls, contact initiations were sustained. A further indication of lesser male attentiveness to mothers in early childhood comes from an early study by Minton, Kagan, and Levine (1971). They observed 27-month-old children at home with their mothers, and reported that boys who were initiating mischievous activities tended to ignore their mothers' initial, low-key remonstrances, so that the mother had to turn to more forceful methods of stopping a boy's behavior than were needed for girls. When young children move out of the home into group-care settings, similar differences in orientation are apparent. As early as toddlerhood, boys in group-care settings have been seen to be less responsive than girls to the reactions of teachers to their behavior; they *are* sensitive, however, to the reactions of other boys (Fagot, 1985). Fagot found that the young girls in the group-care settings she observed were oriented to, and influenced by, the responses of both teachers and other children. Girls also spent much more time interacting with adults than did boys (Fagot, 1994).

By the time they enter the first grade, boys show strong orientation toward other boys. Grant (1985), in her observations of first-grade classrooms, was concerned with the level of attentiveness each child showed toward teachers as compared to peers. She documented high levels of attentiveness to peers, much of which represented a distraction from teacher-pupil interactions. What emerged was a picture of considerably higher attention to peers, and interaction with them, among boys than among girls. Indeed, the boys' attentional orientation to each other was higher than to the teacher. Here is an illustration from Grant's field notes:

> Children are assembled on a rug, while (teacher) reads a story. She tells them: "Pay attention. I'll be asking you some questions about what I'm reading." Andre attempts to attract Ralph's attention and engage him in a pencil-poking fight. Ralph says Shsss. Janet tells them Shsss. Ralph finally fights with pencils with Andre. Mickey giggles. Teacher frowns at them, says nothing, keeps reading. Ralph whispers to Andre, "It's snowing out there (looks out the window). Let's you and me throw snowballs at recess." Andre grins, nods head to indicate yes. Mickey says, "Mr._____ (Principal) won't let you throw snowballs." Andre tells Mickey, "Well, man, he ain't going to see us." (Grant, 1985, p. 71)

The girls in these classrooms, by contrast, directed their attention more to the teachers than to each other.

Closing Ranks to Protect Risk-Taking

Part of boys' separation from adult society involves their risky, limit-testing enterprises. Some of the things grade school boys do—for example, passing around a can of beer, or a cigarette, or a pornographic picture—are clearly understood by boys as something adults would not condone. Such activities are surrounded by mutually understood peer-group rules about not tattling to adults.[30] The boys become a closed group protecting each other from the prying eyes of adults. In their discussion of rule transgression, Thorne and Luria give us some important observations:

> Rule transgression in public is exciting to boys in their groups. Boys' groups are attentive to potential consequences of transgression, but, compared with girls, groups of boys appear to be greater risk-takers . . . It is dubious if an isolated pair of boys (a pair is the modal size

of girls' groups) could get away with the rule-breaking that charac-
terizes the larger male group. A boy may not have power, but a boys'
group does. Teachers avoid disciplining whole groups of boys . . . Boys
rarely identify those who proposed direct transgressions and, when
confronted, they claim (singly) "I didn't start it; why should I be
punished?" . . . Boys are visibly excited when they break rules together. They are flushed as they play, they wipe their hands on their
jeans, some of them look guilty . . . Boys experience a shared, arousing context for transgression, with sustained gender group support
for rule-breaking. Girls' groups may engage in rule-breaking, but the
gender group's support for repeated public transgression is far less
certain. The smaller size of girls' gender groupings in comparison
with those of boys, and the girls' greater susceptibility to rules and
social control by teachers, make girls' groups easier to control. Boys'
larger groups give each transgressor a degree of anonymity.   (Thorne
and Luria, 1986, p. 181)

Thorne and Luria suggest that in their rule-breaking activities, boys are
playing to each other as an audience, and that the contagious excitement
which is involved in the limit testing (including the shared excitement of
taunting marginal or isolated boys) contributes to bonding among boys.
Probably, also, the implicit rules against tattling to adults help to develop
mutual trust among a group of boys.

Boys' and Girls' Friendships

For girls, participation in same-sex social groupings is almost synonymous
with the formation of friendships: they tend to congregate in pairs or trios
who identify each other as friends. And there is reason to believe that even
during the preschool years, girls take more pleasure in interacting one on
one than boys do. In an artificially contrived situation in which a child
interacted either with a single puppet or with a group of puppets, preschool girls showed more interest and positive affect in the dyadic situation
than boys, while boys expressed more positive affect when interacting in
larger groups than in a dyadic interchange (Benenson, 1993). Thus we see
precursors to the kind of social lives children lead in the middle childhood
years, with girls concentrating mainly on reciprocated friendships, while
boys invest in two kinds of social relationships: their larger male groups

and their same-sex friendships. Some evidence for this comes from the work of Benenson and colleagues (Benenson, Apostoleris, and Parnass, 1997). They have shown that by the age of 6, boys engage in dyadic interaction quite frequently, just as girls do. What is different is that boys are also greatly involved in coordinated group activity with larger groups of peers, something that is much less true of girls.

Pairs of girl friends express intimacy in a variety of ways: they use endearing terms to each other, stroke or arrange each other's hair, sit close together with shoulders touching or arms intertwined, and face each other with direct eye contact. In middle childhood, girls' friendship alliances are shifting ones, and girls' conversations reveal considerable concern over who is a friend and who is not. "You can't be my friend anymore" is a potent threat. Girls often cement their close friendships by mutually disclosing secrets and confessing weaknesses or fears—something that makes them vulnerable to gossip by former friends. The breakup of friendships seems to be a more intensely emotional process among girls than among boys.

Some of the games girls play on school playgrounds—hopscotch, jump-rope—involve more than two or three girls. Also, as we have seen, girls sit together in larger groups in school lunchrooms. But these larger groups generally do not seem to cement themselves into genuine groups of girls who meet together frequently, identify each other as group members, or participate in joint activities outside the immediate context of the game or lunchroom. As we have seen, too, larger groups of girls are less likely to form stable dominance hierarchies or play structured games, so these groupings are more like loose associations than structured, coherent groups. Most of the social time girls spend during out-of-school hours is with one or two friends, and it is doubtful whether they often have a strong sense of group membership in a larger category of girls. (This may be changing, though, as more girls become involved in girls' athletic teams.)[31]

Among boys, a meaningful distinction can be made between friendships and membership in larger groups. As we have seen, boys do form larger, structurally coherent male playgroups. A boy who is a member of such a group will often have, in addition, a reciprocal friendship with one or two other boys. Boys' friendships tend to be less intimate than those of girls, in the sense that there is less mutual self-disclosure, less physical closeness and eye contact. As boys progress through the middle-childhood years, they more and more avoid affectionate touching of their male friends; body contact takes the form of exchanging high fives or friendly punches. Male friendships appear to be based primarily on interest in, and participation in, the same activities.

Summary and Comment

The answer to the question whether distinctive cultures emerge in all-girl as compared to all-boy groups is: Yes, they do. It is clear that boys' groups and girls' groups have somewhat different agendas, a major difference being that boys seem to be much more intensively involved than girls in issues of dominance and the maintenance of status. This difference can be seen in styles of discourse and the fantasy themes of pretend play, as well as in the behavioral modes of enacting and resolving conflict.

In Chapter 1, we saw that the tendency for children to congregate with same-sex playmates was robust indeed. The distributions of boys' and girls' choices of playmates of a given sex diverged so strongly that their joint distribution was essentially binary (see Figures 6, 7, and 8 in Chapter 4).

How divergent are the cultures of the male and female childhood playgroups, once segregation has occurred? In some respects, they appear to be nearly as divergent as segregation itself. The incidence of rough-and-tumble play, and of fighting (though this is infrequent even for boys) is much greater in male groups than in female groups. With respect to the themes enacted in fantasy play, the two sexes are also quite divergent, though perhaps not so strongly as in rough-and-tumble play. When it comes to styles of discourse and styles of conflict resolution, gender divergence is probably narrower. I have suggested that scores on discourse styles are in a sense diluted: when boys play together, dominance issues are sometimes salient, sometimes not. My hypothesis is that boys' discourse styles diverge from the female pattern especially strongly when dominance issues are at play; otherwise the styles of the two sexes may be more similar.

So far, I have been talking about same-sex peer groups, particularly male ones, as though they were monolithic. And indeed, on playgrounds for preschoolers or first- and second- graders, there may appear to be one primary boys' group within which dominance relations are mutually understood. Boys do differ, however, with respect to how involved they are in the activities of the primary boys' group, and some individuals remain on the periphery. During the late grade school years, and certainly by the time children have reached middle school, one sees the formation of subgroups along lines of mutual interests. As noted above, boys who display exceptionally high levels of aggression or risk-taking are not especially popular with mainstream boys, but they do find each other, and as time goes on they congregate more and more with each other. Similarly, boys with mutual interests in computers, or athletics, form subgroups, and these groupings are recognized by other children and given names—the "jocks," the "nerds," the "brains." Among girls such groupings are not so clear. The main basis for distinction among girls appears to be *popularity*. The "top girls" are the ones who are style-setters: they know how to dress and take pains about their grooming. They are competent managers of social activities while being "nice" to others. They wield social power in the sense that they can influence which girls are "in" and which "out" of the popular category. And as puberty approaches, they are the girls who are viewed by other girls as popular with boys.

Distinctive patterns of interaction emerge in male and female peer groups. So far, however, we know very little about whether these descriptions apply equally to the different kinds of subgroups that emerge toward the end of the middle-childhood period. It is likely that the most distinctive male patterns—vying for status, competitiveness, ego displays, risk-taking—are more salient in some male peer groups than others.

We should be aware, too, that some children of each sex do not become very deeply involved in *any* same-sex peer group, but remain loners through much of their childhood. Thus some children are much more intensely exposed than others to the socializing environment of a same-sex peer group. And among the majority of children who do spend significant time playing in a same-sex peer group, individuals differ greatly in the behaviors they enact and the relationships they establish within these groups. Among boys, not every member of a given peer group is equally engaged in showing off or wrestling, issuing dares or shouting other boys down. And of course, in a stable dominance hierarchy, the experiences of boys at the top of the totem pole are necessarily different from the experiences of those at the bottom. Within girls' groups, not all are equally engaged in trying to maintain positive relationships among group members, and some girls are clearly more given to relational aggression than others. These individual differences are of great importance for individual personality development, and they undoubtedly have their roots both in genetic predispositions and in earlier socialization experiences, both of which vary among the children of a given sex. Thus there is usually considerable personality variation among the different members of a peer group.

Barrie Thorne[32] argues that these within-sex differences are so great as to render group differences irrelevant, and urges that "the contrastive framework has outlived its usefulness" (Thorne, 1994, p. 108). It is my position that if one thinks about group differences as a comparison of the average scores of males with those of females on some measure of individual personality dispositions, the contrastive framework has indeed been outgrown. But if one thinks of groups as entities which have their own dynamics, their own cultures—properties that pertain to groups as groups and are not describable in terms of the characteristics of the members— then the contrastive framework remains both useful and necessary. It may be the case—probably *is* the case—that a small number of central or leading children are much more active than others in establishing a group's culture. Yet this does not change the fact that all members of the group must find ways to adapt to whatever the group culture is. We all have both individual and group identities. At some periods of life, and in some settings, certain group identities are more important than at other times and in other settings. In this chapter, I have presented evidence to support the view that boys and girls are indeed exposed to two somewhat different cultures of childhood, and in Chapter 6 I will discuss the implications of involvement in a same-sex peer group for the formation of a group identity based on membership in a same-sex collective. The question of how much difference it makes to have been part of a same-sex culture in childhood is an open one. In the last part of the book I will explore how much carry-over there is to the gendered relationships that are formed later in life.

We should not assume that the two sexes are entirely disconnected from each other in childhood, however. Boys and girls are intensely aware of each other, and there are changes with age in the nature of the cross-sex interactions that occur and in the way cross-sex contacts are perceived and managed by children. I take up these matters in the next chapter.

3

Cross-Sex Encounters

As we have seen, children progressively associate more and more with others of their own sex during their free time, as they move from the preschool years into middle childhood. These trends inevitably mean that whatever interests young children may have in associating with the other sex are sidelined, subordinated, sometimes even forcibly repudiated. The changes that occur are illustrated by the experiences of a little girl—daughter of a colleague—as she traversed the years from 4 to 9.

As a preschooler, this little girl was bright and energetic, full of ideas and curiosity. She loved going to school, and played vigorously with both boys and girls. She was a popular playmate for children of both sexes. When she entered kindergarten at age 5, however, things changed. Early in the school year she came home from school considerably upset, and told her mother that the boys had said she couldn't play with them any more, because she wasn't tough enough. She said to her mother, "But I want to be able to do *everything*, and the boys won't let me." She and her mother had a discussion about what it meant to be tough, and whether she wanted to try to be tougher. She and the other girls devised their own solution, however: they organized a girls' group that had dramatic play confrontations with the boys. Each group appropriated a corner of the school playground for a fort, and boys were not allowed to enter the girls' fort (nor could girls enter the boys' fort). On one occasion when the little girl was not feeling well and her mother wanted to keep her home from school, she protested that she *had* to be in school that day because a "war" was planned between the boys' and girls' groups, and she simply couldn't miss it. All of this mock combat was a source of high excitement and adventure—presumably for children of both sexes.

When the girl entered the first grade, things changed again. During the first week of school, she came home crying. She said the boys had chased her, and had gotten her down on the ground with her arm twisted under her so that she was hurt. They had also started pulling at her clothes. She told her mother, "They said they were going to make me naked." Her mother told her that she must never allow boys to do anything of this sort: that she was justified in biting or scratching or kicking—anything to stop boys from treating her this way. But she said, "Oh mom, I couldn't do that." The next day, she went up to the boys' leader and told him, "I don't want to play chase any more." He said "OK," and there were no further confrontations. From then on, she played exclusively with girls. At this writing, she is 9 years old. Her mother reports that at a teacher conference, the teacher had nothing but glowing praise for the child's academic work, and commented on how popular she was with the other girls. She did say, however: "There's just one thing: she *hates* boys!"

Girls' Wariness about Boys

We do not know how often direct confrontations of this kind occur. But young children—particularly young girls—show a certain wariness, indicating an awareness that such confrontations *might* occur. In the Introduction I described a study in which Carol Jacklin and I brought unacquainted pairs of toddlers (aged 33 months) to a laboratory playroom, and watched to see what kind of play would occur between same-sex and different-sex pairs of children. Both boys and girls played much more actively with a same-sex partner. Especially interesting, however, was what occurred in mixed-sex pairs: girls in such pairs frequently withdrew to stand next to their mothers, or stood passively to one side watching the boy play with the single attractive toy that had been provided. In girl-girl pairs, this kind of behavior was seldom seen. It was evident that the girls were reacting specifically to the presence of a boy.

In preschool, children of the two sexes get along reasonably well together. There are certain boy-girl friendships in which the pair play together frequently and comfortably, although the incidence of such cross-friendships diminishes as the children proceed through the age range from 3 to 6. And preschool children frequently participate in mixed-sex groups where all are engaged in similar activities. (This kind of grouping is especially common in activities organized by adults.) Nevertheless, as we saw in Chapter 1, the relationships between children of different sexes progressively become more distant, more wary, less comfortable than is the case for their relationships with same-sex peers.

An illustration of this progressive distancing comes from the work of Borja-Alvarez and colleagues (1991), who set up situations for second- and third-graders in which one child (the "guest") would be instructed to try to join in with the play of a pair of other children who were already involved in a game (the "hosts"). Sometimes the guest would be trying to join a pair of hosts of the guest's own sex, sometimes a pair of the other sex. They found that guests of both sexes were "less constrained" (for example, more willing to ask directly to be included in the game) when approaching a same-sex pair of hosts. Male hosts were more likely to ignore the entry attempts of a guest child of either sex, so that it took more intrusive entry strategies to get their attention. But a girl guest generally did not use the strongly attention-getting entry strategies more characteristic of boys, and so her entry attempts were often unsuccessful when she was dealing with male hosts.

The fact that children spend most of their extracurricular time with others of their own sex means that children of the other sex become somewhat alien. Although each sex has stereotypes about the other—for example, girls think boys are mean, or rough, or too noisy, while boys think girls cry too easily—they sense that there are things about the social world of the other sex that are unknown or not understood (and perhaps secretly intriguing). Children of both sexes have a certain lack of confidence that they know how to talk to or interact with someone of the other sex. Nor do they see any reason why they should want to. Examples are found in Schofield's (1981) interviews with sixth- and seventh-graders:

Interviewer: In your class, do the boys mix more with the boys or the girls?
Harry: The boys!
Interviewer: Why?
Harry: Well, there's boy talk and girl talk.
Interviewer: I've noticed in the lunchroom that very often boys sit together and girls sit together. Why do you think that is?

Bob: So they can talk. The boys talk about football and sports and girls talk about whatever they talk about.   (p. 68)

Sandra: If you talk with boys they (other girls) say that you're almost going with him.
Interviewer: What does the boy think?
Sandra: I don't know. I can't tell what a boy thinks. It's hard.
Interviewer: You mentioned that you have deep conversations with your girlfriends. Do you ever have conversations like that with boys?
Sandra: Never. I mean, it never crossed my mind.   (p. 69)

We can see this sense of alienation from the other sex as an outcome of the gender segregation that has been a fact of life for most children during the years preceding adolescence. How does the avoidance of the other sex get started?

Reactions to Boys' Playstyles

Many girls do not like boys' rough play style, and withdraw from it. To judge from Strayer's work on dominance hierarchies, when an angry confrontation occurs between a boy and girl of preschool age, the girl is more often the one to back down. Perhaps by virtue of their rougher style, boys often succeed in monopolizing play space and materials.[1] An example may be seen in the work of Charlesworth and colleagues, mentioned earlier, in which quartets of children were compared in the way they competed for access to a movie-viewer. Charlesworth and LaFreniere (1983) used this procedure with mixed foursomes of preschoolers, each group being composed of two boys and two girls. When the viewing time was averaged across groups, the boys got three times as much access to the viewing position as did the girls. It would seem that though dominant girls are able to manage other girls so as to get what they want, their techniques of persuasion don't work well when pitted against the more physical, confrontational style of boys.

Interesting examples of this asymmetry are given by Dunn and Morgan (1987). On one of the playgrounds in northern Ireland where they observed the free play of young children, bikes and tricycles were the most popular toys, and they were almost entirely monopolized by boys. Boys competed for access to them. Dunn and Morgan (1987) describe this competition as follows: "Some boys used intimidating aggression to get bicycles from other children, such as standing in front of the bicycle, holding it stationary, and shouting . . . Unlike boys, [girls] showed a reluctance to get involved in a challenge for the possession of a bicycle" (p. 275). Girls got access to bikes only when a teacher intervened and provided the opportunity, or on the rare occasions when a bike stood unused. In one instance a girl noticed that one of the bikes was unoccupied, and said to her girlfriend, "Quick, we can go and play with the bikes now." When they were asked why they never played with the bikes, they said it was because the boys took them. When asked whether the girls ever took them, the children said, "No, just the boys." They had no explanation for why this was so.

A parallel example comes from observations in a large playroom in a northern California school (Greeno, 1989). Quartets of five- and six-year-old children (composed of two boys and two girls) were given access to a range of play materials in a large room. Two girls were jumping on a pair of child-size trampolines, facing each other and laughing. One girl glanced over her shoulder and noticed that the two boys were advancing toward them from the other end of the room. She squealed, "Oooooh! Here they come!" The girls jumped off the trampolines and moved quickly away, leaving the trampolines to the boys.[2]

There is an interesting side effect of girls' wariness about boys' playstyles: girls are more likely than boys to stay close to an adult, if one is present. It was previously thought that this simply reflected some greater trait of "dependency" in girls, but in Greeno's work, this tendency for girls to maintain closer proximity to an adult was found only when boys were present, not when girls were playing in all-girl settings. Apparently, girls were operating under an assumption that, when boys were present, having an adult nearby made them safer from whatever they feared or disliked about boys' playstyles.

And, indeed, the girls may be right about this. Powlishta and Maccoby (1990) observed boy-girl pairs of preschool age competing for access to a movie-viewer. At least under some conditions, girls got a greater share of movie-viewing time when there was an adult present than when the two children were alone in the room.

Mutual Influence

Why do girls leave the field to boys when they don't have the protection of an adult's close presence? Do girls feel overwhelmed by boys' physical power? The fact is that boys and girls don't differ greatly in size during the first ten years of life. Boys may have somewhat greater grip strength, on the average, though the differences are small. But girls do not usually engage in physical tests of strength with different boys to see which boys they can dominate and which ones they can't, and then withdraw only in the presence of boys they know are stronger. Rather, their wariness extends to boys with whom they have had no previous interactions.

The study of toddlers in mixed-sex groups described in the Introduction provides a clue to girls' withdrawal from interaction with boys. In that study, Jacklin and I examined the moment-to-moment sequences of social exchanges between partners. We found that when a boy issued prohibitions to a partner of either sex, the partner was likely to stop doing whatever it was that had elicited the boy's protest. When a girl protested, her objection influenced the behavior of female partners, but not that of male partners. It is a reasonable inference that the girls were giving up on efforts to negotiate a fair share of time with the boys because the boys were ignoring their attempts to do so.

A similar asymmetry was noted by Fagot (1985) in the play of two-year-olds enrolled in a daycare center. She reports that boys were influenced by (changed their behavior in response to) inputs from male playmates, but not from female ones. Girls, by contrast, were responsive to inputs from playmates of either sex.

Serbin and colleagues (Serbin, Sprafkin, Elman, and Doyle, 1984) examined how the patterns of influence between preschool playmates change over the age range 3½ to 5½. This is a time when children increase greatly the frequency with which they attempt to influence the behavior of a playmate, by making suggestions about how they should play or by issuing directives or prohibitions. Influence attempts are utilized as children learn the skills of coordinating their play activities with those of other children. But of course if play is to be coordinated, it is important not only for children to express to their play partners what they are trying to do, but also for them to listen and respond when their partners make reciprocal influence attempts. What the researchers found was that girls and boys were changing in different ways during this age period: the increase in influence attempts among girls mainly took the form of a greater frequency of polite suggestions to their play partners; boys' increases took the form of more and more direct demands, with little or no increase in the use of polite suggestions. Furthermore, boys were becoming less and less responsive to polite suggestions from playmates as time went on. We see here an asymmetry: the developmental changes boys were undergoing were such as to make them progressively less responsive to girls.

Freedom of Choice

We saw in Chapter 2 that adults are more likely to back off from interfering with boys' activities when boys are in groups, presumably because they find boys' groups somehow more volatile or potentially threatening than individual boys. Very probably, girls too are more intimidated by boys in male pairs or groups than they are when they encounter boys one at a time.[3] Indeed, the male behavior that many girls find aversive—yelling, physical roughness, confrontation—is most likely to occur when a boy is in the presence of other boys. Through encounters with individual boys in the neighborhood, with brothers, or with the sons of their parents' friends, girls can have opportunities for more manageable interactions in which they can feel in a better position to hold their own.

Even on school playgrounds, children do play in mixed-sex groups: both Maccoby and Jacklin (1987) and Crombie and Desjardins (1993) found that in the early grades, over a quarter of children's playtime was spent in mixed groups. And there are individual girls who particularly like male-type activities and feel free to cross gender lines and join otherwise all-male groups. Their success in gaining entry is often based on exceptional athletic skills; in addition, such girls will sometimes bring prized athletic equipment to school, and in this way become part of the informal group of boys who are planning the set-up of games.

Thorne (1994, pp. 127–132) provides an interesting account of a girl, Jesse, who was fully accepted as a member of male groups on the playground, but who also played comfortably as a member of girls' groups. Jesse successfully crossed the "gender divide." She was the only African-American child in her fifth-grade classroom, and one of a small minority of black children on the playground. She was exceptionally skilled at soccer, baseball, football, basketball, and dodgeball, and had good social skills as well, so that she was "buddies" with several boys as well as being fully accepted in girls' groups. She was assertive both physically and verbally, so that when playing a game of four-square with other girls, she was able to fend off raiding groups of boys by directly confronting them. Indeed, she had the reputation among the boys of being able to beat up any boy in the school. Thorne notes that Jesse successfully evaded any heterosexual implications of her association with boys, and did not participate in the gossip about who "liked" whom. Several other girls were accepted as members of boys' athletic teams, but they did not become "buddies" outside the games in the way Jesse did.

It is important to note that tomboy girls seldom receive criticism or rejection from other girls because of their interest in male activities and playmates. This means that individual girls have considerable freedom to choose how much contact they will have with boys. Girls who don't like boys' playstyles can immerse themselves in the all-girl cultures of middle childhood, or if they aren't particularly drawn to these cultures, can be loners. In either case, they can avoid interaction with boys except in the brief encounters of borderwork, discussed below. Girls who like boys' games and activities can find opportunities to join them, although to win acceptance they must be not only skillful at games but willing to use more assertive means of entry and self-defense than they would need for participation in girls' groups. The central point is that during middle childhood, gender segregation allows girls to be relatively free of the constraints which close male presence might place on their activities, while at the same time allowing for some variation in the range of cross-sex encounters individual girls will have.

Boys have less freedom of choice. While Thorne documents the case of one high-status boy who joins girls' games as well as being a central member of his male peer group, it is rarer for a boy to cross over in this way than for a girl to do so, and most boys do face taunting from their peers for cross-sex interests or playmate choices.

Borderwork

While children play mainly in their same-sex groups, there is a margin where the two kinds of groups come into contact. The sociologist Barrie Thorne (1986, 1994) has used the term borderwork to describe the nature and meaning of these between-group encounters. She and her colleague Zella Luria (Thorne and Luria, 1986) observed the activities of school-age children on their playgrounds and in classrooms, hallways, and lunchrooms. They worked in several different schools in two widely separated geographical locations, and were able to identify gendered patterns of behavior that occurred reliably across a variety of settings. Sometimes they saw a team of girls competing against a team of boys (as in kickball), or two boys competing against two girls in a game of four-square. They noted that when disputes arose about whether a ball was "in," children sometimes recruited others of their own gender to back them up, and the encounter became one of "the boys" against "the girls."

Raiding and Chasing

Although several girls might sometimes raid the activities of a group of boys, the usual pattern was the reverse. Boys might grab a ball that girls were playing with, or run through and disrupt their jump-rope game. An example:

> Two second-grade boys begged to "twirl" the jumprope for a group of second-grade girls who had been jumping for some time. The girls agreed, and the boys began to twirl. Soon, without announcement, the boys changed from "seashells, cockle bells" to "red hot peppers" (spinning the rope very fast), and tangled the jumper in the rope. The boys ran away laughing. (Thorne, 1986, p. 175)

An episode of this sort is sometimes a provocation for a group of girls to chase a boy or a group of boys. There are other provocations: a taunt of "you can't get me!" or poking and running, or grabbing a possession from a child of the other sex. A chase ensues. If girls capture a boy, the ritual usually calls for the girls to kiss the boy triumphantly, with applause from other girls and taunts from other boys. Children recognize such sequences with special names, which differ somewhat from one locale to another, but have a common theme: "chase and kiss," "kiss-chase," "kissers and chasers," "kiss or kill." Both sexes understand that when a girl catches and kisses a boy, she has insulted, or demeaned, or in some way contaminated him. Thorne says that boys, more than girls, interpret physical contact with the opposite sex as "polluting" (as evidenced, for example, by the fact that girls are more often charged with giving "cooties" to boys than vice versa).

The Sexualizing of Cross-Sex Contacts

At least by the early grade school years, children have begun to interpret cross-sex contacts in romantic or sexual terms. A child who is seen in the company of a child of the other sex is teased for "liking" or "loving" the other child. And children sometimes invent games of romance and marriage in which other children are recruited into cross-sex role-playing (not always willingly). These kinds of interactions were noted by Lloyd and Duveen (1992) when they recorded the naturally occurring dialogue of children in a British infant school (children aged 5 and 6). An example:

A group of girls have focused their attention on two boys, Darren and Oscar. The girls are talking about who is going to kiss whom:

Edith: Joan kiss Darren, and Oscar kiss . . . you!
Joan: (Starts for Darren, who runs.) Hey!
Edith: Come here. (Grabs Lulu, and moves her toward Oscar, not unwillingly.) No, kiss! Kiss her on the lips. Kiss her on the lips. Come on!
Lulu: No way!
Edith: Go on! Kiss Her! Kiss her!
Christine: (Makes a dash for Oscar.) I kissed him.
Oscar: I kissed *her.*
Edith: Oooh!
Oscar: (Points at Christine.) I'm going to marry her. (p. 167)

Children's readiness to interpret cross-gender contacts in sexualized terms was also shown in some observations by Sroufe and colleagues (1993) at a coeducational summer camp. The children in the study were ten- and eleven-year-olds. In one episode, a boy was seen leaving a girls' tent, where he had gone to get his radio. The boys who saw him immediately began to tease and taunt, saying, "He's with the girls!" "Did you kiss anyone, Charlie?" Charlie then chased and hit each boy in turn, presumably to reestablish his place in the boys' group. Sroufe and colleagues say they saw many similar episodes in which children actively maintained the boundaries between the two sexes by teasing children who had violated the unwritten segregation rules.

There's a good deal of ambivalence in children's covert interest in members of the other sex. Such an interest may be strongly denied, perhaps to ward off teasing by others, but also no doubt to avoid acknowledging romantic interest even to oneself. A scene I observed at a local swimming pool is illustrative:

Two third-grade girls are splashing in the shallow end of the pool. Girl 1 says, "Guess who just came out of the men's room?" Girl 2 says, "Who?" Girl 1: "The one you hate!" Girl 2 squeals, "Oooh!" and they retreat across the pool. The two boys who had just come out of the men's room advance toward them, jump into the pool, and proceed to splash the girls, who scream excitedly.

Comments made to an observer by a group of third-grade girls provide an additional example:

Susan asked me what I was doing, and I said I was observing the things children do and play. Nicole volunteered: "I like running, boys chase all the girls. See Tim over there? Judy chases him all around the school. She likes him." Judy, sitting across the table, quickly responded: "I hate him! I like him for a friend." "Tim loves Judy," Nicole said in a loud sing-song voice. (Thorne and Luria, 1986, p. 186)

Children themselves seem aware that a declaration of "hating" a given child of the other gender is by no means a denial of interest in that other child, and indeed can be very close to "liking."

Among small groups of girls who are friends, an interest in a particular boy may be explicitly acknowledged:

The girls and boys from one of the fourth-grade classes sat at separate tables. Three of the girls talked as they peered at a nearby table of fifth-grade boys. "Look behind you" one said. "Ooh" said the other two. "That boy's named Todd." "I know where my favorite guy is . . . there" another gestured with her head while her friends looked. (Thorne and Luria, 1986, p. 184)

Such self-disclosures are expressions of intimacy among girls, but as Thorne and Luria note, they carry a risk of being teased if a "friend" goes public with the information.

When children tease each other about "liking" or "loving" another child, the teasing is always about cross-sex attractions. Although boys may hurl the epithet "fag" at another boy, no observer has yet reported a boy teasing another boy about a specific male-male attraction, as in "Ha, ha! Johnny likes Jimmy!" The absence of such teasing implies that latent sexuality is interpreted by children exclusively in heterosexual terms.

As children approach adolescence, cross-sex teasing begins to take on explicitly sexual overtones, as in an instance reported by Schofield:

Daniel . . . comes running up to Sara . . . He grabs her, putting his arm around her shoulders. She tries to get away, but before she can completely extricate herself, Joe . . ., who has run up behind Daniel with a camera, snaps a picture. The two boys run away laughing gleefully. Joe says: "We've got the evidence!" Eric . . . jokes with a wide grin, "He tried to rape her." (1981, p. 71)

Schofield (1981), commenting on the common pattern of "pushing and poking" courtship behavior, notes that such episodes have virtually no content other than their indication of sexual or romantic interest. There is no relaxed or extended conversation between a boy and girl in such instances, and these encounters do not constitute a basis for cross-sex friendships.

The Rules of the Game

Although boys' groups and girls' groups monitor their members' contacts with the other sex, such contacts are not altogether forbidden. There are some circumstances in which cross-sex contacts are permissible, others in which they are not. Children may not be able to articulate what the rules are, but their behavior reveals some coherent principles. On the basis of their detailed observations of ten- and eleven-year-olds at a coeducational summer camp, Sroufe and colleagues (Sroufe et al., 1993) inferred what the rules are that children seem to be following. The rules are shown in the accompanying box.

The basic principle seems to be that a child must not display an intent to be in the company of an other-sex child. If cross-sex contact is to occur, there must be some element in the situation that makes it clear that the contact was not voluntary. Sroufe and colleagues provide evidence that some children are more active than others in maintaining gender boundaries and enforcing the gender "rules." They further report that the children who do this are generally competent and popular. The children who most often violate gender boundaries, they observe, are especially unpopular with peers. I am reminded of Thorne's observation (1994) that it is the group of popular children on grade school playgrounds who most clearly exemplify the two distinctive cultures of male and female groups.

As children approach adolescence, their sexual and romantic interests in the other sex become more explicit. Yet some of the "rules" are maintained. In particular, the last of the Sroufe rules—including an aggressive element in an approach to someone of the other sex—is often seen. There may, however, be more than one meaning here. Not only does an aggressive

Knowing the rules: Under what circumstances is it permissible to have contact with the other gender in middle childhood? (Source: Sroufe et al., 1993, p. 456.)

Rule: The contact is accidental.
Example: You're not looking where you are going and you
                 bump into someone.
Rule: The contact is incidental.
Example: You go to get some lemonade and wait while two chil-
                 dren of the other gender get some. (There should
                 be no conversation.)
Rule: The contact is in the guise of some clear and neces-
                 sary purpose.
Example: You may say, "Pass the lemonade," to persons of the
                 other gender at the next table. No interest in them
                 is expressed.
Rule: An adult compels you to have contact.
Example: "Go get that map from X and Y and bring it to me."
Rule: You are accompanied by someone of your own gender.
Example: Two girls may talk to two boys though physical close-
                 ness with your own partner must be maintained
                 and intimacy with the others is disallowed.
Rule: The interaction or contact is accompanied by dis-
                 avowal.
Example: You say someone is ugly or hurl some other insult or
                 (more commonly for boys) push or throw some-
                 thing at them as you pass by.

facade help shield the actor from teasing by peers, but it may also protect the actor in case the advances prove to be unwelcome. Schofield (1981), observing children aged 12–14, noted instances of ambiguous approaches, in which, for example, a boy would run his fingers across the back of a girl's neck in a touch that was halfway between a caress and a poke. Schofield says:

The children's concern with rejection and failure in cross-sex relation-ships is highlighted by the fact that virtually all of the widely used courting techniques are structured in a way that lets the students deny the reality of their romantic interest or through other means protects them from embarrassment should their overtures be met with indifference. For example, as discussed above, touching and "bothering" are recognized as an indication of romantic interest. They can, however, be treated as something quite different, such as an attempt to annoy, because no direct declaration of romantic interest is required. (Schofield, 1981, p. 72)

Schofield concludes that although pre- and early-adolescent boys and girls are intensely aware of each other as possible sexual or romantic partners, they also are concerned about possible rejection by the other sex, and continue to have strongly sex-differentiated interests and activities. The result, she argues, is rather ritualized and constricted forms of interaction between the sexes. The participants in these rituals, of course, often see through the behavioral facade to the covert meaning. One girl, for example, said that Boy A liked Girl B. When asked, "How do you know?" she said: "He throws her books on the floor."

Summary and Comment

Girls—especially in early childhood—tend to be wary of interacting with boys. Many find boys' playstyles too rough. And there is evidence that girls find boys unresponsive: a boy is not usually as open to influence by a female partner as a girl is to influence by a partner of either sex. Both these factors should mean that girls in general find interacting with boys unrewarding. Yet there are substantial numbers of girls who are interested in male-type activities and are not put off by male playstyles. In middle childhood, girls who are talented at sports can often win acceptance into male playgroups and participate in mostly male team sports. Girls who cross gender lines in this way usually do not have to pay a price in the form of rejection by other girls; they can maintain good relations with children of both sexes. We have little evidence concerning boys' reactions to girls' playstyles. The evidence presented in Chapter 2 suggests that boys may have difficulty participating in the sustained interactive sequences, or the turn-taking routines, that girls' playstyles involve. Also, boys undoubtedly see girls as weak or "wimpish" because they more often cry, stay closer to adults, and fail to respond in kind to direct challenges.

Despite the many forces keeping the two sexes apart, there are also forces drawing them together. There are a number of situations and settings in which gender has relatively little salience, and in which children of the two sexes can interact comfortably and constructively. Nowadays these are primarily settings, such as coeducational classrooms, that have been organized by adults. At one time there were many neighborhoods in which children of both sexes participated freely with their brothers and sisters and neighbor children in street or yard games—steal-a-step, Rover-red-Rover, King of the Mountain—but this happened in neighborhoods where there were many children and parents considered the neighborhood safe enough so that children could be allowed simply to "go out to play." Nowadays most neighborhoods, even in small towns, have many fewer children; also there are fewer neighbors home during the day to keep a watchful eye on children playing near their houses. And parents are almost universally concerned about the safety of their children with strangers who come into the neighborhood. Thus one of the milieus for relatively comfortable cross-sex interaction in childhood is disappearing.

The major setting in which children encounter non-kin members of the other sex is the school. On playgrounds, segregation is the rule, but cross-sex interest and attraction are nevertheless covertly present. Such attraction often manifests itself in the form of sexualized taunting and gossip. Yet the children themselves erect barriers against cross-sex attraction, and behave as though they are enforcing a taboo on cross-sex contact for the very reason that such contacts have sexual implications. Most of the observational studies that have revealed this pattern have been done since the sexual revolution of the 1960s and 1970s, and we do not know how much children's awareness of the other sex as future sexual partners has been fostered by the more open presentation of sexuality prevailing in recent times, particularly on TV and in films. My guess is that an undercurrent of sexual awareness was always present among children of grade school age, sparking both covert interest and overt avoidance between the sexes. Probably, however, this basic tension has been intensified by the sexual revolution.

I have argued that the reduction of contact between the sexes during middle childhood is a social phenomenon that protects girls from male dominance and coercion. When girls live their lives primarily within adult-monitored structures (the family, the classroom) or in all-girl groups, they are free to develop social and academic competencies in accord with their individual interests and talents. For boys, the situation is different.

We have no reason to believe that contact with girls threatens the development of their individual competencies (scholastic abilities, musical talents, and so on) in any way. But having settings in which they operate outside the sphere of influence from either adults or girls allows them to work out the complexities of male-male relationships: maintaining individual status among male peers while at the same time becoming part of a cohesive male group that can hold its own in competition with other male collectives.

Up to now, I have been giving a mainly descriptive account of the gendered social world of childhood and the way members of the two sexes function within it. The urgent question now is: How and why do these patterns of behavior and relationships come about? These questions will be the topic of Part II.

II

The Explanatory Web

4

What Needs to Be Explained

So far, I have been merely describing the major gender-linked phenomena of children's social development. We have seen that it is especially when children are interacting with their peers in pairs or larger groups that a child's gender matters. It is time now to talk about the hard questions: how and why these gender-differentiated social patterns come about. I will be particularly attentive to the factors impinging upon children between the ages of 2½ and 6, when the separation of the sexes is increasing at an especially rapid rate.

There are three major phenomena that need to be explained. The first is *gender segregation:* the strong tendency for children to congregate with others of their own sex when they have a choice of social partners. This is the most robust gendered phenomenon of childhood. As far as we know, it is found universally, although distinctive cultures do differ in how widespread childhood gender segregation is. The second is the *differentiation of the interaction styles* occurring within all-male as compared to all-female groups. And the third is *asymmetry:* we need to understand why boys' groups are in some sense more cohesive than girls' groups: more sexist, more exclusionary, more vigilant about gender-boundary violations by their members, and more separate from adult culture. We have seen that girls are the ones who first begin to avoid the other sex and to positively prefer playmates of their own sex. We need to understand, then, why the cross-over occurs: why, some time during the preschool years, boys become the ones more active in separating themselves from the other sex.

Multiple, Interwoven Causes

These three phenomena may rest on the same root causes. Or their origins may be similar in some respects, different in others. One thing we need to have in mind from the beginning: there is probably no single primary cause for the complex phenomena described in Chapters 1, 2, and 3. There is surely a complex causal web whose components feed into each other. In the chapters that follow, I have classified explanatory concepts under several major headings, but this does not imply that the explanatory principles are independent of each other. For example, although biological and social-shaping forces are discussed separately, it may be that societies adopt the stereotypes and roles they do in part as an accommodation to biological forces. And biological forces are themselves sometimes responsive to social conditions. Gender cognitions, too, can hardly be independent of other factors. The content of stereotypes and scripts reflects, to some degree, the realities of social behaviors that emerge from biological and social forces, though gender cognitions can distort, magnify, or discount elements of social reality. All the elements of the explanatory web influence each other.

We have seen that the tendency for children to choose same-sex playmates has its beginning some time during the third year of life, and becomes progressively stronger between the ages of 3 and 6. It is reasonable to expect, then, that there may be a limited set of factors that get the tendency started in very young children, but that these factors are then supplemented (or even replaced) by other factors as children grow older. Once same-sex social groups have begun to form, we may find that some of the same factors that caused the sexes to separate in the first place operate to produce distinctive styles of interaction in male as compared to female groups. There may, however, be new factors emerging from group process that were not present when segregation first began. It is important to pay attention to the timing and sequencing of possible causal factors.

Variations in the Robustness of Gender Phenomena

I noted in the Introduction that psychologists have devoted much attention to identifying differences in the average scores for men and women on a variety of characteristics. There has been some controversy concerning the size and importance of the differences that have been found. Some writers have claimed that the differences are so small, and the overlap of male and female distributions so great, that sex differences are trivial and can safely be ignored. But in an influential paper summarizing the results of a number of meta-analyses, Alice Eagly (1995) claimed that the typical size of sex differences is similar to the effect sizes found in studies of a large variety of other psychological factors, and are large enough to have important social consequences, particularly for people whose scores fall at the higher or lower ends of the distributions for their own sex.[1] Figure 6 shows distributions of the two sexes on a hypothetical dimension for which the mean sex difference is .35 standard deviations (Eagly claims .35 to be typical, although others would claim that the typical difference is smaller; for example, Hyde and Plant [1995] suggest a figure of about .25.)

Figures 7 and 8 show distributions taken from Jacklin's and my observational study of playmate choices on school playgrounds for approximately 100 first-graders (attending a number of different schools). The scores shown are for the percent of social play time (that is, of time in which the child was engaged in play with one or more other children) that was spent either exclusively with female playmates (Figure 7) or exclusively with male playmates (Figure 8). As Figures 7 and 8 show, a large majority of the children—approximately four out of five of each sex—spent less than 5 percent of their time playing exclusively with a child or children of the other sex during the recess periods in which they were being observed. (By far the most common score for cross-sex play was 0 percent of time.) About half the children played almost exclusively with others of their own sex, but in addition, there were quite a few children who spent varying amounts of time in mixed-sex groups. This means that a girl, for example, typically spent no time playing in a dyad with a boy, and no time in a situation with two or more boys in which she was the only girl. She either spent her play time entirely with girls, or spent a portion in situations where one or more boys were involved but in which at least one other girl was present. The mirror-image situation prevailed for boys, who were very seldom seen playing exclusively with a girl or girls; some played exclusively with boys, others spent some portion of their play time in mixed groups including at least one other boy. I do not know how typical our findings are of other regions or other cultures. But the results shown in Figures 7 and 8 indicate strongly that in the matter of playmate choice, we are dealing with a gender phenomenon that is qualitatively different from the usual picture of sex differences shown in Figure 6. The sex difference in playmate choice is extremely robust; the distributions for the two sexes hardly overlap. The distributions are more than simply bimodal; indeed, playmate choice is close to being a binary matter, although there is some degree of variation within each sex.

Consider now the range of behaviors discussed in Chapter 2—the ones that appeared to differentiate the patterns of interaction seen in male and female playgroups. Does the magnitude of these differences more closely resemble what is shown in Figure 6, or what appears in Figures 7 and 8? We do not have definitive data to answer this question, but an educated guess is that the various facets of differentiation distribute themselves somewhere in the region between the two patterns. Rough-and-tumble play, direct aggression, and the themes enacted in pretend play and story-telling are quite highly differentiated by sex, and their incidence in the two sexes probably resembles the pattern shown in Figures 7 and 8 more than that in Figure 6. Most aspects of discourse styles, by contrast, are probably not so robustly different, and though perhaps more different than the "typical" difference shown in Figure 6, still show considerable overlap. No doubt, the degree of differentiation of any of these features varies, and

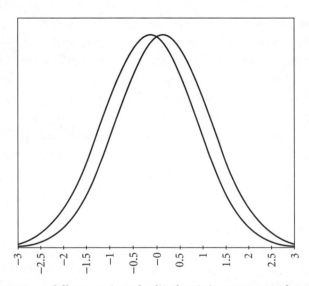

Figure 6. Mean sex differences (standardized units) on a range of psychological attributes. (Either sex may have the higher score.) (Source: based on Eagly, 1995.)

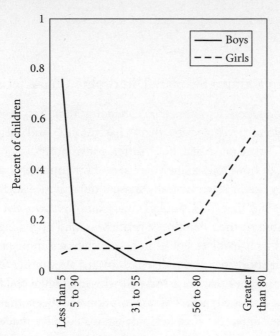

Figure 7. Percent of social play time with girls only at age 6½. (Source: based on data in Maccoby and Jacklin, 1987.)

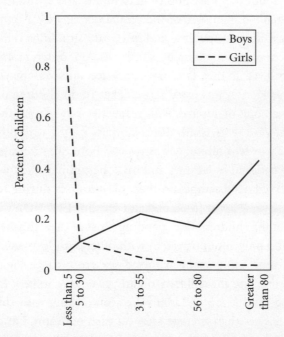

Figure 8. Percent of social play time with boys only at age 6½. (Source: based on data in Maccoby and Jacklin, 1987.)

depends on the nature of the activity a same-sex group is engaged in at any particular time.

Explaining a Strongly Dimorphic Characteristic

In the Introduction, I outlined a viewpoint that has been commonly accepted among psychologists: that "masculinity" and "femininity" are personality dimensions; that boys differ consistently among themselves with respect to how "masculine" they are—how tough and assertive, how involved they are in stereotypically masculine activities such as sports or rough play—and that girls, similarly, vary among themselves in terms of their "femininity": their daintiness, gentleness, and appealing and modest manner, and their involvement in stereotypically feminine kinds of activities. Research efforts have been directed toward attempting to discover the socialization regimes that are associated with individual children's becoming more or less sex-typed. The assumption has been that if we could identify these "antecedent" conditions, we would have made major gains in understanding why boys as a group behave in one way, girls as a group in another.

I have no doubt that measures of masculinity and femininity *do* capture important, stable dimensions of individual personality. A boy who scores as highly masculine at one time and in certain situations is likely to do so on other occasions, in different situations, on different measures. My question, however, is this: Is a preference for same-sex playmates a personality dimension in this usual sense? That is, do children of a given sex differ stably among themselves with respect to how strong their same-sex preference is? And if so, is this dimension associated with other measures of masculinity or femininity? My answer to both questions: probably not.

When the children in Jacklin's and my longitudinal study were 6½ years old, we observed a subsample on their playgrounds during recess on two occasions one week apart (Maccoby and Jacklin, 1987). On each occasion, we found that the children were spending most of their time with same-sex playmates, and only about 6 percent with other-sex playmates, the remainder of their time being spent in mixed-sex groups (see Figure 3). There was variation among the children, on any given day, in how frequent their cross-sex play was. A few children were seen playing with children of the other sex at higher-than-average rates on each occasion; but, importantly, it was not the same children who did so in Week 1 and Week 2.[2] It was *not* the case that certain individual children consistently preferred to play with children of the other sex while most did not. Rather, it was as though there were a few situations in which the children knew that it was "OK" to play with a child of the other sex, and in such situations any child would do so, while in the majority of free-play situations, cross-sex play was not OK and no child would engage in it.

When the children were 4½, we assessed short-term stability on a much smaller subsample, and found no significant week-to-week stability in the strength of same-sex playmate preferences. But there were indications in the data that a modest degree of stability might be present for girls at that age. There may have been a few girls who were consistently joining a boys' playgroup, while we could not identify boys who consistently joined girls' playgroups.

Not surprisingly, we found no connection between a given child's same-sex preferences at age 4½ and the same child's preferences at age 6½. Individual consistency over a two-year time span could only be expected for a characteristic which reliably distinguished individual children from each other at each age, and this condition was not met in our study.

Lloyd and Duveen (1992) examined the stability of same-sex preference over the greater part of a year in their sample of children in British infant schools. They assessed the proportion of play time that individual children spent exclusively in same-sex playgroups during the fall and again the following summer, and found a low correlation between the two time periods. They say, "It is impossible to predict with any certainty what a child's summer-term rating would be from her or his autumn-term rating. Social gender identity, as measured on this index, is not consistent, but dependent on context" (p. 89).

Some other researchers have reported that they do find some consistent differences among individual children with respect to their frequency of association with the other sex (Turner, Gervai, and Hinde, 1993; Thorne, 1993; Bukowski, 1990). As mentioned in Chapter 3, certain tomboy girls like to play boys' games and are accepted into boys' playgroups; and some boys (a smaller number) are seriously interested in trying out such girls' games as twirling on parallel bars, and are willing to brook the disapproval of the other boys in order to join girls' groups engaged in such games. Their situation in both the male and female groups is likely to be tenuous, however (Thorne, 1993, pp. 125–126). More evidence is needed concerning how stable the individual differences among children are with respect to the strength of their same-sex playmate preference. I believe it is likely that this stability will prove to be weak at best, and that in considering same-sex preference, we are not dealing primarily with a personality dimension, but with something that distinguishes children of the two sexes from one another on the basis of their membership in one of two distinct categories: male and female.

The point is an important one. Insofar as children of a given sex differ stably from others with respect to their preference for same-sex playmates, we can focus on those factors which could produce such variation, clearly including variations among families in the amount of sex-typing pressure they place upon their children. But if same-sex preference is *not* a stable personality variable, our search for causal factors would turn in a different direction. We would need to find causal factors which differ for the two sexes, but which are fairly uniform *within* each sex. In other words: phenomena which are strongly sex-dimorphic call for binary explanations. Some biological factors fit this requirement. So do any aspects of socialization—such as assigning categorically different kinds of clothing or hairstyles to children of the two sexes; piercing the ears of infant girls but not infant boys; or using categorically different forms of address—where nearly all girls are treated one way and nearly all boys another. So do some aspects of gender cognition, such as the knowledge that one is either a male or a female. But other popular kinds of explanation, such as within-family pressures on boys to be assertive or girls to be compliant, fit the requirements much less well.

Partner Compatibility

Partner compatibility occupies a middle ground in a model of explanatory factors. It would make sense for young children to prefer to play with other children who are interested in the same toys and activities, or who have similar or complementary interaction styles that enable them to play comfortably together. We have already seen that toy preferences are differentiated at an early age, and that the playstyles of young boys and girls are indeed different in some respects, with boys' play being more arousing—rougher, more "physical," with higher levels of excitement—and more oriented toward issues of dominance, while girls' play more often involves the enactment of domestic themes and the use of more "collaborative" styles of discourse. It may be the early-appearing aspects of these sex-differentiated toy preferences and playstyles that draw children toward others of their own sex. But if this is so, we would then have to move one step back, and ask ourselves why the toy preferences and playstyles differ in the first place.

Now, let us consider whether partner compatibility contributes to gender segregation. If it does, it will become one of the phenomena to be explained in succeeding chapters. Thus the chapter on social shaping will consider how and whether adult pressures directly push children toward selecting same-sex playmates. But it will also consider whether socialization pressures contribute to the development of playstyles that make same-sex partners more compatible.

Compatibility of Toy and Activity Preferences

We might plausibly expect that children would be drawn together by interests in the same toys or activities. Perhaps girls meet each other and become playmates because both go to the doll corner in preschool, or prefer to play with cooking equipment, or have a mutual interest in the jungle gym. Perhaps boys congregate together because they, more than girls, are attracted to blocks, bows and arrows, or toy cars and trucks.

If children segregate because of same-sex similarity in toy and activity preferences, we ought to find that they develop the toy and activity preferences first. We need to know, then, *when* children first show distinctive toy preferences, and whether these preferences already exist at the time they begin to show same-sex playmate preferences (usually, during the third year of life). Certainly, the folk wisdom contained in parents' reports suggests some early differentiation. Many parents who have children of both sexes report anecdotally that their small sons and daughters, even in their second year, seem to like different play materials and like to do different things with the same toys. Boys are said to be more interested in cars, trucks, and airplanes, as well as guns and swordlike objects, and to like making noises that are appropriate to these toys: motor sounds, siren noises, shouts of bang-bang. Boys are also said to be more interested in building blocks and mechanical toys, including robots. Infants and toddlers of both sexes like teddy bears and other stuffed animals, but girls are thought to be more interested in dolls, and many parents notice that even at the age of 2, girls especially like to dress up in party clothes and adorn themselves with jewelry and hair ribbons.

Systematic studies confirm that these observations by parents are generally quite accurate. They do describe the preferences of many boys and girls as early as the second year of life,[3] though sex-typed toy preferences usually develop earlier in boys and may not be well established in girls until after the second birthday.[4] Particularly well documented is boys' greater interest in transportation toys. At the toddler age, however, there are many children of each sex who do not conform to the stereotypical pattern. The divergence of the two sexes in preferences for certain play materials is gradual, and becomes more consistent after the second year.

We see then that many young children have developed sex-typed toy preferences at or before the time when they begin to prefer same-sex play partners. Toy preferences could, then, be a factor drawing same-sex play-mates together. However, research to date indicates that toy preferences do not play any substantial role in gender segregation. First, recall (from Chapter 1) that it is girls who first develop same-sex playmate prefer-ences—earlier than boys—while sex-typed toy preferences develop earlier among boys than among girls. More compelling, though, is the fact that among the three-year-olds studied by Serbin and colleagues (see the more detailed description of the study below), the "segregators"—the children who already had clear preferences for same-sex playmates—were no more likely than other children to have sex-typed toy and activity preferences.

Observing older children (aged 4–5), Jacklin and I (Maccoby and Jack-lin, 1987) came to similar conclusions. We noted that play was sex-segre-gated when children were playing with sex-neutral toys as well as when they were playing with dolls or trucks. Furthermore, we had tested some of our sample children a year before they entered preschool, to determine how sex-typed their toy preferences were, and found no relation between the sex-typing of these toy preferences and their subsequent tendency to prefer same-sex playmates.[5] The evidence so far indicates, then, that if young children find something especially compatible in the play of other children of their own sex, it is not compatibility in toy preferences that matters.

Playstyles Compatibility

Is it compatibility of playstyles, rather than compatibility of toy prefer-ences, that draws children toward others of their own sex? Lisa Serbin and colleagues have carried out research that is directly pertinent to this ques-tion (Serbin et al., 1994). They observed 57 children who were enrolled in five Canadian preschool classes. The children averaged 35 months of age at the beginning of the preschool year, and they were observed frequently during portions of the year so that the development of their social preferences could be charted. In addition, the teachers provided systematic ratings of the children's interactional styles. Not all the children in these classes displayed a same-sex playmate preference, but 66 percent of the girls and 21 percent of the boys did so, the rest of the children being gender-neutral in their choices. The researchers did not report any instances of a child's showing a significant preference for playmates of the other sex. Thus it was possible for the researchers to compare the interaction styles of children who were already segregating with those who were not. Also, they could compare the interaction styles of children who frequently played together, to see how similar they were.

The results pointed to playstyle compatibility as a factor clearly associated with gender segregation. First of all, children engaged in more active interaction, and less passive watching, when playing with a child of their own sex. This is consistent with the studies by Jacklin and Maccoby (1978) and Lloyd and Smith (1986) reported in the Introduction. Also, when children were compared with their most frequent play partners, it was found that children who most often engaged in rough, vigorous play most often had play partners who were also active and not given to focused, sedentary play. Children rated as "socially sensitive" by the teachers tended to have "best friends" who were also rated socially sensitive. And, the "segregating" boys—those who were showing systematic same-sex partner preferences—were among the most active/disruptive, according to the teachers' reports; they were more active/disruptive than the nonsegregating boys. "Segregating" girls, by contrast, were rated higher than other children on "social sensitivity." Thus it was the children who were most sex-typed behaviorally who most often played with same-sex partners in these preschool groups.

Do the results of this study constitute solid proof that it is the gender differentiation in playstyles that brings about same-sex playmate preference? Unfortunately, not quite. If we see that boys whose play is rough and active, and who are described by teachers as disruptive, are playing mainly with other boys rather than girls, does this mean that boys who come to school with already-developed tendencies toward vigorous, active/disruptive play seek out other boys because they are similar to themselves? Or does it mean that once boys have begun congregating together for whatever reason, vigorous and active/disruptive playstyles emerge as a function of the dynamics of male group play? From the existing evidence, we cannot see which way the causal arrow points.[6] All we can say at present is that the Serbin findings are consistent with the possibility that playstyles are one factor underlying the onset of gender segregation. Further evidence for this possibility is found in the fact, discussed in Chapter 3, that young girls are often wary of boys' rough playstyle, and tend to withdraw from it.[7]

In sum: it is a plausible hypothesis that differences in playstyles are both a cause and a consequence of gender segregation. As we consider explanatory components in the following chapters, differential playstyles will be one of the phenomena to be explained.

As we consider the three major components in the explanatory web—biology, socialization, and cognition—it will become apparent that the different components do not bear equally on the three phenomena to be explained. The biological component will be especially relevant to segregation itself, though it will also bear upon interaction styles. The socialization component will be more relevant to playstyle compatibility and the differentiation of the cultures that prevail in male and female groups. The cognitive component will bear upon both these phenomena. We will find that the three dominant explanatory viewpoints have less to say about the third component: the asymmetry that prevails between male and female childhood groups, though this issue will appear peripherally in each chapter.

5

The Biological Component

If there are any biological predispositions underlying development of the male and female patterns of social behavior reviewed in Chapters 1–3, they never act alone. In humans and other species, the form that instinctive behaviors take depends on the environmental inputs that activate them. An obvious example: human infants are preprogrammed to acquire language, but which language they learn depends on which language is spoken to them. To ask whether nature or nurture is more important in these developmental events is not a meaningful question. It is analogous to asking whether the area of a rectangle is determined more by its length or by its width.[1]

Nature and nurture are jointly involved in everything human beings do. All our actions are constrained by our species characteristics—the shape of our bodies, our upright posture, the design of our hands permitting an opposed thumb-finger grasp, and above all, the structure of our brains. It is the very structure of our brains that makes possible the storage of the vast amounts of information we derive from experience—in other words, it is nature that enables us to profit from nurture.

Are children of the two sexes genetically distinct in any way that would lead to the differentiation of social behavior in childhood? We know that the two sexes share a very large majority of their genetic material, so the initial assumption must be that the two sexes will be genetically equivalent with regard to a vast array of the characteristics of our species. Still, the presence of both X and Y chromosomes in males and two X chromosomes in females does underlie the differentiation of the two sexes with respect to their reproductive physiology. The question is: Does the differentiation spread beyond the genitalia, the internal reproductive organs, and the secondary sex characteristics, in such a way that the two sexes absorb somewhat different lessons from similar experiences their environment provides? Or in such a way that they select different elements from the vast environmental potential for utilization and learning? Or is it the case that children of the two sexes start out equivalent with respect to their reactive and selective constraints?

These are questions about which there has been a great deal of theorizing and speculation, and concerning which we do have some relevant data. Let me begin by considering the theorizing that has emerged from an evolutionary perspective, in which it is claimed that the two sexes differ with respect to behaviors that will serve their "inclusive fitness."

Evolutionary Theory

To begin with, it is important to distinguish between evolutionary science and behavior genetics. Both are concerned with inherited characteristics in the largest sense. But behavior geneticists are concerned with within-species individual differences. They examine some characteristic that varies considerably within the species (for example, in humans, height, intelligence, or a temperamental trait such as sociability or timidity) to see whether similarities among individuals are related to their degree of genetic relatedness. Comparisons of identical twins with fraternal twins, or comparisons of parent-child correlations for adopted versus biological children, have been favorite techniques for identifying genetic factors in individual differences. In twin studies, however, only same-sex pairs are included, and the findings are therefore not pertinent to the question of how (or whether) biological sex contributes to physiological or behavioral differentiation.[2]

Evolutionary scientists, by contrast, are concerned mainly with species-wide characteristics, and study how the adaptive characteristics of a species foster survival within the ecological niche the species occupies. They argue that the more important a species characteristic is for survival, the less within-species variation there will be with respect to that characteristic, because the less adaptive variations would quickly die out. Thus within-species individual differences are of little interest to evolutionary theorists, except that within-species variation preserves—in reserve, so to speak—

traits that might turn out to be more adaptive variants in the face of sudden, large environmental change.

In writings by psychologists, sex differences are usually classified under individual differences, but in the writings of evolutionary theorists, the two sexes are treated as subspecies (morphs). The focus is on the characteristics of males as a group and females as a group rather than on within-sex variability.

In evolutionary theory, the adaptive characteristics of the human species are thought to have evolved during the long period of time during which fairly small bands of humans roamed the savannas, hunting game and gathering wild cereals and fruits. As far as we know, through the time when humans evolved, we have always been a social species; human infants, and indeed isolated adults, could not survive alone. Thus we are endowed with the propensity to develop social behaviors, just as are the members of other social species. Individual humans are driven by three great biological imperatives:

- To survive to reproductive age
- To reproduce
- To rear offspring until *they* reach reproductive age

Any species that survives must have adaptive characteristics serving the first two imperatives. The third becomes important for species in which the young are not self-sufficient at birth or hatching. The longer the period of vulnerability of the young, the more important the third imperative becomes.

In bisexual species, there is no reason why individuals of the two sexes should differ with respect to the physiology and adaptive behaviors that fulfill the first imperative. Both males and females must obtain food and water and escape from predators. To this end, the digestive tracts of the two sexes are the same, and so are their food-getting and self-protection equipment (anteaters of both sexes have long snouts to probe anthills; ungulates of both sexes can run fast, and can use their sharp hooves to kill snakes). The theory would argue that the sexes should not differ with respect to the perceptual, conceptual, or motor skills needed for individual survival, so that among humans, there would be no reason to expect sex differences in adaptive qualities such as intelligence.

But the two sexes in bisexual species do have different reproductive roles, and so should be expected to differ with respect to the adaptive characteristics arising from the second imperative, and usually from the third as well. Reproductive tracts are differentiated, and only females give birth or lay eggs. Behavioral and morphological differentiation are linked, so that, for example, only male ungulates have horns, which they use in male-male combat over access to mates. In mammalian species, only females lactate, and thus invest more in the early care of the young.

The claims of the sociobiologists are well known, and I need not treat them in detail here. A few of the major ideas can be summarized briefly:

- Strictly speaking, motives and behavior patterns do not evolve and cannot be inherited. It is the physiological structures and processes underlying motives and behavior patterns that evolve. Evolution selectively favors the genes controlling those physiological characteristics that underlie certain motives and behavioral patterns: specifically those that serve the "inclusive fitness" of species members. Daly and Wilson define inclusive fitness as "the organism's contribution to the replication of its genes in both descendants and collateral kin."[3]

- The inclusive fitness of males is served by impregnating many females, thus leaving behind as many genes as possible (unless this strategy imperils the survival of the offspring), and by insuring paternity via keeping other males away from female mates. It is notable, however, that among different species of mammals, and among different subspecies of primates, there is considerable variation in the amount of paternal investment in the care of the young.

- Since females can produce fewer offspring, the survival of the offspring they do produce is especially important to their inclusive fitness. In species in which the infants have a long period of dependency on adults, females will have evolved to expend considerable energy in caring for the young. In species and ecological niches in which male parental investment contributes to the survival of offspring, it is in the female's interest to select mates who will invest in parenting, to keep the male involved, and to ward off other females who might compete for the male's resources.

The validity and implications of these propositions are widely debated, particularly as they apply to humans in industrialized societies. An important point for present purposes, however, is that they deal with how individuals of the two sexes may be predisposed to behave *after they have reached reproductive maturity.* The differentiations in social behavior that need to be explained take place before this time. Why should a young male who will later seek to father many children avoid girls and engage in male-male rough play during his childhood years? To ask this question makes us aware how little we know about the adaptive functions of play in childhood for later successful functioning.

Some clues may be found, however, in experimental work in which young animals have either been afforded or denied opportunities to play with age-mates.[4] This work indicates that rough play serves to socialize the young animals' aggressive tendencies, and, for males, to establish their place in the male dominance hierarchy. Considering that males will be the more aggressive sex later on, and will be predisposed to engage in combat over females, it becomes important for the survival of the social group that fights among adult males be kept within bounds. Adult males, after all, are usually strong enough, and equipped with sufficient weaponry (such as the adult ape's long, strong incisors) to be able to kill each other. Deadly fighting within the in-group would threaten the survival of all members of the group. Experiments with nonhuman primates show that when young males have the opportunity to play-fight and form dominance hierarchies, they learn with whom to fight, when to fight, and how to signal that they don't mean their behavior to be a serious threat—in other words, how to live in a male social group without overly aggressive encounters. And what they learn appears to go beyond the regulation of aggression; it extends to more active forms of cooperation and collaboration. These lessons presumably carry over into adult life, where they serve the interests of both the individual and the troop.

The functional significance of juvenile females' greater interest in infants seems straightforward: it is presumed to give young females practice in the skills of infant care and thus improve their subsequent maternal behavior. Several primatologists have traced the acquisition of "mothering" skills by juvenile females, showing that young (prepubertal) females are initially awkward, but with experience become nearly indistinguishable from maternal animals in their ability to soothe infants, and to carry and hold them competently.[5]

What evolutionary purpose could be served by the segregation of the sexes in play? Here we are on more uncertain ground. One possibility is that it functions as part of a system to prevent incest, and thus minimize the risks of inbreeding. Animals may be predisposed to lose sexual interest in any other animal with whom they have been closely reared, so that they will not mate with close kin. We do not yet have primate experiments in which male-female pairs have been caged together from childhood, and compared with pairs reared apart, in terms of their subsequent sexual interest in each other. With humans, however, there is an interesting natural "experiment" that is informative. In some parts of southern China, it has been customary for potential marital couples to be affianced by their parents when the children are still very young. In some cases, the little girl goes to live in her future parents-in-law's household, and grows up with her future husband. The anthropologist Arthur Wolf (1995) has studied these couples, and reports that when they become pubescent they lack sexual interest in each other, and sometimes resist consummating the marriage. Proof of their low level of sexual attraction may be seen in the fact that such marriages have exceptionally low rates of fertility and high rates of adultery and divorce. Wolf's findings are consistent with observations that boys and girls reared in close proximity in the children's houses of the Israeli kibbutzim tend not to marry each other when they become mature. It may be, then, that children's spontaneous avoidance of cross-sex others who are not kin serves the biological function of keeping these others within the pool of potential mates.

Evolutionary theory may also offer an explanation for certain asymmetries between the sexes in their childhood social behavior. In particular, the tendency for boys' groups to become more separate from adult society than girls' groups may also be seen as a social arrangement for the prevention of incest. Among most nonhuman primates (chimpanzees being a rare exception), young males are "peripheralized" when they are old enough to survive away from close proximity to their mothers. Young males congregate on the edges of the troop while the young females remain close to the center, with the adults of the troop. When the young males approach adulthood, they are usually driven out of the troop altogether, and must migrate to a different troop where they must find a place for themselves in the new troop's social hierarchy and carry out their adult mating activities. This exchange of males among troops presumably has evolved because it reduces the risks of inbreeding.

It is instructive that in the few remaining human societies in which the conditions of life are most similar to the conditions in which our species evolved, young males are also peripheralized.[6] They are sent away from the camping place of the tribe, and a young man rejoins the tribe only when he gains the permission of a girl's family to join the family as her mate.

This brief account reflects the focus of much of evolutionary theory on the adaptive activities of *individuals,* with the maximizing of each individual's inclusive fitness as the driving force of the evolved behavior patterns of members of a species. In recent developments in evolutionary theory, self-interest is seen as necessarily constrained by the requirements of in-group coordination. Several different kinds of human groups are distinguished, in which individual-group relations are constructed ("repeatedly assembled") in each new generation in order to afford the enactment of evolved, necessary functions (Caporael, 1995). Each configuration is associated with a group size, and the set of configurations can be seen as a nested hierarchy. The group size that is optimal for each function is reliably replicated in succeeding generations; if a group grows too large for its function it will undergo fission (rather than disintegrate). In the individual, genes will be nonfunctional unless the appropriate social context is constructed. There are several "core configurations":

1. *The dyad.* This social grouping is characterized by intimate coordination, such as that occurring in mutual imitation between a mother and infant, or in the reciprocal actions of sexual partners.
2. *The small face-to-face group.* Evolved from foraging and hunting, this group involves families or work groups when they carry out a joint enterprise.
3. *The band (deme).* Larger than the small group, the band maintains the conditions in which small face-to-face groups can function. In nomadic societies, these would include management of the group's movement from place to place. Presumably, they would also include protection from predators capable of threatening the band.
4. *The macroband.* This over-arching group is formed when bands gather seasonally for the exchange of individuals, resources, and information.

The assumption is that human beings have evolved to possess behavioral potentials for functioning within each of these kinds of groups. The appropriate behavior is presumably different for the different kinds of social groups, and is called into play whenever the social conditions exist that afford the specifically relevant evolved behavior. The implication is that we may be equipped to be a member of an intimate dyad, but that this behavior may not be relevant to (and will not carry over to) functioning in a small, task-oriented face-to-face group.

Clearly, children of both sexes function successfully in each of these core configurations. A group of girls playing jump-rope or four-square on the school playground are operating at the second level, just as a group of boys are who, as a group of four or five, are building a fort. It is interesting that the stable playgroups identified by Strayer (1980) in a number of preschools were usually made up of four or five children. This appears to be the group size that is optimal for carrying out the enterprises (or enacting the scripts) involved in much of the free play among children of this age. Caporeal's analysis (1995) draws our attention to the fact that the interactions in these playgroups are qualitatively very different from those in which the children are involved at home when interacting dyadically with a parent.

When children are about age 5, some gender divergence appears in the size of playgroups. Girls play in smaller groups and more of their interactions with peers occur in dyads. Indeed, Benenson (1993) reports that girls are more comfortable in a dyadic than in a group interaction condition[7]—smiling more and maintaining greater eye contact—while this difference is not seen in boys. Boys, by contrast, spend more of their time in social configurations that allow the behaviors called for at Levels 2 and 3. And we have seen that boys appear to distance themselves from dyadic intimacy with their mothers sooner than girls do. The two sexes differ, then, in the amount of experience they accumulate in utilizing the evolved behavior appropriate to each configurational level.

So far, the more recent evolutionary theorizing has not given an *explanation* of this gender divergence—only another way of stating what we already know about the social-behavioral functioning of the two sexes. We would still need to ask: Do girls start out with a more fully evolved set of mechanisms (and their associated behaviors) adapted for dyadic functioning, while boys are better prepared to produce the behaviors needed for Levels 2 and 3? It seems unlikely that the sexes differ in readiness for dyadic interaction. For one thing, infants and toddlers of the two sexes do not differ in their capacity to enter into intimate relationships with their mothers; and rough-and-tumble play, a key ingredient of the male playstyle, is as well adapted—perhaps better adapted—for play in dyads as for play in larger groups. It is still possible, of course, that boys are better prepared for participation in larger social structures, for example for finding a place in a dominance hierarchy. At this point, the possible connections are speculative. The important point here is that the two sexes may differ in evolved behaviors that are appropriate for functioning in groups of different sizes, and that we cannot expect behavior in groups always to have its roots in the experiences individuals acquire in dyadic relationships.

Yet we must not forget that even if boys were more fully adapted for functioning in larger groups, this fact would by no means encompass some of the major differences in playstyles documented in Chapter 2. Play in male dyads has certain components that are clearly different from play in female or mixed dyads. We must consider the possibility that the two sexes are differently adapted for interacting *with specific categories of social partners.* We are familiar with this idea from the ethological writings on nonhuman primates and other mammals, where it is shown that the topography of fighting behavior between two males is qualitatively different from behavior patterns seen in male-female or female-female dyadic interaction. Differential adaptation for functioning in groups of different sizes, then, is only one of a possible set of social-context–specific adaptations that might distinguish the two sexes.

Comparisons of Humans and Other Primates

From an evolutionary perspective, of course, it is a basic assumption that humans evolved from "lower" forms of life, and that we share many characteristics with other mammals and in particular with other primates. Indeed, it is now known that we share a remarkably high proportion of our genetic structure with our nearest primate relative, the chimpanzee. Jared Diamond in his book *The Third Chimpanzee* places the figure for shared DNA at 96 percent. The small portion that is not shared, of course, makes an enormous difference, and might function to override some similarities in the very sphere of development of interest here: gender differentiation. However, assuming that we humans do, indeed, share an evolutionary history with our nonhuman primate cousins, it becomes relevant to ask how and whether gender differentiation takes place in the social behavior of young nonhuman primates.

In a review of many observational studies of great apes, baboons, and seven species of monkeys, Meany and colleagues (Meany, Stewart, and Beatty, 1985) report highly consistent findings on rough play (or what they call play-fighting).[8] In all the primate species studied, male infants and juveniles have been seen to engage in this kind of behavior with much greater frequency than females. This is true of primates observed in the wild as well as those raised in cages or large enclosed spaces. More recent work (Lovejoy and Wallen, 1988) at the Yerkes primate laboratory in Atlanta is fully consistent with the 1985 review. In the Atlanta work, one-year-old rhesus males (approximately comparable to four-year-old to five-year-old humans) initiated rough play with age-mates approximately three times as often as did females. Meany and colleagues report that in primates younger than a year, sex differences in rough play are less evident, but as the animals grow older the male play grows rougher and the sex differences more pronounced. It is important to note that rough play is initiated primarily by males toward other males. It is also important that sex differences in rough play are more consistently found across species and studies, and are larger in magnitude, than sex differences in aggression.[9]

Preference for same-sex playmates is widely observed in young monkeys and apes. No doubt the male interest in rough play contributes, but it may not be the only factor responsible for sex segregation in play.

Among monkeys and apes, the play behavior of the two sexes is different in another important respect: juvenile females show much more interest in young infants. This finding, too, is consistent across many primate species (Meany, Stewart, and Beatty, 1995). Lovejoy and Wallen (1988) report that female rhesus yearlings were three times as likely as were male yearlings to approach and remain near infants. Also of interest is the fact that female yearlings spent considerably more time close to the adult females of the troop—close to their mothers and close to other adult females as well. Young males separated themselves from their mothers at an earlier age, and moved earlier into high rates of time spent with same-sex playmates. Interestingly, when monkey mothers resume estrus and their sexual activity, they also pull away from interacting with their infants and toddlers. Under these conditions, male infants increase their active play with peers, while females turn to increased grooming of other members of the troop (Barman, Rassmussen, and Suomi, 1994).

Some of the play among the young of nonhuman primates is sexual in nature. There is play-mounting of other animals (the male pattern) and "presenting" (the female pattern). Play-mounting is much more commonly seen in young males, although young females occasionally do it (especially if they have only other females available to play with). "Presenting" is more common in young females.[10]

To summarize what we know about the similarities between human children and young monkeys and apes:

- Both show gender segregation in play, at similar phases of development.
- The playstyles among young males are different from those seen among young females: males show more rough-and-tumble play, more mock aggression (as well as more real aggression).
- The two sexes are asymmetrical in their relation to adults: males separate from the adults of the group sooner and more fully than do females.
- Juvenile females are more interested in infants than are juvenile males, and interact with them more.[11]

These similarities strengthen the case for the claim that these behaviors in human children have emerged from the common evolutionary history we share with other primates. At least, it seems that in their most basic features, the juvenile sexually dimorphic behaviors which were the focus of Part I of this book do not require any conditions that are unique to human cultures. The sociobiological claims about the functional utility of sexually dimorphic behavior—what evolutionary "purpose" they serve— are intrinsically interesting but remain difficult to prove. And whatever the reasons why these patterns have evolved, we still need to know about the *processes* and *structures* whereby they become manifest. Are the brains of the two sexes organized differently? Do their neuroendocrine systems respond differently? If evolution really has equipped children of the two sexes with different predispositions to engage in certain patterns of social behavior, we ought to be able to identify some differential physiological processes that underlie the behaviors in question.

States of Activation in Boys and Girls

Metabolism Rate

It has long been suspected that there may be a physiological difference between boys and girls in terms of the sheer amount of energy they have to expend. It is known that the metabolism rate—the rate at which the body burns its fuel—increases greatly from birth to 24 months. Indeed, this rate is much higher between the ages of 2 and 4 than it is at any other time of life. Especially interesting is the fact that the basic metabolism rate reaches a higher level in boys, and remains at its peak longer. In girls, it reaches its highest level at about 24 months and declines thereafter. In boys, the decline does not begin until at least a year later (Eichorn, 1970, p. 233, figure 5). Of course, the fact that boys have an especially high metabolism rate during the crucial age period from 2 to 4 need not imply that they are necessarily more active; they may simply use up more energy in sustaining a given level of growth or bodily activity. Nevertheless, it is plausible that boys' higher metabolism rate may mean that they do expend more energy in the course of a day, and this might affect male playstyles in a number of ways: in the form of especially vigorous movements, frequent movement or restlessness, more rapid arousal to bursts of activity, or some combination of these.

Activity Level

Individual children differ considerably in how physically active they are. There is a range within each sex: some boys are quieter than most girls; some girls are more active than most boys. And especially important: any individual child's activity varies greatly depending on the opportunities for activity afforded by the situation a child is in at any given moment. Here the question is whether, over and above these variations, there is a tendency for boys to be more active overall than girls. If there is such a difference, it may have a bearing on the kind of playstyles that predominate in male and female playgroups.

Activity level is assessed in a variety of ways. Some researchers have attached "actometers" to children, recording the amount of arm or leg movement that occurs in a given period of time. Others have observed children at play, and counted the number of times a child moves from one place to another, or rated the vigor of the child's movements (comparing jumping and running with slower-paced activities). And parent reports have also been used.

These sources taken together indicate that in the first two years, sex differences in activity level are minimal, and are not found consistently from one sample to another.[12] In the preschool and grade school years, boys are often found to be more active than girls, but the size of the sex difference depends on the situation in which activity is assessed.[13] Girls of preschool and grade school age enjoy certain kinds of highly active outdoor play—jumping rope, jumping on trampolines, climbing on jungle gyms—when they have the right equipment, enough space, and freedom from interference by boys. When the children in the Stanford longitudinal study were preschoolers, each child was brought, along with two same-sex playmates, into a carpeted playroom equipped with a child-sized trampoline, a beachball, and (for part of the session) a large inflated Bobo doll. The girls spent nearly twice as much time jumping on the trampoline as did the boys (Maccoby, 1988). Furthermore, when the same children were observed in free play, the girls were as active as the boys when in the outdoor preschool play areas. Indoors, however, the girls were less active, while the boys were as active indoors as outdoors. These findings suggest that the girls were not less active in any general sense, but they, more than boys, may have moderated their activity level in response to the situational constraints of indoor classrooms.

When children are playing alone, sex differences in activity level are minimal. The differences appear primarily during play with peers. This fact first came to light in the 1970s, when Halverson and Waldrop (1973) reported that preschool girls displayed about the same activity level whether they were playing alone or with playmates; boys, however, were about as active as girls when playing alone, but increased their activity substantially when interacting with playmates. These results have been confirmed by subsequent research.[14] Since we know that preschoolers spend the bulk of their play time with same-sex peers, these results imply that boys are stimulated to high levels of activity by other boys. In short, we can see high rates of activity as a *consequence* (or at least, an intrinsic element) of male-male play, rather than as a cause of male playstyles.

We seem to have come full circle. If we had found that boys were generally more active than girls, we could have viewed activity level as probably a manifestation of sex-differentiated metabolic processes, and it would have seemed plausible that boys would be drawn to each other as playmates because they shared an interest in especially active forms of play. But such reasoning loses its force if male activity level is higher than female activity level primarily in the context of male-male play. Then high male activity level becomes merely a component of the rough, high-energy male play patterns that need to be explained. In making this point, I am overstating the case somewhat: there may be a residual overall sex difference in activity level, apart from the social-context effects.[15] But such a difference, if it exists, is much more modest than has been supposed.

Eaton and Yu (1988) offer an intriguing idea: that girls are less active than boys because they are more mature. Maturation rates in the two sexes will be discussed more fully below, but for the present note the following points: we do not know exactly at what age children are most active, but there is evidence that at least from preschool age onward, activity level declines. If girls are maturationally ahead of boys in some relevant respect, they should decline in activity level sooner; and, at any given age, when they are being compared with less mature boys of the same age, they would be less active. Eaton and Yu assessed activity levels in 83 children in the age range 5–8 years, and assessed each child's physical maturation on the basis of the proportion of estimated adult height the child had attained.[16] Girls were more physically mature than boys at each age. And, on average, the boys in this sample had higher activity levels than the girls of similar age. Furthermore, children who were more physically mature for their age were significantly less active. Did the sex difference in maturity, then, explain why the boys were more active than the girls? Yes, but only partly. The sex difference in activity level was reduced when boys and girls of equal maturity were compared, but some difference remained.[17] Especially interesting is the fact that maturity seemed to be associated with lower activity level only for boys. The sex difference in activity level is partly accounted for, then, by the more immature boys, not by the more mature girls.

When we compare the two sexes in terms of how active they are, we must consider the possibility that the sexes differ not only in the *amount* of their activity, but in the very nature of the activity itself. This possibility is highlighted in the reports of parents who were interviewed about their two- to four-year-old children (Goodenough, 1957). Goodenough reports that parents talked about their young sons' activity in the following terms: "a force barely under control"; "a bomb shell"; "a great deal of unnecessary energy, so much he doesn't know what to do with it, can't use it all up" (1957, p. 302). Such language was seldom used in describing the high-energy activities of young girls. Of course, it is possible that parents' perceptions were influenced by their stereotypes concerning what children of the two sexes ought to be like. Still, there is reason to believe that their reports also reflect something real about the qualitative differences in boys' and girls' active behavior. For one thing, activity level is part of a different cluster of characteristics in boys and girls. In my work with Jacklin, we found that the highly active toddlers of both sexes made more bids for their mothers' attention than did more placid children. But the more active girls were likely to bid for attention by smiling, offering objects, or vocalizing pleasantly; highly active boys were more likely to resort to fussing, demanding, or obstructing. These same children were seen two years later in play sessions with their mothers and fathers. It was the girls who had been most active as toddlers, and the boys who had been *least* active, who sustained the highest levels of cooperative play with their parents (both mothers and fathers) at the later time (Maccoby and Jacklin, 1983). Additional evidence comes from Fagot and O'Brien (1994) in their study of two cohorts of toddlers. They report: "Parents rated active boys in a more negative manner than active girls. This was true for both ratings of temperament characteristics and problem behaviors" (p. 395).[18] It would seem that high-energy behavior in boys is more likely to have an unrestrained, *hyper*active quality than is the case for girls—a quality that can interfere with cooperative interaction with parents, and perhaps with peers as well.

Arousability

Although it runs counter to some stereotypes about females being more "emotional" than males, there have been suggestions in the literature that males may be more excitable than females, in the sense that they become physiologically aroused at a faster rate than females under certain stressful or challenging conditions, and calm down more slowly. Such arousal could have either a positive or a negative emotional tone—it could show itself either as happy shouting and laughter or as displays of anger or frustration. If such a sex difference existed in early childhood, it might cause girls to back away from boys who are becoming quickly aroused, while boys might react with reciprocal quick arousal.

Much of the work on the rates of rise and fall of arousal levels in the two sexes has been done with adults. Gottman and Levenson (1988) cite a number of studies showing that males excrete more adrenaline under a variety of stressful conditions, with some evidence suggesting that they are slower to return to pre-stress levels. In their own laboratories, Gottman and Levenson monitored the level of emotional arousal in husbands and wives who were in the midst of a marital dispute, and found that the men's level of emotional arousal went up faster and higher than that of their wives, and returned to baseline more slowly.

Results for children are scattered and less consistent. Frankenhauser and colleagues in Sweden (Frankenhauser, 1975) did find a greater output of adrenaline among twelve-year-old boys than girls of the same age when the boys were under the stress of a crucial academic examination, but subsequent work in this laboratory with younger children has not yielded consistent results, and more often than not, children of the two sexes have emerged as similar rather than different (for example, in their reactions to the stress of being in the hospital).[19]

Especially intriguing is the work of Eisenberg and colleagues.[20] In Fabes's summary of this work (1994), the initial hypothesis was that boys are in some sense more generally arousable than girls. Using skin conductance as the measure of arousal, researchers compared preschoolers' responses to two films: one was a calm, gentle depiction of dolphins swimming in the sea, the other an "evocative" film in which a child was shown being cruelly teased. During the latter film, boys showed faster increases in their level of emotional arousal, reached higher levels, and dropped off more slowly than did girls. Another study, however, showed that this male reaction might be quite specifically linked to certain film content. In this later study, researchers compared children's reactions to a sympathy-inducing film and a threatening one in which children alone in a house saw a stranger lurking outside. Here, the girls showed more arousal than boys to the sympathy-inducing film, while boys were more aroused than girls by the threatening one. In the end, the conclusion appears to be not that boys are more generally arousable, but that the two sexes tend to be emotionally aroused by somewhat different things, although there are certain situations that elevate emotional responses in both sexes (such as being examined by a doctor, going to the hospital). Perhaps the most striking difference is that boys seem to be more aroused by threats, challenges, and competition.

These findings do not cast much light on same-sex playstyle compatibility. If it had turned out that boys were more generally arousable, we could have concluded that being prone to quick arousal was a factor drawing boys together (although we would still have had to ask whether boys are equally drawn to highly arousable girls). But if boys are specifically aroused by threats, challenges, and competition, that arousal is only an additional piece of evidence about male playstyles: that when engaged in competition or meeting challenges, boys become especially excited (usually *enjoyably* excited). This is something that was already evident in the qualitative descriptions of the male-male playstyles, and what needs to be explained is why this particular set of contexts is especially arousing (or especially pleasurable) to boys rather than girls.

Maturation Rates in Boys and Girls

We saw in Chapter 2 that young girls appear to be able to sustain longer bouts of interaction with each other than do young boys, and that boys of ages 2 and 3 are involved in more frequent conflicts. These findings suggest the possibility that girls in their third year begin to prefer each other as playmates because they are in some sense more mature, more able to regulate their behavior in such a way as to coordinate it with that of a partner. If this is so, it would help to explain why girls are the first to prefer same-sex playmates.

In human children, and indeed in the young of other species, maturation does not occur evenly. Some physiological systems mature faster than others, and the maturation of the different systems is not necessarily synchronized, so that a given child may be more mature than other children with respect to some systems but not others. Therefore, we need to consider the maturation rates of the two sexes with respect to a number of different systems. During the first two years of life, children are of course growing rapidly, in height, weight, and head circumference. The skeleton matures, in the sense that soft cartilage and bones harden. This early period of life is also a time of other important maturational changes. There is a predictable timetable for the eruption of baby teeth, beginning to sit up, beginning to crawl, beginning to walk. There is reason to believe that these transitions are related to the maturing of components of the nervous system. Long-standing evidence is that boys and girls do not differ consistently with respect to the rate at which they begin to sit up, crawl, walk, or climb (Bayley, 1965). Furthermore, their rates of physical growth during the early years are almost identical, although girls are slightly ahead in the hardening of bones (Tanner, 1970). It has been alleged that the sexes differ in adulthood with respect to the lateralization of the brain—in terms of how differentiated the two halves of the brain are in their functioning. In a comprehensive review, however, Kinsbourne and Hiscock (1983) concluded that sex differences have not been established in either the rate or the degree of hemispheric lateralization in childhood. Recent MRI data reopen the issue, and it remains unresolved.

The cycles of sleep and waking change dramatically in the first two years. As every parent knows, young infants do not sleep through the night, but as they grow older they can sustain longer periods of both sleeping and waking, and the number of transitions from one state to the other declines. By preschool age children have adopted a diurnal sleep-wake pattern quite similar to that of adults. Children differ in how quickly they make the transitions through the sleep-wake stages: some infants can sleep through the night much earlier than others; some give up their daytime naps earlier than others; and certain children are consistently ahead of the average trend in their sleep-wake development, others consistently behind. Thus one can see a child's sleep pattern as an index of maturity, and here again, the two sexes do not differ (Jacklin, Snow, Gahart, and Maccoby, 1980).

So far, then, we find boys and girls maturing at very similar rates with respect to a number of important aspects of development. There are some areas, however, in which girls appear to mature faster, and these are now examined in more detail.

Language Development

Toward the end of the first year, many infants begin to say their first words, and give indications that they have some rudimentary understanding of words spoken to them by their parents. Certainly, the onset of a child's ability to use and understand language should have a considerable impact on the kind of interaction that is possible with social partners. It is widely believed that girls have a head start in language development, but the truth of the matter has been difficult to pin down empirically. In a review of studies up to 1974 (Maccoby and Jacklin, 1974), Jacklin and I reported that at that time there was no clear evidence for sex differences in early language development. Findings since that time have been mixed, but a number of studies are pointing to an advantage for girls.[21] Naturalistic studies have been plagued by small sample sizes, and in laboratory work, boys have sometimes been more resistant to the testing procedures, so that their level of language competence has been more difficult to assess and may have been underestimated. At this time, the best guess is that girls acquire vocabulary somewhat faster than boys between the ages of about 14 to 20 months, after which time the boys begin to catch up (see Huttenlocher et al., 1991). In addition, there is reason to believe that regardless of vocabulary size or *receptive* language competence (the ability to understand the speech of others), girls *use* language more at an early age. That is, they initiate talk more often with parents, peers, and teachers (Fagot, 1977; 1978). In their meta-analysis of gender effects in children's talk, Leaper and Anderson (1996) report that girls do talk more than boys, especially as toddlers, *except* when interacting with boys, when they talk somewhat less.

Intriguing bits of evidence continue to appear in the research literature concerning the possibility that male and female brains may be organized differently with respect to language functioning. For example, Shucard, Shucard, and Thomas (1987) found that as early as 6 months of age, female infants show more electrical activity in the left hemisphere than the right when listening to verbal stimuli, while male infants show the reverse pattern.[22] Techniques for noninvasive study of brain function are being rapidly improved, and we can hope for more detailed information concerning the development of the language functions of the brain in the two sexes. Meanwhile, let us simply note that there are hints of a neural substrate that enables girls to progress faster (or at least differently) with respect to language.

Inhibitory Mechanisms

In infancy and toddlerhood, boys are somewhat more likely than girls to get into mischief of various kinds—for example, to pull books or records off shelves, pull curtains, play with wall plugs or sockets, try to get out of cribs or shopping carts.[23] Children are not born knowing that they may play with some objects and not others. Girls' being less mischievous might mean that they have learned the distinction between permissible and impermissible objects better than boys have; or boys and girls may have learned equally well, but boys may be less willing (or able) to comply with what they know is expected. These possibilities raise a host of questions: Do parents make less forceful efforts to teach boys what is allowed and what is not? Are girls more attentive to, more responsive to, their parents' reactions? Do boys have stronger reactions when their ongoing actions are interfered with, or are their mechanisms for regulating such reactions less mature?[24] For the present, consider what is known about the maturation of inhibitory (self-regulatory) mechanisms.

Adele Diamond (1985, 1988) studied infants' performance on a task that presumably requires inhibiting a prepotent (practiced) response in order to make a less practiced but correct response. The task, originated by Jean Piaget, involves hiding an object in one place, then moving it (in full view of the infant) to another hiding place. Younger infants tend to look for the object in the original hiding place (making what is known as the A not B error). Diamond found regular improvement on this task between the ages of 8 and 12 months: with increasing age infants could tolerate increasing delays between the time the object was hidden and the time they were allowed to look for it, before they made the mistake of looking in the original hiding place. Boys lagged behind girls in the amount of delay they could tolerate. In work with rhesus monkeys, Diamond reports, frontal lobe lesions interfered with performance on this task, but not on tasks that require only memory, not inhibition of a prepotent response. She suggests, then, that male infants, on average, lag behind females in the development of inhibitory centers in the frontal lobes.

This is a provocative hypothesis. A number of other things we know would be consistent with it. Whiting and Edwards (1988) noted that in the many different cultures they studied, mothers quite consistently began training daughters earlier than sons to behave properly and to help with tasks, "as if responding to a developmental difference in the rate of social maturation." In support of their interpretation, my colleagues and I (Martin, King, Maccoby, and Jacklin, 1984) found that girls can be successfully toilet trained at an earlier age than boys, suggesting that girls may be able to inhibit sphincter action at an earlier age.

Boys' greater mischievousness could be interpreted as difficulty with inhibiting a prepotent response such as reaching for a forbidden object. Higher activity levels, too, could be seen in this light: perhaps boys impose less regulation on their activity. The fact (reported above) that preschool girls moderated their activity levels when moving from outdoor play to indoor play while boys did not suggests greater self-regulation by girls.[25] The much higher rates among boys of hyperactivity (or the so-called attention deficit syndrome, ADS) suggest that at least some boys have less ability than girls to inhibit irrelevant, off-task behaviors.

The end of the second year of life and the beginning of the third may be a time when girls make especially rapid gains—more rapid than boys— in self-regulatory abilities. We saw in Chapter 2 that the end of the second year and the beginning of the third year is the time when agonistic behaviors drop off for girls, but not for boys. It is also a time when angry frustration reactions (including crying and temper tantrums) diminish rapidly in girls but remain high in boys (Goodenough, 1931; Van Leishout, 1975; Fagot, Hagan, Leinbach, and Kronsberg, 1985).

Rothbart and colleagues (Rothbart, Posner, and Rosicky, 1994) found that the period between 24 months and 36 months is a time of particularly strong development of "effortful control," a temperamental dimension which has to do with young children's ability to inhibit a prepotent response in the interests of keeping their attention focused on an intentional activity (see Rothbart and Bates, 1997). Rothbart and colleagues cite evidence that this form of self-regulation is related to the maturation of areas of the mid-frontal lobe of the brain. It is not yet known whether there is a sex difference in rates of maturation of the relevant brain structures, though to judge from the work of Diamond, and from the behavioral evidence I have noted, there may well be.

Recent work indicates that the sex difference in inhibitory control continues into the third and fourth years. Kochanska and colleagues (Kochanska et al., 1996) have assessed children's "impulse control" in a variety of ways, by examining their ability to (1) wait for a desirable outcome (for example, hold an M & M on the tongue for a specified interval before swallowing or chewing it), (2) slow down motor activity, (3) wait for a "go" signal, and (4) lower their voices. They observed a large group of children (101 at the onset of the study) attempting these self-regulation tasks on two occasions: once when their age averaged 33 months and again when they were 46 months old. Boys had considerably more difficulty with these tasks, and their self-regulatory scores were as much as one third lower than those of the girls.

The work by Eisenberg and colleagues (Eisenberg et al., 1994, p. 109) points in the same direction: they report that when preschoolers' ongoing activities are interfered with by peers, boys are more likely than girls to "vent" (yell, scream, stomp feet) or retaliate, while girls more often respond with nonhostile verbal self-defense or demands ("Hey! That's mine!" or "It's my turn now") and display what the authors call "constructive coping," which they interpret as a manifestation of self-regulation. Of course, girls' ability to handle conflict by negotiating rather than "venting" might have a good deal to do with their greater command of verbal modes of coping.

The idea that boys may be more impulsive than girls is not a new one (see Maccoby and Jacklin, 1974, pp. 99–101), but early work on the subject yielded sporadic results. Interest in self-regulation has grown in recent years (see Fox, 1994), and methods of assessment have improved considerably. The claim that the ability to regulate impulsive and emotional behavior develops earlier (or more strongly) in girls is gaining plausibility.[26] Still, the question remains open as to whether this delay in boys (or at least, *some* boys) is an outcome of slower maturation of inhibitory centers in the frontal lobes, as Diamond has suggested. There might be other reasons for boys' lower levels of self-regulation. One alternative possibility is that girls' greater command of language in the second and third years of life may contribute to their self-regulation.[27]

We have seen, then, that although the two sexes are very similar with respect to many aspects of maturation, there may be some important domains—verbal ability, emotional self-regulation—in which girls mature more rapidly. In the section on activity level, we also saw some evidence that boys' slower physical maturation (as indexed by the proportion of predicted adult stature achieved) might be implicated in their higher activity levels. The question remains: What bearing could these differences have on gender segregation?

Jacklin and I have argued elsewhere (Maccoby and Jacklin, 1987) that boys' greater activity level probably is not a significant factor in gender segregation. We noted that segregation is as great in situations where the sex difference in activity level is minimal (outdoors) as it is in situations where boys are more active (indoors). Furthermore, it is not the more active boys and the less active girls who most consistently prefer same-sex playmates. And activity levels—and sex differences in activity—decrease during the age period from 4 to 6, a time when gender segregation is strongly increasing.

There are similar problems when it comes to trying to explain gender segregation in terms of the hypothesized sex difference in self-regulation or impulse control. We must remember that same-sex attraction has two faces. To explain segregation in terms of temperamental compatibility, we need to show not only that one sex shows consistently more of some characteristic such as emotional self-regulation, but also that children of a given sex differentially notice, like, or respond reciprocally to the characteristic that is more typical of their own sex. Conceivably, boys who are themselves weak in self-regulation (given to intense, quick emotional displays) might like this same characteristic in other children, while a girl might not, whether or not she was given to intense emotional displays herself. However, Eisenberg and colleagues (Eisenberg et al., 1993, p. 1418) have reported that undercontrolled boys are *not* popular with other boys, while for both boys and girls, children who are "constructive copers" tend to be popular with their peers.[28] This suggests that girls ought to be more popular play partners with *both* boys and girls. We have not made much progress in trying to understand why boys in particular are attracted to each other as playmates. It would be more understandable if children of both sexes were attracted to children who were somewhat more mature than themselves (girls usually), on the grounds that they could more easily sustain bouts of interaction, and have fewer conflicts, with a mature playmate.

Prenatal Hormonal Priming

Most of the research on the physiological process related to sex-dimorphic behavior has examined the effects of sex-steroid hormones. Early studies indicated that young primates of the two sexes did not differ greatly with respect to the concentrations of male or female hormones to be found in their blood during the prepubescent time when sex-differentiated patterns of behavior were clearly appearing. Thus even if it could be shown that injecting extra amounts of testosterone into young animals during the juvenile period would make them more prone to rough play (an *activating* effect), this would not explain why male juveniles engaged in such play more often than females in the absence of supplementary androgens, during an age period when young males on the average hardly differ from females in the amount of available androgen. An alternative hypothesis was proposed: that sex-steroid hormones are implicated in behavioral sex differences through their prenatal *organizational* or *sensitizing* function. It was known that after the fetal gonads are formed in the first trimester of gestation, the male testes pour out substantial amounts of androgens; that the sex differences in blood concentrations of testosterone are much greater prenatally than they are at the time of birth; and that during the long period of childhood up till the onset of puberty the circulating levels of testosterone are quite low in both sexes.[29] If sex-steroid hormones are implicated in behavioral differentiation, it was argued, it must be the case that the two sexes are *pre*programmed—or "sensitized"—through the action of the relevant hormones in utero, to behave in different ways after birth at times when no currently activating effect of hormones is occurring.

Goy and colleagues (Phoenix, Goy, and Young, 1967; Goy, 1970, 1973) were the first to put this proposition to a test, and their findings are by now well known. To summarize: An experimental group of pregnant rhesus monkeys were injected with testosterone. Those of their offspring who were genetic females turned out, at birth, to be genitally masculinized, and as they grew old enough to interact with peers, it became evident that their play had been masculinized as well: they engaged in more rough play, and did more play-mounting, than untreated females.[30] Experimental prenatal administration of estrogens did not seem to have much effect on these behaviors in either sex.

Shortly after the early findings of the Goy studies became known, Money and Ehrhardt (1972) began to study the effects of prenatal hormonal sensitization in humans. Of course, they could not administer hormones experimentally to unborn human fetuses, but there were certain cases in which genetically female fetuses were exposed to exceptionally high levels of androgens because of a disorder of the fetal adrenal glands. The adrenals of both sexes, as well as the male testes, produce androgens. The disorder in which excess amounts of adrenal androgen are produced prenatally is called the adreno-genital syndrome, or AGS. AGS females were known to be genitally masculinized at birth, a condition which could be surgically corrected during infancy in most cases, so that the child's physical appearance would conform to its genetic sex. But the point of greater interest was that AGS girls, even after any physical anomalies had been corrected, appeared to adopt male play patterns.[31] Specifically, they engaged in high levels of rough play (higher than their normal sisters) and were reported to prefer male play partners. In addition, they were less interested in playing with dolls than unaffected girls.[32]

More recent work by Berenbaum and Snyder (1995) extends and confirms these findings. They reported fairly strong elevation of the preference for masculine toys and activities in AGS girls (compared to their normal sisters), and a significant elevation in the preference for male playmates in some AGS girls but not others. Thus the findings of the work on prenatally androgenized girls are consistent with the experimental work on monkeys reported by Goy and colleagues.[33]

Critics of this work have argued that it does not provide positive proof of a causal role for prenatal androgens in the differentiation of the social behavior of the two sexes. They note that monkey mothers are greatly interested in their infants' sex; at least, they do a good deal of sniffing of male infants' genitals (more than females'), and there is a possibility that male play behavior is somehow a response to the fact that their mothers "know" the sex of their infants and treat the two sexes differently.

Some more recent work at the Wisconsin Primate Center (Goy, Bercovitch, and McBrair, 1988) bears upon this issue. These researchers replicated some of the early work in which researchers injected testosterone into pregnant monkeys, but added some variations in the timing of these injections. They found that when the injections were given early in gestation, genetic females were genitally masculinized, and when playing with peers they engaged in more male-type play-mounting than did untreated females. Furthermore, the onset of puberty was delayed in these females, a further indication of masculinization with respect to specifically sexual functioning. But their levels of rough play were not elevated. By contrast, when the injections were given late in gestations, the genitalia of the genetic females were normal, while their play patterns were masculinized; specifically, levels of rough-and-tumble play were elevated. The mothers of early-treated females sniffed their genitals as they did with genetically male infants, while mothers of late-treated females did not, instead following the pattern of maternal response to female infants. Furthermore, these researchers did not find any relationship between any aspect of maternal behavior and the nature of an infant's subsequent play with peers. The authors concluded that rough play with peers is not related to genital virilization, and that the two things are independently regulated by hormonal events occurring at different points in gestation. They also concluded that the male pattern of rough play does not appear to stem from maternal differential treatment of infants who are genitally male.

So far, we do not have comparable experimental evidence concerning possible prenatal hormonal priming that may underlie young females' greater interest in infants. Stern (1989), in an extensive review of maternal behavior in mammals (mostly "lower" mammalian species), provided evidence that maternal behavior can be elevated in virgin females by the administration of estrogen and progesterone, if the timing and relative dosages of estrogen and progesterone are carefully calibrated to mimic the changes in hormonal concentrations that occur at or near the time of parturition. The implication is that hormonal factors are at work to produce maternal behavior in females who have recently given birth. But this work does not tell us why young prepubescent females—who do not have the pattern of estrogen and progesterone levels that are associated with giving birth—should show elevated interest in infants compared to juvenile males.

Experimental efforts to induce higher levels of nurturant or parental behavior in males by administering endogenous female hormones have not been very successful. But of course it may be that males are relatively uninterested in infants not because of the lack of female hormones but because of their elevated levels of androgens (either prenatal or postnatal levels). Males of a number of mammalian species (including primates; see Chamove, Harlow, and Mitchell, 1967) have been found to be aggressive toward infants, and aggression (which is androgen-related) is surely a kind of behavior that is antagonistic to nurturance. Some work with "lower" mammals suggests that when males are castrated at birth, they are subsequently more responsive to the young of their species, while females who have received androgens prenatally show reduced responsiveness (Stern, 1989, p. 149). To date, there is little work with primates concerning the possible nurturance-suppressing effects of androgens, although the findings of Ehrhardt and Baker (1974) concerning the lack of interest in dolls on the part of AGS girls would be consistent with such an effect. Some further relevant work is in progress. At the Yerkes Laboratory, Kim Wallen is treating genetically female monkey fetuses early or late in gestation with endogenous androgens. These animals will be compared postnatally with untreated females, in terms of their interest in infants.

There is some evidence that androgens may also play a role in the rate at which infants separate from the adult females of a monkey troop. Wallen and colleagues (Wallen, Maestripieri, and Mann, 1995) administered an androgen antagonist to a group of male rhesus neonates, and found that they spent more time in proximity to their mothers than untreated males. Their separation from their mothers, the shift into associating primarily with other young males, was delayed, and in this respect their social behavior was more like that of a young female.

Summary and Comment

Although humans, monkeys, and apes are all primates, they are obviously vastly different. Is there any reason to think that research on other primates is relevant to humans? I think we must take this work seriously, for two reasons: First, the sex-differentiated behavior patterns of interest here—the much higher incidence of rough play in young males, the greater interest in infants on the part of young females, and the preference for same-sex peers as playmates—are very similar in humans and nonhuman primates. And second, the work with human children, limited though it is, does point to prenatal priming processes in humans that are similar to the processes that have been pinpointed more precisely in monkeys.

If we do take the primate research seriously, there is no denying the fact that it points to a role for prenatal sex-steroid hormones in priming or predisposing the two sexes to develop somewhat different patterns of social behavior in postnatal life. What do we know about any sex differences in specific physiological mechanisms that are set up by this prenatal differential priming, and that then in their turn lead to the documented differences in the social behavior of boys and girls?

In considering energy physiology and energy expenditure, I noted that from infancy on boys have a higher basal metabolism rate, and asked whether this has implications for the rates at which the two sexes expend energy in the form of bodily activity. Research shows that while there may be an overall base-rate difference in activity level, there is considerable variation, from one situation to another, in whether boys are more active than girls, and in how great the sex difference is. In particular, boys appear to be stimulated to bursts of high activity in the presence of peers—probably especially when with other boys. When girls interact with other children, there is little increase in their activity level over what they display when playing alone. A similar picture emerged from examination of levels of physiological arousal. The claim that boys are more arousable in any general sense was not substantiated, but it did appear that children of the two sexes become emotionally aroused over different things. In particular, boys, more than girls, are excited by threats, challenges, and competition. The implication of these two sets of findings is that prenatal hormonal priming mainly predisposes children of the two sexes to respond somewhat differently to specific kinds of social stimuli, rather than generating general temperamental differences.

The arousal that boys experience when involved in situations of challenge and competition with other boys appears to be something that they like and seek. In traditional psychological language, certain challenging responses from peers appear to be more "reinforcing" for boys than girls. In this sense, a boy's positive arousal in response to these peer challenges is an intrinsic element in boys' preference for male playmates, and in the higher levels of rough, active play in male groups. It may also be an element in asymmetry, leading boys to have stronger same-sex preferences than girls.

Brain organization was considered indirectly, via studies of maturation. Maturation is, of course, controlled by developmental changes in the brain, but research identifying the neurophysiological processes involved in maturation is in its early stages. Rates of maturation are very similar for the two sexes with respect to many important aspects of development. But recent studies suggest that there are at least two areas of growth where the two sexes may have somewhat different timetables. One is language development, and the other is the development of the inhibitory capacities that underlie emotional self-regulation. In both of these areas, there are scattered, intriguing findings pointing to faster maturation for girls, on the average, in the second and third years of life. Possibly, too, girls' development in these areas may not be just faster, but also *different*. At least, recent evidence points to a somewhat different form of cerebral organization of the language function in boys and girls.

If girls, as toddlers and young preschoolers, are better able to use language in interacting with peers, and better able to control their frustration reactions, this ought to make them more compatible playmates for peers of both sexes. For boys, however, the attraction of playing with someone who can sustain longer bouts of harmonious interaction is counterbalanced by the fact that they are attracted to another child who displays the very uninhibited, boisterous behavior that is implied by lower levels of emotional self-regulation. On the basis of these possible differences in maturation rates, we can begin to understand why girls would be the first to establish a clear preference for female playmates: they would find boys too "wild," too uninhibited, and not responsive to the rudimentary forms of verbal negotiation young children are able to employ. Boys would be initially ambivalent, finding different things attractive about playmates of the two sexes. With increasing age, however, it would appear that boys' preference for male playstyles wins out; and probably, they are pushed in a segregating direction by other factors as well, such as their increasingly firm sense of male identity (see Chapter 7).

Is there anything in the foregoing analysis of biological factors that would lead to the asymmetries noted in Chapter 2? The work on prenatal or perinatal hormonal sensitization did point to a biological underpinning for the male tendency to separate earlier and more completely from the family of origin. This tendency might manifest itself in terms of males being more oriented toward each other, more sensitive to the reactions of same-sex partners than to those of other-sex partners, more exclusionary both toward adults and toward girls.

There is some good evidence that our evolutionary history has equipped children of the two sexes with predispositions for engaging in somewhat different forms of play. Has evolution also equipped each sex with differential reactions to specific categories of social others, so that boys and girls are drawn to same-sex others and wary of (or indifferent to) potential playmates of the other sex, over and above the attractiveness of the playstyle any individual other child may display? Here we lack relevant evidence. Consider the work by Goy and colleagues, in which genetically female monkeys were treated with testosterone late in gestation, so that they were not genitally masculinized, but showed male patterns of rough play. What we need to know is whether these females were accepted as playmates by young genetic males. We would like to know the same thing about AGS girls. At the moment all we can say is that some of the sex-differentiated predispositions, such as the tendency to be emotionally aroused or excited by challenge, or to engage in intense spurts of physical activity, may be more readily triggered by a specific category of social others—in boys, by same-sex playmates.

If there are some probable biological components in the set of causal factors underlying gender differentiation in social behavior, does this imply that biology is destiny? By no means. All primates have an enormous capacity for learning, which implies that they can adapt their behavior to the demands of the specific time, place, and sociocultural milieu in which they live. Humans in particular, with their extraordinary capacity for language and conceptual thinking, weave their biological predispositions into the fabric of their various cultures. It is time now to consider two other kinds of processes that are involved in the gender differentiation of social behavior: social-learning processes and the acquisition of gender cognitions. The question is how these processes might combine with biological predispositions to bring about culture-specific adaptation in the social behavior of the two sexes.

6

The Socialization Component

As noted in the Introduction, it is commonly believed that any behavioral differentiation of the sexes stems mainly from differences in the way boys and girls have been socialized: that they have been rewarded for what people in their society consider to be sex-appropriate behavior, and punished (or, at least, given negative messages) when they cross gender lines and behave in ways considered appropriate for the other sex. Parents are considered to be major actors in the socialization drama, especially in the early years, since at that time they are the ones who are most frequently in a position to administer contingencies for their children's activities. Some of the things that parents do may be quite unconscious, as when they arrange a little girl into a modest sitting position when she climbs up next to them on a couch. Presumably, parents operate from stereotyped knowledge and beliefs about what is appropriate for a child of a given sex, and train their children accordingly. And parents are probably influenced by future-oriented hopes and expectations concerning what they want a son or daughter to become.

In its broadest sense, sex-role socialization involves not only the direct shaping of "appropriate" behavior by parents and other agents, but also the child's own acquisition of stereotypes. Once children know what is considered appropriate for their own sex, the theory goes, they will use this cluster of knowledge and beliefs to regulate their own behavior so as to conform to the self-relevant sex-role prescriptions. One way to accomplish this is to choose same-sex models—more than other-sex models—for imitation and identification, selecting especially same-sex models who are thought to be good exemplars of own-sex characteristics. This kind of self-socialization will be considered in the next chapter. Now I merely note the basic premise underlying the claims for the power of sex-role socialization: that the adults of each generation pass on to each new generation of children, by means of teaching and example, the culture of gender— beliefs, myths, and rules of sex-appropriate behavior—that pervade the particular society in which the children are growing up.

In this chapter, I will examine what is known about the differential socialization of children of the two sexes, to see whether there are differences that could plausibly lead children to prefer same-sex playmates or develop different patterns of play within their same-sex playgroups. Since these patterns appear fairly early in children's lives, I will focus mainly on *parents* as the agents of differential treatment of boys and girls, and also on parental beliefs about gender as these may relate to the gendered phenomena of childhood that I have set out to explain. At the end of the chapter I will consider the larger extrafamilial socialization contexts, and how these fit into the overall social-shaping picture.

How will we know whether parental socialization practices are contributing to gender differentiation in children's social relations with peers? Certainly if parents, on average, treat children of the two sexes differently with respect to some aspect of social behavior, we might expect to see a corresponding difference when we compare the average scores of boys and girls on the social behavior in question. Thus if parents more often reinforce boys for aggressive behavior, or react negatively to such behavior in a girl, we would expect to find more conflict and fighting among boys in their same-sex groups. But the comparison of averages would not give a complete picture. In order to pin down the role of parental socialization, we would have to show that it is the very boys whose parents have been most permissive (or least punitive) toward their sons' aggression whose sons do the most fighting in the peer group. If a boy's selection of a peer group, or his behavior within his peer group, is unrelated to the way his parents have socialized him, then the fact that there is more aggression in boys' groups in general is harder to explain. At the very least, we would have to consider the possibility that the characteristics of children's sex-segregated groups are not strongly determined by the characteristics of the individual children who make them up.

Pressure to Segregate

We have surprisingly little information about whether parents put direct pressure on young children to play with others of their own sex. When parents set up playmate opportunities with another child, convenience presumably plays a strong role: the most available other child might be a near neighbor or the child of a parent's friend. In either case, the sex of the other child would not be the determining factor. And within the home, of course, the sex of siblings is a chance matter, and children play with the sibling nearest to themselves in age regardless of gender. In neighborhoods where it is safe simply to send young children out to play (usually with instructions about how far away from home it is permissible to go), the children may have few choices among children close to their own age, but if there are enough children for preferences to come into play, the choices are the children's own, not their parents'. I have not seen systematic reports on what happens when parents go with a young child to a park or playground—whether parents steer their children toward same-sex playmates. My own observations and those of young parents whom I have asked about this are that parents in parks usually say simply, "Go play with the other children," and give their children free rein in choosing which activities and social configurations they will enter, intervening only when some sort of trouble or danger presents itself.

In the usual case, children seem to develop an interest in same-sex playmates without any need for direct adult pressure. Of course, some children may become wary of the other sex as a result of parental warnings. If a two- or three-year-old girl comes crying to an adult because a group of boys have pushed her down, we can easily imagine the adult saying to her, "Maybe you'd better stay away from the boys. They're too rough." (It's harder to imagine similar warnings given to a boy about playing with girls.) It would be difficult to distinguish the effect of such warnings from the effect of a child's direct experience with the other sex in episodes that led to the adult warnings. In any case, in the large array of socialization studies no reports have come to light indicating that adults do urge young children to avoid the other sex, for whatever reason.

Until there is evidence to the contrary, then, it seems to be a reasonable assumption that parents do not play an active role in selecting same-sex playmates for their children when the children are young enough to need to have their parents involved in setting up their play opportunities.

When children are older, some parents—probably especially fathers—may become concerned if a son shows signs of being a "sissy." When a boy shows a preference for playing with girls, this is often seen as a symptom of effeminacy by both adults and other boys. It is plausible, then, that parents would try to steer a son toward playing with other boys if they were concerned about his masculinity. However, we do not have direct evidence that they make such attempts, or succeed in them.

Parents' Stereotypes

We all know that the first thing parents ask when a baby is born is, "Is it a boy or girl?" (although nowadays many parents already know the answer, from prenatal ultrasound scans). In a study done in the 1970s, parents got their first view of their newborn infant through a hospital window, and were asked to describe the child. Although the infant boys and girls in this study did not differ on objective measures of size or activity, parents saw their infant sons as robust, strong, alert, and large-featured, while they saw daughters as fine-featured, small, delicate, and "soft" (Rubin, Provenzano, and Luria, 1974). These parental reactions seemed to indicate that, from the very beginning, the way parents perceived their infants was strongly biased by their expectations about femaleness and maleness, and the findings of this study suggested that the way parents react to their children might be more influenced by their beliefs than by the child's actual characteristics.

Following this early work, a number of researchers have asked adults to respond to an unfamiliar infant or toddler who is introduced to them as either a boy or a girl. In these studies, a "stimulus child" is selected whose appearance is not particularly sex-typed, so that the same child can plausibly be labeled for some observers as a boy, for others as a girl. The virtue of this kind of study is that if adults react differently to the child depending on this arbitrary gender label, we can be confident that it is the adult's perceptions and beliefs, rather than the child's actual characteristics, that are causing the differentiation. In some studies, the adult observers merely view a videotape of the child in action, and are asked to describe the child and say how they would react to it. In other studies, the gender label is given to a live infant, with whom the adult interacts.

Early studies indicated that the gender label made a difference in adult reactions. For example, Condry and Condry (1976) found that when adults saw a videotaped incident in which a child appeared to be upset, they were more likely to label the child's state as anger for a presumed boy, and as fear for a presumed girl. More recent work, however, has not provided strong support for the view that a gender label in and of itself has much effect on an adult's response. Stern and Karraker (1989) have reviewed 23 gender-labeling studies. In some cases, adults were asked to rate the characteristics of a videotaped infant labeled as either a boy or a girl. In other cases, an adult interacted with a live infant.[1] There were relatively few instances in which an adult's rating of an infant on a particular characteristic varied with the gender label that had been applied. And when a labeling effect was found in one study, it was usually not found in other studies rating the same characteristic.

Results were somewhat more consistent with respect to the sex-typing of toys adults offered to the live infants: half the studies reported either that "girls" were offered dolls more frequently or that "boys" were more often offered a masculine toy such as a toy football or hammer. But the amount of interaction with the infant, and the adult's warmth and responsiveness—as indexed by touching, smiling at, talking to the infant—were not affected by the gender label.

We must remember that these studies present the adult with an artificial, contrived situation. Although in some studies the adults did have children of their own, many did not, and in any case the infant they were observing or playing with was not their own. Perhaps parents' gender stereotypes have a cumulative impact, and show themselves mainly when parents interact with a child on a daily basis. Or perhaps, on the contrary, the better parents know an individual child, the more their reactions may be governed by the actual characteristics of the child rather than by their stereotypes about what a male or female child should be like. We need to turn to more naturalistic situations, in which parents interact with their own infants and toddlers. And whenever possible, we need to go beyond such global measures as "amount of talking" or "total responsiveness" to a child, and examine what parents are talking to children about and what specific child behaviors they are responding to.

Of course, if we find that parents respond differently to sons and daughters, this might result from differences between the moods or needs or reactions of boys and girls that call for distinctive parental treatment. However, at least during the first two years, children's "eliciting" behaviors in most respects have little to do with their sex. Therefore, if parents do in fact treat infants and toddlers of the two sexes differently, it is a plausible inference that they do so largely because of their own preconceptions and training objectives.

Parent-Child Interaction

General Comparisons of Parental Treatment of Daughters and Sons

There now exist scores of studies in which researchers have visited the homes of parents to observe and record details of the way parents and children react to other as they carry on the activities of daily life. In addition, parents have brought their young children to laboratory rooms in which the interactions of adults and their children can be observed under standardized conditions. In a 1974 review of the body of research that then existed, Jacklin and I concluded that young children of the two sexes are treated very much alike by parents (Maccoby and Jacklin, 1974). We found no overall trend of parents differentiating between boys and girls with respect to the amount of warmth displayed, their responsiveness to the children's initiations, the amount of talking to the children, or the amount of restriction placed upon their activities. The only consistent trends were for girls to be offered dolls more frequently than boys, and for boys to be handled somewhat more roughly. In her review in 1983, Huston came to similar conclusions.

In their more recent comprehensive review of the research literature, Lytton and Romney (1991) found no differences in parents' treatment of sons and daughters with respect to the total amount of interaction, the amount of talking to the child, warmth, nurturance, responsiveness, or restrictiveness.[2]

A more recent meta-analysis by Leaper and colleagues (Leaper, Anderson, and Sanders, in press), focused specifically on talk between parents and children, found that mothers talk more to daughters than to sons. There was not enough research on fathers to determine whether they, too, treated daughters differently from sons in this respect. But parents did treat sons and daughters very much alike when it came to being assertive or "affiliative" (warm) toward them.

Also of interest is the fact that research has not shown any consistent tendency for parents to encourage independence or assertiveness more in boys than in girls, or to foster emotional closeness (attachment) in girls more than in boys. Thus parents do not appear to socialize children in conformity with frequently-held stereotypes concerning what is gender-appropriate.

Lytton and Romney did identify a tendency (of borderline strength) for parents to stimulate motor activity more in boys—to handle them more vigorously and do more roughhousing with them. The clearest, most consistent area of differentiation was in parents' encouragement of sex-appropriate activity as rather narrowly defined: offering sex-typed toys to children, or reacting positively to "sex-appropriate" activity (such as a boy using a hammer, a girl using cooking utensils) and negatively to "inappropriate" activity.

In the Stanford longitudinal study of three cohorts of children from birth to age 6, Jacklin and I observed interactions between parents and their children (usually mothers, but sometimes fathers as well) at ages 9 months, 12 months, 18 months, 33 months, 45 months, and 6 years.[3] On some occasions, the observations were made in a laboratory playroom, at other times in the families' homes. During some sessions, the parents were asked to engage the child in simple, age-appropriate tasks; at other times, the children were engaged in free play in the parents' presence. In addition, parents were interviewed (or filled out questionnaires) on their methods of dealing with their young children. To summarize very briefly: In the first two years of the children's lives, there were few consistent differences in the parental treatment of sons and daughters. Parents were even-handed in terms of the affection they expressed to their children, and in their responsiveness when children made bids for attention or care. When asked to involve their children in simple tasks at 12 and 18 months, mothers gave equal amounts of encouragement and direction to sons and daughters (Maccoby, Snow, and Jacklin, 1984). One difference did emerge: when there was a choice of toys, parents were more likely to offer a doll to a daughter than to a son.

When one cohort of children were 45 months old, we visited their homes, bringing an array of toys, some of which were sex-typed and some sex-neutral. Each parent engaged in a 15-minute play session with the child and the provided toys. Both parents offered masculine toys more to boys, feminine ones more to girls, and the toy choices of the children were also sex-typed. The play themes that were acted out jointly by the parent-child pair were also geared to the sex of the child (Jacklin, DiPietro, and Maccoby, 1980).[4]

There is evidence that the kinds of toys and play themes offered to children make a difference in the kind of play that occurs between an adult and a child. Leaper and Gleason (1996) set up play sessions between preschoolers and their parents (separate sessions with the mother and with the father) in which part of the session was devoted to assembling a toy car (masculine activity) and part to a more "feminine" activity: playing with the props for a toy grocery store. The nature of the talk that occurred between parent and child differed according to the play activity, and for a given activity, verbal exchanges did not differ according to the sex of the child. The pair exchanged more information in the toy store scenario, and parents did more verbal guiding of the child during the car assembly. This study suggests that providing different toys for children leads them to adopt different kinds of themes or scripts for their play, and thus may have implications for the kind of interactive experiences boys and girls have during play. In our home visits with 45-month-olds and their parents, parents were more likely to pick out toys that invited high-activity play (such as a toy football) when playing with their sons. No doubt partly in consequence of these choices, both parents engaged in rougher, more arousing play with sons than with daughters. The father-son dyad displayed the highest levels of roughhousing: three times as much rough play occurred between fathers and sons as between mothers and daughters (Maccoby and Jacklin, 1983). Our studies, then, are consistent with earlier work in indicating that differential socialization of boys and girls by parents during the early years primarily takes the form of offering sex-typed toys, supporting stereotypically "sex-appropriate" play themes, and playing more roughly with boys than with girls. We found that young boys and girls were treated very much alike by their parents when it came to the amounts of affection shown, the level of demands and restrictions, the amount of positive, negative, or neutral interaction that occurred, or the responsiveness of parents to the child's bids for attention or help.

Do the differences in in-home socialization summarized above help explain gender segregation, or the nature of the two cultures developed in male and female groups? Certainly parents' roughhousing with boys might predispose boys to play roughly with their peers, and we have seen that boys' rougher playstyle contributes to gender segregation. But the expected connections have not so far been found. The amount of rough play observed in the Stanford study when a given pair of parents were playing with their child at age 45 months was unrelated to the amount of rough-and-tumble play with peers that we recorded when that same child was in preschool the following year.

Another very plausible possibility is that sex-typing "pressure" from parents—their encouraging sex-appropriate play, providing sex-typed toys, reacting negatively to signs of effeminacy in a boy or tomboyishness in a girl—supports the development of sex-appropriate behaviors and preferences in children of each sex, and that these behaviors and preferences in their turn lead children to prefer same-sex playmates and adopt distinctive styles of play in their same-sex groups. These connections seem so obvious that it is surprising how difficult it has been to find empirical evidence for them. In our own observations of parents interacting with 45-month-old children, Jacklin and I found that the frequency with which parents offered sex-typed toys or entered into sex-appropriate thematic play was unrelated to the strength of the children's sex-typed toy preference when this was independently assessed (Jacklin, DiPietro, and Maccoby, 1984).[5] And indeed, children at nursery school do not necessarily choose toys similar to the ones they have at home, often being more interested in novel materials, so the fact that parents have offered dolls to girls and toy cars to boys at home does not mean that their children will be especially interested in these toys when they get into nursery school and have a wide array of toys to choose from.

The negative findings from our longitudinal study are not definitive. Our sample at 45 months was small, and although the play sessions were conducted in the naturalistic setting of the home, the situation was artificially set up and may not have revealed what goes on in everyday life. We need confirming (or disconfirming!) evidence from other samples of children, and other kinds of situations. But Jacklin and I are not the only ones to have found little or no connection between such sex-typing factors present in a home as traditionality of the parents' attitudes, activities, or division of household labor, or sex-differentiated direct reactions to the children, and how sex-typed the children become.[6] These negative findings warn against making untested assumptions that a child's experiences when interacting with parents will lodge in the child's psyche as a stable personality trait called masculinity or femininity, which will then automatically carry over to the child's play with peers.

Punishment and Parental Power-Assertion

In our review of then-existing studies (Maccoby and Jacklin, 1974), Jacklin and I reported that boys received more physical punishment than girls. Lytton and Romney's review also revealed a trend toward more frequent use of physical punishment as a means of control with boys than with girls. This difference appeared to be especially strong in countries outside North America, although there were too few non-American studies to be definitive.

Whiting and Edwards (1988) give a fuller picture of cross-cultural findings, and report that power-assertive forms of control, including physical punishment, are more often directed toward boys in most, but not all, of the cultures they studied. The major exception was a village in India, where boys were much more highly valued than girls, and were indulged and protected more. Research in Western countries has also pointed to more power-assertiveness in parental reactions to sons than daughters. Studies find that boys receive more negative reactions, more imperative directives (as distinct from reasoned requests or cooperative give-and-take approaches), and more simple prohibitions than do girls.[7]

Whiting and Edwards offer a straightforward explanation for the greater use of power-assertion in the socialization of boys:

> Across cultures and age groups, boys are less compliant to their mothers than are girls. Thus boys may require more control—firm, strong and definite "structuring"—because they are, on average, less sensitive to the needs of others and therefore less compliant or responsive to their mothers' directions. This does not mean that boys are "uncontrollable," but rather that they elicit a more intrusive and power-oriented control pattern from mothers than do girls. (1988, p. 128)[8]

There is ample evidence that parents tend to react to negative behavior in their children—whining, resistiveness, demandingness, mischievous or destructive behavior, temper outbursts—with imperative, peremptory kinds of directives and sometimes counter-coercive measures, including punishment. If negative behavior were indeed more common in young boys, it would be understandable that there would then be more imperative, more peremptory parental reactions toward them. Such a sequence appeared in one of the Stanford studies, when fathers and their twelve-month-old children were observed in a waiting room. Fathers issued approximately twice as many vocal prohibitions to their infant sons as to their daughters, but this difference was entirely accounted for by the fact that the boys more often attempted to touch forbidden objects (Snow, Maccoby, and Jacklin, 1983). It is surprising that boys should have been getting into mischief more often than girls at such an early age. As we saw in Chapter 5, it is not until about the end of the second year or the beginning of the third that we commonly see a strong divergence between the sexes in terms of the uncontrolled, impulsive behavior that would be expected to elicit negative, imperative reactions from parents, although there may be some precursors to this divergence at an earlier age. In any case, there is enough divergence between boys and girls of ages 2–4, in terms of negative or thoughtless behaviors, to contribute to parents' being more imperative or punitive toward boys. Indeed, in their observations of two-year-olds and their mothers at home, Minton, Kagan, and Levine (1971) found that mothers became more imperative toward sons precisely when the boys had failed to comply with earlier, milder instructions. In addition, of course, parents may feel that boys are inherently tougher—that they can absorb rigorous discipline without the sort of physical or psychological trauma that a girl might suffer.

I have suggested in Chapter 5 that if girls achieve self-regulation earlier than boys, while boys show higher levels of resistive or impulsive behavior after the age of 2, that this divergence has its origins at least partially in biological maturation. Still we must be aware of other possibilities. Fagot and colleagues (1985) observed a sample of children in play groups at two ages: when they were 13 months old, and again nearly a year later. At 13 months, boys and girls tried equally often to communicate with the adult teachers, and they used similar means of gaining the teachers' attention. But the teachers more often responded to a girl's communication attempt if she used gestures, gentle touches, or vocalizations (babbling, mainly), while boys were more successful in getting the teachers' attention if they whined, cried, or screamed, or forcefully pulled at the teachers' clothes or hair. A year later, the boys were using more negative methods of communication, while the girls were relying on more positive communication acts, including rudimentary speech. The obvious implication is that, when the children were age 13 months, the teachers' reactions were such as to reinforce different communication styles in children of the two sexes, and that the boys' greater use of coercive approaches later on, at approximately the age of 2, might well be the outcome of these earlier teacher reactions.[9] And of course, if the boys had been "trained" to be more coercive, it would not be surprising if this would set in motion coercive cycles between parent and child so that the parents would then adopt more power-assertive tactics with boys than with girls.[10]

Fagot and colleagues suggest that there may be a fairly narrow window of time—probably the first half of the child's second year—during which inputs from parents and teachers shape certain sex-typed behavioral tendencies in children, and that these tendencies then become firmly established and fairly impervious to being changed later when the reactions of adults are less sex-differentiated. I am skeptical as to whether socialization inputs and their effects can be as time-limited as this. The question remains open, however.

The fact that parents use firmer, more imperative or punitive tactics with young sons than young daughters does not tell the whole story when it comes to power-assertion by parents toward sons and daughters. There are certain respects in which parents appear to be more power-assertive toward daughters. For example, Leaper and colleagues (1989) report that fathers are less compliant toward their preschool daughters than toward their preschool sons—something that Jacklin and I also found in our 45-month home observations (Maccoby and Jacklin, 1983). Several studies have reported that mothers try to control or manage the behavior of young daughters more than that of young sons, granting girls less autonomy,[11] and this is reminiscent of what we saw in Chapter 2: that teachers feel more free to intervene in the activities of girls' groups than boys' groups. There are some interesting questions here: Do mothers indeed feel in a weaker position when it comes to managing sons? Do they allow boys, more than girls, to dominate them? Do they wait for a more serious provocation from a son before taking action? Do they back off from making demands or attempting to teach when a boy rather than a girl puts up resistance?[12] Do they sustain a boy's ego (and thus empower him) by expressing admiration for a performance that would draw only a matter-of-fact reaction from parents of a girl?[13] So far, there are only provocative hints in the literature that processes of this sort may be at work, but I suspect they do occur in many mother-son dyads and may indeed be quite pervasive and powerful.

If parents, for whatever reason, use more power-assertive styles of discourse with boys than with girls, this clearly may have a bearing on the kinds of communication styles that are seen in boys' peer groups. When boys, more than girls, use more imperative demands and fewer conflict-mitigation strategies with their peers, this may be a direct reflection of the kinds of communications they are accustomed to receiving from their parents. What is missing, however, is any direct information that this is the case. After all, not all boys receive levels of imperative communications from their parents at home that are higher than the usual levels received by girls. Is it mainly the boys who *are* treated imperatively by their parents who are biased toward this style of discourse in their peer groups? We do not know. If it is not, then we have to find out how a modest overage of imperative discourse, directed toward *some* boys by *some* parents, translates into group process among peers.

The Special Case of Aggression

In Chapter 2, we saw that direct, physical aggression is primarily a male-to-male phenomenon. It sometimes occurs as a spin-off from rough-and-tumble play, when someone gets hurt and becomes angry. I argued that this does not mean that most boys are aggressive, but only that aggression can occur sporadically as boys are engaged in male-type activities that are usually merely high-spirited. We also saw that boys, more than girls, are more concerned to avoid being seen as weak. Although presumably most boys would rather avoid a fight—and the risk of getting hurt—they try not to back down in the face of a challenge, so there are some circum-stances in which almost any boy will fight. Beyond these general trends, there is a relatively small subset of children who are consistently involved in fighting or bullying more often than other children; such children are far more likely to be boys than girls. Studies of such children have revealed a kind of paranoia in the way these boys perceive others: they are especially likely to believe that others mean to do them harm; they carry a chip on their shoulders, and believe they are acting in self-defense when they react aggressively to certain ambiguous behavior on the part of others who actually intended no harm (Dodge, 1980).

Clearly, the greater frequency of episodes of direct conflict among boys' groups is part of the male childhood culture that we seek to explain. It becomes important, then, to know what role parents (and other socializing agents) play in training or encouraging boys to be confrontational toward their peers. Are parents more likely to tell a son—rather than a daugh-ter—to stand up for himself when challenged? To fight his own battles rather than running to an adult for help? To expect hostility from other boys?

We have a good deal of information concerning the in-family conditions that are associated with high levels of aggression in children. But most of this research has been done with all-male samples, and has focused on factors that lead to some boys being more aggressive than others. No doubt researchers have concentrated on boys because aggressive behavior more often reaches "problem" levels in boys than girls, and not infrequently evolves into serious levels of criminality as aggressive boys become young men. Thus it has been considered especially important to try to understand the causes (and possible cures) of aggression in males. In an important early study of aggression in adolescent boys, Bandura and Walters (1959) compared the families of boys who had a record of repetitive antisocial aggression with the families of boys who were not aggressive but were socially interactive (not passive or withdrawn). Interviews with the parents revealed substantial differences between the two groups in parental attitudes, and in the parents' reports of how they had reacted when their sons were involved in fights with other children. An interview with the mother of an aggressive boy is illustrative:

I. Have you ever encouraged Earl to stand up for himself?
M. Yes, I've taught young Earl, and his dad has. I feel he should stand up for his rights, so you can get along in this world.
I. How have you encouraged him?
M. I have told him to look after himself and don't let anybody shove him around or anything like that, but not to look for trouble. I don't want him to be a sissy.
I. Have you ever encouraged Earl to use his fists to defend himself?
M. Oh yes. Oh yes. He knows how to fight.
I. What have you done to encourage him?
M. When he was a little boy, he had a little pair of boxing gloves. His dad has been an athlete all his life, so his dad taught him.
I. Has he ever come to you and complained that another fellow was giving him a rough time?
M. Oh, yes, when he was younger. I told him, "Go on out and fight it out yourself." (Bandura, 1973, p. 95)

It is important to note that although the parents of aggressive boys were especially likely—by comparison with the parents of nonaggressive boys—

to encourage their sons' belligerence in the ways illustrated above, they did not tolerate aggression toward themselves; indeed, they were quite punitive when a boy attempted to direct anger toward his parents.

In an extensive program of research on aggressive boys, Patterson and colleagues (Patterson, 1982; Patterson, Reid and Dishion, 1992) have studied the socialization of aggression by directly observing parent-child interactions in the home. Their hypothesis is that children learn a cluster of what they call "coercive" behaviors in interaction with their parents, and then make use of this repertoire when interacting with peers. Thus rather than focusing on how parents react to their children's fighting with other children, Patterson and colleagues concentrate on the moment-to-moment reactions of parents and children to each other, searching for ways in which parents may be inadvertently teaching (reinforcing) aggressive rather than pro-social behaviors. These researchers have found that rates of coercive behavior (hitting, teasing, yelling, humiliating) are higher among all family members in the families of chronically aggressive boys: in these "clinic" families more often than among the normal controls, these kinds of negative power-assertive behavior occur at higher than normal rates from parent to child, from child to parent, and between siblings. The studies by the Patterson group have not yielded consistent results as to whether aggressive boys receive especially high levels of reinforcement for their coercive behaviors, by comparison with nonaggressive boys. But it is clear that they receive very little support for any positive behaviors they show (Snyder and Patterson, 1995), while nonaggressive children do receive such support. Evidently, nonaggressive children develop viable, positive behavioral alternatives to aggressive behavior—behavior patterns which they can utilize for problem-solving when conflicts arise with peers. Among aggressive boys, the training for such alternative behaviors is notably weak. Another way of looking at this is to say that context matters. A parent's refusing to allow a child to be aggressive, or punishing aggressive behavior, has a different effect if the parental reactions occur in a context of a generally supportive, warm home atmosphere than if they do not.[14]

There are some unresolved issues here. One thing that needs explaining is the greater incidence of conflictual behavior within the male peer culture than within the female peer culture. If home training has an effect, does this mean that the way children have learned to behave with parents and siblings spills over into their interactions with peers, as Patterson believes? Or is it the case that the major effect of parental socialization comes via what parents allow or expect their children to do when playing with other children outside the home, *not* via the way children are trained to behave toward other family members? The existing research does not allow us to choose between these alternatives. Both possibilities are viable at our present state of knowledge.

It seems intuitively obvious that if there is more aggression among male than female peer groups, boys must have been exposed more heavily than girls to the kinds of home conditions that the researchers cited above have identified as making some boys more aggressive than others. Yet it has proved surprisingly difficult to get evidence verifying this obvious assumption. Is it really true that boys, more often than girls, are encouraged to hit an aggressor back, or that girls have received more reinforcement than boys for nonaggressive alternative behaviors? If we look back to the remarks (reported above) by a mother who was interviewed by Bandura and Walters, it is hard to imagine parents encouraging a daughter to be combative in the way this family had dealt with their son. Yet consider the following comments by several English mothers interviewed by John and Elizabeth Newson in the 1960s. The interviewer asked, "Do you ever tell [child's name] to hit another child back?":

M1. Yes, I do. If another child hits her of her age, like. I have always stopped my children from kicking or biting or scratching or anything; but I have got so fed up with the children here. I have told them that they have to go out and they have to kick and bite and— do all the other things these children do. (Newson and Newson, 1968, p. 126)

M2. I say "Go and hit Susan back, else Mummy'll smack you" and she knows. I do try to make her hit back, yes. I don't want to make her a bully. But I do try to make her defend herself. (Newson and Newson, 1968, p. 127)

M3. Well, she's been playing with boys at school, and they have been knocking her down, and I told her then to knock *them* down, because she's got to stand up for herself. She did start telling tales to the teacher and that, and I said, you know, she's got to hit them back and fight her own battles. (Newson and Newson, 1968, p. 127)

In the Newsons' interviews with 700 English mothers of four-year-olds, there were some mothers who said they encouraged physical self-defense, and others who did not (these being mainly the upper-middle-class mothers). But encouraging children to fight back was reported as commonly by mothers of daughters as by mothers of sons. In our review of this and other studies through 1973 (Maccoby and Jacklin, 1974), Jacklin and I found that parents were, on average, equally permissive (or nonpermissive) toward aggression in sons and in daughters. In their more recent (and more methodologically sophisticated) review, Lytton and Romney (1991) reached the same conclusion.[15] They included information from fathers, and reported that fathers as well as mothers treated sons and daughters similarly when it came to encouraging or discouraging children's aggression. In their review, however, Lytton and Romney do not distinguish aggression toward parents from aggression toward playmates, and this distinction may be a crucial one. Furthermore, most of the studies reviewed by Lytton and Romney, as well as those reviewed by Jacklin and me, relied on the reports of parents concerning how they had reacted (or would react) to aggressive behavior in their children. It is difficult to get reliable observational data on parents' real-life reactions to their children's aggression toward parents or peers. Relying on parents' reports has its dangers: parents are not always aware of the subtle (or mixed) messages they are sending to their children.

Perhaps we can get useful information from the children themselves, by asking them what kind of reactions they would expect to get from parents and peers if they behave aggressively. Perry, Perry, and Weiss (1989) studied children (fourth-, fifth-, sixth-, and seventh-graders, mean age 10 years) with this question in mind. Children of both sexes said they expected less parental disapproval for retaliatory than for unprovoked aggression; for boys, their expectations for parental disapproval were lowest if their aggression was not only provoked, but directed against another boy. In sum, boys in middle childhood sense that their parents are more tolerant about male-male fighting than other forms of aggression.

As the interview excerpts quoted above show, parents feel considerable ambivalence about their children's fighting, and although the Newsons did not find that this ambivalence was greater for four-year-olds of one sex than the other, it may be that by the time the children have reached middle childhood, parents may feel that it is especially important for a boy not to be a "wimp." Bacon and Ashmore (1985) studied parents who had both a son and a daughter between the ages of 6 and 11, asking them what they considered to be "bad" or "not normal" behavior in each of their children. The parents felt that hostile-aggressive behavior was unequivocally bad in their daughters, but were more ambivalent about it in their sons. Fathers, although they considered a boy's hostile-aggressive behavior to be bad, were equally concerned about "sissy" behavior, which they considered undesirable. Insofar as not being a sissy calls for standing up for oneself even to the point of physical fighting, fathers appear to have been sending a mixed message to their sons. Also, fathers were more likely to rate aggressive behaviors as "normal" for boys than for girls.

In sum: most parents and other adults do not like aggressive behavior directed toward themselves by children, though they vary in terms of how strongly they prohibit it. For present purposes, the important point is that they are no more likely to permit such behavior from a boy than from a girl. When it comes to fighting among peers, however, many parents place value on not interfering—on allowing the children to settle their own arguments among themselves—and some parents, of both boys and girls, actively insist that their children defend themselves. Many parents do try to steer their children away from physical means of settling disputes with peers, and toward reasoning and compromise. However, many parents and other adults seem to see fighting among boys, even though deplorable, as something to be expected—something "natural." Although the evidence is thin, there is reason to believe that fathers in particular are likely to encourage their sons to defend themselves, even if this involves physical fighting. Mothers, it would appear, are quite even-handed in their reactions to aggressive behavior shown by children of the two sexes.

Talk with Children about Emotions

Above, I identified a tendency for parents to use a more power-assertive communication style with their sons than with their daughters. Recently, an additional difference has emerged in studies of the kinds of communications that occur between parents and children of the two sexes: a tendency for parents (perhaps especially mothers) to talk more with their young daughters about emotions. Judy Dunn and colleagues (Dunn, Bretherton, and Munn, 1987) recorded conversations between mothers and toddlers (aged 18 months or 24 months), and examined what kinds of things mothers talk about to these very young children. The researchers were particularly interested in talk about feeling states. A number of such states were considered: liking or disliking an event or person or object;

being afraid, surprised, sad, upset, or angry; expressing sympathy or concern.

Dunn and colleagues give several examples of a mother's focusing on feeling states. In one instance, the child referred back to an argument with the mother at breakfast, when the child hadn't wanted to eat the cereal the mother had offered. The mother said, "Crying, weren't you? We had quite a battle." In another case, the mother's feeling-state language came in response to the child's own introduction of such language: the child wanted some chocolate cake. When the mother refused, the child said: "Why? Tired!" The mother replied, "You tired? Ooh!"

Mothers' usage of feeling-state language to eighteen-month-old boys was only about two thirds as frequent as to girls of this age, and when the children were 24 months old, the difference was greater: now mothers initiated feeling-state talk with daughters 3.3 times per hour, compared with 1.6 times with sons. Reciprocally, girls used (and initiated) more feeling-state language than boys at the age of 24 months.

As children acquire more language, and conversations between parents and children become richer and more complex, the greater use of talk about emotions to girls continues. Radke-Yarrow and colleagues report that mothers of children in their third year use more emotion words with daughters than with sons.[16] There appears to be a difference not only in the *amount* of emotion-talk that takes place with sons and daughters, but in its nature as well. In two studies, Robyn Fivush (1993) told parents that she was interested in young children's memories, and asked them to discuss special novel events with their children (aged 30 to 35 months). In the first study, only mothers were involved, but in the second, fathers were included as well. Fivush found that parents sometimes attributed emotional states to a child, as for example:

Mother: You were so happy.
Child: Yeah.

Sometimes a parent elaborated on the emotion attributed to the child:

Mother: Were you scared?
Child: Yeah.
Mother: I had never seen you so scared.

Or, a parent might bring in causes or consequences of an emotional state.

In a third study conducted by Fivush (1993), mothers were asked to discuss four specific kinds of emotional events with their children: events involving the experience of happiness, sadness, anger, and fear. In all three studies, discussions of emotions were almost always initiated by the parent, and boys and girls did not differ in their use of emotion words. Parents, however, talked in somewhat different ways with sons and daughters: they talked more about sadness with daughters than sons, and were more likely to explore explanations of sadness and to try to resolve sad emotional states with daughters.[17]

With sons more than daughters, conversations were about anger or conflict. Boys sometimes introduced the idea of retaliation:

Mother: Who bites you?
Boy: Uh, ummm, Johnny bites me.
Mother: Yeah, and what do you think when Johnny bites you?
Boy: That I will shoot him.
Mother: You're gonna shoot him?
Boy: (nods yes)
Mother: When he bites you?
Boy: Yes.

There were no instances in which a girl introduced the possibility of retaliation. It is evident from these examples that the children themselves are contributing actively to the direction the conversation takes. But drawing upon these and many other examples, Fivush concludes that parents make their own contribution, partly through attributing certain emotions to their children, but more commonly through elaboration and explanation. Fivush says that the mothers in her study seemed more willing to accept anger and retaliation in boys than in girls. When the mothers attributed anger to boys, the boys tended to agree, and the mother would reconfirm, as in the sequence: Mother: "You were mad, weren't you?" Child: "Yeah." Mother: "Yeah . . ." With girls more than with boys, mothers focused on reestablishing harmony between the child and others with whom the child was in conflict. It is interesting, too, that in choosing what emotional episodes to discuss with their children in the third study, mothers more often referred to socio-emotional episodes with their daughters (episodes in which other people were involved or had caused the emotional states). With sons, by contrast, mothers more often chose to talk about something the child experienced alone.

The tendency of mothers to focus on socio-emotional themes with daughters is further underscored in Smetana's work: In her observations of children aged 26 and 37 months with their mothers at home, she noted that when children did something naughty (something that impacted on the rights or well-being of other family members), mothers tended to talk with girls about the distress they were causing for others, a parental technique sometimes called "other-oriented induction." With boys, the mothers were more likely just to raise their voices and tell them to stop.

It should be noted, too, that although it is true that parents talk about emotions more with girls, girls also talk about emotions more with their parents than boys do. Emotion talk is a two-way process, and it is sometimes difficult to say how much contribution each member of the dyad makes to initiating or sustaining parent-child conversation about emotions.

What are the implications of the fact that parent-daughter pairs appear to talk about emotional states more frequently than parent-son pairs? Could this make a difference in the kind of culture that girls develop among themselves in their play groups? Clearly, it could. There is evidence from two longitudinal studies (Dunn, Brown, and Beardsall, 1991; Dunn, Brown, Slomkowski, Tesla, and Youngblade, 1991) that children who spend their early years in families with frequent parent-child talk about emotions are better able to recognize others' emotional states at a later age, and better able to take the perspective of other people, than are children who were not exposed so much to emotion-talk.[18] It seems that sensitivity to the emotional states of others should promote just the kind of cooperative, reciprocal discourse more often seen in girls' groups than in boys' groups. But we have no evidence that it is the very girls who experience the most emotion-talk with their mothers who are most active in establishing the cooperative norms of girls' discourse. Such evidence would greatly strengthen the case for a connection.

We should be aware, too, that understanding the emotions of others may not always lead to cooperative, empathic interaction. It might instead contribute to skill in teasing or manipulating others (see the discussion by Dunn, Brown, and Beardsall, 1991, p. 454). So far, we cannot be sure whether early emotion-talk is a factor that underlies girls' greater use of conflict-mitigating, collaborative discourse in their same-sex groups, though it is a strong possibility. Nor can we be sure whether it was girls' readiness for such talk at an early age, or the mother's greater readiness to engage in such talk with a daughter, or both, that carries over to subsequent relationships with peers.[19]

Teaching Boys Not to Display Feelings

Not only do parents talk less to boys about feelings. There is evidence that they actively suppress emotional displays in boys. Block (1978) summarized studies in a number of northern European countries as well as the United States, finding that boys were consistently more likely than girls to be the objects of parental pressure not to cry and not to express feelings. In a longitudinal study, Jeanne Block (1978) found that parents of preschoolers were quite active in trying to "down-regulate" their sons' emotional displays. In Chapter 5, we saw that girls were making somewhat greater progress, during the toddler and preschool years, in regulating their own emotional states than were boys, so it is likely that parents were applying added regulatory pressure to boys partly because their sons were more given to impulsive emotional outbursts. Still, parents deem it especially important for boys not to display the kind of weakness or vulnerability or "babyishness" that is implied by crying and other displays of poor emotional control. The fact that their extra pressure on boys is effective is indicated by Buck's (1975) report that by the age of 6, mothers can more easily "read" a daughter's than a son's emotional state.

The Reciprocation of Emotional States

Although parents talk more about emotions to daughters, this does not imply that they express different emotions toward daughters and sons. As noted earlier, parents appear to be as affectionate toward young sons as toward daughters, and equally kindly and helpful in the sense that they are equally responsive to bids for attention or help from daughters and sons. Most of the research on parental responsiveness to infants and toddlers has been done with mothers, but what is known about fathers indicates that they, too, are as much involved in care-taking with young daughters as with sons, and show similar amounts of affection toward them. However, measures of parental responsiveness and affection are one-way scores; they assess a parental behavior apart from the degree to which the behavior (or emotional states) of the parent and child are synchronized. Recently, there has been increasing interest in emotional reciprocity, especially in the sharing of *positive* emotional states between parent and child. There have been claims that mothers establish a more intimate or "enmeshed" emotional relationship with daughters than with sons (Chodorow, 1978), and such a view would be supported if a greater frequency of positive emotional reciprocity were shown in mother-daughter pairs.

A number of researchers have attempted to see whether mothers were in some way inducting children of one sex more than the other into a mutually empathic system of interaction. Using detailed observations of mothers interacting with infants or toddlers, researchers have watched to see whether mothers match their own emotional expressions to those of the child. Leaper (1995) suggests that such matching may indeed be greater between mothers and daughters than between mothers and sons, but only in the context of traditionally female activities.

In general, however, matching or reciprocation of affect has not been shown to be greater between mothers and daughters than between mothers and sons. Consider first studies of infants: Haviland and Malatesta (1982) reported that mothers matched an infant *son's* expression of interest, surprise, or joy more than they did a girl's.[20] Tronick and Cohn (1989, p. 83) also found that there was greater matching/synchrony by mothers with infant sons than with infant daughters. But Martin (1981), when he assessed the degree to which mothers matched the intensity (and changes in intensity) of an infant's arousal level, found no sex difference. In the Stanford longitudinal study, two cohorts of children aged 18 months were observed in interaction with their mothers, and in both samples the number of "positive exchanges" between mother and child was very similar (and not significantly different) for boys and girls.

Kochanska and colleagues (Kochanska, Askan, and Koenig, 1995; Kochanska, 1997) worked with somewhat older children, observing episodes of interaction between approximately 100 mothers and their children at ages 33 months and 46 months. They report that when a mother-child pair frequently show positive emotions at the same time, the child, in other situations, will show more of what Kochanska calls "committed compliance"—that is, will comply with a mother's directive willingly or spontaneously, with little pressure. Furthermore, these researchers suggest that when children have experienced high levels of reciprocated positive affect as toddlers, a year later they will more readily incorporate or "internalize" adult norms of behavior. The Kochanska group found that girls have consistently higher scores on both committed compliance and internalization. Does this mean that girls, more often than boys, have a history of having frequently shared positive emotional states with their mothers? Surprisingly, no, at least not in the Kochanska sample as this form of reciprocity was measured. Episodes of shared positive feeling states were equally common in mother-daughter pairs and mother-son pairs, at both 33 months and 46 months.

Cross-cultural studies also do not point to greater mother-daughter enmeshment. Dora Dien (1992) describes the mother-*son* relationship as more enmeshed in Chinese society than the relationship between mothers and daughters. Whiting and Edwards (1988) did not have an explicitly reciprocal score for mother-child pairs, but they did have a score called "sociability," which implies two-way positive affect. In the various cultures they studied, mothers were equally "sociable" with young sons and daughters. We see, then, that research indicates that an equal degree of affective synchrony prevails in the interactions of mothers with infants and toddlers of the two sexes. This may be true with preschoolers as well, although the evidence for this age is limited. Thus there is no support so far for the hypothesis (Chodorow, 1978) that mothers construct a more empathic or enmeshed relationship with daughters than with sons in the early years via the matching of emotional states in infancy and toddlerhood.

The Kochanska report echoes some earlier research indicating that when mothers are nurturant and empathic, and when there are high levels of positive mother-child interaction, this is associated with high levels of empathy and concern for others in their young daughters, but not in their young sons.[21] This is not a universal finding, but taken together with the more recent Kochanska work it underlines the possibility that young girls are more open than young boys to affective inputs from their parents (perhaps especially from mothers).[22] If, then, the mother-child bond were shown to be more intimate, more mutually responsive than the mother-son bond—and so far, this has not been shown—it would not necessarily imply that the mother has more actively drawn her daughter than her son into such a bond. Again and again, we seem to face the same chicken-and-egg question as to whether it is the mother's socialization pressures or the child's characteristics that first establish the trajectory that a mother-child relationship will follow.

Are Fathers More Active Than Mothers in Gender Socialization?

In some ways, fathers seem to play the role of a grown-up male peer to their sons: they sometimes react to a son the way they interacted with other boys when they themselves were young. Such paternal reactions can start when a boy is very young. Consider one father's response when his toddler boy falls and hurts himself:

Mother says: "Come here, honey. I'll kiss it better."
Father: "Oh toughen up. Quit your bellyaching." (Gable, Belsky, and Crnic, 1993, p. 32)

This father might be thinking ahead to the time when his son will have to cope with the derision of other boys if he becomes a "crybaby." Or, the father may simply be reacting as he would to any male's signs of weakness. In either case, he is playing a more active role than the mother in trying to instill male-typical ways of behaving in his son. We see the same thing at work when we compare the reactions of mothers and fathers to their children of preschool age, when the children are enacting sex-appropriate or sex-inappropriate scripts. Langlois and Downs (1980) set up two play-rooms, one equipped with "masculine" play materials (an army game; a tollbooth with cars; cowboy outfits) and the other with "feminine materials" (dollhouse; cooking equipment; dress-up clothes). When a child had begun playing with the materials in one of these rooms, either the mother or the father was brought in to join the child's play, and the parental reactions were observed. When a father saw his son engaged in feminine activities, he was five times more likely to show a negative reaction than if he saw a daughter playing with masculine materials. Mothers, by contrast, were much less negative than fathers about a boy's cross-sex behavior, and reacted similarly to a daughter or son's being engaged in "sex-inappropriate" behavior.[23]

Siegal (1987) summarized the findings of 39 studies in which it was possible to compare fathers and mothers with respect to their treatment of sons and daughters. The studies were not all consistent, but the trend was clear: that fathers were indeed more likely than mothers to differentiate between sons and daughters.[24] The fathers' differential parenting behavior often took the form of being stricter with boys, more negative or confrontational with them. But in some studies there were other trends as well: a few reported that fathers took more interest in boys, or played with them in more arousing or "physical" ways (see also Power, 1994). And when boys arrive at grade school age, their fathers are more likely to take them (rather than their daughters) to sporting events, or play ball with them. At the same time, fathers tend to be less sympathetic toward shows of dependency from a son than from a daughter (Russell and Russell, 1987).

Fathers may also play a stronger role than mothers in "feminizing" daughters, though this is less clear. In the 1960s, Hetherington (1967) examined the in-home conditions that were associated with a little girl's becoming especially "feminine." She found the fathers of such little girls liked women, and showed appreciation of pretty clothes and hair-dos, and sweet, appealing ways, in their little daughters. Since that time, there has been little interest in this aspect of fathering, but there is no reason to believe that the connection between fatherly appreciation of femininity and little girls' gender development would be any less strong now than it was 30 years ago.

My major conclusion is that fathers, more than mothers, do try to "toughen up" their sons. Fathers also maintain a stance of male dominance toward their sons, as an older boy might do. And fathers who share the common pattern of male homophobia may distance themselves somewhat from emotional involvement with their sons.[25] To some extent, then, fathers appear to be participating in the induction of boys into male peer culture. At the same time, there are countervailing forces: fathers, of course, are aware that their sons, just like their daughters, are young and vulnerable. So fathers of sons play two roles: that of parent-to-child and that of male-to-male. It seems reasonable that the younger the child, the more the parent-to-child role must take precedence. In any case, fathers clearly feel powerful ties to both sons and daughters: ties of love and ties stemming from the need to provide teaching, protection, and daily care. These things depend very little on the sex of the child, and both parents are largely even-handed with respect to them.

We have seen that fathers, at least under some circumstances, are more power-assertive with sons than with daughters—the implication being that they are "softer" with daughters. This may mean that they think boys are inherently tougher—better able to withstand pain and harshness—or that they need to be treated as though they were tough in order to make them so. There is a fairly consistent pattern here: a tendency for fathers to put especially strong pressures on their sons not to show weakness or signs of effeminacy. In addition, as children grow into middle childhood, each parent is likely to draw a same-sex child into shared sex-typed activities: mothers involve girls more in the preparation of meals (Goodnow, 1988) and fathers involve their sons more in both active and spectator sports, and in nonindustrialized societies, fathers involve their sons more in male occupational activities.

Summary and Comment

Childhood culture is different from adult culture in many ways. Childhood culture is far more gender-segregated than is adult culture. Also, the content of children's games is passed on from one generation of children to another, not from adults to children. And interaction styles are different, too: especially among younger children, interaction is more "physical" (particularly among boys) and briefer than it is among adults. We may expect to find, then, that there is much that happens in children's playgroups that probably will not be best understood as an outcome of socialization pressures exerted by adults.

When we try to understand the impact of adult socialization agents on gender differentiation in childhood, the next important point to remember is the fact, documented in this chapter, that in many respects adults treat children of the two sexes in very similar ways. We have seen that when people are reacting to an unfamiliar infant or toddler, their reactions do not depend consistently on whether they believe the child to be a boy or a girl. In most respects, the same may be said of the way parents deal with their own sons and daughters: they are equally responsive to boys and girls overall, equally affectionate toward them, and place similar restrictions or demands upon their activities. These conclusions emerge from a large body of research in which parents have been observed, either at home or in a laboratory playroom, as they interact with sons or daughters ranging in age from infancy to middle childhood.

We do not see, then, a process in which parents are fostering the development of different global sex-typed personality traits in sons and daughters: we do not see socialization patterns that would lead to girls becoming more passive or dependent or "sociable," or boys becoming more assertive. And indeed, children of the two sexes do not typically differ with respect to global personality traits.

Within this pattern of overall similarity, however, certain trends toward gender differentiation may be seen. Parents treat little daughters more gently in terms of the quality of physical handling, and are more likely to roughhouse with young sons. They also behave somewhat more power-assertively toward a son in situations where they need to obtain compliance to a demand. Parents talk more with girls about emotions and about interpersonal events and causes of events. And parents react more positively when they see their children behaving in "sex-appropriate" ways as fairly narrowly defined (not defined in terms of global personality traits). That is, many parents like to see a little girl playing with dolls, pretending to cook, putting on dress-up clothes or trying on her mother's high-heeled shoes; or to see a little boy playing cowboy, or playing with trucks or carpentry tools. Indeed, parents usually provide children with sex-typed toys (along with a range of sex-neutral toys), and as we have seen, this parental behavior supports different kinds of play activities in the two sexes. Also, many parents tend to react negatively when a child engages in activities that are thought to be sex-inappropriate. These negative reactions are especially directed toward boys: both parents are more accepting of "tomboy" tendencies in a daughter than of "sissy" tendencies in a son. Fathers react more strongly than mothers toward cross-sex activities in their children, particularly in their sons. Parents, then, give girls more leeway than boys when it comes to sex-typing.

I should note that most of the differences in parental reactions to sons and daughters are small in magnitude (though, of course, small effects may accumulate over time and snowball in their impact): the distributions for parental treatment of boys and girls overlap greatly, and studies are not consistent in their findings. The exception is emotion-talk to children, where research conducted so far is consistent from one study to another, but even for this feature of socialization, the sex difference does not begin to approach the binary pattern established in playmate preferences.

No evidence has emerged that shows parents exerting direct pressure on their young children to play mainly with others of their own sex. At least, parents in modern industrial societies do not appear to do so. Nor do parents exert influence by example; in the home setting, adults do not segregate by sex, and so do not provide a model for sex segregation as something that adult society expects. Of course, differential socialization by parents might lead to gender segregation by a different route: if all or most parents reinforced girls for one set of characteristics and boys for another, children would presumably begin to find other children of their own sex more compatible, by virtue of their shared characteristics. I noted earlier, for example, that being played with roughly by their parents might predispose boys to rough-and-tumble play with other boys, who presumably have been similarly socialized. But the small amount of correlational evidence available so far does not support this scenario. For example, research to date does not show that the amount of roughhousing parents do with a son is related to the amount of rough-and-tumble play that child will engage in with peers, or to the child's preference for male playmates.

When it comes to sex-typing pressures from parents, such as providing sex-appropriate toys, it is plausible that the children who are most subject to such pressures would be the ones most likely to adopt sex-typed preferences for toys and activities, and who would then in turn prefer to play with other children with similar preferences—children of their own sex. So far, efforts to uncover such connections have been disappointing. Individual children seem to move into mainly sex-segregated playgroups regardless of how strongly their parents have reinforced sex-appropriate behavior at home. Indeed, their playmate preferences appear to be quite independent of how sex-typed their choices of toys and activities are.

To summarize my first main point: In-home socialization probably plays only a minor role in gender segregation. Although there are certain respects in which parents do treat sons and daughters differently on the average, individual children's preferences for same-sex playmates appear to be unrelated to whether or not a child has been subjected to greater or lesser degrees of sex-typing pressure from parents.

When it comes to the interaction styles that develop in all-male versus all-female playgroups, in-home socialization probably has a greater impact, although, as I discuss below, it is difficult to be sure. In addition to the greater frequency of parents roughhousing with sons, and their somewhat more tolerant attitude toward boys' fighting with their peers, parents use a more power-assertive, imperative style—including more physical punishment—with sons than they do with daughters, and it is plausible that boys learn to use the interactive styles that their parents use toward them (see Carli, 1995). These sex-differentiated parental practices could foster the rough, imperative interaction styles that boys exhibit in their playgroups. Similarly, the greater frequency of emotion-talk between parents and daughters could impel girls toward the more other-oriented, conflict-mitigating styles seen in female playgroups.

To summarize my second main point: In-home socialization is probably a more important factor in the kinds of interaction styles children develop in their same-sex playgroups than it is in producing gender segregation per se. There are a number of respects in which the direction of the sex difference in parental treatment matches, or is consistent with, the direction of the difference in playgroup interaction styles. Thus the characteristics that children of the two sexes develop in the course of interaction with their parents may well carry over, to some degree, to the way the children behave in interaction with same-sex playmates.

And in relation to asymmetry, my third main point is: Parents, especially fathers, appear to put more pressure on boys to be "masculine" than they do on girls to be "feminine." This parental behavior could contribute to the asymmetries noted in Chapter 2: the fact that boys' groups are stronger, more active in policing gender boundaries, and more given to pressuring each other not to be effeminate. It is not so clear, however, how parents' putting greater sex-typing pressure on boys could lead boys to distance themselves from *adults,* as well as from girls.

Note the word "probably" in my second point. There are some unresolved issues that keep us from being confident about the connections between in-home socialization practices and peer-group interaction styles. A major difficulty is the question of who is influencing whom. In the case of parents' using more power-assertive types of pressure on boys, there is good reason to believe that this happens because boys get into mischief more often and are less responsive than girls to milder forms of parental pressure. Similarly, boys may be played with more roughly because they somehow invite such play. And in the case of emotion-talk to children, there may be something in girls' readiness to engage in such talk, or at least to listen to it, that encourages their mothers' greater use of such talk with daughters. If parents are adapting their behavior to the eliciting characteristics of their children, might it not be the children's initial characteristics, rather than any effects of the parents' response, that carry over to the peer group? I would argue that interaction is always a two-way street, with each participant in the parent-child interactive chain influencing the other. And the two participants may contribute different things. For example, though it may be the child's temperament that influences the parental response, it may be the parent's interaction style, rather than the child's temperament, that has the most important influence on the style that develops in the children's playgroup. The relative contributions of parent and child have not been sorted out, however, and my best guess is that both matter.

An additional problem: There are difficulties in translating children's individual characteristics into group process. Parents presumably influence only their own individual child. And families differ considerably in how strongly the parents teach, or model, sex-typed interaction styles. If parents are influencing the playstyles that emerge in same-sex playgroups, it ought to be the very children whose parents have encouraged these styles who emerge as style-setters in the children's groups. There is very little research on the socialization histories of the children who emerge as leaders, or style-setters, in children's groups. We know from some work by Charlesworth and LaFreniere (1983) that when four-child groups are competing for a scarce resource, it is the boys who individually rank high in dominance in their preschool setting who win out in the competition, doing so by the use of male-style strategies: pushing, threatening, commanding. If we were able to show that these dominant boys had come from families who used more physical punishment than other parents, did more rough-housing with their children, gave them only masculine toys, or encouraged them to hold their own with other children even if this required fighting, we would have completed the chain of evidence leading from parental socialization to sex-differentiated interaction styles. So far, the evidence is lacking that would allow us to establish this chain. Existing correlational studies have not shown clear connections between what individual parents are doing in terms of sex-typing pressures and how strongly their own children contribute to the sex-typed interaction styles that characterize sex-segregated peer groups.

Judith Harris (1995) has proposed what she calls a *group-socialization* theory. Her claim is that elements of culture are passed on from parents *as a group* to children *as a group,* and then the group of children socialize each other. The characteristics of a peer group do derive from what the parent generation has taught them. But if a particular pair of parents are providing their children with models, or using socialization pressures, which do not conform to the practices of the larger culture, then the child will take on the characteristics prescribed by the larger culture. Harris illustrates this process by reference to an immigrant child learning a new language—a different language from the one spoken at home. This child picks up the language, or dialect, spoken in the peer group, a language or dialect which most members of the peer group learned from their parents. But the transmission is a group process, not an individual one.

Harris' formulation is intriguing. Can we really see the transmission of language and the transmission of sex-typed childhood culture as analogous? One problem is, as I noted earlier, that childhood culture is in many respects quite different from adult culture, so that whatever effects adult socialization agents are having on children's playgroups do not take the form of the transmission of identical elements. And in the case of language, the whole group of parents in a given cultural group speak very nearly the same language and the same dialect. This uniformity does not hold true for the socialization of gender. As we have seen, parents differ very greatly in whether, and how much, they maintain one set of socialization practices for boys and another for girls. It is possible, though, that enough parents have roughhoused with their boys and talked about emotions with their girls that a majority of children, when they enter their same-sex peer groups, will have had these sex-differentiated experiences and will incorporate them into the group process.

We need to know more about the ways in which group interaction styles emerge from the characteristics of the individual children who make up the group. Is there a kind of critical mass, such that if there are enough children who share a certain style learned earlier, these children can succeed in socializing the other children so that their style comes to pervade the interactions of the whole group? Or is it the case that the children who become style-setters in a group are the ones who have been socialized so that the interaction style they display fits best with some underlying disposition that most members of a given sex share? Or fits best with stereotypes, widely held in a culture, as to what modes of behavior are sex-appropriate? Clearly, these issues are important ones for a research agenda.

It is time to note, again, that my account so far may very well be too culture-bound. Most of the research on which my account is based has been done with children in modern industrialized societies. In smaller, more traditional social groups, the differential training of boys and girls may start much earlier and be much more powerful. Consider some observations made in an African village, where little girls as young as age 2 were seen to step to the side of a path and lower their eyes whenever a male approached them along the path.[26] Clearly, they had been trained in deference to men and boys, and presumably boys had also been trained to expect deference from females—to believe that males are the favored or superior sex. Children presumably can make such inferences early in life if they live in a society where, for example, the two sexes do not eat together—where the men and boys eat first, being waited on by the women, who have prepared the food. Inferences concerning the relative status of the two sexes derived from experiencing such cultural practices obviously could contribute strongly to children's congregating almost exclusively with playmates of their own sex, and to some of the asymmetries favoring male playgroups that I have noted. Indeed, Whiting and Edwards (1988, p. 277) note that it is in the very societies where men most clearly have higher status than women that boys make the earliest and strongest efforts to distance themselves from women and girls—from their own mothers, as well as from other females. In less industrialized cultures, too, segregation can be fostered by the assignment of different chores to boys and girls, so that they are found in different spaces: domestic chores for girls keeping them close to home while boys' chores, such as herding animals, take them some distance from home. My account so far, then, has pointed to a smaller role for socialization pressures from adults in modern industrialized societies than may be valid for a number of other cultures.

Although I have stressed the different interaction styles that emerge in male and female playgroups, I have said very little about the *content* of children's play. Here the cultural impact is great. In India, little girls use whatever materials are at hand—mud, sand, dough—to pretend that they are preparing chapatis and cooking them over a make-believe fire in a stone hearth. Girls in Mexico play at grinding corn and making tortillas; girls in the United States pretend they are making chocolate-chip cookies and baking them in an electric or gas oven. The content of children's play obviously derives from the scripts that their adult culture provides, and parents may be a major—though not the only—providers of the scripts that are learned. Certain aspects of male play, such as dominance struggles and themes of heroic combat, may be cross-culturally universal, or nearly so, but the content of the scripts depends on what weapons are available in a given culture and on what kind of cultural heroes are known to children.

As we saw at the beginning of this chapter, a common view is that boys and girls diverge in their childhood social behavior because adults treat them differently, and thus instill different habits, preferences, and skills. This conception is part of a more general view about socialization of children: that it occurs through processes whereby adults pass on to each new generation of children the rules, values, and beliefs that govern social behavior in the culture where the child is growing up. In this view, socialization occurs through the training of individual children. The characteristics of groups are a kind of sum or average of the characteristics of the individual children that constitute them.

There are a number of reasons to be dissatisfied with this approach. For one thing, as we have seen, childhood culture is in many ways not a direct reflection of adult culture. Further, the phenomena which need explanation—gender segregation, the distinctive male and female childhood cultures—are *group* processes, and we have seen that within-family processes do not translate well to group peer processes. But most important, the common view of socialization is too static. It does not take account of culture change. In the twentieth century, we have seen extraordinary changes in sex roles and in the relations between the sexes. We know what some of the social forces are that have brought about these changes: the widespread availability of contraception; the education of women; the employment of women; and the ideological changes embodied in the women's rights movement. In systematic ways, each new generation has been different from its parent generation. We could almost see this situation as a *failure* of socialization, if we think mainly in terms of intergenerational transmission.

Does this mean that I am discounting "socialization" as a force for gender differentiation? No, although it does mean that I am claiming a more limited role for parents in this socialization than others have done. Peers clearly have a socialization role. Indeed, peers may be more effective carriers of social change than the parent generation is. (After all, many children acquire computer literacy, or skill in video games, from age-mates and from somewhat older young people who are much closer to their own age than their computer-illiterate parents or grandparents are.) But there may also be forms of direct transmission of changing gender ideology and changing cultural gender-related practices that bypass both parents and peers.

We have already seen that children's behavior is governed not only by what they have been directly taught but also by what they have inferred through observing the culture around them. Certain cultural views about gender are embodied in myths, plays, and stories as well as in daily life. They are "in the air," and can be picked up by children from a host of sources. In the next chapter, we take up the role of cognitive processes—children's knowledge and beliefs (stereotypes, schemas) about what is sex-appropriate—and consider the conditions under which such knowledge and beliefs will be adopted as guides to children's own behavioral choices.

7

The Cognitive Component

We humans are unique among living creatures in our use of language for communicating with others and even for communicating with ourselves. And using language implies that we have coded and conceptualized our experience, and stored a great deal in memory that we can access via categorical codes. As children grow up, they accumulate a fund of information and beliefs about gender: how males and females behave in the real world, how they are *expected* to behave, what social roles they usually play, and what the prototypes are that encompass the ideal or glamorous qualities of males and females. We know how greatly societies differ in what they prescribe as appropriate behavior for people of the two sexes. We may expect, then, that children in different societies will acquire quite varied gender concepts.

A number of writers have assigned a causal role to gender cognitions in children's development of "sex-appropriate" behavior patterns.[1] The fundamental cognitive hypothesis is this: when children know the sex identity of themselves and others, and become aware of what activities and preferences are considered appropriate for each sex, they will be motivated to adopt own-sex distinctive behavior.

We may refer to this as the self-socialization hypothesis. Of course, adoption of behavior socially prescribed for one's own sex can never be independent of the kinds of direct socialization pressures discussed in Chapter 6. The hypothesis posits, however, that in addition to the control over their own behavior that children gain from their experiences of being rewarded or punished for certain things, children tend to adopt own-sex behavior simply because it has been defined as being appropriate for their own sex. Indeed, children may come to believe that there would be social consequences for sex-inappropriate behavior, even if they have never experienced or directly observed such consequences. The content of gender stereotypes—beliefs about what is sex-appropriate—comes from the child's own observation, from being instructed by knowledgeable members of the society, and from the gender-relevant content of the society's myths and prototypical or ideal images. (In the modern world, these include large contributions from TV fare.) But the learning of gender labels must come first, according to the theory, since children could not infer what are "male-type" or "female-type" activities from observing people engaged in these activities if they did not know the sex of the actors. Nor could they apply their knowledge to regulating their own behavior if they did not know their own gender. Thus gender-category labeling is fundamental to all the other processes of gender cognition.

People do not always do what they know to be "proper" or "expected." While it is true that individuals cannot conform to conventions unless they first learn what they are, adoption of conventional standards is by no means automatic. First of all, as Bandura's (1992) theory of "self-efficacy" stresses, the individual must feel confident of possessing (or being able to acquire) the skills and attributes needed to enact the prescribed roles. But beyond this, there is such a thing as rejection of social stereotypes. The vast changes in the social roles of women that have occurred in the twentieth century could not have occurred were it not for the refusal of a coterie of tough-minded women to accept the restrictions implied by traditional definitions of what kinds of education women should have, whether they should be permitted to vote or own property, what kinds of work they could or should do, what kinds of relations they should have with men.[2] In the effort to understand the differentiation in childhood of boys' and girls' social lives, we need to distinguish what children *know* about the gender stereotypes that define what is typical for members of each sex, and what they *accept* as applicable to themselves.

Studies of gender cognition have focused mainly on the role of such cognitions in the development of sex-typed behavior in individual children. The research has been concerned mainly with the processes whereby children develop "masculine" or "feminine" personality traits, and has searched for factors that determine how strongly sex-typed individual children of each sex become. As I said in the Introduction, in this book I am only marginally concerned with individual differences in the degree of sex-typing. It is to be expected, then, that much of the work on gender cognition will not be directly relevant to the purposes of this book.

In this chapter, I examine the usefulness of cognitive theory for explaining three phenomena: gender segregation itself, the differentiation of interaction styles within same-sex peer groups, and asymmetry. With respect to segregation, we need to ask whether, in order to segregate, children need to be able to code others as "same sex as me" versus "different sex from me." Alternatively, it may be the case that gender segregation can occur in the absence of such cognitions. It might be, for example, that young girls avoid playing with boys because they are wary of male playstyles, rather than because they know that boys belong to a different gender category than they do themselves.

Still, the "same as me" categorizing ought to have powerful effects. The social psychologist Tajfel (1982) showed that when people believe that they share membership in a group, several things predictably follow: there is an attraction to in-group members, preferential treatment of in-group members, greater value assigned to in-group members, and a kind of homogenization of the out-group—out-group members are lumped together and thought to have a few predominant characteristics, while members of the in-group are seen as more varied, more differentiated. Tajfel was able to show these effects when group membership was experimentally created on the basis of quite trivial shared characteristics.[3] We can only assume that sharing a gender category would be much more powerful in producing the in-group attraction and preference that manifests itself as segregation. Gender stereotypes, when young children begin to acquire them, might also contribute to same-sex preferences. Still, when we consider that young nonhuman primates segregate themselves by gender, presumably in the absence of the kind of cognitions about group membership that humans are capable of, we must entertain the possibility that in humans, too, knowledge of gender stereotypes, or even knowledge of the gender identity of self and others, may not be necessary for segregation, though they may enhance and support any tendencies to separate that occur for other reasons.

I will also ask to what extent the different interaction patterns that develop in male and female playgroups reflect not only categorical coding of the sex of self and others, but also learned stereotypes. In other words, one question will be whether, in their same-sex playgroups, children are adopting certain modes of interaction because they know they are considered appropriate for their own sex. And finally, I will ask whether children's acquisition of cultural knowledge and beliefs leads to asymmetry—to boys' groups being more separate than girls' groups both from other-sex children and from adult society.

Cognitive explanations are not entirely distinct from the other types of explanation we have been considering. As noted earlier, children's knowledge and beliefs are constructed in part from the social-shaping processes discussed in Chapter 6. Furthermore, children presumably make inferences, from observing the behavior of boys and girls, concerning the ways in which the behavior patterns of the two sexes are distinctive. To the degree that these behavior patterns reflect the kind of biological factors discussed in Chapter 5, cognitive explanations are not independent of biological ones.

In the first two sections of this chapter I consider two gender-cognitive phenomena separately: (1) knowledge of gender identity and (2) knowledge of gender stereotypes and scripts. These two aspects of gender cognition can be seen as quite distinct. In categorizing self and others as to sex, we make use of binary categories: individuals are coded as unequivocally either male or female.[4] Gender stereotypes, however, are prototypes. There is a cluster of characteristics that define what we think of as "masculine" or "feminine" behavior, and individuals vary in terms of how closely they resemble the prototype. Masculinity and femininity, then, become personality dimensions, and individuals can be arrayed along these dimensions in terms of the degree to which they display the attributes defining them. Gender identity, by contrast, does not vary in degree.[5] I will ask whether a child's having acquired knowledge about cultural stereotypes has an impact on any of the three phenomena I have set out to explain. It will be my contention that the recognition of the gender identity of self and others is more important for gender segregation than is gender stereotyping. Stereotyping may have an impact on interactive styles, but we will see that this, too, is problematic.

In the third section of this chapter, I will consider how children use their gender cognitions—their categorical coding of gender, their stereotypes, their schemas and scripts—to regulate their own behavior. I will thus differentiate between *knowledge* of gender prototypes and their adoption. Do children seek to match their own behavior to what they understand to be "appropriate" for their own sex? If so, at what age do they do this? Are there conditions under which they feel free to deviate from stereotypes? Most important: Is the way children interact with each other in same-sex groups shaped in any way by their shared understanding of the way persons of their sex *ought* to behave?

A final section of the chapter is concerned with "group think"—with the ways in which shared meanings are constructed through group process.

Gender Identity

By *gender identity* I mean the understanding that one is either a male or female person, and the incorporation of this understanding into the concept of the self. I begin by tracing a developmental trajectory, and then consider how the achievement of gender identity fits into the explanatory web.

Perceptual Distinctions

What do infants and toddlers know about their own sex identity and that of other people? On first thought, the question may appear nonsensical, when we consider that infants have no language with which to label people's gender. Or the question may seem unanswerable, since we cannot ask infants what they perceive or what people seem similar or different to them. There are, however, techniques which enable us to find out what categorical distinctions infants can make. We can take advantage of the fact that infants become bored if they are shown the same picture, or hear the same sound, again and again. More important, they lose interest if they are shown a series of pictures in the same *category* (such as many different makes of cars). But their interest reawakens if a new category (say, breeds of dogs) is introduced. We can trace their level of interest by the simple device of watching to see how long they look at a newly presented picture. If it is novel in some important respect, the infant will look at it longer than if it seems too similar to what has gone before.

Cynthia Miller (1983) wanted to discover whether infants aged 6 months could tell the difference between male and female voices. The voices could be heard whenever the infant looked at a visual display—the voice stopped if the infant looked away. With this arrangement, it was possible to tell how interested an infant was in a voice by monitoring how long the infant looked at the visual display when a voice was being played. In all, 12 different male voices and 12 different female voices were used. When several female voices were presented in succession, the infants gradually lost interest; but if the sound track switched to a male voice, their interest revived. The same happened with a switch from male to female voices. Clearly, the infants were making a categorical distinction between male and female voices.[6] Miller was able to show that infants could tell the difference between the two kinds of voices even when the fundamental frequency of the speech was controlled; thus they were not merely noticing the differences between low-pitched and high-pitched voices.

Leinbach and Fagot (1986) were interested in infants' ability to distinguish between male and female faces. They used real-life pictures of men and women with a variety of clothing, hairstyles, and facial expressions. They found that infants of 9 and 12 months would quite consistently show more interest in a newly presented face if it showed a person of a different sex than the previously presented faces. True, infants could distinguish between different people of the same sex, but they gradually lost interest when a series of same-sex pictures was presented, and showed renewed interest when the categorical switch was made.

Not only can infants distinguish the faces and voices of the two sexes, but they can tell which faces and voices go together. Poulin-Dubois and colleagues in Montreal (Poulin-Dubois, Serbin, Kenyon, and Derbyshire, 1991) presented infants of 9 and 12 months with a male and female face simultaneously, and accompanied the pictures with either a male or a female voice played over a loudspeaker. The infants spent more time looking at whichever face matched the voice they were hearing.

It is clear, then, that by the end of the first year infants can distinguish between men and women on the basis of both their appearance and their voices, or the two combined. Whether they use other cues as well—smell? body movements?—we do not know.[7] Also, we do not know how well they can distinguish among infants or children on the basis of their sex, since in much of the research, only pictures or voices of adults have been presented. Probably, they can make gender distinctions among younger persons as well.[8]

Perhaps it should not come as a surprise that by the end of their first year infants can distinguish among other people on the basis of their faces and voices. Certainly they can recognize their own family members and distinguish them from strangers. In the case of distinguishing males from females, however, they are not just distinguishing individuals, but are making a *categorical* distinction based on gender. Although it may seem surprising that such distinctions can be made without verbal labels, we should remember that perceptual categorizing is commonplace among nonhuman species, which also lack language. Specifically with respect to sex: nonverbal animals in bisexual species react differentially to male and female conspecifics; so infants are doing nothing more remarkable than what other nonverbal creatures do. Categorizing others of one's own species by their sex is probably nearly automatic, requiring very little in the way of cognitive elaboration. Still, when verbal labels and a variety of newly learned associations with gender are acquired, these of course add new distinctiveness to the early, nonverbal categorizing that is already in place by the time language becomes available.[9]

Categorical Membership

It is not easy to discover when a child first understands what his or her own sex identity is. There are anecdotes about young children's reactions to being teased. Saying to a girl, "You're really a boy," or teasing a boy by calling him by a girl's name, can elicit an outraged reaction from the child, but we don't know at what age children first begin to defend their sex identity as a central part of the self.

Researchers have struggled to find ways of asking questions about gender identity that are meaningful to very young children.[10] A favorite approach has been to ask children to sort a series or pictures or objects into two piles or boxes, one "for boys," one "for girls." The researchers usually begin by asking the children to sort familiar objects or pictures—such as square objects into one box, round ones into another, or pictures of dogs into one box and pictures of cats into the other—to make sure that they understand how to sort objects or pictures when asked. Most children can sort reliably by age 24 months or earlier, so the method can be safely used from this age onward. A male picture is usually displayed above one box and a female picture above the other, and children are asked to sort pictures of "things for girls (women)" into one box, "things for boys (men)" into the other.

Studies using such methods have come up with quite a consistent picture. Here is a summary of what they show.[11]

Own gender identity: At age 24 months, most children do not know their own gender: they cannot answer correctly "Are you a boy (girl)?" or sort their own pictures reliably into a box for their own sex. By age 2½, many children perform above chance on these measures, and by 36 months, own gender identity is quite well established for most children.[12]

Gender matching: Children might be able to label their own gender and that of other people accurately, and still not know which other people are "same as me" with respect to gender. We have little information about how early this matching process occurs, but some recent work indicates that boys achieve same-sex matching at a surprisingly early age, possibly earlier than girls.[13] In any case, by age 36 months, most children of both sexes can give appropriate answers to questions about which other people (or doll figures) are similar to the self with respect to gender (Thompson, 1975). Among children aged 4 and 5, there is evidence that being of the same sex as another child is more important to boys than to girls.[14]

At the time that young children are forming their sex-identity concepts, many do not know about the genital differences between the sexes. When asked to identify the sex of nude dolls, they rely more on the length of the doll's hair, or on upper-body conformation, than on genital structure (Thompson and Bentler, 1971; see also Bem, 1989). No doubt, too, children draw on first names, on the gendered pronouns that adults use in referring to other people, and on a wealth of cues from dress and perhaps body language as well.

Some years ago, Kohlberg (1966) introduced the idea that achieving gender identity is not an all-or-nothing thing. He said that there are way-stations reached in predictable order. He noted that children may be able to answer correctly the question "Are you a boy (girl)?" by the age of 3 or 4, but that at those ages the child may not realize that one retains the same gender over a lifetime. Some preschool-aged boys, even though they knew that they were boys, did not realize that they could only grow up to be "daddies" rather than "mommies," and in his own studies Kohlberg found that some young children thought that if a pictured boy was dressed in girls' clothes and had been given long hair, he had changed into a girl. Kohlberg claimed that it was only after attaining "gender constancy"—the belief that gender is unchangeable regardless of such superficial transformations—that children began to use gender classifications to pay special attention to same-sex models, and monitor and direct their own behavior into "sex-appropriate" channels. He thought that full gender constancy was usually not achieved until age 6 or 7.

In the ensuing years, many studies have explored gender constancy and its role in sex-typing. There is still disagreement among scholars on the interpretation of the existing body of work.[15] I believe, however, that we can now say with some confidence that most children develop a firm, stable gender identity considerably earlier than Kohlberg thought, and that being able to resist being misled by inconsistent perceptual cues may not be as important as he believed.

For present purposes, the important point is that children's formation of a core gender identity, and their knowledge about the gender of others, begin to take form at about the same time that they begin to prefer same-sex playmates. Thus this aspect of gender cognition may well be a contributor to gender segregation.

Gender Identity As a Contributor to Gender Segregation

Do we have any direct evidence that having achieved a firm gender identity *does* contribute to a child's preferring same-sex playmates? The meager evidence is mixed. Fagot and colleagues (Fagot, 1985; Fagot, Leinbach, and Hagan, 1986) worked with children aged 20–40 months, assessing their ability to apply accurate gender labels to pictures of boys and girls, men and women. They found that children who could label gender accurately spent a higher proportion of their social play time with same-sex other children, compared to others of their own age who did not yet have command of gender labeling.[16] By contrast, Smetana and Letourneau (1984), studying children who ranged in age from 27 to 70 months, found that throughout this age range, a child's tendency to choose same-sex playmates in free play was unrelated to whether the child could label accurately the sex of his or her self and others.

Serbin and colleagues (1994), studying children from 26 to 40 months of age, found that gender identity was no more fully developed in the children who preferred same-sex playmates than it was in those whose playmate choices were more gender-neutral; but we should note that the large majority of children in this study had already achieved gender identity. This finding means, then, that among young children almost all of whom know their own gender identity and that of other children, some have also developed same-sex playmate preferences while others have not. On the basis of this study alone, we could conclude that gender identity may be a necessary but not sufficient condition for segregation.

The achievement of gender identity probably comes at about the same age for children of the two sexes, although, as noted above, boys may be able to match the gender of self and others at a somewhat earlier age than girls. The achievement of gender identity, then, does not explain the fact that girls display same-sex preferences at a younger age than boys. There is some indication in existing studies that the in-group favoritism discussed above may be stronger in girls than boys at grade school age.[17] But this does not help us to understand why, in middle childhood, boys' groups are more exclusionary toward the other sex than are girls' groups—in fact, the opposite would be expected.

The foregoing exploration of gender identity as a causal factor contributing to the onset of gender segregation has revealed a number of ambiguities. The fact that the two processes occur in synchrony makes it plausible that they are causally linked. Yet the evidence for linkage is inconsistent, and the studies summarized above leave unresolved the question of whether being able to label one's own gender and that of other children is either a necessary or a sufficient condition for a child to begin preferring same-sex playmates. It is certainly possible that some other factor, such as wariness of the playstyle of the other sex, fosters the onset of cross-sex avoidance whether or not the other child has been identified as "different from me" with respect to gender. But although achieving gender identity is surely not the only factor in the emergence and maintenance of gender segregation, it must contribute in some way to these processes.

By the time children reach preschool age, it is clear that labeling self and others as to gender has become an integral element in gender segregation. We saw in Chapter 1 that when a child is asked to approach an unfamiliar child, the approach is more frontal and closer if the other child is of the same sex as the approacher (Wasserman and Stern, 1978). This happens before a child has any knowledge of the other child's individual playstyle, and indicates that the child has made a categorical distinction as to whether the other child is male or female, and acts accordingly in ways that imply categorical cross-sex avoidance.

It is worth noting that only a very modest preference for associating with others who are "same as me" with respect to gender identity (or avoiding others who are different) can result in substantial segregation. In an analysis of residential segregation by race, Schelling (1971) was able to show that if each householder held only the mild preference that three out of five nearest neighbors should be of the same race, initially mixed neighborhoods would undergo a cascade of sequential residential moves and emerge as substantially segregated. Thus collective results in groups of children can be much more pervasive than would be expected on the basis of the strength of individual "same as me" preferences alone.

Group Identity

So far I have been discussing a child's achievement of gender identity as a possible stepping stone toward, or a possible amplifier of, tendencies to join same-sex groups and adopt distinctive interaction styles. We should consider now the possibility of a reverse process: that segregation contributes to the formation of gender identity. In raising this question, I shift my focus. I have been talking about gender identity as though it were a matter of knowing one's own gender, and knowing the gender identity of individual other people. Long ago, William James pointed out that our identities not only are individual, but include our membership in social groups. For many people, it is part of their core identity to be a member of a clan, a religious group, an ethnic group, or a nation. If one identifies with a group, one shares its values and its goals, feels pride in its functions and accomplishments, and feels distress when the group is threatened. We often perceive others in terms of their group identity. This identity can be signaled by group-membership markers, such as uniforms, rings or lapel pins, or fan-club baseball caps or T-shirts. We also infer group membership in terms of who associates with whom, especially when a group carries out coordinated activities with others in pursuing a joint enterprise, as is the case with a jazz group, a Marine honor guard, a sports team, or a board of directors (see Brewer and Harasty, 1994).

Abelson (1994) has noted that the salience of group membership varies: sometimes a man will think of himself simply as an Italian-American individual, but at other times, perhaps on a celebratory occasion such as Columbus Day, he will think of himself as a member of an Italian-American collective. Abelson has been able to show that under conditions in which an out-group's collective identity has been made more salient, the in-group collective identity also becomes more salient, so that, for example, people seek backup from members of their own group when faced by a perceived threat from an out-group collective.

Are these distinctions meaningful when it comes to gender identity? If so, we would see that children sometimes function in terms of their individual gender identities, but at other times see themselves as a member of a "we boys" or "we girls" group. In the same sense, other children could be seen and reacted to either as individual boys or girls, or as members of a group of "those boys," or "those girls." Although there has been essentially no research on collective gender identity as such, the descriptive material presented in Chapters 2 and 3 suggests strongly that there are situations in which children do take up a collective gender identity. In referring to children in the classroom or on the playground collectively, they say "the boys" did this, "the girls" did that. We saw instances in which a group of boys disrupted a girls' game, and the girls, as a group, gave chase. We saw that children claim certain playground territory, or certain tables in the lunchroom, as "belonging" to one sex or the other. In their borderwork, children are careful to maintain boundaries between groups of the two sexes. We do not know how far children's group gender identity extends. It is doubtful that children see themselves as part of a group made up of all adults and children of their own gender. Still, children do identify with storybook and film characters, and real-life celebrities, of their own sex; so the sense of membership in a gender group is not confined to small face-to-face groups.

I suggest that the sense of identity with one's same-sex collective grows directly out of gender segregation; and further, that in childhood, boys may have a stronger sense of membership in a same-sex collective than girls.[18] For one thing, as we have seen, boys' groups tend to be larger, and to have a clearer group structure. They seem to have a distinctive set of activities, of which team sports are the quintessential example, involving both in-group cooperation and between-group rivalries. And boys, more than girls, set themselves apart both from adults and from children of the other sex, and are more coercive toward group members who show signs of cross-sex interests. From preschool age on, boys are attentionally oriented to each other, playing to other boys as an audience. They maintain strong norms about not tattling on other group members who transgress rules or engage in risky behavior. All these things suggest that for boys their identity as members of a group of "we boys" must have considerable salience. As boys grow older, the male playgroup subdivides into recognized subgroups with specialized interests, so that there are shifts in the boundaries of the male group with which any individual boy identifies. And, throughout childhood, there are "loners" who are only minimally involved in any group.

If gender-based group identity is indeed stronger for most boys than most girls, it follows that girls will often *perceive* boys as being part of the gender collective "those boys," while boys will see girls more often in their individual female identity. This is not to deny that some male sexist attitudes do depersonalize girls and women, treating them as members of a derogated out-group. But, perhaps, boys and men less often see women and girls as members of a coherent female group that has collective objectives and collective influence. Girls, however—and adults as well— probably do see boys' groups as having a collective agenda and power.

It is likely that the conditions that make our individual gender identity salient are quite different from those that activate our group gender identity. In particular, heterosexual attraction is the quintessential condition for individual gender salience, but this is a condition that runs directly counter to a sense of identity with one's own gender group.

Knowledge of Gender Stereotypes, Scripts, and Metaphors

Gender Stereotypes

As early as the third year of life, children begin to form beliefs about the gender-typicality of certain familiar household objects and items of clothing. Through the preschool years, the list expands, and increasing numbers of children will sort pictures of such items as a hammer, baseball, shirt and tie, razor and shaving cream, into a box for men, and pictures of a dress, vacuum cleaner, cooking pot, cosmetics, handbag, into a box for women. Certain toys, such as trucks and dolls, also increasingly come to be seen as more appropriate for children of one sex than the other. Children develop stereotyped beliefs that certain *activities,* as well as toys and other objects, are more appropriate for one sex than the other.[19]

Children not only come to know which toys are associated with each sex, and which items of clothing and which hairstyles are sex-typical; they also come to believe that certain occupations—in industrial societies, such occupations as carpenter, police officer, truck driver—are masculine, while others—secretary, nurse, teacher—are coded as female occupations. Of course, there are many objects and activities which are *not* seen as being especially associated with either sex. But standard tests of stereotypical knowledge and beliefs indicate that there is widespread agreement among children concerning these matters, and very little individual variation. On some standard measures of stereotyping that have been widely used, most children appear to reach "ceiling" by about age 7,[20] but more varied measures indicate that additional stereotypes continue to be formed and old ones expanded or modified through the grade school years.

The development of gender stereotypes occurs equally rapidly for boys and girls, and the content of the stereotypes is very similar for children of the two sexes. Both sexes know which toys are preferred by each sex, which household objects are more likely to be used by mothers, which by fathers, and so on. However, children are likely to hold somewhat more positive stereotypes about children of their own sex than those of the other sex. In the preschool and early grade school years, both sexes claim that children of their own sex have "good" traits ("happy," "gentle," "soft-hearted," "adventurous," and "sure of self") regardless of whether these traits are stereotypically masculine or feminine; at the same time, they depict the other sex as more often having "bad" traits ("weak," "emotional," "messy," "cruel").

There is some evidence that children learn first about the stereotypes associated with their own sex, but by age 8 or 9, most children have a firm understanding of the sex-role expectations and definitions their society has established for both sexes (Martin, 1989, 1993).

The specifics of which items and ideas become sex-typed and which are gender-neutral depend on the information children receive from the culture in which they live. Some information is similar across cultures (for example, that men are taller than women, on the average). Other items, such as modes of dress that differentiate the sexes, differ greatly from one society to another. Children's stereotypes generally reflect their cultural norms.

Gender Scripts

The knowledge that young children acquire is not just a matter of knowing the gender-relatedness of individual objects or specific isolated acts. Rather, knowledge is *scripted:* children learn what *sequence* of events to expect.[21] They know that when getting dressed in the morning, you put on your underwear before your outer garments; they know that the main course of a meal comes before dessert, and so on. Gender-related knowledge is scripted too: children not only know that a hammer is a "masculine" object; they have a whole carpentry script, including such items as knowing that you first position a nail point-down on a board before you strike it with the hammer. Certain scripts are gendered, while others, such as the scripts for brushing teeth or eating dinner, are not. There is evidence that boys have a firmer grasp of masculine than feminine scripts, while for girls, the two kinds of scripts are equally well understood (Boston and Levy, 1991).

Gender Metaphors

Although children know at a fairly early age what activities, what items of clothing, what toys and utensils are typical of each sex, they are slower to make inferences concerning personality characteristics that might differentiate the sexes.[22] We might conclude from this that young children's stereotypes are based on objective, observable gender differences. Yet there are certain gender stereotypes that children hold that go considerably beyond what is given in the objective information that children have available to draw from. For example, if a stuffed animal is equipped with large fierce-looking teeth, preschoolers are more likely to classify it as "for boys" than if it looks more benign. Similarly, fire, lightning, sharks, and gorillas are classified as masculine by preschool children, as are things that are large in size, dark in color, sharp, or rough to the touch (such as sandpaper). Things that are soft, small or delicate-looking (clouds, ducklings, butterflies), smooth and with rounded contours (soap), or pastel in color are classified as "for girls." And angry facial expressions are coded as male, happy ones as female (Leinbach, 1993; Hort, Leinbach, and Fagot, 1992).

We do not know where these metaphorical gender meanings come from. The kinds of qualities associated with maleness are clearly related to the kinds of play materials boys prefer (guns, swords, monster and dinosaur masks or toys), and to the play themes (danger, struggle) they like to enact. We can understand, then, that boys would derive the metaphorical meanings described above. Likewise girls would recognize, in metaphors, the themes that characterize their own play. It is less clear why children should subscribe to the metaphors for the other sex, but the fact is that children of both sexes do share the metaphorical meanings of maleness and femaleness. Perhaps their metaphors are simply generalizations abstracted from a variety of experiences with individuals of the two sexes. For example, children could certainly discover that men's voices are usually louder and deeper than women's voices (and hence more threatening?). Perhaps their mothers and other familiar women have smiled at them more often than the men the children have known. And men are, on the average, larger than women. Metaphorical meanings could then be simply associationistic extensions from real-life experience, though there has been no systematic effort to find connections between such experiences and metaphorical beliefs.

Psychodynamic explanations have been offered as well (Erikson, 1952, for one). We could even imagine that some sort of Jungian racial unconscious is at work. Whatever the source, these metaphorical meanings of maleness and femaleness probably have some importance in their own right. Preschoolers apply them to hypothetical individuals about whom nothing is known except their gender. Hough and colleagues (1980) showed preschoolers videotapes of two infants, one labeled a boy and the other a girl, and then, presenting still pictures of the two infants they had just seen in action on video, asked the children to choose, by pointing to one infant or the other, descriptive labels for them from pairs of opposite trait names: big/little, nice/mean, and so forth. More often than would be expected by chance, the children chose the following adjectives for the infant labeled a boy: smart, big, strong, hard, mad, fast, loud, mean; for a "girl," the choices were: dumb, weak, soft, little, scared, slow, quiet, nice.[23] In actuality, the infants did not differ on any of these characteristics.

The sense preschoolers have that males are somehow more powerful or threatening translates into images they have concerning dominance and authority within the family. Anderson (1978) asked preschoolers to play-act little scenes, taking in turn the roles of two doll-characters, one described as a mother, the other as a daddy. The children depicted the "daddies" as giving more orders to the mothers than vice versa, while "mothers" were more likely to give "hints." Matthews (1977), observing same-sex pairs of four-year-olds engaging in free play with the toys provided in a playroom, recorded instances of fantasy play in which the children enacted the roles of father and mother. Boys depicted mothers as being homebound, engaged in housekeeping and child care. Boys tended to see the relation between their parents as one in which the mother was helpless or inept (for instance, mother asks the daddy to plug in the iron), while fathers were depicted as leaders and being in control in both their husbandly and fatherly personas. Girls depicted mothers as generous, nurturant, and skillful managers (the one who knows where everything is), while fathers were considered appreciative ("Thank you, wife, that was a good supper") and masterful and directive toward their wives. Both boys and girls depicted household work as optional for fathers.[24]

These studies were conducted in the 1970s, when the household division of labor was probably more sex-typed than it is today. Even so, considerable division of labor still prevails, and it is reasonable to believe that children's stereotypes are based at least in part on their realistic observations of the work assignments and the dominance relations between their parents. It may be, however, that there is in addition a kind of merging in their minds of their observations at home with the metaphorical meanings described above. It is likely that children see their fathers as more masterful and directive toward their wives and children than they are in real life. There is some evidence that children are more compliant to their fathers' directives than to their mothers', a tendency which might stem as much from the perceptions as from the reality of greater male authority.[25]

The Flexibility of Gender Stereotypes and Beliefs

Some writers have suggested that children's gender concepts become less stereotyped, more flexible, through the middle-childhood years. It is true that, in some ways, ages 5–8 may be the most "sexist" period of life. At this age, children tend to be "essentialists," in that they usually do not attribute sex differences to environmental causes, but believe they simply follow from being either a male or female person (Taylor, 1995). And at this time, gender stereotypes are quite rigid, and children see deviations from them as positively *wrong*, not just misguided.[26] Furthermore, children of this age make predictions about the characteristics and preferences of children they don't know almost entirely on the basis of those children's sex, ignoring other available information that might tell a different story. Older grade school children give more credence to environmental factors in sex-typing. In addition, they can utilize other information jointly with knowledge of another child's gender to draw conclusions about an unfamiliar peer. They also begin to see possibilities for acceptable variation in what is appropriate for a boy or girl to do. And they become more able to consider simultaneously ways in which the two sexes are alike, as well as ways in which they are different.

Despite the fact that with increasing age children are able to bring to bear these more sophisticated levels of thinking about gender, it does not appear that children become more flexible in any general sense during middle childhood. Their knowledge and beliefs about what activities and occupations are typical of, and considered appropriate for, males and females only become more fully established with age (Signorella, Bigler, and Liben, 1993; Martin, 1989; and Serbin, Powlishta, and Gulko, 1993). Furthermore, studies in the 1980s indicated that older grade-schoolers are less tolerant than younger children of peers who engage in clearly cross-sex behavior (see Stoddard and Turiel, 1985; Carter and McClosky, 1984). More recent studies have suggested, however, that with increasing age, children become more likely to believe that certain sex-stereotyped activities *can* (or *should*) be undertaken equally by both sexes.[27] In one recent study (Serbin, Powlishta, and Gulko, 1993), the number of children saying that both sexes could legitimately engage in a variety of activities rose with age, being twice as great for sixth-graders as it had been at kindergarten age. Katz and Ksansnak (1994) documented a clear increase with age, from middle childhood through high-school age, in children's acceptance of nontraditional activities, for themselves and for others. Indeed, some older children exhibited what Slaby (1990) has called "self-generated disengagement": a personal choice to disregard societal norms as invalid, irrelevant, or unjust. These more recent findings may indicate that efforts to expand the horizons of children's thinking about possible roles for the two sexes have borne some fruit with the upcoming generation of children. Girls in particular show increasing flexibility when asked which sex *can* or *should* perform activities or take up occupations which have traditionally been labeled appropriate mainly for one sex (Signorella, Bigler, and Liben, 1993; Katz and Ksansnak, 1994).

Does Knowledge of Stereotypes Contribute to Gender Segregation?

We have seen that knowledge of gender stereotypes and the tendency to prefer same-sex playmates more or less proceed in synchrony. The onset of segregation occurs at about the same developmental period in which children first begin to understand that certain toys, household objects, and activities are associated with one sex rather than the other. Knowledge of stereotypes, then, is a plausible candidate for a factor that might foster gender segregation. In fact, however, the connection between knowledge of gender stereotypes and preference for same-sex playmates is weak.

In the study of toddlers described in Chapter 4, Serbin and colleagues (1994) found that the children who had begun to prefer same-sex playmates did not have any greater knowledge of gender stereotypes than did the children who were "non-segregating." Martin (1994) found only a very weak relationship between preschoolers' tendency to prefer same-sex playmates and their beliefs concerning differences in boys' and girls' playstyles.[28] Serbin and colleagues, studying children ranging from kindergartners to sixth-graders found no relation between knowledge of gender stereotypes and children's same-sex peer preferences. Powlishta (1995) also found no connection between individual children's preference for same-sex partners (as observed while mixed groups of third- and fourth-grade children were working on a task) and their knowledge of gender stereotypes. Taken together, these studies do not point to any significant role for the acquisition of gender stereotypes as a mechanism underlying the onset or maintenance of gender segregation.

There has been considerable interest in the possibility that if gender stereotypes become more flexible, less rigid, as children progress through the age range 6–11, children might not feel the need to adhere as rigidly to the "rules" of gender as they did when younger. They might "outgrow" some of their strong sense of membership in a gender group, and might begin to experiment with playing games identified with the other sex or even become more willing to associate with children of the other sex. We have seen that the research on flexibility is equivocal, with some work pointing to children's becoming more tolerant concerning cross-sex interests and activities, while other (mainly earlier) research points to the opposite.[29] In any case, the simple fact is that even if gender stereotypes do become less rigid throughout middle childhood, children's preference for same-sex playmates does not decline. There are increases, during this period, in children's choices of same-sex other children as people they would like to play with, sit next to, or engage in some activity with. In fact, among the fourth-, fifth- and sixth-graders studied by Serbin and colleagues (1993), most children made nearly 100 percent same-sex choices. We have one more indication, then, that gender stereotypes, whether flexible or not, seem to have little bearing on gender segregation.

Stereotypes might, however, influence the kind of activities that go on in same-sex groups. If they function to make boys' activities different from girls' activities, they must do so through the joint action of stereotype knowledge and gender identity. As we have seen, boys and girls have very much the same knowledge and ideas concerning what is considered appropriate for children of the two sexes. But once sex identity is established, children of each sex might seek to adapt themselves to what they know is considered appropriate for their own gender. Most of what we know about these kinds of adaptive processes has come from studies of individual children, not children in groups. But the questions are much the same:

What we need to know is whether, and to what extent, children use the stereotypes as a guide to their own actions—in other words, for self-socialization.

Self-Socialization

Studies of self-regulation with regard to gender appropriateness have dealt almost entirely with the adoption of sex-typed toy and activity preferences. Thus they deal with the processes involved when boys adopt "masculine characteristics," girls "feminine" ones. They have not dealt directly with self-regulation as it might affect the choice of same-sex playmates, differentiation of interaction styles, or asymmetry. Still, they may yield some clues as to how self-regulation might be involved in these domains.

As an example of a study aimed at the question of children's efforts to match an own-sex stereotype, Perry and colleagues (1984), working with children aged 2–5, administered tests of the children's knowledge about which toys and activities were "for boys," and which "for girls"; they also assessed the children's own preferences. They found that boys' sex-typed toy preferences were developed at an earlier age than their awareness of which were "boys' toys" and which were "girls' toys," and thus their toy and activity preferences could not have emerged from efforts to match a stereotype (for girls, the two things developed in parallel). Other studies also have found that sex-typed toy preferences develop before children have acquired the gender stereotypes that they presumably could use to guide such preferences.[30]

Self-Evaluation

We see, then, that knowledge of stereotypes is not a necessary condition for the development of certain aspects of sex-typing. It might still be true, however, that once stereotypes *are* acquired, children use them to guide their own behavior into "sex-appropriate" channels, thus supplementing whatever other factors may be leading children in this same direction. Bussey and Bandura (1992) investigated this kind of self-regulatory process in preschoolers. In their view, self-regulation involves having a self-accepted standard for how people of one's gender ought to behave, and then evaluating one's own behavior against this standard. They sought to establish that preschool children, once they had come to believe that certain toys were considered to be "for boys" or "for girls," would evaluate their own toy choices in terms of this standard of sex-appropriateness.

What they found was that both three-year-olds and four-year-olds, when presented with the opportunity to choose among an array of toys, made choices that were clearly sex-typed. Furthermore, when all other toys were removed except one stereotyped for the other sex, children—especially boys—resisted playing with them. One boy threw the baby doll across the room and turned his back on it. A girl, left with only a dump-truck to play with, said, "My mommy would want me to play with this, but I don't want to." Clearly, some of the children had strongly held preferences which corresponded closely to the stereotypes concerning which sex should be playing with certain toys. There was, however, an age progression in the process of self-evaluation. Although three-year-olds expressed toy preferences that accorded with the stereotypes, they did not systematically rate themselves as more satisfied with what they were doing when playing with a sex-appropriate toy, or less satisfied when playing with an other-sex toy. Such relevant self-evaluations *were* found for four-year-olds, however. Furthermore, for four-year-olds, self-evaluations and sex-typed behavioral choices were correlated, while no such correlations appeared for the younger children. We see, then, that during the preschool years, children make a transition from "is" to "ought." Three-year-olds, almost all of whom know their own gender identity and also know a good deal about which toys are "for boys" or "for girls," nevertheless do not appear to translate this knowledge into beliefs about what they *should* be doing, or to use their knowledge for self-regulation. But by the time they are four, not only do they make sex-typed toy choices, they evaluate such choices positively. We see here the onset of the "moral imperative" that sex-appropriate behavior seems to take on in early middle childhood. And the self-evaluations that children bring to bear from the age of four onward presumably reinforce their same-sex preferences, and strengthen their resistance to cross-sex activities (again, more strongly so among boys).

The research described above was designed to uncover processes whereby children participate in socializing themselves to adopt certain specifically sex-typed behaviors (in the Bussey and Bandura case, toy choices). We may assume that these processes are also involved in children's development of preferences for sex-typed clothing, hairstyles, nicknames, and so forth. Are they involved in choices of same-sex playmates, or in the development of sex-typed playstyles and the group processes that distinguish boys' and girls' playgroups? To deal with this question, we must be more specific about what self-evaluation entails. Consider the following cases:

1A. A girl doesn't like rough play. She has discovered that boys' play is often rougher than girls'. She thinks, "I don't like to play with boys; they're too rough."

1B. A boy enjoys rough play and chasing. He has discovered that most girls don't like this kind of play. He decides that girls aren't much fun to play with, and begins to avoid them.

2A. A girl observes that boys' play is usually rougher than girls' play. She thinks, "I am a girl, so I ought to play the way girls play—not so roughly." She approves of herself when she is playing quietly, disapproves of herself for playing roughly.

2B. A boy has observed that boys do more chasing and roughhousing than girls do. He thinks that since he is a boy, he ought to engage in chasing and roughhousing, and approves of himself more when he is playing this way than when he is playing quietly.

These putative inner "conversations" are not meant to be taken literally. When children are influenced by such considerations, they may or may not be consciously aware of them. Still, these cases illustrate an important distinction. All the cases involve self-regulation of a sort: in every case children are intentionally guiding their own behavior in a certain direction. And stereotyped beliefs may underlie this self-guidance. Martin (1994) has shown that boys who believe that boys do more chasing than girls are more likely to associate primarily with other boys; and that girls who say that girls play more indoors, while boys play more outdoors, are also more likely to play mainly with other girls. But it is not clear whether we are dealing with Category 1 or Category 2 here. If a girl likes indoor play, she is likely to be attracted to playmates who she believes also like indoor play. This does not necessarily mean that she is trying to conform to what she believes is appropriate or "expected" behavior for a girl. Strictly speaking, only the cases in 2A and 2B are examples of guiding one's behavior on the basis of a self-adopted standard concerning what is acceptable or proper for a person of one's own sex. In the example given by Bussey and Bandura, it is plausible that the emotional reaction of a boy who throws a baby doll across the room and turns his back on it arises from his having accepted a standard for what is OK or not OK for him, as a boy, to do (although, alternatively, he may dislike playing with dolls for other reasons). It is less clear whether standard-based self-regulation is involved in the case of rough-and-tumble play. Martin (1994) suggests that rough-and-tumble play is not cognized as a "gender imperative"—not something that boys believe they are supposed to do in order to be boylike, and I believe she is right.

Especially interesting is the example of the girl who doesn't want to play with a dump-truck even though she knows her mother would approve of such play. This child may be resisting a stereotype her parents want to impose, adopting instead a standard from peers as to what kind of play is sex-appropriate and attempting to conform to this standard. But she may instead simply be avoiding the dump-truck because she doesn't like to play with dump-trucks, without regard to whether this is a behavior that is socially approved or disapproved by members of a salient reference group. In the latter case, she would not be self-regulating on the basis of a standard at all.

It is extraordinarily difficult to determine whether, or how much, a given bit of sex-typed behavior is being self-regulated on the basis of a self-accepted standard of sex-appropriateness. It seems likely that such self-evaluation is important in boys' avoidance of certain activities that are understood to be "for girls," and this may extend to avoidance of play with female playmates. It seems much less likely that certain aspects of male play—in particular, roughhousing and struggles over dominance—reflect self-evaluative efforts by boys to meet a standard of how a boy ought to behave. Girls are generally less strongly motivated to avoid "masculine" activities, but as they move into middle childhood they do become especially interested in feminine items of clothing and adornment, and in romantic themes and stories. It remains an open question how much these interests are driven by the desire to conform to a standard of femininity. The fact that "tomboys" gain considerable acceptance from peers of both sexes must mean that girls have considerable freedom to adopt or not to adopt such standards for regulating their own behavior.

Imitation of Same-Sex Models

Selective imitation can be a means of self-socialization. Children may infer that they can best learn behaviors relevant to their own sex by observing, and emulating, same-sex models rather than other-sex models. As Bussey and Bandura say, same-sex imitation "seems to rely on classifying males and females into distinct groups, recognizing personal similarity to one group of models, and tagging that group's behaviors in memory as the ones to be used as a guide to behavior" (1984, p. 1297).

Some years ago, Jacklin and I reviewed the then-existing body of relevant research, and concluded that although children do learn a great deal by imitation, they do not systematically imitate own-sex models more than other-sex models, at least not during the first six years of life (Maccoby and Jacklin, 1974). Since that time, the issues concerning same-sex imitation have been considerably clarified. Perry and Bussey (1979), working with eight-year-old children, presented films of models engaging in unfamiliar activities. In one condition of the experiment, all four male models selected one set of activities to perform, all four female models selected a different set. In another condition, three men and one woman carried out one set of activities, while three women and one man did another. And in still another condition, half the men and half the women chose each set. When children were subsequently offered the opportunity to choose among the same activities they had seen modeled, the children in the first condition—high within-sex consensus among models—consistently imitated the same-sex models. In the second condition of only moderate model consensus, there was less same-sex imitation, but more than would have occurred merely by chance. In the third condition, in the absence of model consensus, the boys and girls did not differ in their activity choices.[31] Perry and Bussey also discovered that children consistently failed to imitate a model of their own sex if that model had previously been shown behaving in a manner different from that of the other own-sex models.

These studies indicate that when children are in a situation where they must make some choices among an array of unfamiliar activities, they will use information from the number (or proportion) of models of each sex that they see performing the activities as a guide to the sex-appropriateness of the different activities. But individual same-sex models will not be imitated preferentially unless there is reason to believe that they are somehow representative—that their choices are a reliable clue to what "all the men" or "all the women" prefer to do. This interpretation is confirmed in the work by Barkley and colleagues (1977), who found that when seven-year-olds observed male models doing either masculine or feminine things, or female models doing either feminine or masculine things, they imitated whichever model was engaging in the activities they already knew were appropriate to their own gender. They showed no additional tendency to imitate same-sex models. Thus in the special case where children have no preexisting information about the sex-typing of an activity, model consensus created by an experimenter gives them information that they would usually have to accumulate over many observed instances as to which sex normally performs which activities. In short, experimental subjects can be given the materials from which to form a stereotype. The more powerful implication of the Perry and Bussey work is this: the mere knowledge that people of their own sex make a certain choice—a choice different from that of people of the other sex—exerts an influence on children's own choices. Thus although not all children adopt gender stereotypes as guides for their own behavior, many do, at least in situations where they have no other basis on which to choose.

What are we to conclude, then, concerning the power of same-sex models to influence children's adoption of sex-typed behavior? A commonly accepted theory has been that children acquire their gender-stereotypical behavior through imitation of same-sex models. But if a child's imitation of a given same-sex model depends on the child's understanding of how gender-typical that particular model is, it would appear that certain preexisting stereotypes must already be in place to prime children to imitate only culturally legitimate models. Once they have identified such models, they can acquire new information, new stereotypes, new modes of behaving, from observing and imitating them. In sum, the work on model consensus shows that models, *in the aggregate,* do play a role in shaping "sex-appropriate" behavior.

The studies discussed above examined how and whether children imitate same-sex *adult* models. Thus they bear upon the transmission of culture from one generation to the next. Consensus among adult models is one source of information that children can draw on, along with what they learn from instruction and other sources, concerning the sex roles and expectations their culture has established for the two sexes. Children know a great deal about the sex roles of the other sex, as well as their own, but though they may *know* what is appropriate for both sexes, they choose to adopt preferentially, and practice, the elements relevant to their own sex. As we saw in Chapter 6, little girls in cultures around the world can be seen imitating, in their play, the daily activities of their mothers and other women, while little boys often enact, in their play, the scripts of male occupations and other activities (pretend plowing, soldiering). Such observations are persuasive evidence that same-sex imitation is a powerful conduit for the transmission of sex-role cultures across generations.

In American society, it is striking how girls' interests in stories and TV dramas, and their play with Barbie dolls, focus on themes of glamour, romance, and marriage. In their play, girls seem to be socializing themselves for their future roles in relation to men. Boys' TV preferences, and the play themes in boys' groups, are quite different. Their preferred themes of adventure and heroism do not seem to involve much in the way of preparation for future roles involving relationships with women (as lovers, husbands, co-parents).

When children adopt childlike versions of adult sex roles, their choices may not be directly relevant to the phenomena under discussion here. We may ask whether, for example, girls use conflict-mitigating strategies in their discourse with each other because they have discovered that girls and women, more often than boys and men, deal with each other in this way. This returns us to the question noted above: whether children are trying to conform to "gender imperatives" when they display the modes of interaction commonly seen in all-male as compared to all-female play groups. I am doubtful as to whether this process is an important factor in the differentiation of interaction styles, but evidence is lacking.

The question becomes even more fundamental when we ask about gender segregation itself, and the possible role of adult models in bringing about the childhood patterns described in Chapter 1. It is no surprise that adult cultures pass on to new generations of children the stereotypes that reflect their culture-specific version of what roles and behavior are appropriate for people of each sex. The transmission occurs in part via children's observation and imitation of what people of their own sex do. But this formulation of the sex-typing process does not fit what we know about childhood gender segregation very well.

As I have noted at several points, gender segregation in childhood is not a matter of children imitating what they see adults doing. If there is any consensus among adult models concerning whether they do, or should, associate with people of the other sex, the consensus reflects more the seeking of association with the other sex than the avoidance of it. Thus gender segregation is not a matter of transmission of gender-relevant elements of culture from adults to the next generation. We cannot see children's avoidance of the other sex as a matter of self-regulation in which children attempt to adapt themselves to the gender-role requirements of adult culture. No doubt children make self-regulating efforts to adapt themselves to *child* culture. For example, preschoolers, in avoiding children of the other sex with increasing frequency, are influenced by their knowledge that other children of their own sex usually avoid them, and would disapprove of a child who did not. But if the cultural transmission is from child to child, rather than from adults to children, we must ask why childhood culture differs from adult culture in the first place, with respect to the degree of gender segregation that is displayed. In asking this, we have simply returned to the original question, without making much progress toward an explanation.

"Group Think"

It has been one of the primary themes of this book that gender is expressed in childhood largely at the social level. Separation into same-sex social groups permits the emergence of distinctive male and female childhood cultures which have characteristics over and above the characteristics that inhere in individual children. So far, in considering gender cognitions, I have discussed children's acquisition of their individual gender identities, and each boy's or girl's acquisition of gender stereotypes, in terms of the impact these might have on their gendered social behavior. But it is time to consider that social cognitions can also function at the group level: that there is such a thing as group cognition, which can even be thought of as the heart of group culture. It is well known that individuals who find that they are out of step with the dominant opinion in a group they have joined are likely to conform to the dominant opinion (at least outwardly). But group cognitive processes go much beyond the idea that individual children are influenced by others in their group. In fact, meanings are co-constructed in groups, in such a way that the group product is different from the initial position or set of assumptions of any individual group member (see Perret-Claremont, Perret, and Bell, 1991). Communication among group members grows out of these shared meanings.

Co-Construction of Meanings

Members of any social group, if they continue to interact with each other over a period of time, construct a form of verbal shorthand. They can use cryptic messages and words with idiosyncratic meanings. Lengthy explanations of what one person means are no longer needed because group

members can take for granted certain assumptions and mutually understood references that underlie another group member's brief remark. Even
in a single experimental session, the processes of developing such specialized mutual understandings can be shown to be at work. An example
comes from the research of Krauss and Russell (1991), who used a referential communication task where a subject (the sender) had to describe
an ambiguous drawing to a partner (the receiver) in such a way that the
partner could pick out the intended item from among an array of other
drawings. In early trials senders devised elaborate descriptions, but in
successive trials, they reduced the length and complexity of the communication step by step until it became quite cryptic. Thus a drawing that
might initially have been described as "looks like a martini glass with legs
on each side" was described with successively shorter phrases until, in the
latest trials, it was simply called a "martini." These simplifications depended on the sender's receiving feedback from the receiver that the
successively shorter messages had been understood. In short, the sender
and receiver were constructing a shared referential meaning. The pair were
much more able to do this if they could see each other. They were using
"back-channel" signals, in the form of facial expressions and body language, to signal the development of mutual understanding.

In real-life groups, group members talk about their interpretations of
what is going on, and often refer back to prior shared experiences in
constructing their joint interpretations of current events. Newcomers to a
group, not having shared these prior experiences, may not understand
what long-standing group members are talking about, and it takes time
for them to establish a common experiential base that fosters their sharing
of the group culture. Of course, it often happens that previously unacquainted people already share common ground. If you and a new acquaintance discover that both of you are members of the Elks' Club, or of the
same fraternity or sorority, or come from the same hometown, you can
make assumptions about what the new acquaintance already knows or
believes, and can decide on that basis how much explanation or detailed
description to use in conveying information or making a conversational
point (Krauss and Fussell, 1991). Sharing membership in a gender category is surely a powerful basis for assumptions concerning how much
common ground is already shared with a new acquaintance. Recall the
child described in Chapter 3 who said that it "never entered her mind" to
sit down and chat with a boy the way she would with a girl, because she

wouldn't know what to talk about; or the boy who couldn't imagine what girls talk to each other about. In the segregated playgroups of childhood, the continuing interaction among group members involves the co-construction of meanings and assumptions common to the group, but not shared by members of the other sex.

Forging Shared Scripts

Group members acquire knowledge and expectations about what others in their group will probably do in given circumstances. And to ensure the effective functioning of a group in pursuit of a goal, these cognitions must be shared by all members of the group. In her fascinating study of the process whereby a group of initially unacquainted boys were forged into a winning Little League team, Shirley Brice Heath (1991) emphasized that they all had to learn to be aware of each other's whereabouts on the field, and to share expectations concerning who would move to where when certain events occurred. The coach took an active role in forging these shared understandings. During one training session, he said, "What would have happened if Rob had bunted? What about the man on second?" teaching the group to share cognitively the scripts that they would have to act on collectively during a game. Even when no coach is present, groups of boys and groups of girls can forge such shared scripts as they talk about what they are doing, and what each should be doing, in the process of carrying out a group enterprise.

Distributed Cognition

Some researchers have studied what they call "distributed cognition." They note that there are many kinds of group enterprises for which no single individual can have all the relevant information, but that different people know different relevant things and by pooling their information they can assemble a body of information sufficient to carry out the task. However, the way information flows and how it is pooled differs from group to group, depending on the structure of the group. As Edwin Hutchins (1991) says, "If groups can have cognitive properties that are different from those of the individuals in the group, then differences in the cognitive accomplishments of any two groups might depend entirely on differences in the social organization of distributed cognition and not at all on the cognitive properties of individuals in the two groups" (p. 285). Social psychologists have been noting for some time that individuals often fall into a cognitive trap by forming a hypothesis and then paying more attention to new incoming evidence that confirms their hypothesis than to new incoming evidence that contradicts it (the so-called confirmation bias). Hutchins suggests that group processes can serve to correct this bias in individuals, because members bring diverse interpretations of events to the group. But he suggests that this correction emerges more readily from consensus-based group structures than from hierarchical ones. Groups that operate with a consensus structure, however, have their own liabilities when it comes to effective group cognition: they may have more trouble reaching decisions.

We saw in Chapter 2 that boys' groups tend to have a hierarchical group structure, while girls' groups more often have a consensus-based structure. Hutchins' analysis would lead us to conclude that these differences in social structure have consequences for the way in which boys' groups and girls' groups pool their information, make decisions, and interpret situations. We are only in the very early stages of considering how group cognition differs from, or amplifies, individual cognition, but it is clear that the kinds of differential group processes operating in boys' and girls' groups involve distinctive cognitions at the group level—cognitions that underlie the way groups do, and can, function as groups.

Summary and Comment

There are two major hypotheses concerning the role of gender cognitions in the behavioral differentiation of the two sexes in childhood: First, knowing one's own sex and that of others leads to being attracted to others who are "like me"; this tendency implies both preferential attitudes toward like-sex others and preferential association with them. Second, when children learn gender stereotypes—what the cultural standards and practices are concerning how people of the two sexes behave and how their society *expects* them to behave—they will attempt to adapt themselves to these standards and practices by behaving in "sex-appropriate" ways (this is the self-socialization hypothesis). The second hypothesis presupposes that children have acquired the ability to identify not only their own gender but that of others who might serve as appropriate models for sex-typed standards and practices. Thus knowledge of gender identity is primary for both hypotheses 1 and 2. Let us now consider how helpful these two hypotheses have been in the effort to understand the phenomena I have set out to explain.

At a very early age, children categorize themselves and others according to their sex. Once established, these categories form the core around which gender stereotypes are built. When children have coded others by sex, they tend to perceive and remember the others' activities in more sex-differentiated ways than would be justified by unbiased real-life observations. Furthermore, young children soon come to understand that certain other children are the "same as me" with respect to gender, while others are not. At least by preschool age, this understanding clearly has an impact on same-sex playmate preferences (although no one has been able to establish that it is either a necessary or a sufficient condition for the *onset* of such preferences).

Knowing that certain other children match the self with respect to gender contributes to own-sex biases that take a number of forms: not only are children preferentially attracted to others of their own sex, but they also attribute more favorable characteristics to own-sex others. Furthermore, they like certain unfamiliar objects or activities simply because these things are labeled as being "for" people of their own sex (Martin, Eisenbud, and Rose, 1993). We do not know how early these own-sex biases begin to take effect. Probably they are not especially powerful at the time that same-sex playmate preferences first appear, but become progressively more important as contributors to gender segregation as children move into the grade school years. Quite possibly, in-group favoritism initially develops as a *consequence*, rather than a cause, of children's associating more with members of their own sex; but once developed, the sense of group identity that emerges from same-sex association further reinforces segregation.

These own-sex biases seem to reflect the operation of some well-known in-group processes, and they raise the question of whether children have a sense of *group* gender identity. This question has been very little studied, but what we do know about male and female groups in childhood suggests that group gender identity is probably stronger in boys than girls.

Gender segregation could result not only from being attracted to others perceived as similar to the self, but also from the acquisition of stereotypes that make the other sex seem unattractive in some way. If girls come to believe that boys are rough and noisy, they may avoid boys as a general rule, even boys who are not particularly rough and noisy. Boys, who may also believe that boys' play is in some sense more uninhibited, more "physical," would not consider this behavior grounds for avoiding male playmates. This points to a problem. The fact that boys and girls generally have the same stereotypes concerning what are "masculine" or "feminine" activities does not lead them to have the same playmate preferences. Obviously, children of the two sexes find different things attractive in a peer, and this makes it unlikely that it is the stereotypes per se that are driving the preference. This conclusion is strengthened by the research showing that individual differences among children in their degree of gender stereotyping are unrelated to how strongly they prefer same-sex playmates.

We may ask similar questions concerning the distinctive interaction styles that emerge in all-boy and all-girl groups. Is it the gender stereotypes held by the children who participate in sex-segregated playgroups that lead them to adopt distinctive interaction styles? Possibly, but the answer is complex. Perhaps it is only when the members of same-sex groups *share* a stereotype concerning how they ought to behave that they adapt their collective style to what they believe is sex-appropriate. But perhaps more important: though children of both sexes do understand that certain activities are considered appropriate for boys, others for girls, they do not seem to have well-defined understandings concerning the interaction styles that the two sexes usually employ or are *expected* to employ. Their distinctive styles—the more collaborative, conflict-mitigating style among girls, and the more confrontational, "physical" style among boys—appear earlier than the time when children come to believe that girls are supposed to be "nice" and boys "rough." It is unlikely, therefore, that children initially adopt their particular styles because they think it is sex-appropriate to behave in these ways. At least for children of preschool age, these modes of interaction are probably not "gender imperatives," though they may become so at a later time.

A word about asymmetry. Boys and girls generally hold the same gender stereotypes, and acquire them at the same rate. Thus there is more symmetry than asymmetry in gender cognitions. Still, there are some interesting respects in which the sexes differ. There is some evidence that boys have a stronger sense of similarity to others of their own sex; perhaps we could call this a stronger identification, among boys, with their own sex as a collective. There is also evidence that boys have a better understanding of masculine than feminine scripts, while girls understand the two kinds of scripts equally well. Much research points to boys having stronger prejudices than girls against engaging in cross-sex behavior, while girls—especially as they move into the grade school years—have more flexible attitudes concerning what activities and occupations are acceptable for people of both sexes to engage in. Balancing this greater "sexism" in boys is a modest trend for girls to show more in-group favoritism, in that they attribute more negative qualities to boys than boys do to girls.

These asymmetries in gender cognitions match quite closely the behavioral asymmetries noted earlier—the greater cohesiveness, greater distinctiveness, and greater exclusiveness of male groups. Can we say that the asymmetries in gender cognitions underlie the behavioral ones? There is no evidence that children must first develop cognitive asymmetries before they show behavioral ones. The two kinds of processes seem to develop in synchrony, and may be seen as two sides of the same coin. Children elaborate cognitively what they are doing behaviorally. At the time when boys are moving rapidly in the direction of avoiding cross-sex activities, they are acquiring convictions that it is wrong to play with dolls or wear dresses. Girls, who do not so strongly avoid masculine activities, also do not have as strong convictions concerning the legitimacy, or acceptability, of cross-sex activities.

The experimental studies of self-regulation and imitation of same-sex models have shown convincingly that children adopt new sex-typed behaviors by copying what a group of own-sex models do, when there is consensus among the models in the sense that all female models do one thing, all male models another. It is also clear that children monitor their own behavior according to a self-accepted standard of what is appropriate for their own sex. We can see the behavior of models as one of many sources of information which children use to develop their prototype or template of what attributes differentially characterize the two sexes. Children can, and often do, use this information to don the cloak of gendered attributes that their culture provides.

This conclusion is somewhat at odds with what we would have concluded if we had been relying only on the studies of *individual differences* in children's knowledge of gender stereotypes, since variations in the amount of such knowledge prove to be only very weakly correlated with variations in children's degree of sex-typing.[32] I believe that the usual measures of knowledge of stereotypes are too blunt to reveal the processes at work, and that correlational studies have limited value in the study of phenomena such as knowledge of common stereotypes, where there may be very little individual variation and nearly everyone possesses the requisite knowledge. The experimental studies are more powerful, but they have not yet given us the information we most need to have. They have shown that the information about the characteristics of people of the two sexes that children acquire by observing multiple models can and does influence children's toy and activity choices. But the fact that children can acquire stereotypes by observing models of the two sexes, and then use these stereotypes as one element in their own adoption of toy and activity preferences, does not demonstrate that the stereotypes acquired by observation also guide gender segregation, differential interaction styles, or asymmetry.

For the reasons discussed above, I am skeptical about claims that gender segregation stems in any important degree from modeling. When it comes to the *content* of children's play in their same-sex groups, however, the role of cognitive cultural transmission seems clear enough. Consider, for example, a culture in which only women prepare and serve food. In such a culture, it would be unlikely indeed for a group of eight-year-old boys to play-act preparing and serving food. This example suggests that the content of children's play in their segregated groups is heavily determined by the gendered scripts their culture provides, as long as these scripts are distinctive enough so that all the children in a same-sex group share the knowledge of what the distinctive patterns are. We may assume that there is a good deal of contagion, within same-sex groups, of gender-relevant knowledge and beliefs, so that any child who does not originally share a widely held stereotype will soon come to do so.

In our own society there are very few social scripts that are as sex-distinctive as the ones that are found in traditional societies. Nowadays, both men and women cook, both men and women drive trucks and buses, both men and women hold important public offices, both men and women serve in the armed forces and on police forces. Within-sex model consensus in the Perry and Bussey sense is weakening year by year. Consequently, we would not expect to find the content of children's play differing as greatly between male and female playgroups as it does in more traditional cultures. Still, there are strong gender themes pervading modern popular culture: certain spectator sports are entirely dominated by males, and we see these themes reflected in the play of male groups. When it comes to images of the relations between the sexes, romantic themes predominate in TV and movies, and these are picked up and utilized in girls' play. In short, children's gender cognitions are constantly being augmented by an array of inputs from the media, from their parents, and from their observations of many others. These merge with the metaphorical meanings that seem to pervade children's inferences about gender from an early age. To the extent that the themes from the various sources are consistent, and common enough so that children in a given playgroup are likely to share them, they may be expected to pervade the content of children's play.

Do these gender cognitions fully determine the nature of the interactive styles adopted in children's playgroups? Probably not. It is very likely that the distinctive interactive styles in male and female groups are multiply determined. Boys' rough—sometimes aggressive—play, for example, undoubtedly reflects some degree of prenatal hormonal priming. It is probably also affected by the fact that parents and teachers expect this kind of behavior to occur more among boys than among girls, and tolerate it more, even though they may not like it or directly teach it. Whether interaction styles reflect, in addition, the children's own cognitions concerning the right and proper ways for people of their own sex to behave is something we do not yet know.

In this book, I have repeatedly stressed that people behave differently depending on whether they are interacting with a member of their own sex or someone of the other sex. Work on gender cognitions has focused on the way children utilize own-sex stereotypes in the development of sex-typical behavior and dispositions. We know much less about how children cognize the other gender. The sociological concept of altercasting is relevant here: when we develop concepts concerning how individual others—or groups of people belonging to an out-group—are likely to behave, we increase the likelihood that when they interact with us, they will behave as we expect them to. Or, even more interesting, we believe that their reactions conform to our expectations even when they don't. If we think ahead to the adolescent and adult years, when the barriers against cross-sex interaction break down, it becomes pertinent to ask what kind of sex-role stereotypes the members of each sex have prepared for members of the other, considering that their expectations may place some constraints on their cross-sex partners to conform to what is expected. And when they misread the reactions of the partner on the basis of unrealistic stereotypes, the opportunities for misunderstandings are many.

III

Convergence in Adulthood

8

Heterosexual Attraction and Relationships

In Chapter 3, we saw that during the grade school years, boys and girls show interest in children of the other sex, although they play primarily with children of their own sex.[1] Indeed, they appear to recognize that children of the other sex are likely to be their romantic partners in the future and, although ambivalent, they are also excited by the prospect. As we saw, boys' interest in girls more often has explicitly sexual overtones; early forms of "locker-room" talk occur among them. Among girls, romantic themes predominate. Girls are interested in romantic TV fare, and their doll play often centers on courtship, marriage, and glamorous "dating." In childhood, however, these themes occur mainly in the world of fantasies that are either private or shared with others of a child's own sex. Although children do sometimes acknowledge a special interest in one particular other-sex child, the barriers against actual "boyfriend" or "girlfriend" relationships are usually carefully maintained via individual wariness and social pressures to affiliate with one's own sex.

The dominant theme of childhood, as far as gender is concerned, is separation. Adolescence ushers in an entirely new phase in the relationship between the sexes. Now, heterosexual attraction becomes an extraordinarily powerful force, opposing the forces of cross-sex avoidance. Of course, sexual maturation does not always require a shift in orientation toward the other sex. A substantial number of people experiment with same-sex sexuality at some point in their lives, and a small minority settle into a life-long pattern of homosexuality. For them, their adult sexuality does not carry them in an opposite direction from their childhood period of cross-sex avoidance. And, of course, some people live largely asexual lives. For them, too, no strong shift is required. Yet attraction to individuals of the other sex remains the predominant pattern for the vast majority of people as they become sexually mature. In this chapter, I seek to understand how, for these people, the shift occurs.

For most young people, the transition occurs gradually. It will be my contention that the patterns of childhood never simply disappear, and that forming cross-sex relationships in adolescence and adulthood entails reconciling and integrating the preferences and behavior patterns of the childhood period with those that come into being with sexual maturity.

Continuing Segregation

In modern Western societies, the taboos against cross-sex interaction begin to break down at about ages 11–13. But for a considerable period, adolescents continue to spend the major portion of their social recreational time with same-sex friends. Larson and Richards (1991) conducted a study of how waking time was spent by children in each grade from the fifth through the ninth. Each child in the study wore a beeper which was programmed to give a signal at random intervals during the day and evening. When the beeper sounded, the children wrote down what they were doing, with whom, and what mood they were in at the moment.

The study revealed that in the fifth grade the boys were spending *none* of their free time with a female friend, while girls were spending very little time indeed with a male friend. And even by the ninth grade, both boys and girls were spending approximately ten times as much time with same-sex friends as with friends of the other sex only. Intermediate amounts of time were spent in mixed-sex groups. It may be seen, then, that gender segregation prevails strongly during early adolescence, even though romantic interest in the other sex has begun to be explicit and some children have begun to be sexually active. Social contact with the other sex appears to occur mainly in the context of mixed-sex groups. We see here a continuation of the "rule" we saw being observed in childhood: that it is more acceptable, and more comfortable, to be seen interacting with a member of the other sex if one recruits a same-sex friend to be present as well. In adolescence, it is common for a pair of girls to go together to a place where teenagers congregate—an eating place, a shopping mall, a movie theater—where they know they will be able to meet boys. Boys, too, commonly come to such places in male pairs or groups.

Before we attempt to understand the initial negotiations among young men and women in modern society as they become mutually interested in each other, and move toward sexual intimacy, it is important to be aware of the rapid pace of the changes that have taken place in the social context in which such negotiations occur, and also to be aware of the great cross-cultural variation that currently prevails.

Social Customs Surrounding Sexual Maturation

Parents and other relatives have never been indifferent to the fact that a young daughter has grown old enough to become pregnant. In all societies up to quite recent times there have been forms of social regulation of sexuality, with the explicit or implicit purpose of ensuring that if pregnancy occurs, infants will be born into a social unit that can provide care and rearing. Adults have traditionally taken an active role in selecting mates for their young sons and daughters. Through marriage rituals, a man and his family have committed themselves to providing for any children born from the young couple's sexual union. Usually, there has been a reciprocal commitment on the part of the bride and her family: that her husband would have exclusive sexual access to her. This custom presumably served two functions: to reassure men concerning their paternity of children born to the union; and to minimize fighting over women among the males of a social group by setting up clear rules concerning who "belonged" to whom.

For females, especially in Asian and African countries, the age period from about 14 to 20 was a time of active search and negotiation for a husband, and the majority of young women were married before they entered their twenties. For males, the age at marriage covered a wider range, and it was not uncommon for a girl to be married to a much older man, particularly in polygamous societies, where she might be a second or third wife. The negotiations between the families of the prospective bride and groom could be protracted and complex, particularly in social groups where marriage involved an exchange of property from the bride's family to the groom's (dowries) or payments of a bride price by the groom's family to the bride's. Over long periods of human history, romantic attraction and love were not necessary for marriage. Marriage was considered an arrangement formed for the express purpose of establishing households, producing domestic goods, and rearing children.

The official standards of Judeo-Christian and Muslim cultures were that girls should be virgins until marriage. Of course, there have always been numerous instances of nonmarital sexuality and pregnancy, but there have been serious consequences for such lapses. Even when most adults of a society covertly acknowledged that sexual experimentation would occur between young unmarried men and women, it was understood and expected that when a girl became pregnant the young couple would marry, and there was strong social pressure for them to do so.

In the twentieth century, especially in Western industrialized societies, profound changes have taken place in these customs and assumptions, and in the conditions underlying them. Among adolescent girls, the age at menarche has probably been gradually declining. Marriage, however, has been occurring at later and later ages. The period of time during which young people are sexually mature but remain unmarried has lengthened greatly. Not surprisingly, most do not remain celibate during this long period, despite exhortations to do so. Thus sexual activity and marriage have been progressively decoupled.

The "Sexual Revolution"

The "sexual revolution" was under way throughout the twentieth century, but gained considerable momentum in the 1960s.[2] More and more, both men and women were considered to have a right to sexual pleasure and fulfillment. People of all ages were increasingly exposed to explicit sexuality in daily life (via TV, popular music, art), and relatively hedonistic attitudes about sex became widespread. The parent generation had less and less of a role in the choice of partners for their children. The decline in chaperonage of young people meant that they were increasingly able to find opportunities to be together away from the prying eyes of adults. Many factors combined to bring about considerable change in the timing of early sexual experience. Young people's first sexual experience occurred earlier and earlier.[3]

The widespread availability of contraception has meant that young people can be sexually active without a high risk of pregnancy, but the fact remains that many young people do not contracept effectively, either out of ignorance or because of a variety of psychosocial barriers. The result is a fairly high rate of unwanted pregnancies, at least in the United States, where there is more ambivalence about making contraception available to teenagers than prevails in other Western industrialized countries (Brown and Eisenberg, 1995). While unwanted pregnancies previously meant that young people would marry, now the pressures to marry—or the prospects for doing so—have diminished greatly. Rates of both abortion and child-bearing outside of marriage have increased.

These changes have meant that there is now a much different context for the formation of cross-sex relationships in adolescents than the social context that once prevailed. More and more, young people must rely on their own resources to manage their entry into the marketplace of dating and sexuality. In the context of these new freedoms, how are young people of the two sexes positioned to take up negotiations with the other sex over heterosexual attraction and sexual intimacy? Adolescents are emerging from a long period of childhood in which they have spent most of their free social time with others of their own sex. Usually, boys and girls have developed somewhat distinctive interactive styles in the context of their same-sex groups. Also they have developed different expectations concerning the meaning of their relationships with the other sex. Girls have been more taken up with romantic fantasies about such relationships, boys' thoughts have been more focused on explicit sexuality. When real-life encounters with the other sex begin to occur, how do these different styles and expectations work out? Is either sex at a disadvantage? At the outset, let me stress that the answers to these questions will probably not be the same in different cultures and subcultures.

Getting Acquainted with the Other Sex

A major enterprise of adolescent social life is the search for romantic partners. For each individual, it involves considering other adolescents for their potential as partners, and presenting oneself so as to be rated highly by the set of possible partners whom one might like to attract. Adolescents of both sexes are intensely concerned with their appearance, their popularity, and their reputation, but girls appear to be especially preoccupied with these matters. Girls are generally less satisfied with the bodily changes that occur at puberty, when girls put on weight in the form of fat, boys in the form of muscle. For boys, the increasing upper-body strength that attends their sexual maturing is consonant with a positive masculine self-image, while for many girls the naturally occurring changes are not consistent with the slender, willowy image they are increasingly encouraged to project. Upon entering adolescence, then, girls are more vulnerable to a loss of self-confidence about how attractive they are.

Cross-Sex Discourse

Young men and women, in encountering each other, must adapt to a partner who brings to the interaction a rather different style from what they are accustomed to in same-sex friends. Girls are accustomed to turn-taking in discourse, boys are accustomed to trying to hold the floor. Boys are accustomed to being assertive or confrontational without having to worry that such behavior will alienate their male friends: a male partner will usually counter-assert, or counter-confront without feeling that his partner has been inconsiderate. Girls are accustomed to softening their assertions or influence attempts so as to maintain social cohesion, and generally they avoid confrontation, so that dealing with a more directly assertive partner can throw them off balance. Boys, for their part, can be surprised and confused if girls are alienated, or show hurt feelings over their dominating style. Male-female encounters are replete with opportunities for miscommunication, as has been well set forth by Deborah Tannen (1990) in her influential book *You Just Don't Understand*.

Young people of the two sexes usually come to their early cross-sex encounters with a set of beliefs concerning how they should behave in order to be attractive to the other sex. Folklore abounds with advice on how girls should interact with boys in order to hold their interest. This lore may be passed on from mothers to daughters, or circulated among groups of girl friends, or absorbed from books and TV. Common themes are: play up to his ego, introduce topics that you know he knows something about or likes to talk about, don't confront him openly or be too assertive, keep him in a good mood, laugh at his jokes, admire his accomplishments. Folklore seems to be less rich concerning how boys should treat girls. One theme has traditionally been that if a boy is interested in a girl and they go out together, he should "take care" of her. This covers the gamut from small acts of chivalry to staying at her side, paying the check, defending her if necessary, and bringing her safely home. The very terminology of "taking" a girl out on a date, or "bringing" her home, implies that it is the male who is expected to manage the arrangements for their time together, although of course he may consult his partner as to what she would like to do. Such expectations for male behavior have clearly been fading away in recent years, as has the practice of dating itself, but some vestiges remain. In this changing situation, young men are understandably confused as to how much "in charge" they should try to be.

Work by Carli (1990, 1995) throws an interesting light on young women's "playing up" to men. Carli identified what she called "tentative" speech. When expressing an opinion, some people began their statements with disclaimers such as "I'm not an expert on this, but . . ." or "I may be wrong, but . . ."; or they used more "hedges," such as "sort of," "perhaps," "maybe," or used tag questions to soften an assertion: "Men have more accidents than women, don't they?" Carli arranged sessions in which two college students discussed an issue on which they initially disagreed. Some of the pairs were made up of two men, some of two women, and some were a man-woman pair. She found that women used tentative speech more than men, *but only when paired with a man.* Furthermore, a man in a man-woman pair was more likely to be persuaded by a female partner who used tentative speech, and to like her better, even though he rated her as being less competent and knowledgeable when she used such speech than when she did not. When interacting with other women, women did not resort to tentative speech any more often than men did, and if a woman did use tentative speech, a female partner was *less* likely to be persuaded by her than if she used more assertive speech. We see, then, that when interacting with men, women were adapting to what they assumed (rightly, as it turned out) were male preferences about how assertive a woman should be. And this is one more example of a gendered phenomenon that is not accurately described as a sex difference: women are not unassertive in general; their assertiveness depends on the sex of their partner.

This study confirms the folk wisdom concerning how women should act to be attractive to men. Such stratagems seem designed to equip girls for playing a role complementary to the male egoistic interaction style. And to some extent, the less assertive style girls and women use with men is compatible with the styles girls have employed in their female playgroups at an earlier age. At least, girls are accustomed to avoiding confrontation and sustaining positive affect with interactive partners. But girls are also accustomed to interacting with partners who reciprocate their styles: who yield the floor, acknowledge a partner's previous comment, express agreement or approval. With a male partner, they may find themselves waiting for a conversational turn that does not come.

Loss of "Voice"

Carol Gilligan and colleagues (Gilligan, 1982, 1993; Gilligan, Lyons, and Hanmer, 1989) have forcefully presented the view that for females, entry into adolescence involves suppressing, or disguising, crucial elements of the self.[4] During middle childhood, Gilligan holds, girls are generally self-confident, able to express clearly and openly what they believe, what they feel. When they enter adolescence, however, they take on the culturally prescribed female persona of the "good woman," meaning one who is nice, is polite, and who adapts herself to what others want her to be. She also takes on the role of serving others' needs rather than her own. In the process of making these adaptations, girls' true "voices," Gilligan alleges, go unheard. A similar scenario is drawn by Mary Pipher (1994), whose best-selling book *Reviving Ophelia* is based on the study of a group of girls being seen in clinical practice as they make the transition from late childhood to adolescence. Pipher says that adolescent girls "experience a conflict between their autonomous selves and their need to be feminine." She quotes Simone de Beauvoir's comment that girls "stop being and start seeming." Pipher says further, "Adolescence is a time when girls experience social pressure to put aside their authentic selves and to display only a small portion of their gifts."

Gilligan also refers to what she calls a "relational impasse" for girls, deriving from the fact that they, more than males, value connectedness to others. This means that they are strongly motivated to avoid acting in ways that threaten relationships with others. Girls fear that they might alienate others if they speak their minds, and so rein themselves in to protect valued relationships. We saw in Chapter 2 that girls, in interacting with their girl friends, are more likely than boys to use double-voiced discourse, in which they not only pursue their own individual objectives but also take care to maintain positive social relations within a female dyad or group. It appears, then, that the "relational impasse" is something that does not stem entirely from entry into adolescence, but rather is carried over from the interaction styles of childhood.

Harter and colleagues (Harter, Waters, and Whitesell, 1996), in reviewing the work on "voice" in adolescence, note something rather surprising: there has actually been no systematic documentation of the alleged fact that females suppress their voices more than males do. In their recent work, Gilligan and colleagues, and Pipher as well, have sought to understand the changes they see in girls without regard to whether any similar changes may be occurring in boys as they reach adolescence. Their choosing to focus on girls seems entirely reasonable in view of the fact that commonly held social stereotypes concerning femininity appears to call for much more suppression of "voice" in females than in males. The Harter research group has made an empirical check on this assumption by studying large samples of both male and female adolescents, from the sixth grade through the twelfth. They asked these young people whether, and how often, they spoke openly and frankly with certain others (parents, teachers, male classmates, female classmates, and close same-sex friends), as distinct from speaking guardedly and not saying what they really felt or believed.[5] Here are some of the results:

1. Adolescent boys and girls did not differ with respect to the loss of "voice."
2. For young people of both sexes, about a third said that they disguised their true thoughts and feelings in dealing with certain categories of others, but a substantial majority of both sexes did not report doing so.
3. When young people did speak guardedly, they did so mainly in the context of interacting with classmates of the other sex. Both boys and girls were less self-confident in talking with age-mates of the other sex than they were when talking with their parents, teachers, or same-sex classmates or friends. They seemed to be aware that their same-sex interaction styles might not be entirely appropriate for situations where romantic interest might arise. Adolescents of both sexes said they were careful not to embarrass themselves, or "look stupid" in front of the other sex.

These findings make sense in view of the childhood gender dynamics described in Chapters 1 and 2. For children of both sexes, young people of the other sex are largely unfamiliar interaction partners with relatively unfamiliar interaction styles. When adolescents reach the age of wanting to please, and be attractive to, the other sex, it is natural that at least some adolescents of both sexes would be wary in exploring this unfamiliar territory, not wanting to make mistakes that would put them in a bad light. It would appear, however, that many teenagers are quite self-confident about negotiating the new relationships.

Is either sex at a disadvantage? It is puzzling that the Harter group did not find a sex difference in the tendency to cover up true feelings and beliefs when interacting with the other sex. It would appear that the issues boys face in making the transition into cross-sex relationships have been relatively neglected. It also appears that previous work has focused on a subgroup of girls who do cover up their true thoughts and feelings in adolescence—who "lose voice." But these processes may not be nearly as widespread as has been claimed. Harter and colleagues suggest that the cover-up processes are found only in a minority of girls, but we do not yet know how large the proportion of affected girls will turn out to be in new studies with different populations.

Though Harter and colleagues found equal numbers of male and female adolescents who felt they must speak guardedly with classmates of the other sex, there is reason to believe that young women are often at something of a disadvantage in early cross-sex contexts. In mixed-sex problem-solving groups, there is consistent evidence that males are dominant, in the sense that they give more directions and provide more information, and that their opinions are more influential in group decisions than those of females in the group (see Maccoby, 1990, for a summary). Young women, by contrast, express agreement with others more often. And they are more uncomfortable in dyadic interactions with young men in situations where they have not had a choice of partners. An example: Davis (1978) set up "get acquainted" sessions between previously unacquainted male-female pairs of college students. He found that the men exercised control over the rate at which intimacy (defined as self-disclosure) increased. The women adapted themselves to the pace set by the men, but reported afterward that they had felt uncomfortable about not being able to control the sequence of events, and had not enjoyed the encounter as much as the men had. It seems likely that even though a substantial number of young men report that they guard what they say in talking with young women, they nevertheless often manage to dominate the discourse between them, aided and abetted by girls who acquiesce in their dominance.

Intimate and Supportive Speech

When talking with women friends, young men appear to be as willing and able as women to talk about their feelings, their hopes and aspirations, their vulnerabilities.[6] It is primarily in talking with male friends that males conceal these things. We can see this as a concern among males—one that continues from childhood—about dominance and maintaining competitive status with each other. Guarding against self-disclosure is a process that is generally incompatible with intimacy, but it does not appear to loom large when men are interacting with women. Indeed, men's capacity for intimacy with women has probably been considerably underrated because self-disclosure has been studied mainly in the context of people's interactions with same-sex friends. Still, Leaper (1994) and others have noted that while males may reveal their own feelings in talking with women, they do not offer as much support as women do for the expression of feelings on the part of their partners. Women more often than men engage in a form of "active" or "supportive" listening, saying "Mm-Hum" or "I see" or saying things that express understanding and sympathy with what a partner has said. Very likely, girls' history of closeness to their female peer groups prepares them to offer these kinds of support to a boyfriend when they enter romantic relationships.

Leaper (1994) suggests that one reason males are not so well prepared for intimate relationships as they reach adulthood is that, as children, they have congregated in larger groups where less intimacy is called for than in girls' more typical one-on-one friendships.

Moving toward Sexuality

Peer-Group Influence

Initial encounters between the sexes often occur in mixed social groups of teenagers who go places together, or simply "hang out" together, listening to music, watching videos at each other's houses, visiting shopping malls.[7] Peers replace parents as primary sources of social influence where friendships are concerned. The emergence of temporary or more lasting liaisons is a process closely watched by friends of the individuals involved: endless talk goes on, especially among girls, about who likes whom, who is "going with" whom, who has broken up with whom, who is jealous of whom.

The teenage peer group is more than just a locus for gossip. For adolescents, friends provide a primary resource for information about sex and contraception. Among girls, the disapproval of other girls can act as a brake on "wild" or promiscuous sexual behavior, although boys do not appear to inhibit each other's sexual activity in this way. For teenagers of both sexes, however, the opinions and actions of peers are important in setting standards and limits concerning who is a suitable or desirable partner. Younger teenagers are especially concerned about how their peers will rate the partners they are seen with or thought to be "going with," and strive to have the "right kind" of romantic relationships with the "right people." As Brown (1996) notes, in early and middle adolescence teenagers are preoccupied with finding a crowd, fitting in, being popular, and achieving status in their group. Romantic relationships are one means of achieving these objectives, and for young teenagers these considerations are often more important than the relationship itself.

Teenagers tend to overestimate the amount of sexual activity that goes on among their peers, and when they believe "everybody is doing it," they lower their own barriers against embarking on sexual activity (Christopher and Cate, 1984). Sometimes, too, there is direct peer pressure to engage in sexual adventuring—a pressure which may not fall equally on the two sexes. Males more often than females report feeling pressure from their friends to become sexually active (Carns, 1973; Muelenhard and Cook, 1988). Yet when young teenagers issue dares to each other, boys are more likely to be dared to do something physically dangerous, while girls are more often dared to do something sexual (Lewis and Lewis, 1984). Of course, for girls, the risk of pregnancy makes sexual dares physically risky as well. The fact is, though, that we do not know a great deal about what teenagers' same-sex friends are urging them to do, or giving them tacit permission to do. For girls, there are probably mixed messages that urge both restraint and sexual freedom. A few girls may take the lead with bold or provocative behavior, while other girls watch ambivalently, tempted but afraid to go along (Eckert, in press).

Falling in Love

Romantic relationships in adolescence of course involve a great deal more than simple sexual attraction. Although it is true that reports of being "in love" are a direct function of pubertal status, and are therefore at least in part hormonally driven (Richards and Larson, 1993), many young adolescents develop romantic relationships in which there is no explicit sexual component, whatever fantasies there may be concerning future possibilities. The experience of being in love carries with it literally mind-altering emotional states: a rosy glow pervades perceptions; expectations about the future become inflated, and judgments tend to become absolutist and unrealistic.[8] It is sometimes difficult for settled (jaded?) adults to appreciate the intensity of the emotions involved in teenage romantic relationships. Larson and Richards (1994) report that some adolescents experience almost transcendental states of euphoria, and that young people of this age experience much wider swings between emotional extremes—from elation and rapture to despair and vice versa—than do adults. These emotional swings are closely associated with changes in romantic relationships: with falling in love, with breaking up with a boyfriend or girlfriend. Larson points out that extreme emotions of either a positive or a negative kind can cloud rational judgments; for example, he cites evidence that the elation of being in love leads adolescents to underestimate the risks of unprotected sex.

Sexual Intimacy

When a boy and girl begin dating, their intimacy proceeds through a series of predictable stages, from getting acquainted through talking, to the first kisses and light touching, and finally to heavy petting and intercourse. In earlier times, the progression through these stages could take years, and the final stage was often delayed until marriage. In the not-too-distant past, then, young people usually had the opportunity to explore the early stages with more than one partner. In this way they gained experience in negotiating with people of the other sex, and delayed the more consequential involvement in a fully sexual relationship until they were more mature. Nowadays "courtship" can be very brief, lasting only for a few days or even hours, and the progression through the stages of intimacy often occurs at a fast pace. The result, of course, is that the young partners may not know each other very well, and therefore may find it especially difficult to communicate accurately with each other about what each wants and expects of the other.

Contraception. It will be my contention that girls are at a disadvantage under these circumstances, first and foremost because girls are the ones who can become pregnant. Both members of a young couple are almost always aware of this basic fact, though there is still some ignorance concerning exactly how pregnancy comes about. The risk of pregnancy obviously raises questions concerning contraception: how much the young people know about it, whether they have access to it, which member of the couple is considered responsible for it. The first time intercourse occurs between a given couple, it is usually unplanned, and more often than not, unprotected. If contraception is used early in a relationship, it is usually the male who takes responsibility and uses a condom. Many young males, however, are reluctant to use condoms: some find their use embarrassing or pleasure-diminishing, and don't like the interruption of foreplay that is involved. In fact, many males of high school age believe that only females should use birth control (Finkel and Finkel, 1981). As a sexual liaison continues, the responsibility for contraception falls more and more to the girl, who usually relies on contraceptive pills. In recent years, with increasing risks of sexually transmitted diseases, there has been some increase in condom use, but many young males continue to reject the use of condoms and to feel that contraception should be the woman's responsibility. Girls, for their part, find it difficult to exert pressure on a boy to use a condom, particularly if intercourse occurs early in a relationship that she is eager to maintain.

For young girls embarking on sexual activity, the question of whether to use contraceptives can involve agonizing conflicts. To be prepared for sexual intercourse implies that it is planned, accepted, even sought. Such preparation runs contrary to the female self-images of being the person who is pursued by males, the one who "gives in" to male needs, the one who is "carried away" by love. And it is not just the self-image that is at risk when a young girl carries a condom in her purse or is "on the pill." She runs the risk of irretrievably damaging her reputation, whereas a man's being known to be prepared for intercourse would more likely enhance his reputation than damage it. Young women, in other words, face the reality of a continuing double standard where sexual matters are concerned.

Fidelity, reputation, and the double standard. The double standard may not be immediately apparent. Nowadays, egalitarian attitudes about sex are expressed by many young people, especially college students. Many young people, both male and female, also believe that premarital sex is acceptable, as long as there is mutual affection (not necessarily being "in love") and no one gets hurt. Casual sex for both sexes, with no lasting emotional commitment, may be condoned. This attitude is expressed by an eighteen-year-old male as follows: "I view sex as one of the best feelings in the world, one of the best pleasures, and if two people can share it, then that's fine as long as both parties understand that this does not mean there is a relationship involved . . . it just happens to be a physical thing" (Feldman, Araujo, and Winsler, 1994, p. 9).

More often, egalitarian attitudes among young people involve paying lip service to the idea of mutual commitment and mutual fidelity: you should have only one sexual partner at a time, and both members of a couple have a right to expect that the other will not have other liaisons. It is worth noting how often this standard is breached. In a study of community college students, Feldman, Araujo, and Winsler (1994) found that over half had "cheated" on their partners despite an explicit commitment to be monogamous. Although young men value their commitment to their primary partner, they are more open to casual sex with others than are young women. And many young men, although they have had multiple partners themselves, say they want their future wives either to be virgins at marriage or to have slept with only one partner—themselves—before marriage. In an Australian study of sixteen-year-olds (Moore and Rosenthal, 1993), a very large majority of girls expected that when they were involved in a committed relationship, both they and their partners would be faithful. The boys, by contrast, thought that a boy had a right to expect that his girlfriend would be faithful, but could hold himself to a less exacting standard.

The question of "belonging to" your partner is a complex one. Before the sexual revolution, popular song celebrated the "I'm yours" or "You're mine" themes. Engagement and wedding rings were given and accepted, and they were meant to convey that the wearer was "taken"—off limits for sexual overtures by others. But engagement rings were worn only by women, and wedding rings were universal for married women, rare for married men. Thus women were much more frequently marked as "belonging to" someone than were men. Even in modern times, when both sexes wear wedding rings and engagement rings have fallen out of fashion in many social circles, girls are more likely to be treated as belonging to the person they are dating regularly. Men are cautious about approaching a woman known to be another man's partner. They know that approaching her amounts to challenging her boyfriend, and that they would be risking a confrontation with him. The result of these customs is that young women, more than young men, are quickly cut off from exploring other possible relationships, once they appear in public several times with a given partner.

A reputation for promiscuity exacts a much heavier price from women than from men. In the study of Australian teenagers mentioned previously, a substantial number did say, when asked for their reactions to boys' or girls' "sleeping around," that it was equally OK for a person of either sex to do so, or equally unacceptable. In Australia, as well as the United States, there is reason to believe that attitudes are becoming more egalitarian and more liberal. But the double standard is still clearly present, and many teenagers expressed explicit beliefs that there were different standards for the two sexes. When the standards were thought to differ, they invariably tilted in a single direction: promiscuity was thought to be worse for girls than for boys. For example, when asked about girls who sleep around, a male Australian teenager said:

> Sluts, basically. Because they have a mattress on their back, they like having sex. That's the way I look at it, no two ways about it. (What about boys who sleep around?) A stud. Good luck to him. It's okay for a guy to be like that. (Moore and Rosenthal, 1993, p. 97)

Similar attitudes are found in other modern Westernized countries, as illustrated by the comment of a sixteen-year-old English girl in a sample of teenagers who were asked, "How do you feel about girls/boys who engage in one-night-stands?" She answered:

> I would think she is too easy, not a slut but I would say she doesn't feel anything. (Boys?) It doesn't really bother me. It's different. People say we should be equal and the same, but the fact is it is not. For a man to have many sexual partners is okay, but for a girl to have many sexual partners, she is considered pretty low and a guy is considered what a man, a stud. He has had some experience, he is great. (Lees, 1986)

In some social circles, where real egalitarian standards prevail, it may be that girls have no more reason than boys to fear the loss of reputation when they are known to have had a number of sexual partners. But in many social environments, probably in most, there is good reason for girls to be more wary than boys about how they will be judged by others if they enter a sexual relationship. Girls must walk a fine line: the images of popular, attractive girls depict them as being sexy and flirtatious, wearing provocative clothes, being seen with prestigious men. Furthermore, present-day ideology allows girls to acknowledge their own sexual feelings and desires more fully than they once did. A girl does not want to be, or appear to be, a prude. At the same time, she does not want to be known as someone who is "easy." If she too openly acknowledges enjoying sex, she risks being labeled excessively sexual (a nympho) and allowing males to think she will accept casual, uncommitted sex. She wants to maintain a reputation as someone who is able to keep restraints on sexual behavior and is selective where her male companionship is concerned. It is not easy to find the balance between these different images of the female sexual self. Males, by contrast, have much less conflict of this kind.

What Each Sex Wants

Not surprisingly, then, it is commonly reported that as couples embark on the first stages of intimacy, girls seek to prolong the early stages and delay intercourse; boys attempt to accelerate the pace at which intimacy increases. In one study of sixteen- and seventeen-year-olds, the boys said they wanted more intimacy at all levels of dating. Only 8 percent of girls wanted intercourse when they began "going steady" with a boy, but 45 percent of the boys wanted intercourse at this level of dating (McCabe and Collins, 1990). When intercourse is initiated, girls are more likely than boys to experience guilt.

Young men, in their eagerness to accelerate the pace of intimacy, are not above a certain amount of coercion. In a nationwide study of college students (Koss, Gidycz, and Wisniewski, 1987), 44 percent of the women reported having engaged in unwanted intercourse because they felt overwhelmed by men's continual arguments and pressure. Of course, it is not unheard of for males to engage in unwanted intercourse as well, when feeling under pressure to prove their adequacy (see Muelenhard, Goggins, Jones, and Satterfield, 1991).

It is clear that in many young couples, the two partners want different things from the relationship. Males tend to be more oriented to pleasure—not just to the pleasure of sex, but to the pleasure of having fun with the partner. Girls are more often looking for a committed, long-term, loving relationship (Roscoe, Diana, and Brooks, 1987). This difference has been found in a variety of ethnic groups and at all socioeconomic levels, and seems to be characteristic of modern young people in all of the Western countries where studies have been done.

Based on his ethnographic study of African-American teenagers in inner-city settings, Elijah Anderson (1989) has described the pattern graphically, and says that the goals of the two sexes are often diametrically opposed.

The girls, he says, are looking for romance. They watch romantic movies and listen to the words of popular songs, and dream of having a boyfriend who will take them to glamorous places, or a fiancée or husband with whom they can share a nice home in a decent neighborhood. (We can see here the carry-over of hopes and fantasies from middle childhood.) Girls are eager to believe in a boy's good faith when he makes promises about providing these things, and defend a boyfriend against the suspicions of skeptical friends and relatives. When girls agree to sex, it is often done as a means to getting a genuine commitment from a boy.

Boys' primary loyalty is to their peer group and its norms. Manhood is displayed by having sexual relations with multiple females. It is not enough merely to *be* sexually successful; one must be *known* to be successful. Young men therefore brag about their conquests to other males (and probably exaggerate their prowess). Of course, young men are often ambivalent. They fall in love, and genuinely want to please a girl and sustain a relationship with her. But to do so conflicts with the values of the male peer group. Commitment to an enduring relationship with a woman means that a man has given her the right to tell him what to do—something the peer group does not condone. The fact that these attitudes are not confined to inner-city black youth is amply illustrated in studies of young white men and studies of ethnically mixed groups. In the study of community college students mentioned earlier, the authors quote revealing comments by two young men:

> For a male, he's—ah—shooting for prowess and prestige in the male community. You know—trying for trophies, feathers in his cap.

> It's kind of like a measuring stick—how many females you've slept with, it's kinda like a notch on the bedpost. (Feldman, Araujo, and Winsler, 1994, pp. 8–9)

It is important to note that while many young men experience cross-pressures between the norms of their peer group and what their girlfriends want and expect of them, girls are seldom subject to such cross-pressures. Their peer groups generally support a girl's search for close relationships with a boyfriend, although sometimes a girl's female friends will provide a needed reality check against her unrealistic appraisal of her boyfriend's motives.

Are young males more loyal to their male friends? Perhaps. Girls have certainly been known to abandon their female friends in the interests of establishing or maintaining a relationship with a boy. And as we have seen, men are cautious about infringing on another man's "rights" to a particular woman, though this may be more a matter of self-protection than group loyalty.

Variations in Peer-Group Influence

So far, I have been treating adolescent peer groups as though they were monolithic. Of course, in actuality they are far from it. Through the grade school years, peer groups become more and more differentiated according to the interests of group members and the reputation of various groups. In middle schools and junior high schools, most students can identify the different cliques or "crowds," and individuals are known by their membership in such social groups as the "jocks," the "nerds," the "brains," the "druggies," or "the heads"; or an individual may be known as a loner. In most schools there is a group of girls known to be "populars" or "top girls." Although these different peer groups have not been systematically described with respect to the sexual values they hold, there is every reason to believe that some male peer groups are much more "macho" than others—much more given to sexual adventuring, much more likely to share sexually exploitive attitudes toward women. Furthermore, individuals vary in how vulnerable they are to pressures from whatever peer group they belong to.

It is interesting to consider how the experiences children have had in their segregated childhood cultures influence their choice of same-sex peers, and their relationships with the other sex, once they move into differentiated adolescent peer groups. An early longitudinal study carried out before the onset of the sexual revolution (Kagan and Moss, 1962) reported that the boys who had been most fully involved in male peer activities during their grade school years had the least difficulty moving into relationships with girls when they reached adolescence: they were comfortable in beginning to interact with girls and in pairing off with a girlfriend. By contrast, boys who had been peripheral to male peer groups in grade school, or who had been loners, were more inhibited about forming relationships with girls in adolescence, and more often had sexual anxieties. At that time in our cultural history, then, childhood experience in a male peer group appeared to be a positive element in boys' cross-sex adjustment a few years later.

But the times have been changing. The more recent longitudinal study by Feldman and colleagues (1995) reveals that the boys who were best liked by other boys in the sixth grade—and who were presumably centrally involved in male peer-group activities—were the ones who started their sexual activity at an especially young age, and who had had the largest number of sexual partners by the time they reached high school age. They were popular and gregarious in high school. Their gregariousness involved "partying," and drinking at parties often established a group atmosphere in which sexual impulses were allowed free rein. We can see, then, that the changing mores have meant that a childhood experience—being a central member of a pre-adolescent male peer group—that once led merely to comfortable dating, or perhaps early marriage, now leads to lessened sexual restraint in adolescence and a greater readiness to exploit sexual opportunities and display sexual prowess.

There is a darker side to the power of male peer groups among the relatively small group of young men who engage in coercive sex or feel it is legitimate to do so. Alder (1982) reports that young adult males who admit to having physically forced a girl to have sex usually have friends who are also sexually aggressive, and that as a group they define women as legitimate targets, believing, for instance, that "most women enjoy being forced to have sex." Kanin (1985) reports that college men who say they could imagine using force in a sexual encounter were more likely than other men to have experienced pressure from friends—both currently and earlier when they were in high school—to be sexually active. Their friends had recommended accessible girls to them; and there had been episodes in which several friends had had sex with a single girl. And young men who were prone to sexual aggression shared a belief with their friends that it was acceptable to get a girl drunk in order to seduce her.

Obviously, most teenage males do not belong to peer groups that practice and advocate sexual aggression. Young men vary greatly in how much exposure they have had to peer groups that advocate and practice exploitive behavior toward women. Presumably, more pressure of this sort is experienced in locker rooms, fraternities, boot camps, and street gangs than in other all-male settings. Thus some male peer groups, but not all, are seedbeds for the kinds of sexist attitudes and behavior that can place women at risk.

In Chapter 2, I noted that male childhood peer groups were more closed societies than female ones—less open to communication with adults and with children of the other sex. Certain asymmetries continue into the dating period, though there are similarities as well. Adolescents of both sexes continue to spend a good deal of time with same-sex friends. And both boys and girls rely on their same-sex friends for support and standards of partner choice as they make their initial contacts with the other sex. But when males show their softer side to a girlfriend, they are presenting a self that is not easily compatible with the tougher persona they have sought to project within their male peer groups. Girls, too, can "put on an act" with boys that represents a shift from their customary modes of behaving with female friends and adults, but the incompatibilities are probably not so great.

The Balance of Power

As young men and women meet and begin to form close relationships, is there a power imbalance between them? We have seen some indications that there is, others that there is not. Generally speaking, the person who is less in love, is more physically attractive, or who has more alternatives and thus more freedom to leave the relationship, has more power to influence the partner (Peplau, 1979). Possessing a constellation of traits especially valued by the other sex implies power, in that it allows the possessor to pick and choose among suitors. In a study of 37 different cultures, David Buss (1989) asked people to rate 18 characteristics as to their importance in choosing a potential mate. Characteristics included such qualities as dependable, chaste, intelligent, and physically attractive. Interestingly, men and women showed many of the same preferences. Intelligence and kindness were at the top of the list for both sexes. But the sexes did differ on some of their preferred characteristics: women consistently expressed a preference for men who had status and power, while men rated youth and physical attractiveness as especially important in a mate. Thus girls and women who are exceptionally pretty—or lively and "cute" (youthful)—are in a strong position in the rating and dating marketplace. So are boys or men who are looked up to within a social group—stars on the schools' athletic teams, well-to-do men or their sons, admired musicians—and perhaps also males who are simply large and strong. Whichever member of a male-female pair outranks the other in terms of the set of characteristics thought to be desirable by the other sex will presumably have the upper hand in terms of who influences whom within the relationship, at least in the early stages. And quite often, the rankings of the two members of a pair will be quite similar.

In dating couples, it is often quite difficult to determine who has the upper hand. In a sense, it is an advantage for young women that they have not been party to the dominance-striving that prevails among boys during the childhood years. If they had had to fight their way into the male hierarchy as boys must do, they might not have fared well, since for most girls their interaction style is not well adapted to achieving status in a male group. But in adolescence, things are different. Young women are not trying to find a place in a male group. They are relating to boys or men one at a time. Their power with males depends on factors entirely different from those that determine status within a male hierarchy. When two people are in love, each is eager to please the other and be considerate of what the other wants. From this standpoint, there seems to be no intrinsic reason why females would be at a disadvantage with males in a dating relationship.

Yet the two sexes are positioned differently in certain aspects of court-ship. Adolescent girls are perfectly aware of the importance of physical attractiveness in the eyes of the other sex, and many become intensely preoccupied with their hair-dos, their complexions, their clothes, and especially with controlling their weight. There is reason to believe that some—perhaps many—young women concentrate on these things to the neglect of other important aspects of their lives, such as intellectual devel-opment and the acquisition of career skills that would serve them better than beauty in the long run. And for those who cannot succeed in making themselves beautiful, the result can be significant depression. Some men, too, cannot manage to project a persona of confidence, competence, and strength. On the whole, however, the attributes men need to attract women are more compatible with the constellation of attributes they need for competence in other aspects of their lives, beyond their romantic objec-tives.

We have seen evidence of other differentials as well. In Carli's work, described above, young women tended to adopt "tentative speech" when talking with men, a form of discourse which implicitly accorded domi-nance to their male partners. And some young women, especially those who attributed markedly "feminine" qualities to themselves, avoided ex-pressing their true thoughts and feelings in the presence of males, some-times saying instead what they thought their partners would like to hear. This once again amounts to subordination of the self. The existing evidence does not tell us clearly whether this kind of self-subordination toward the other sex occurs more often in women than in men. Certainly, it does in traditional societies, and probably the gender imbalance in some subgroups of our own society is greater than in others. To acknowledge what one's conversational partner has said and be open to a partner's arguments is a characteristic girls bring with them from their experience in female peer groups. Boys more often bring with them tendencies to override what a partner has said. When these two tendencies meet, the result is some degree of conversational dominance for males.

Another echo from childhood is girls' greater interest in establishing and maintaining an emotionally close relationship with a partner. Males bring with them to adolescence a continued greater interest in simply sharing activities, sharing "fun," with a partner, adding now a greater interest in sexuality for its own sake. It is not clear what difference these discrepant orientations should make to the balance of power, but it is plausible that they would make a woman somewhat more eager to please, more willing to adapt to a partner's wishes.

There are, however, factors contributing to an imbalance of power between the sexes which do not represent a carry-over from tendencies established earlier. One of these is the usual discrepancy in age between members of male-female couples. Although a teenager may first "go steady" with someone very close in age, in young couples who have established a moderately stable liaison, the man is usually two or three years older than his partner. Sometimes the discrepancy is much greater. Studies of teenage pregnancy have sought to establish the age of the putative father. Often his age cannot be determined, but when it is, the data show that in a surprisingly large number of cases—perhaps as much as a fourth—young girls have been impregnated by men who are five or more years older than they.[9] Nowadays, with the increasing rates and greater risks of sexually transmitted diseases, many men may be looking for younger, inexperienced partners who are less likely to be infected. Young women, then, may increasingly find themselves attempting to deal with the advances of older men, who, by virtue of their age, seem to have more authority then they.

Another new factor that may affect the power discrepancy in adolescence is the female's vulnerability to pregnancy at a time when she no longer has the traditional protections against male predation. Also, nowadays, she is the one usually thought to be responsible for contraception. She takes more risks when the relationship becomes a sexual one. The double standard means that she is also at greater risk for the loss of reputation if she moves too quickly from one sexual relationship to another. All of which means that women need to be more "choosy" than men, more careful not to let the relationship become too intimate too fast. When a woman tries to put the brakes on the rate at which intimacy progresses, does this give her more power or less in a relationship? Probably there is no general answer, except to say that it is one more factor that differentiates the strategic situation of the two sexes.

Overall, it would appear that there need be no power differential between the members of dating couples, although there may be. Experiences carried over from childhood peer groups appear to tilt the balance of power somewhat toward males. The new factors that come with sexual maturity in the post–sexual revolution era can shift the balance even further in favor of males. But this need not happen when a couple are of similar age and equally in love, and particularly when they are functioning in a cultural milieu where men are not systematically accorded the right and power to manage the lives of women.

As young people move from the early teenage years to the late teens and young adulthood, romantic relationships evolve into more mature forms of intimacy. For one thing, the earliest romantic relationships are usually short-lived, and a teenager may have several relationships that are qualitatively quite unlike one another (retrospectively, teenagers may describe an earlier relationship as a "mistake"). With increasing age, romantic relationships are typically longer-lasting, and come to embody more intense interpersonal attraction and mutual expressions of affection. Couples begin to provide support to each other in coping with daily hassles and stressful events, and relationships become more cohesive in the sense that couples increasingly link their daily lives and enjoy each other's company in a variety of activities. This aspect of intimate relationships has sometimes been called "companionate love" (Hatfield, 1988). A further development takes place when a couple's relationship evolves into a "communal" one (Clark and Mills, 1979), in which couples embark on joint enterprises, share goals, trust each other to act in each other's interests, and develop mutual empathy such that each person's emotional states are to some extent experienced vicariously by the other. The flip side of intimacy is that the more closely two lives are linked, the more vulnerable each person is to a partner's unexpected or hurtful actions. Breaches of trust, promises not kept, even minor slights, can generate very powerful emotions of anger, jealousy, or despair.

Marriage

Marriage is the probable outcome toward which intimate heterosexual relationships progress, and for most people marriage is the most intimate and enduring relationship they experience in adult life. At least 90 percent of Americans marry at some point in their lives, these days often after a period of cohabitation. And even though at least half these marriages end in divorce, remarriage typically occurs within two or three years (U.S. Bureau of the Census, 1992). Marriage represents a new level of mutual commitment, in that the couple publicly enter into a relationship in which goals and resources are shared. There is a vast body of both scholarly and popular literature on marriage, and it is not possible to do justice to it here. In the following sections, bits and pieces have been selected that are pertinent to the central issues of this book: the ways in which the childhood patterns described in Chapters 1–3 are utilized, built upon, and reorganized in the context of adult relationships.

The Meaning of Relationships: A Continuing Divergence

Before marriage men more frequently cite a desire for sexual contact as the primary reason for dating, whereas women cite the desire for intimacy as their primary motive (Roscoe, Diana, and Brooks, 1987). Once couples have established a sexual relationship, and continued into cohabitation and marriage, this sex difference in motivation persists. In a study of a sample aged 22 to 57 years, a majority of the younger women said that they valued sex because of the feelings of love and intimacy that it entails.[10] Only 22 percent—in contrast to 44 percent of young men—said that their sexual activity was motivated by the desire for physical pleasure. The same patterns, with men attaching more importance to physical pleasure, and women to love and intimacy, were reported by Hatfield (1988) and by Leigh (1989). When asked to describe their sexual relationships, men are likely to mention frequency of intercourse and activities that are sexually arousing, while women are more likely to mention themes of comfort, responsiveness, specialness, and communication (Metts and Cupach, 1987). Each sex's orientation to sexuality, then, resembles the qualities of interaction that were experienced in same-sex childhood playgroups, insofar as females seek emotional interchange and males more often seek physical stimulation.

The Negotiation of Roles and Spheres of Influence

When a couple move in together, and particularly when they marry, new issues arise concerning how they shall share the management of the household. To a surprising degree, separation of the sexes can persist even within marriage. In traditional marriages in which the wife manages the household and is responsible for the children while the man is the breadwinner, the two spend large blocks of time apart while the man is away at work. In addition, in some cultures or subcultures, the two have largely separate social lives (for example, a man may spend most of his evenings at a bar or other drinking club with male friends, while the woman socializes mainly with women friends during daytime breaks from child care and housework). Japan provides a well-known modern example of this pattern (Bumiller, 1995). Even couples who spend more time together are likely to have an agreed-upon division of household labor: one member of the pair pays the monthly bills; one person takes major responsibility for laundry and for grocery shopping and food preparation. The birth of children usually brings about a further division of labor (discussed in Chapter 10).[11] In some families, men are responsible for "outside" work—maintaining the car, mowing the lawn, cleaning the garage—while women do the "inside" work. As is thoroughly documented, women usually carry a much larger share of household responsibilities, whether or not they are working outside the home (see Hochschile, 1989). There has been some change in the balance in recent years, with men participating more fully in household tasks. But most households do not approach equal sharing, and working women consistently experience more "overload" due to their household responsibilities than do working men (Wortman, Biernat, and Lang, 1991).

Does the division of labor imply a power differential? Not necessarily. It can be a matter of convenience, in which each willingly cedes to the other a sphere of decision-making authority, and tries not to interfere with or second-guess the other's choices. For example, many men do not expect to participate in decisions about interior decoration of the home or the menu for daily meals, and many women leave decisions about car repairs or choice of insurance policies to their husbands. Indeed, Connell (1987) makes the point that the sexual division of labor may diminish the power differential that might otherwise prevail in traditional societies. He says, "a marked sexual division of labor actually places some limits on the patriarch's ability to exercise power, since women monopolize certain kinds of skill and knowledge" (1987, p. 125). In many households, however, a power hierarchy is maintained along with a strong division of labor. A husband may see his wife as his "executive" in her sphere of work, reserving to himself the right to exercise veto power over her decisions, or constraining her choices by virtue of his power over the family purse strings. But there clearly are cultural groups in which the mother is the central figure and the father has little real authority within the family, however much authority he may have outside the domestic sphere (Bronstein, 1994; Parsons, 1964). Regardless of the division of labor, families in modern Western societies cover the whole range from male-dominated to female-dominated, with a substantial group falling in the middle and genuinely sharing decision-making power.

When it comes to the subtleties of power that have to do with mutual influence, it becomes almost impossible, in many couples, to say who has the upper hand. It depends on which member of the couple is more eager to please the other, and which feels more free to ignore the other's wishes. Initially, at least, these things are in part a matter of relative status, which can be quite independent of gender. One member of the couple may be at a disadvantage because of having "married up" in one sense or another: an unattractive man married to a beautiful woman, or a working-class woman married to a wealthy, high-status man, will feel more vulnerable than the spouse. Much depends on which member of the pair feels more secure in the relationship—more confident that the other will not leave—and perhaps also on which person has more alternatives if the relationship should fail. Probably, neither males nor females need have an overall advantage when it comes to these factors. There is reason to believe that such considerations will continue to make themselves felt even between partners of fairly long standing, although their importance may diminish with time.

Marriages do not remain static. With time, the importance of physical passion usually diminishes—perhaps more so for men than for women. For marriages that endure and remain satisfying, there is often a switch to a more companionate, more "communal" kind of relationship. When this occurs the issue of power—who is in charge, who "wears the pants"—may also diminish in importance.[12] Insofar as a couple have the same goals and operate as a team, with each trusting the other to act in their joint interests and each responding empathetically to the other's emotional states, the question of who has "won" an argument becomes relatively unimportant, and both partners strive to avoid conflict. There is evidence that as relationships become deeper and last longer, any overall asymmetry that may have existed initially in one person's power to influence the other diminishes considerably (Heiss, 1962; Leik, 1963; Shaw and Sadler, 1965). There are also marriages, however, in which the power balance switches toward the husband with the passage of time. This can happen if the husband's initial interest in pleasing his partner was based primarily on his sexual interest in her. If the relationship does not switch to a communal one, and if his sexual interest diminishes with time, he becomes less motivated to adapt to his wife's needs, while her willingness to adapt to his may have different roots and may not diminish at the same rate.

Still, no matter how egalitarian (or reciprocal) the overall balance of power may be, there are always plans and decisions that need to be negotiated, and certain differences in negotiation style are seen that are reminiscent of the interaction patterns we saw earlier in life. Women make more efforts to generate or maintain good moods in their partners (Huston and Ashmore, 1986). Men continue to use more imperative styles when they want to influence their partners, while women are more likely to make suggestions, ask questions, or otherwise use indirect approaches (Falbo and Peplau, 1980).[13]

The negotiation of sexuality can be one of the most delicate processes in marriage. Many couples use mood-setters—music, candlelight, wine—to enhance mutual attraction, and the language of glances and tones of voice is celebrated in song and story. While some spouses may inquire bluntly, "How about it, honey?" many more use more subtle nonverbal approaches to assess a partner's readiness, and body language is also used to convey reciprocal interest or a "not tonight" response (Cupach and Metz, 1991). It is clear that in marriage or a cohabiting relationship, a man is more likely than a woman to be the one who initiates a sexual episode (Byers and Heinlein, 1989; Blumstein and Schwartz, 1989; Brown and Auerback, 1981). Whether this reflects a stronger sex drive in men, or long-standing socialization of women not to take sexual initiative, we do not know. Although the stereotype is that women often decline (perhaps resorting to the famous "headache" excuse), the fact seems to be that women usually respond positively to their partners' signals of interest.

According to the existing studies, women in established relationships are no more likely to decline a partner's sexual invitation than are men. Women's negative responses are numerically more frequent because their partners' invitations are more frequent.

There are some changes with time in these matters. Men make sexual overtures to their partners less frequently as time goes on—perhaps because of a decline in their sex drive—and many women become more comfortable, as time goes on, about indicating sexual interest to their partners. Whatever the reason, the roles of the two partners in initiating sex become more egalitarian as time passes, at least in marriages in which the partners express satisfaction with their relationship (Blumstein and Schwartz, 1983).

The Negotiation of Conflict

The highest emotional highs and the lowest emotional lows experienced in adult life typically occur within the context of the marital relationship. Over the years couples share extremely intimate moments. Yet the very intimacy that links two people also lays the groundwork for feelings of deep resentment, sadness, jealousy, and anger.

Couples clearly differ in the degree to which they experience positive and negative emotions in their marriages, as well as in the strategies they enlist to cope with relationship conflicts. Most couples develop characteristic styles of dealing with conflict: some have tacit agreements to avoid discussing conflicts; others have frequent and open airing of hostilities (Gottman, 1993); others have fairly dispassionate modes of negotiation. Because each spouse's emotional well-being is so clearly linked to the other spouse's, in order for marriages to remain happy a style must evolve that allows both partners to achieve satisfactory resolution of conflict. Indeed, couples' success in resolving conflictual issues predicts marital outcomes better than the frequency with which they share positive emotional experiences (Markman, 1992). In a significant number of marriages, conflicts are not resolved effectively. And, not surprisingly, when they are not, the likelihood of divorce increases (Gottman and Levenson, 1992). Remaining in unhappy marriages places women—but not men—at increased risk for physical and mental abuse (Markman, Renick, Floyd, and Stanley, 1992) and depression (Beach, Jouriles, and O'Leary, 1985).

The ability to handle emotional conflict in marriage depends, to a great extent, on the ability to deal simultaneously with one's own negative feelings and the negative feelings expressed by a partner (Markman, 1991). Issues that arouse strong feelings in both partners are very difficult to resolve when spouses adopt different coping strategies. And not surprisingly, men and women do differ in the way they deal with marital conflict. In general, men avoid conflict with their wives, and try to end discussions about conflictual issues either through conciliation—which may be a brief "Have it your own way"—or through withdrawal. Women, by contrast, are more likely to push toward more genuine resolution of conflicts. An example, taken from Gottman's observational studies of conflict discussions between husbands and wives, illustrates the point:

Wife: (worried voice) Is something wrong?
Husband: (distant voice) Nope. Not a thing.
Wife: I can tell that you're annoyed at me—I can see it in your face. What's wrong?
Husband: (sounding annoyed) I already told you, there's nothing wrong. Will you lay off me? I just need some time to myself.
Wife: Are you angry because I was talking on the phone with Margie during supper? Or because I made a date with the Wilsons on Saturday without asking you first? I thought for sure you'd want to go.
Husband: (looking away) I already told you. There's nothing wrong. (Gottman, 1994a, pp. 138–139)

Gottman refers to what this husband was doing as "stonewalling." Other examples of stonewalling: When a wife brings up a touchy subject, her husband leaves the room; if they are talking on the phone, when a conflictual topic comes up, he says, "Sorry, gotta run"—and hangs up the phone; if they are in the car (where she may think she finally has him as a captive audience), he turns up the volume on the radio. Stonewalling is something that husbands do frequently, and that infuriates wives, who experience it as disapproval, and feel cut off from any means of reaching a resolution of a conflict.

Why does this pattern occur? Gottman (1996) sees it as a part of a larger pattern, in which some men resist accepting influence from their wives—a pattern which in itself reflects a feeling on the part of some men that a man needs to be in control where women are concerned. The processes revealed here may have their origins much earlier in life: we saw in Chapter 3 that boys were unlikely to respond to girls' influence attempts, while they did respond to those of other boys. Gottman finds that a husband's unwillingness to accept influence from his wife predicts marital distress and, ultimately, divorce (Gottman, 1994).

Marriage researchers have postulated a number of different reasons for the gendered styles of husbands and wives. Christiansen and Heavey (1990) view these styles as an example of a more general "demand/withdrawal" dynamic of interpersonal interaction. They argue that, regardless of gender, a person who desires change will make demands and a person who is being asked to change will withdraw. According to their view, the pattern becomes gendered because women are often in a subservient position relative to men. In households where the husband is the major wage-earner, women often need to ask for money. And in households (the majority) where it is assumed that the wife is more responsible than the husband for household management, she often needs to ask for his help with the children or with household chores. In consequence, the theory goes, wives make more demands on their husbands than vice versa. In an experiment in which two conflictual topics were discussed, one in which wives wanted change and one in which husbands wanted change, partial support for this hypothesis emerged. Wives showed more withdrawal behavior when their husbands asked for change and vice versa. Nevertheless, husbands remained more withdrawing and wives more demanding overall, apart from who was making demands. So the Christiansen and Heavey hypothesis gives us only a partial explanation, and we need to look further.

Perhaps husbands are simply indifferent to conflict, or unaware that it exists. But this is clearly not the case. In Gottman's and Levenson's laboratory, the marital couples who come in as volunteer subjects are monitored for a number of physiological reactions (such as changes in heart rate) while they are engaged in discussing issues on which they disagree. These researchers have found that when men stonewall, their heart rates are elevated, and it is evident that they are emotionally aroused (more aroused, usually, than their wives). Gottman and Levenson (1993) offer an additional hypothesis: they believe that during arguments with their wives men disengage verbally and emotionally because they cannot tolerate high emotional arousal as easily as women can—or at least, that men cannot easily tolerate the physiological arousal that accompanies *negative* emotions.[14]

The differences between husbands and wives in conflict-resolution style in some ways resemble the styles we saw in the same-sex groups of childhood, but, in important ways, they do not. We saw that when conflicts arose in these segregated groups, girls were more likely to negotiate with each other: to try to understand their partner's point, and to find a solution satisfactory to both. Boys were more confrontational, and were more likely simply to assert, and reassert, their own point of view, and to become overtly angry. The female pattern appears to be what wives are trying to employ in conflicts with their husbands. But husbands do not appear to be reacting to their wives in the same way they reacted to conflict with other males: with aggressive, power-assertive tactics. Furthermore, in other settings males do not seem to have any great difficulty in tolerating the high levels of negative arousal involved in male-male confrontation and fighting.

Consider, then, an alternative hypothesis: that men become aroused during conflicts with their wives because they cannot (or are reluctant to) use the tactics that seem "natural" and that they have been accustomed to using with men and boys. Boys fight with other boys, not with girls, and males far more often direct aggression toward men than toward women (Daly and Wilson, 1988). In fact, a male would lose face if he was seen fighting with a girl. It is reasonable to believe that most boys and men develop inhibitions against hitting, or threatening, girls and women. (Whether this stems from being trained by parents not to hit girls, and not to be too rough with them, or whether the roots are deeper, we cannot say.) It is a long-standing tradition that if a woman slaps a man because she feels he has overstepped the bounds in his sexual advances, he is expected not to slap her back. In short, she counts on his inhibitions, feeling confident that he will not retaliate with his full (and greater) physical strength. In the marital context, men surely recognize the risks to their relationship with their wives if they were to employ the confrontational, power-assertive tactics that they are accustomed to using in conflicts with men; they genuinely do not want to hurt their wives' feelings—to make them cry, or make them angry. At the same time, many men have not developed the kind of skills in resolving conflict through negotiation that women are likely to have. According to this reasoning, spousal conflict would be intrinsically more frustrating to men than women because men cannot use their accustomed modes of dealing with conflict, and don't have good alternative modes at hand. It becomes understandable that men both become more aroused and use withdrawal as a mode of coping with conflict.

It may seem strange to talk about the inhibition of male aggression toward women, when we know how frequently wife-battering occurs. What may well happen is that in some couples and in some situations a man finds he cannot successfully withdraw or successfully negotiate; he reaches the limits of his ability to inhibit his anger. Then he strikes out, but at this point, because of the very effort he has made to hold his anger in, he is so aroused that he becomes uncontrolled, violent. If he has been drinking, the disinhibition occurs more readily (Fagan and Browne, 1994). Women, and sometimes the children too, get hurt. We may assume that men, particularly men who engaged in physical fighting with other boys during their childhood, have an assaultive repertoire that is much readier for activation (or disinhibition) than is the case for their female partners.

I do not mean to imply that women are blameless in marital conflicts. They certainly do their share of heaping verbal abuse on a partner, and not infrequently become angry enough to throw objects (Straus and Gelles, 1986).[15] Whether a quarrel escalates to the level of physical violence depends in part on whether one partner, or both, move to break the spiral. Seen from this perspective, male stonewalling is not entirely dysfunctional. It stops fights, and keeps them from escalating. At the same time, it leaves problems unresolved, and if unresolved problems accumulate over time, the marriage becomes less and less satisfactory, probably especially for women.

It is difficult to know how important men's greater physical strength, and their greater experience with direct aggression, is for the balance of power between couples. As noted above, spousal abuse is a fact of life in a substantial number of marriages. Probably for an unknown number of other couples in which the man has never assaulted his spouse, the woman recognizes the possibility that he might do so, and moderates her behavior toward him so as not to elicit angry outbursts. No doubt, threatening gestures or tones of voice from a larger, stronger male will often be enough to cause a female partner to back off and wait until a more propitious time to try to negotiate some issue with him. In some families, the opportunity to negotiate seldom comes, and the man's use of physical coercion or the threat of it becomes a central element in tipping the balance of power in his direction. In many other cases, however, the man either successfully inhibits whatever aggressive impulses he may have, or the woman's sources of power are sufficient to redress any imbalance between them that would otherwise result from his aggression.

Summary and Comment

The onset of puberty brings with it a strong increase in interest in the other sex. Taboos imposed by childhood playgroups against contact with the other sex begin to break down. Thus it is a time for the disruption of existing patterns—for discontinuity. Still, the changes are not as abrupt or as deep as might be supposed. Gender segregation continues to prevail well into adolescence, with youth spending most of their free social time with same-sex friends. Initially, contact with the other sex occurs mainly in the context of mixed-sex groups, and it is guarded and exploratory.

The sexual revolution that accelerated so greatly after the middle of this century has left young people with few of the adult-managed arrangements and social constraints that once governed courtship. Nowadays, many young people are essentially on their own to negotiate their entry into the sexual marketplace. Members of same-sex peer groups are active in monitoring and guiding each other as they begin the process of seeking and forming romantic relationships with the other sex, and young people also rely on the scripts provided by TV and films for clues as to what is acceptable and expected.

A main question posed in this chapter has been: How are the two sexes positioned for negotiating with each other as they form heterosexual relationships? Of course, both boys and girls are eager to make themselves attractive to the other sex, but this need appears to place a greater burden on girls. Girls know (and research shows) that, to boys and men, a woman's physical appearance ranks very high on the list of attributes that determine how attractive she is. Girls become intensely concerned about their clothes, their makeup, their hair-dos, and their weight, and many girls become so preoccupied with these matters as to lose sight of other objectives, such as educational achievement. Appearance is a less important factor in the attractiveness of boys and men to the other sex, and they are less vulnerable to concerns about it.

The discrepant interaction styles developed earlier in same-sex playgroups are also often mentioned as factors that can easily lead to male dominance of male-female conversations, and to difficulties for young women in being heard by a male partner. Such difficulties do indeed arise. But these discrepancies might not be especially important were it not for the fact that they can be woven into a larger dynamic: a process whereby girls and women "play up" to male egos as a way of attracting and holding the interest of young men. It has been claimed that upon entering adolescence, girls typically adopt self-subordinating strategies and shut down their earlier robust ego development, suppressing their true "voice" and behaving instead in ways they think others—particularly males—want them to behave. We have seen that while some girls undoubtedly do subordinate themselves in these ways, many do not.

Why the variation? It surely depends in part on a young woman's subculture, and on the kind of relationship with men she feels teenage romances are ultimately directed toward. A young woman can see self-subordination as a useful strategy if what she wants—and thinks is possible—is to draw a partner of her choice into a traditional long-term relationship. Implicitly, she offers the bargain of becoming a compliant wife in return for a man's support. But if she lives in a subculture where male-female relationships are notoriously short-lived, and where men can seldom be counted on to provide support in the long run, she has less reason to adopt a self-subordinating posture. Presumably, many young women today look forward to being wage-earners themselves, not to a traditional marriage in which only the husband works. Such expectations can bring a self-confident sense of being able to control one's own future, and insulate young women against a "loss of voice." No doubt the continuing spread of a more egalitarian ideology concerning relationships between the sexes can have the same effect.

It is in negotiations over sexuality itself that young women may be at the greatest disadvantage. They, after all, are the ones who can become pregnant, and in many situations are the ones expected to take responsibility for contraception. If pregnancy occurs, a young man no longer needs to fear an irate father who will insist on his marrying and supporting a pregnant daughter. It is the girl and her family who must face the consequences. Apart from the issues of pregnancy, a double standard for sexual behavior still exists, and this places girls at considerable risk for the loss of reputation when they become sexually active. Typically, young men pressure their girlfriends to move toward sexual intimacy at a more rapid pace than the girls would like to set. As young people negotiate about sex, the fact that members of the two sexes typically want different things from a romantic relationship becomes important: boys more often are seeking a relationship which will offer a variety of pleasurable joint activities, including sex; girls are likely to be looking for a more lasting and more exclusive relationship based on love and emotional support, rather than wanting sexuality for its own sake. In the new context of heterosexual relationships, then, we see some echoes from the earlier kinds of friendships developed in middle childhood, with girls' friendships being more marked by intimacy and emotional closeness, boys' friendships based more on enjoyable joint activities.

Such continuities can also be seen among older, more established couples who are cohabiting or married. The women in such couples are more active in trying to maintain good moods in spousal interactions. We see here something quite similar to the "dual-voiced discourse" observed among girls in childhood. There is a curious reversal, however: while girls, in childhood, are the ones more likely to avoid confrontation when disagreements arise, in married couples it is the men who tend to withdraw from conflict with their wives. They seem to avoid the direct, power-assertive tactics that they used in conflict situations with their male peers, but at the same time are reluctant to enter into an extended, lower-key negotiation with their wives. Issues of "face," or power, appear to be involved here in subtle ways.

The question of which sex typically has more power in long-term relationships has proved difficult to answer. Such relationships cover the whole range from male-dominated to female-dominated, with most being in an intermediate range. I take this variation as evidence that there is nothing in human biology that biases the relationships of adult couples toward male dominance, although in many societies male dominance within marriage is buttressed by a variety of social norms and practices. How viable a particular dominance relation will be probably depends on the cultural context in which it is found. In modern societies, there is evidence, albeit fragmentary, that dominance issues between the members of a couple tend to fade into the background as they take on a joint agenda to which both contribute and from which both benefit.

9

The Two Sexes in the Workplace

Heterosexual relationships in adolescence and adulthood are almost necessarily one-on-one. By contrast, interaction among people who share a workplace usually occurs in the context of a group structure. As we will see, this makes a considerable difference for same-sex and cross-sex relationships in the workplace.[1]

The discrepant situations of men and women in the workplace have usually been interpreted as manifestations of discrimination against women. There is plentiful evidence that discrimination exists at all levels, and is a powerful force affecting women's opportunities for job training, for being hired, and for being promoted. I will argue, however, that discrimination per se is not the whole story. The different childhood histories of the two sexes may have a variety of implications for the way men and women relate to coworkers of their own sex and those of the other sex. We have seen that when children have a choice of social partners, they tend to gravitate toward same-sex others and avoid children of the other sex. On this basis alone, we might expect to see tendencies toward gender segregation in the workplace as well. But by the time they enter the world of work, most people have been involved in dating and forming heterosexual relationships. Perhaps via this route, and via experiences working in mixed-sex groups on school-based projects, they have learned to be comfortable associating with people of the other sex as well as their own in task-oriented situations. Thus gender integration, rather than segregation, might turn out to be the dominant pattern in the workplace. So the first question to answer is: In the daily life of the workplace, to what extent does gender segregation, versus gender integration, prevail?

Given that some degree of segregation is revealed, the second question is: What are the dynamics that sustain or modify it? We saw in Chapter 2 that boys' groups were in some respects more cohesive, more exclusionary, than girls' groups. We may expect, then, that men in the workplace will be more likely to band together to exclude women than women will be to exclude men. Of course, this issue may be moot, if it turns out that men often have the power to exclude women while the reverse does not hold. In any case, if men do form all-male groups in the workplace, the implication is that they will also be likely to depersonalize their female coworkers and treat them as members of an out-group.

The strong tendency to separate into single-sex groups during childhood created the opportunity for different styles of interaction to emerge in all-boy as compared to all-girl groups. As we saw, boys were much more competitive with each other, more concerned with dominance issues and with protecting turf, while girls in their groups were more democratic, more collaborative, more likely to avoid direct confrontation with each other. We saw in Chapter 8 that the different male and female styles emerging out of childhood affected the interactions between the members of romantically involved couples, sometimes creating misunderstandings or difficulties in conflict resolution. When men and women interact dyadically in the workplace, the same kinds of disjunctions in interactive styles might be expected to occur.

Most workplaces are hierarchical almost by definition. There may be many or few levels in the workplace hierarchy, but there will always be one or more individuals directing and supervising the work of others. It is possible that the styles boys utilized in childhood allow them to adapt more readily to the workplace hierarchy. They may start with an advantage over women when it comes to competing with others for promotion, and to knowing ways of relating to others above or below them in a hierarchy. But women may find themselves better prepared to enter into the new-style management techniques, which involve seeking consensus among coworkers and avoiding overly authoritarian modes of supervision.

The prevailing pattern of gender separation in childhood kept boys and girls from having to compete with each other for a place in a joint hierarchy. Thus issues of dominance between males and females were usually circumvented or at least muted. Cross-sex interaction occurred mainly as "borderwork" when male and female playgroups encountered each other, and in these situations children of each sex usually had the back-up of their same-sex age-mates. Or encounters with the other sex occurred within the fairly gender-neutral contexts structured by adults, where hierarchical lines of authority flowed from adults to children, not from children of one sex to the other. In Chapter 8, we saw a mixed picture where dominance between the members of a male-female couple was concerned. True, there was a tendency for adolescent girls to "play up" to male egos in the early stages of courtship, while at the same time they were uncomfortable with male controlling styles in situations where the partners had not chosen each other. These trends suggest that males tend to assume a dominant role toward women in young adulthood, and that women may collaborate with them in allowing this to happen when pair relationships are being formed. In established couples, however, actual dominance may go either way, although in some male peer groups and some cultures there is a shared ideology supporting the right of males to be in control of women.

In this chapter, I will be concerned with the kind of hierarchical or dominance relationships between men and women that emerge in the workplace. (The available information will come mainly from Western industrialized societies.) One of the major social changes in recent years has been the movement of women into several levels of management, and it will be interesting to see whether the developmental histories of the two sexes seem to have a bearing on the way they manage cross-sex hierarchical arrangements.

Gender Segregation

The Prevalence of Segregation

When young people have finished their schooling and begin to try to find a job, they encounter an occupational world which is permeated by gender differentiation. Many kinds of jobs are held almost entirely by individuals of one sex. And the very process of searching for a job is gender-biased. People tend to find jobs through informal, word-of-mouth information networks. These networks are largely sex-segregated: women find out about job openings from other women, and men get job leads mainly from other men (Hanson and Pratt, 1995). In this way both men and women are channeled into jobs usually held by persons of their own sex.

How extensive is gender segregation in the workplace? The simple answer is: very extensive. Many jobs become known as "women's jobs" or "men's jobs," and the gender designation of occupations is surprisingly stable. Though occupations do sometimes switch their designation from male to female, or (less often) female to male, Strober and Catanzarite (1994) estimate that in the early part of the twentieth century, only 2 percent of occupations changed their designation from one sex to the other. The gender specialization of out-of-home work has a long history and a wide reach. It prevails in preliterate societies, but also in advanced industrial ones in which the two sexes have fairly equal access to education and the rights of citizenship. Not only does gender segregation occur at the level of *activities*, with men and women typically performing different kinds of work; but the two sexes tend to work in different *industries*: worldwide, women make up the substantial bulk of the workforce in the garment industry, while in mining, the workforce is almost entirely male.

A distinction is sometimes made between "primary" and "secondary" jobs (Sayed and Tzananatos, 1995). Primary jobs have fairly high levels of skills adapted specifically to the work of the employing firm; they tend to have good wages, good promotion opportunities, job security, and good benefits. Secondary jobs require less in the way of job-specific skills; they have lower wages, fewer benefits, fewer opportunities for advancement, and higher turnover. Women are much more highly concentrated in secondary jobs than are men.

Segregation is obvious when the two sexes work in spatially separated places. There are many situations where large groups of women work in a large space doing semiskilled work: for example, assembling semiconductor components or sewing clothes. Segregation of this sort is common worldwide, as the recent revelations about sweatshops in the garment industry have revealed. In such occupations, women can work day after day without encountering a male coworker. Hanson and Pratt report the comment of a woman who worked in a footwear factory: "I've worked here for ten years but I've never been upstairs. That's where the men are" (1995, p. 182). In this factory, "upstairs" implied a status differential as well as a spatial one.

There can also be spatial separation between men's and women's work, even when the jobs are at roughly the same hierarchical level, for example, in an industrial laundry:

The white male population tended to be spatially segregated from women and immigrant men. The laundry was brought in from hospitals by white Anglo male truck drivers, and then hand-sorted by Jewish and Polish men. It was then moved through the washer and dryer by a conveyor belt and robots, monitored by white male workers. Male general laborers transported the cleaned laundry to an ironing room where mostly women ironed it. It was then moved into a folding room where it was folded by hand by women, and taken to a shipping area, where male and female packers boxed it. (Hanson and Pratt, 1995, pp. 181–182)

Evidently, packing was the only part of this multifaceted operation in which men and women worked side by side doing the same kind of work.

A common but different form of gender segregation occurs in situations where men and women work together in the same space but at different status levels. (This is sometimes called vertical segregation.) I will discuss this pattern more fully below, when I consider the hierarchical relationships of men and women in the workplace.

Employing a commonly used overall measure of segregation (the Duncan index), one study conducted in the early 1980s reported that although the index of segregation in the United States had been declining during the 1970s, the level of segregation nevertheless remained quite high.[2] Surprisingly, workforce segregation was equally high, by this index, in Sweden in the mid-eighties, despite the long history of efforts in Scandinavian countries to provide equal access to occupational opportunities for men and women.

The verdict as to how segregated an occupation is depends on how narrowly the occupation is defined. The occupation "machine operator" might not be very segregated if all kinds of machine operators are pooled. But if sewing-machine operators are distinguished from the operators of lathes, the degree of gender specialization is much greater. Because of problems of this kind, we cannot say precisely what proportion of working people work primarily in gender-segregated jobs; however, existing studies indicate that a substantial majority of employed people do so. As Reskin says, "Few occupations employ men and women in proportion to their representation in the labor force, and workers seldom work with persons of the other sex in the same establishment, much less in the same location or on the same shift" (1993, p. 245).

There is plentiful evidence, then, that gender segregation is a pervasive phenomenon in the workplace, just as it was in childhood. I cannot give a full account here of the factors that have been identified as leading to workplace segregation, but here is a quick summary.

1. In childhood and adolescence, the two sexes diverge in terms of their interest in certain kinds of work, and in their expectations concerning what occupations they can realistically expect to enter.

2. Their divergent interests and expectations lead to different choices in terms of what courses to take, what after-school jobs to look for, what post–high school training programs to enter. Adults play a role, too, in tracking young people of the two sexes toward different kinds of training and apprenticeships.[3] By the time they are ready to enter the labor force, their education and training have often prepared them to enter occupations already dominated by their own sex.

3. Over and above training and preparation, a formidable set of institutional barriers exist that stand in the way of women's gaining access to male-dominated jobs (resistance by male-dominated unions; word-of-mouth recruiting) (Reskin and Roos, 1990).

4. When men and women have moved away from the parental home and established their own households, the typical division of household labor comes into play in the work roles of the two sexes. Because of their heavier responsibilities for household duties and child care, women more often seek part-time work, and more often than men prefer to work close to home, minimizing commuting time. These constraints typically impel women toward working in female-dominated occupations (Hanson and Pratt, 1995).

5. Men have more freedom to leave low-paying jobs, and more access to high-paying ones (Reskin and Roos, 1990). Also, at all levels of an occupational structure, men are more likely to gain promotion to the next higher level. Thus women find themselves clustered together in the lower-level (lower-paid) jobs.

These processes are well documented as being powerfully implicated in workplace segregation. Yet I suggest that the story of segregation is not complete without considering, in addition, the same-sex and cross-sex dynamics emerging out of patterns developed in childhood and adolescence.

Change in the Patterns of Segregation

How much movement has there been in the past 20 years toward genuine gender integration in the workplace—men and women working side by side at the same level in the same occupation? Researchers do not agree on the answer to this question, though there has probably been some diminution in segregation.[4] Certain trends emerge:

1. When there is a change toward greater integration of an occupation, the change is usually a one-way street: it involves women breaking in to formerly all-male occupations rather than vice versa. True, there has been a small increase in the number of male nurses and secretaries, but such trends do not begin to balance the movement of women into "male" (and usually higher-paid) occupations.
2. There has been more change toward gender integration in professional occupations than in nonskilled or semiskilled manual or clerical jobs.
3. What looks like the integration of an occupation is sometimes only the half-way point of a movement toward resegregation.

Kanter (1993) notes that although women did make considerable progress during the 1970s and 1980s in gaining access to management levels in corporations and professions, the recent surge of "downsizing" of workforces has resulted in a substantial shrinkage of available jobs at the middle-management level. Because of the intense competition for the jobs that remain, the trend toward increasing representation of women at these levels may be losing its momentum.

Point 3 deserves some comment. There are fascinating instances in which women gain entry to a formerly all-male occupation, whereupon the men begin to leave the occupation and it becomes predominantly female (Reskin and Ross, 1990). Secretaries were once almost exclusively male. (It was thought that females couldn't handle a complex piece of machinery like a typewriter! Also, parents were wary of allowing their daughters to work closely with men in positions of authority, who might "take advantage" of a young woman.) But once secretarial jobs began to be filled by women, fewer men applied for such jobs, and secretarial work rapidly became almost entirely a female occupation. Strober and colleagues,[5] in analyzing several occupations that switched from being predominantly male to being predominantly female, note that men tend to leave an occupation when it becomes bureaucratized or loses autonomy, or when the opportunities for advancement are curtailed. When they leave, opportunities for entry are opened up for women. Whatever the reasons, the major point here is that when occupations do change their gender composition, there is a tendency for them to go all the way—from one form of segregation to the other.[6] This tendency is by no means universal, however. The increasing representation of women in law and medicine, for example, has not occasioned male flight from these professions, but rather has brought about some real gender integration.

Reskin and Roos (1990) made a detailed study of 33 predominantly "male" occupations in which there was an increase in women's representation, according to official records of occupational distributions for the two sexes.[7] They found that appearances were deceiving. Although women appeared to have broken in to some male occupational strongholds, in many cases new women entrants were "ghettoized" (isolated) or shunted into the lower-paid specialties within a larger occupational classification (as when women went into family law rather than tax law). Or the occupation was in the process of being resegregated, with men leaving the occupation. Their conclusion was that occupational segregation by sex remains a strong reality in many workplace settings, even where some change toward greater integration appears to have occurred.

What happens when new industries appear in a modern world in which women are well educated and an ideology favoring gender equality is widely shared? We might expect these new industries to be more integrated. But a careful examination of the computer industry done in 1983 by Game and Pringle revealed that at that time, this new industry was as fully segregated by gender as long-established industries: data-entry clerical jobs were filled almost entirely by women; men predominated as salespeople, systems managers, and managers.[8] It is evident that there are structural features that cause gender segregation to replicate itself in new situations where there is no established tradition to account for this outcome.

Nevertheless, we should note that since Game and Pringle wrote about the computer industry, there has been a substantial increase in the representation of women in computer jobs. Furthermore, even though women have been earning a decreasing proportion of bachelor's degrees in computer science, information science, and computer engineering, women have not been increasingly "ghettoized" into lower-level enclaves in the computer industry. Instead, they have been increasingly represented at all levels (Wright and Jacobs, 1995).

The Reasons for Segregation

Much has been written about the many factors, large and small, that combine to produce workforce segregation. At one time, it was widely thought that occupational segregation resulted from the two sexes' having different talents and capacities. For example, women were thought to have greater finger dexterity, and so, the argument ran, they would be better at certain assembly jobs requiring fine motor movements, and would cluster together in such jobs. The consensus of research is that such factors are not very important. Most women can easily do most "men's" jobs, if they have the relevant interest, education, and training; most men, suitably trained, can easily do most "women's" jobs. There are some possible exceptions. Men, for instance, may have an advantage for jobs that require very heavy lifting, considering their greater upper-body strength. But it is worth noting that heavy work (such as digging trenches for street repairs or carrying heavy burdens) is done as often, or more often, by women as by men in many parts of the world, and most "men's" jobs do not require heavy lifting.

People do not leave behind their attitudes toward the other sex, or their previous experiences with the other sex, when they enter the workplace. There are several aspects of people's developmental history that I believe come into play more strongly than has been recognized so far: (1) the differential interaction styles emerging from segregated childhood cultures probably have an impact on the way people relate to same-sex and other-sex others in the workplace; (2) all-male peer groups commonly exist in the workplace, and they function in ways similar to those that prevailed earlier in life; and (3) when sexual or romantic attraction occurs between men and women who encounter each other at work, they bring into the workplace elements of their experience in the dating culture (see Chapter 8) and their sexual attitudes toward the other sex. These forces create complexities in the workplace, and can conflict sharply with the kinds of relationships that are called for by work functions or occupational hierarchies.

In examining the dynamics of the same-sex and cross-sex interactions prevailing in the workplace, I will need to rely on rather selective studies, because much of the relevant research involves observations of the daily interaction patterns in a limited number of offices or factories, or interviews with people at various levels of the hierarchies in a selected set of companies. Thus we do not know how widely we may generalize from the settings that have been studied to other workplace contexts; nor do we know how typical the people are whose experiences are recounted. Still, the observations and interviews do enable us to identify some processes that demonstrably do occur in the workplace, however typical or atypical they may be, and that bear clear resemblances to the gendered forms of behavior that I have traced in earlier periods of life.

Male and Female Interaction Styles

In her well-known book *You Just Don't Understand* (1990), Deborah Tannen described the ways in which typical talk among women is different from typical talk among men, and identified ways in which these different styles of discourse could lead to misunderstandings between heterosexual couples. In her more recent book, *Talking from 9 to 5* (1994), she considers how these sex-linked discourse patterns are manifested in the workplace. She notes that a good deal of informal chitchat goes on in offices, talk that is not related to work but that serves to form and solidify social bonds, to keep lines of communication open, and to defuse work-related tensions. Not surprisingly, she finds that same-sex office-mates tend to drift toward sex-typical topics: men chat with each other about such things as cars, sports, and technology; women more often chat about clothes and hairstyles, or domestic concerns and children. It is generally recognized that there is such a thing as "man talk" and "girl talk," and people usually find it easier to get to know a new coworker who is of their own sex because they feel more comfortable about finding an informal topic of mutual interest.

But as we have seen in Chapter 2, styles of discourse go much beyond the content of what is being talked about. For one thing, the sexes typically differ in how humor is expressed. Boys and men josh each other, engaging in razzing, teasing, and pretend hostility. When women don't respond to this kind of banter, men often think women have no sense of humor. Among girls and women, a more common form of humor is self-mockery. Women can mistake men's humor for genuine hostility, while men can mistake women's for true self-abnegation, which seems to them out of place. Studies have shown that women and men get along more comfortably in the workplace if the women are able to participate in male-style banter (Tannen, 1994, pp. 72–75).

Differences in discourse styles sometimes come to the surface in the workplace when a supervisor criticizes a worker's product or asks for changes that may be unwelcome. Women, with their habitual avoidance of confrontation, tend to soften critical messages. Men, accustomed to being more direct, are less uncomfortable about delivering criticism, but when they are on the receiving end of criticism, they may miss the unwelcome message that a woman has sugar-coated. Tannen gives an example: A woman manager had to ask a male employee to redo an unsatisfactory report. In talking to him about the problem, she began by offering limited praise for the things about the report that were acceptable, and then went on to tell him, as tactfully as possible, how and why it needed to be considerably revised. When the new version came in, it had been changed in only minor ways, and the changes were not responsive to her critique. At the next meeting both were incensed: She thought he had ignored her directions; he thought she had changed her mind ("you told me before it was fine!"). For him, her initial praise became the message, while for her the softening phrases were merely face-saving devices, not meant to negate the central critical content of her message. This form of politeness, customary among women, was something the female supervisor expected others to understand. As Tannen shows, indirection is by no means exclusively a female mode, but when used, it can prompt a coworker to say, or at least think, "Why don't you say what you mean?"

Another gender disjunction is involved in the exchange of compliments. Women are accustomed to exchanging compliments routinely, men much less so. If a man is asked, "What did you think of my talk?" or "What did you think of my report?" he is likely to embark on a serious critique, while a woman is more likely to take the question as a courtesy ritual: to assume that a compliment is in order and look for something to praise. In the same way, apologies are more routine, more ritualized, among women, who frequently say "I'm sorry" in the course of ordinary conversation. Such phrases are not meant to be taken as serious apologies, but men—for whom apologies are generally not routine—may take them as such and wonder what exactly a woman has done that she needs to feel apologetic about.

Women's more collaborative orientation is also implicated in workplace communication, and can have real consequences for their career development. Tannen notes that women often fail to take individual credit for their workplace accomplishments, saying for example that "we" collectively finished a successful piece of work, where a man would be more likely to say "I" finished it. Men often create informal opportunities—such as joining a supervisor for lunch—to make sure that their successes are known to the people who will make decisions about upcoming promotions. Women are more likely to believe that all that is needed for promotion is to do a good job. They hesitate to "brag," preferring to take it for granted that supervisors will notice and reward good work. Male supervisors sometimes interpret women's hesitancy about putting themselves forward as a lack of self-confidence. If self-confidence is seen as a quality that is necessary for success at high-level jobs, these male perceptions of female coworkers can contribute to the "glass ceiling" that women often encounter when it comes to promotions.

Male Peer Groups

Beth Milwid, in her book *Working With Men* (1990), reports the experiences of 125 women working at various management levels in professional or industrial settings where their colleagues were almost entirely male. Here are some examples of the situations they described:

> Three men in our office [are] standing at a hallway intersection, talking . . . another man goes up and slips—slips!—into the conversation with no trouble at all. I walk by and the conversation comes to a screeching halt. No one says anything until I've gone past. The idea that I might try to join the conversation? Forget it. Never! (p. 68)

> It's very difficult, breaking into men's informal groups. If you're too cold and aloof, the men won't want to be with you because you're not the typical fun, sensitive, vulnerable woman. If you let it show that you are in fact vulnerable, you break the strong "professional women" image that you have to show at work. There's a very fine line that you have to tread. (p. 77)

I was in a meeting the other day, and our president made a bunch of comments about how, if we did something, he was going to buy us all a drink and a whore. And I said, "Well, that isn't going to help me much." And he said, "Oh, I forgot, I thought we were all guys." (p. 98)

You're not invited to lunches during the day. In the three years I've been here, I don't ever remember my boss asking me out to lunch, yet he'll ask all the other brokers out. I think he feels strange around me. I'm not saying he hasn't helped me. He has. But he always does it with a kind of a "don't come too near" attitude. (p. 70)

This last woman's boss may have wanted to avoid the appearance of initiating an office romance. Men and women in the workplace find it difficult to fall into easy camaraderie with each other without fearing that their friendliness will be misunderstood as signs of sexual interest (see the discussion of sexuality below). But regardless of such implications, it is simply easier for people to associate informally with others of their own sex. It is especially when groups from the office engage in nonwork social activities, then, that the presence of women seems difficult for men to cope with:

Every May, the entire management group goes on a fishing trip up north. The trip costs about $100 per employee . . . That spring (when I became a manager) I remember having a discussion with my boss and saying, "Well, I don't imagine I'm going to get asked to go on the fishing trip." Sure enough, beginning that May, the men would go fishing, and the company would give each woman manager $100. (Milwid, 1990, p. 71)

In business organizations, higher-level jobs often involve a good deal of traveling, to visit field offices or meet potential clients or customers. Sometimes business gets done outside the usual working hours, during informal gatherings in a hotel bar or nightclub. Women are often ambivalent about whether they can or should join the men in these situations: "As a woman, you feel left out. The men don't want you to go drinking with them after work. And certainly it is rather strange if a woman goes to the local bar where the guys are going to down twenty in a night. It's just not appropriate" (Milwid, 1990, pp. 69-70). Women recognize, however, that when they skip the informal male gatherings, they are being excluded from some of the talk that is relevant to the business deals that were the purpose of the trip.

Milwid sums up her own experience working in the office of a big-city mayor:

> Day after day, I sat in those meetings trying to laugh at the jokes, trying to keep up with the latest names in football, tennis and golf—in other words, trying to learn a new job and a new male culture all at the same time. I knew I didn't fit in and wasn't taken seriously, but I was determined to give it my best shot. (1990, p. 2)

Clearly, many men are accustomed to a form of camaraderie in their all-male work groups that they find it difficult or impossible to maintain in the presence of women. The parallels between these patterns and those seen in the all-male groups of childhood are obvious. Part of the problem is that men's talk commonly includes locker-room sorts of references to women as sex objects—talk that would be embarrassing if it were heard by a female colleague. In addition, there are frequent references to masculine topics of interest, such as sports and cars, that women typically know less, and care less, about.

Not surprisingly, men can mobilize themselves powerfully to keep women out of their comfortably male groups, not only their clubs, associations, poker parties, and so forth, but also the workplace. White males in particular become "gatekeepers," protecting their workplaces from invasion by females through various forms of harassment.[9] As a consequence, when women move into male occupations, they often leave again quite soon (Jacobs, 1989).

Quite a few of the women interviewed by Milwid said that the exclusionary and sexist attitudes and practices illustrated above were mainly found among older men—those over 50. Younger men, they said, seemed to take working with women more for granted. The higher echelons of management, of course, tend to be occupied by older people than do the lower levels; consequently a woman is likely to encounter more social exclusion from male coworkers the higher up in an organization she goes. These age differences, if they are widespread, suggest that with the passage of time the upper levels of management may provide a more open social environment for women, as the younger, more liberal-minded men are promoted to positions of power.

Female Peer Groups

Much less has been written about problems faced by men when entering largely female occupations, but the existing work suggests that their situation is by no means analogous to that of women entering male occupations. In studies of nontraditional occupations, Williams (1989, 1995) interviewed males who had entered several "female" occupations, including nursing, elementary school teaching, social work, and work as librarians. (She also interviewed a number of female coworkers of these men.) She points out that when men enter these professions, they enter structures which usually have men at the higher supervisory levels of the organization. They tend to establish good rapport with these higher-level males, in part because they share "male" interests such as an interest in sports. Furthermore, males in nontraditional jobs are usually free from harassment by supervisors. For example, male nurses say they have almost never experienced having a doctor throw anything at them, while female nurses frequently report that this has happened to them. Men in nontraditional jobs sometimes report that their judgment gets more respect from supervisors than is accorded to female coworkers' judgment, and they tend to be promoted more quickly. They say they believe rapid promotion happens in part because they can respond to the calls for emergency overtime work more readily than can women, who have to balance their domestic and work responsibilities.

As far as informal relations with female coworkers are concerned, people of both sexes report fairly comfortable talk about job-related matters. But job-related interactions do nevertheless reflect assumptions about sex-related characteristics. Women are reported to rely on greater male strength for a number of job-related tasks—lifting patients into a wheelchair, subduing violent patients, carrying heavy cartons of books, dealing with disciplinary problems in the classroom. Women may also ask for help from male coworkers with technical matters, such as fixing a computer. But there clearly are barriers to inclusion of males in some of the informal social activities that are based in the workplace. These barriers are felt by people on both sides of the gender divide. Men are sometimes reluctant to join women—and women sometimes exclude them—when they are talking "girl talk," as at the lunch table; and male nurses may not be invited to join a nurse's softball team or to attend a bridal shower (Floge and Merrill, 1985).

Despite these examples of females excluding males, it seems clear that the efforts of male workplace peer groups to exclude women have been a much more powerful force in maintaining gender segregation than have the efforts of women to exclude men. The difference mainly reflects the fact that changes encouraging greater gender integration in the workplace usually take the form of women attempting to enter male-dominated occupations rather than vice versa.

Sexuality

Adults have multiple agendas. For the majority of people, a central aim is to find work that is either fulfilling or at least acceptable and that provides economic support. For heterosexual people, another central life task is to find and maintain a satisfying intimate relationship with a person of the other sex. And there may be in addition an interest in sexual adventuring for its own sake. For most people, their main concerns in the workplace have to do with the work they are there to do. Their sexuality is on the back burner. As we have seen, many people work in settings where they seldom or never encounter coworkers of the other sex. When a workplace does include both sexes, there are usually informal codes of conduct that impose restraints on workplace flirtations. Awareness of a coworker's attractiveness may surface in the form of mild banter, or be expressed as gallantry or "charm." But many people, perhaps most, live their work lives without going beyond these very modest expressions of sexual interest.

For some people, however, the workplace provides an opportunity to meet potential partners. Nowadays we have become so aware of the widespread occurrence of sexual harassment in the workplace that we tend to lose sight of the more benign side of mutual attraction: many lasting, mutually satisfying relationships have begun when people met at work. The fate and meaning of sexual approaches in the workplace depend on many things: how closely the two people's work roles intersect, how mutual the interest is, the motives of the two people, how well each understands the other's intent, and whether any element of exploitation is present. Many would argue that any kind of romantic involvement between coworkers will interfere with getting the work of an office or workshop accomplished. There is the danger of favoritism between people who are mutually attracted, and when romantic relationships break up, jealousy and anger interfere with former lovers' ability to work together. Still, there are many instances in which people have managed to work effectively together even when they are, or have been, romantically involved.

There is a great deal of ambivalence among both men and women concerning the image they should project in the workplace: whether they want to be seen as sexually attractive as well as collegial. Women in particular give considerable thought to how they should dress. Women who "dress for success" may wear a severely tailored business suit, but they will usually use makeup and carefully chosen hair-dos to enhance their attractiveness, and wear high heels and sheer hosiery.

Some women do not set aside, while at work, the sometimes unconsciously flirtatious modes of interaction they have been accustomed to using with men in social situations. A businesswoman commented:

> If you as a woman indicate, either consciously or unconsciously, that you're sexually available—or sexually interested—it immediately puts the man in the mental space that he has with his wife or his lovers. Then he has to deal with you as a domestic woman, and you definitely don't want that in business. I think that for a lot of women, this process of subtly coming on to men is not conscious. Many women have never learned another way of relating to men. After many years in this field, I've come to the conclusion that women have as much difficulty relating to men as men have relating to women. (Milwid, 1990, p. 120)

Whatever the truth of this woman's insight, the fact remains, as we saw in Chapter 8, that more men than women are interested in casual sexual adventuring. The literature on sexual harassment strongly suggests that it is far more common for men to make unwanted sexual advances to women in the workplace than vice versa. Perhaps some men are misled by women's unconscious signals, but we may suspect that unwanted advances by men occur whether or not such signals are present. It is part of the traditional sex roles in courtship for the man to be the one who takes the initiative, and for the woman either to accept or reject his advances. Although many men do not bring a desire for sexual adventuring to the workplace, some do. They look over the women in their workplace, alert for cues as to who is likely to be "available," and they may assume that a woman is interested unless there is very clear evidence to the contrary. Any attractive woman becomes fair game so long as she is unattached. As one women manager interviewed by Milwid said:

> I believe the atmosphere at work is really different for a married woman. The men don't make the same snide remarks or suggestive comments to a married woman that they do to a single woman. The single woman is treated much more loosely and not nearly as professionally. If you're single, the men treat you as if they're saying, "Well, you're just here, honey, because we like the way you look." Whereas with married women, the message is, "We hired you because you have skills." Now if a married woman acts single, she's going to get the comments too. But if she has pictures of her kids on her desk and brings her husband to the baseball games and the company parties, she's treated a whole lot differently. (Milwid, 1990, p. 114)

Another woman also stressed the importance of a husband: "The come-ons you get when you're married are more subtle than they are when you're divorced. When you're married, the men know your husband, and they aren't going to be disrespectful of another man" (Milwid, 1990, p. 114). Men's awareness of other men's reactions is not confined to wariness of, or respect for, husbands. There is the further matter of being able to win points in one's male peer group via sexual conquests. When an attractive single woman is present in a workplace, there is likely to be a good deal of interest among the men concerning who will win out in competition for her favors.

The workplace can offer opportunities for sexual exploitation. There are women who use their sexual attractiveness to gain workplace advantages— to be hired, to get promotion, to get a competitive advantage over cowork-ers in attracting or keeping customers for a business enterprise. The kind of sexual exploitation men engage in is usually of a different sort. They are almost never in the situation of being able to gain advantage by "sleeping their way to the top." Rather, they may take advantage of being in more powerful positions in organizations where both sexes work; they can use their power to demand sexual favors from women in return for promotion, job protection, or favorable performance ratings. It is this kind of exploitation that is usually involved when issues of sexual harassment come to the fore.

The popular literature is full of stories concerning women's experiences in dealing with men's unwanted advances in offices or shops. In many cases, the "advances" do not take the form of direct propositions. Rather, there is sexual teasing, including comments about a woman's face or body, that occurs in the midst of work-oriented interactions in such a way as to make it clear that what the woman is saying is not being taken seriously— that instead, the man's focus is on her as a sex object. (An example: in a meeting of sales representatives, a female representative stood in her turn to report on her region. She began, "I have two points . . .," and a male member of the group spoke up, "You certainly do, honey, and they look great!") In other instances, of course, direct sexual propositions do occur. In such situations, women know that if they become angry, or make a complaint, they risk losing their jobs, or may sacrifice their chances for promotion.

Women in the business world also find themselves the objects of sexual advances from customers or potential customers. They must deal with these situations in ways that will not lose business for their companies and that will keep their own sales record (as well as their personal sexual integrity) intact (Milwid, 1990). A common strategy for dealing with both in-house and customer-related situations is to make light of them—to make a joke, avoid "making waves." Many women try to respond in such a way as to protect the man's ego and save him from embarrassment, as well as to avoid angering him and thereby endangering their own jobs. The case of a woman on a field trip who had gone out to dinner with a group of male coworkers in a hotel is instructive. During the dinner, the man next to her groped her, and after the meal, invited her to his room, saying, "You know, I really like you and I could do a lot for your career." Her reaction:

> My first thoughts were, "My God, what's going to happen to me if I say no? I could get fired." And so I found a way of saying no that would be easily accepted. It was "Look, I'm really attracted to you, but you're married and I'm Catholic, and I don't believe in that sort of thing." You have to protect their egos. You have to find a more politically acceptable solution than slapping someone in the face— even though that's what I was inclined to do. I would have slapped him if he hadn't been in my direct reporting line in the corporation. (Milwid, 1990, pp. 94–95)

A different form of exploitation occurs when employers use the women in the office or salesforce to entertain visiting dignitaries and potential customers. A woman who feels she is not taken seriously during the business negotiations with a customer will nevertheless be invited to the dinner celebrating a successful negotiation, and it will be clear to her that she is expected to look her best and to make the men feel good.

> They [the customers] love to flirt with me. They want to put their arms around me, they want to dance, they want to dance close, and when they drink too much, it becomes a very sticky situation. The whole time you're trying to maintain a professional demeanor, yet at the same time you're expected not to keep things *too* professional. Above all, remember, you never want to alienate the customer. It's a very hard game to play. (Milwid, 1990, p. 80)

The women interviewed by Milwid were unanimous in their belief that business and romance don't mix—that sexuality should be kept out of the workplace, even if a woman is strongly attracted to a male coworker. Many also thought that in the early phases of a woman's presence in a workplace, it was almost inevitable that some men would explore the possibilities of a sexual relationship, but that if the woman consistently fended off such advances and remained entirely work-oriented, the initial phase would pass and it would become possible for men and women to settle down into a friendly coworker relationship.

Gender-based Hierarchy

Inequities in the workplace can arise because people have had relatively little experience interacting with people of the other sex except in the context of heterosexual bonding. In consequence, people often use pre- viously acquired sexual scripts in workplace contexts where they are inap- propriate or actively dysfunctional. Even when sexual scripts are suspended in the workplace, however, there is an absence of well-established patterns of other kinds of interaction to fall back on. Many people are made uncomfortable by the prospect of informal interaction with a coworker of the other sex working alongside them at a same-level job. As we have seen, mutual avoidance is a common solution, and this can take two forms. One is separation: working in different places in single-sex work groups, or choosing only same-sex partners for informal social interaction in the workplace. The other is gendered hierarchy, where people of different sexes work together but are distanced from each other by virtue of being at different levels in an organizational structure.

In the not-too-distant past, most doctors were men, who worked closely on a daily basis with female nurses and receptionists who were clearly subordinate to them. This pattern has not disappeared despite the influx of women into the ranks of physicians. In many occupational settings today, most of the executives, supervisors, or higher-level professionals are men, assisted by female secretaries, clerks, aides, or lower-level managers.

It is important to note that there has been a very large increase in the number of women classified as "managers" according to the occupational classifications of the U.S. Census. In 1970, only 18 percent of people so classified were women. In the early 1990s, the proportion of women managers had risen to 40 percent, and the change probably reflects a real rise in women's positions in the workplace hierarchy, not just a reclassification of existing work assignments that bestowed on them fancier job titles (Jacobs, 1995). However, the fact remains that when women become managers, they usually supervise other women. Women supervising men remains much more rare, and their access to the higher levels of management where real power and authority are exercised remains limited.

When women enter a workplace they frequently find a male hierarchy already established. Whether a woman's entry creates tensions for herself or others in the workplace presumably depends on the level of the job she takes and the source of any authority inherent in the job. She may come in at a subordinate level, as, say, a clerk or receptionist. But if she comes in at the same level as male coworkers, she will be faced with the unaccustomed process of jockeying for position among them, and competing with them for the attention and approval of the people higher up in the hierarchy. If she comes in as a manager or supervisor who has male subordinates, she must learn how to deal with people who may want her job, or who may find it difficult to adjust to being supervised by a woman. Some men believe so strongly in male superiority that they resist women's advancement up the workplace hierarchy. Such men sometimes say quite explicitly that it would be "an insult to their intelligence" to be supervised by a woman (Harlan and Weiss, 1982). And there are fairly widespread male beliefs concerning the "natural" (male-dominant) relation between the sexes. In adulthood there is a strong stereotype associating power with masculinity (Ragins and Sundstrom, 1989), just as there was in childhood, so that women in supervisory positions generate ambivalent reactions in men: are they to treat this woman as a powerful person or a feminine person? If she is seen as feminine, then a man with traditional attitudes might feel it is appropriate to be protective and chivalrous, or at least courteous, while at the same time failing to take her seriously where work-related matters are concerned; clearly, he would expect to be the person who "takes charge" when they interact. Can he forget that a female supervisor is female, and adapt himself to a situation where she is the one who takes charge? It is much easier for men—and perhaps for many women too—to slip into a traditional male boss/female secretary or male doctor/female nurse kind of work relationship in which the "appropriate" power relationships between the sexes are maintained in the workplace hierarchy. Such traditional attitudes may be weakening, but they are still prevalent enough to impede the promotion of women in many situations.

Such male attitudes seem to emerge as much from the romantic-dating culture as from the culture of childhood. In childhood the power aspects of the relationships between the two sexes are subdued by virtue of segregation and by the pervasive presence of the adult-child power differential (though we did see some signs that boys considered girls to be "not tough enough," and in this sense weaker than themselves). There are other aspects of childhood culture, however, that might have some carry-over to workplace hierarchies: We might expect that women in the workplace would especially value the social contacts and friendships formed there, and be less motivated to compete for advancement up the corporate ladder. Furthermore, the more democratic, less hierarchical nature of female social groups might mean that women have less experience with, and would be less comfortable in, situations where they must exercise supervisory responsibility over others.

Rosabeth Kanter, in her important book *Men and Women of the Corporation* (first edition, 1977), challenged the assumption, widely held at that time, that women would bring a "feminine" style to managerial jobs. She and others did not find that women (more than men) use the workplace mainly for the satisfactions of friendship and social contacts. She found women to be fully as work-oriented as men. Her contention was that the job itself is what determines how its holder will perform, and she reported that men and women handled supervisory responsibilities in much the same way. More recent analyses of supervisory job performance confirm this view (Kanter, second edition, 1993; Powell, 1990). Fagenson (1990) reports that whether people in an organizational hierarchy manifest "masculine" characteristics depends on their level in the hierarchy, not on their sex. Thus although we might have expected that the nonhierarchical style prevailing in girlhood groups would lead to some difficulty for women taking on supervisory responsibilities, this has not been found to be the case, at least not among the women who have risen in hierarchies to managerial levels. (Of course, there may be a selective element here, such that the women who were least fully socialized by female peer groups in childhood into a nonhierarchical mode are the women who prove to be most able to rise in occupational hierarchies in adulthood.)

Recent work by Moskowitz and colleagues (1993) adds depth to these conclusions. They asked people to make reports, while they were at work, about each sustained interaction (one lasting five minutes or more) they had with a supervisor, a supervisee, or a same-status coworker. Participants answered a set of questions about each event. One set was aimed at determining how dominant ("agentic") or submissive the participant had been toward the other person, as indicated by such behaviors as giving an opinion, giving information or directions, or setting goals, as distinct from ducking responsibility and waiting for the other to act. The other set of questions dealt with how friendly or agreeable ("communal") the participant had been, as indicated by such actions as listening attentively or providing help, as distinct from showing impatience or withholding information. Both men and women were found to be more dominant, more agentic toward people they supervised, and more submissive toward people above them in the hierarchy, and there were no sex differences in the amount of dominance or submissiveness shown toward each of these categories of others. In other words, men and women were fitting into the workplace hierarchy in essentially identical ways, with behavior tailored to the status differential between themselves and their interactive partners. This work is consistent with the earlier research in indicating that women in the workplace do not have difficulties handling supervisory responsibilities. The findings on "communality," however, show a different aspect of workplace dynamics: women were more communal with women than men were with men, regardless of status relationships. So here we do see some carry-over to the workplace of the same-sex interaction patterns of childhood.

If women have difficulty fitting into a corporate hierarchy, it probably has more to do with relationships upward in the hierarchy than with relationships downward with people they supervise. Promotions depend on cultivating informal connections with the people who will make the promotion decisions, and success at one's current level depends on having the support of these same people. A woman with a very high-ranking job in a corporate structure says:

> There's a lot of gamesmanship here. Business is much like a game, and there's always a person who is ahead, the winners and the losers, and the concept of "a team"—who's going to carry the ball on a project and who's going to follow up. I think all of this is really tough for women to understand. I don't think every man working for a corporation has a clear sense of the game either, but I do think that, in general, women haven't been exposed to it as much. (Milwid, 1990, p. 139)

As we have seen, the experience of finding, keeping, and improving a position in a hierarchy begins much earlier for males than for females, having its roots in the hierarchical structure of male childhood peer groups.

The reasons for the "glass ceiling" in the managerial hierarchy, and the inflexibility of promotion patterns at lower levels, have been analyzed and debated extensively. Sometimes the problem is one of simple discrimination, based on stereotypes concerning characteristics of women that are thought to interfere with successful performance in supervisory roles ("too emotional"; "can't be trusted"). Kanter's view was that the difficulties women have in rising to the higher levels of management have little to do with how well they handle supervisory functions once they are in a managerial role. Rather, they have to do with what qualities men at the highest levels look for when they decide whom to promote. Kanter notes that high-level jobs almost always involve high-risk decision-making. Speaking about the patterns that prevailed in the 1970s and earlier, she says, "The high uncertainty inherent in the most powerful managerial jobs made trust important, thus evoking a preference for confining power to people resembling those already in power. This cloning effect perpetuated discrimination at the top" (Kanter, 1993, p. 292). In traditional corporations with well-established career paths, she found that women were consistently disadvantaged in terms of power and opportunities.

Since the late 1970s the corporate climate has changed in important ways, and in some respects Kanter claims that the changes have made the barriers against women less formidable. Certain things, however, have hardly changed. Kanter refers to what she calls "the comfort factor": the tendency for higher-level executives to pick, for their confidants or most trusted aides, people with common backgrounds as well as similar experiences and tastes in life outside of work. She says that in the present leaner, less "command-oriented" corporate world

> the comfort factor is especially important in higher risk jobs. The best leadership positions are fraught with uncertainty: the judgment quotient is high and the measurable technical content low. The time frame for asserting the impact of decision is long, and the trust factor is more critical. Therefore the sometimes-unconscious bias toward people resembling those already in leadership positions has continued. The persistent problem for women and minorities has been to find someone who would take a chance on them, backing them for a risky assignment. (Kanter, 1993, p. 316)

I can only add that the gender element in the comfort factor, making people of each sex more comfortable with like-sex others, has a long history. So long as men occupy the highest positions in workplace hierarchies, this and related factors will mean that the "glass ceiling" is still a formidable barrier, despite the rapid changes that are going on in corporate culture.

Summary and Comment

There are very clear parallels between certain features of the relationships between men and women in the workplace and those that prevailed earlier in the life course between boys and girls, although there are differences as well. First and foremost among similarities is the widespread prevalence of gender segregation in the workplace, reminiscent of the ubiquitous formation of separate boys' and girls' playgroups in childhood. As we saw in Chapter 3, "borderwork" along the boundaries of same-sex childhood playgroups involves a certain amount of sexual teasing, a forerunner of some of the light and not-so-light sexual banter that goes on in the workplace. Also, boys' groups often engage in forms of talk about sex that foreshadow some of the attitudes toward women as sex objects that enter into men's orientation toward women in some work settings. Among children, friendly overtures across the gender divide are interpreted by peers as signs of romantic interest, and this, too, foreshadows some of the gossip in the workplace and the ambivalence people feel about making a social approach to a coworker of the other sex. There is also a divergence of interests between the sexes in childhood, such that boys and girls, in their same-sex groups, tend to talk about different things. These differences in interests persist into adulthood. Differences in interests, along with the barriers created by the possibility that friendly social overtures to people of the other sex will be misinterpreted, mean that people who have coworkers of both sexes gravitate toward others of their own sex for lunch and informal social chatting, just as they did in childhood.

In their same-sex playgroups, hierarchy and jockeying for dominance pervade the social structures created by boys, while egalitarian relationships, collaborative discourse, and democratic leadership styles are more characteristic of girls' groups. In the informal social life of children with their peers, girls generally do not have to try find a place in a male hierarchy, and boys do not have to adapt themselves to the female style of interaction. The issue as to which sex dominates the other seldom comes up, although adults do treat groups of boys as though they had more autonomous power than groups of girls. In a sense, then, the workplace is a new playing field, where previous social experience does not provide a clear precedent for how the two sexes will fit into a joint hierarchy. Although we might have thought that female inexperience with hierarchies would put them at a disadvantage in functioning within a workplace hierarchy, there is no evidence that women have difficulty handling supervisory responsibilities once they have obtained jobs in which they can exercise them. Thus their socialization in female groups has not meant that they lack the qualities needed for working with people on the lower rungs of the ladder in the workplace hierarchy. Women do appear, however, to have more difficulty jockeying for the attention and patronage of those higher up, and the fact remains that men usually cluster toward the top, and women toward the bottom, of these hierarchies. If there are any echoes from childhood here, they probably reflect the tendency of existing male hierarchies to perpetuate themselves via exclusionary and mutually trusting male networks.

To some of my readers, the analyses above will no doubt seem old-fashioned. Many professional women are now part of organizations—law firms, medical clinics, some university departments—where men and women work together and have equal status. Where less elite jobs are concerned we have all noticed, too, that certain jobs are unisex—both sexes work at check-out counters in the supermarket; both men and women staff airline ticket counters. We have become accustomed to the idea that a judge, or a pilot, or a bus or taxi driver, can be a woman. The world of work is beginning to seem considerably more gender integrated than it once was.

Much of what has been said in this chapter about barriers to occupational integration pertains to situations in which a small number of women have entered workplaces that were formerly all-male. It is reasonable to believe that as increasing numbers of women enter a workplace, forming a critical mass, it will come to seem more natural for them to be there—men will become accustomed to their presence, and many of the tensions that characterized the initial entry of a few women should fade away. The changes in attitudes and behavior that have accompanied women's increasing representation in many occupations serve to underline the fact that the structural constraints discussed earlier are not absolute. They can be considerably modified. The fact that there is a generational shift in attitudes, with younger people taking gender equality in the workplace more for granted, also holds promise of greater cross-sex acceptance in the future.

Nevertheless, there are still some sobering impediments to change. Although much of the material I have used in this chapter was published in the 1980s or even earlier, so that it might reflect a past reality more than a present one, more recent studies (such as Reskin and Roos, 1990; Hanson and Pratt, 1995; and Sayed and Tzannatos, 1995) have continued to document widespread segregation, both horizontal and vertical. The structural constraints of gender undoubtedly remain stronger in blue-collar settings and business offices than in the academic and other professional settings with which I—and probably most of my readers—have most of our day-to-day experiences.

I would hazard the guess, too, that integration is proceeding faster in occupations where people do not interact closely on a day-to-day basis, even though they are working in the same organization at the same status level. Men and women selling real estate or insurance, for example, may meet together in occasional staff meetings, but most of their work is carried out individually with minimal coordination with the work of other salespeople. Some kinds of computerized work can now be done at home, quite separately from that of other same-level employees. The acid test comes when the side-by-side work of same-level employees must be coordinated in face-to-face interaction. Such coordination is beginning to be achieved in mixed-sex teams in certain settings, notably in police forces and the military services, where the command structure is strong enough to permit a pro-integration policy to have some success in overriding the gendered structural constraints that would otherwise have a strong impact. Nevertheless, there are well-publicized instances where sexual tensions have a disruptive impact in these settings.

10

Men and Women As Parents

When men and women become parents, they start the long process of forming a kind of relationship that is in many ways quite new, compared with those they have experienced at early periods in their lives. True, as young children they were members of a parent-child relationship, but to be the child in such a relationship is vastly different from being the parent. New parents have experienced intimacy in their spousal relationship, so they are not strangers to intimacy, but the kind of intimacy called for in the relationship with a child is different: there is intense love, but there is a much larger component of protection, nurturance, and empathy, as well as control and discipline, than is involved in a relationship with another adult. Thus, like the other relationships discussed so far, a parent-child relationship is constructed over time, involving the transformation and adaptation of existing interactive dispositions, not simply the transfer of an unmodified set of relationships skills already developed in other settings.

In this chapter, I will be concerned with two main issues: the way in which the roles and relationships of the two parents vis-à-vis each other are affected by parenthood, and the nature of the relationships each parent forms with children. With respect to the second issue, it will be of interest to see how, and whether, the sex-differentiated styles of interaction apparent in other contexts manifest themselves in the context of parenting.

It has been a major claim of this book that boys and girls, or men and women, have different relationships and different styles of interacting with others of their own sex, as compared with persons of the other sex. The reader might expect, then, that in this chapter I will present a strong contrast between the way parents relate to children of their own sex versus children of the other sex. This issue will be discussed, but the main message of the chapter will be that although the two parents may bring different skills and different styles to the parent-child relationship, their adaptation to the parental role involves primarily reacting to the qualities of children as children, rather than to the gender match between parent and child. At least, I believe this is true when children are young.

The birth of children profoundly changes the lives of an adult couple. In some ways, the arrival of children might be expected to bring a husband and wife closer together. They have taken on a major new joint enterprise, with all that this means in the way of shared objectives, shared interests, and the family-centered activities generated by joint child-rearing. There can be new levels of understanding and appreciation of each other, too: men who have been present at the birth of their children not only report what an intensely moving experience it is for them, but often say that they have gained new respect for what their wives must go through for the sake of bringing a family into being. For women, the father's presence and support at the time of birth can signal a valued promise of his commitment to the child-rearing enterprise. But whatever increased emotional closeness the birth of a child may bring about, there seems to be an almost inevitable shift toward greater differentiation in the roles of men and women when the "family" composed of only a man and woman is expanded to include children.

The Division of Child-Care Responsibilities

In all known societies, women, whether they are working outside the home or not, assume most of the day-to-day responsibility for child care. In traditional societies and subcultures, considerable division of labor between husband and wife usually already exists before the birth of children, regardless of whether both are working outside the home; thus in many childless households, the woman carries more responsibility for household duties while the man carries the major responsibility for bread-winning. A child's arrival augments the discrepancy by adding many more new functions to the mother's than to the father's agenda.

Even among modern young couples where both are working and where both expect, before the first child is born, that they will share child-care duties equally, the reality usually turns out to be different.[1] The arrival of an infant affects the daily life of the mother much more than that of the father.[2] The mother assumes a larger share of household duties—not only child care, but housework as well—while the father may increase his working hours so as to augment the family income. Those who have attempted to reverse the traditional pattern, with a father staying home with an infant or young child while the mother works, have found that this arrangement is seldom maintained for any substantial period of time (see Russell, 1982; Radin, 1988).

The fact that women do the lion's share of child-rearing has been thoroughly documented. Stone (1972) reported the amount of time spent in child care by housewives, employed women, and employed men in 15 countries, showing that while employed mothers spent considerably less time with their children than did housewives, they still consistently spent much more time than did employed fathers. Stone found that when fathers were with their children, their wives were usually present as well and doing most of the child care, while women (both those employed and housewives) spent considerable time alone with the child, without the child's father being present. More recent reports from modern Western countries tell the same story. For example, Belsky and colleagues (1984) observed 72 pairs of parents at home with their infants. They found that the mothers interacted much more frequently with the infant, not just for routine caretaking but also with stimulation, soothing, and displays of affection, while fathers were more likely to read or watch TV.[3]

It has been found consistently that the differences between the involvement of mothers and fathers with their children declines as the children grow older, so that it is with infants and toddlers that the mother most predominates as the primary parent. But even when the children have reached school age, it is still the mothers who take most responsibility for caring for the children and directing their daily lives (Russell and Russell, 1987).

Of course, there have been many widowers who have successfully reared children, but often they have done so with the help of female relatives or hired female housekeepers, particularly while the children were young.[4] In recent years, there has been a great deal of talk about the "new fatherhood," and it has become something of a middle-class ideal that fathers should participate much more in the day-to-day lives of their children than traditional fathers once did. And indeed, we can all point to families in which young fathers are intensely involved—where they do an equal share, when they are home from work, of diapering, feeding, and bathing children; where they may have turned down promotions to jobs that involved a lot of travel, so that they could spend time with their families; or where they have taken extended time off from work to care for children while their wives complete education or advance their careers. Such cases are the exception, however. When mothers of young children go to work, there is usually little increase in the amount of time the fathers spend with the children—in one study, the increase was only 45 minutes per week (Barnett and Baruch, 1988). When mothers go to work, or increase their working time from part time to full time, what appears to happen is that they usually hire substitute caregivers—other women—rather than relying upon their husbands to fill the child-care gap. There are many exceptions, of course: for example, families in which the two parents work different shifts so that there is always one parent available for child care while the other works (Presser, 1989).

Among some fathers there is active resistance to taking a larger role in child-rearing—perhaps more commonly (or more openly) in traditional societies. A recent newspaper article (*New York Times,* October 6, 1996) on the declining birthrate in Japan reported male disinclination to participate in child care as a factor influencing the child-bearing decisions of working Japanese wives. One woman reported: "Our fourth child was on condition that my husband help more. But then after I had the baby, he kept saying he was too busy, so I ended up doing all the work by myself." The director of the Tokyo Institute of Population Problems said, "The main reason for the decline in fertility is that women have advanced. They want to get ahead in the world, but they're also asked to care for children and do all the housework. Men never do that stuff." The fact is that the day-to-day routines of caring for young children, however rewarding they may be in some respects, are often onerous or boring, and incompatible with many attractive adult pursuits. Over the centuries, people who could afford it have left much of their children's care to servants, or have delegated it to older siblings. In male-dominant societies, it is a kind of work which men can usually manage to avoid, leaving it, by default, to women.

In recent years, there have probably been overall decreases, rather than increases, in male participation in the lives of their children. Griswold (1993) refers to what he calls men's "flight from the family" during the last several decades, involving lower rates of marriage (and more fathering of children without marriage), deferral of marriage until an older age, and increased divorce. Since mothers retain custody of the children after divorce in the large majority of families, fathers' involvement in day-to-day child-rearing necessarily diminishes in most divorced families, and may indeed cease altogether. Furthermore, divorce usually means a shift from fathers to mothers of much of the traditionally male responsibility for supporting the children financially (Maccoby, Buchanan, Mnookin, and Dornbusch, 1993). It is a reasonable conjecture that while there may have been increased variability in the role of fathers—with some fathers becoming more involved with children, others less—there has been little overall shift of child-rearing responsibilities from mothers to fathers during the last half-century, and the shift may actually have been in the other direction.

Lamb and colleagues (Lamb, Pleck, Charnov, and Levine, 1988) have made a useful distinction among several components of parental involvement: *interaction* is a parent's direct contact with a child through caretaking and shared activities; *availability* is a parent's being present or accessible to the child whether or not interaction is occurring; and *responsibility* is the role a parent takes in making sure the child is taken care of, and in mobilizing resources for the child (arranging for medical care or substitute child care, for instance). Reviewing a wide range of studies, Lamb and colleagues report that in intact two-parent families fathers are involved in about one third as much interaction with children as are mothers; that fathers are "available" to the children about half as often as mothers; and that the largest discrepancy concerns *responsibility*, where mothers are nearly ten times as likely as fathers to be the one who leaves work to take a child to the doctor, who stays home with the children when no one else is available, who arranges for nonparental child care, or who takes the children to lessons, sports practice, or social events.

Explanations for the Discrepant Parental Roles

Why do men and women not participate equally in day-to-day child-rearing activities? There are a number of possibilities. Probably, no one explanation is sufficient. Several factors undoubtedly conjoin to produce powerful forces toward gender differentiation at this important stage of life.

Sex Differences in Reproductive Biology

In Chapter 5, I noted the sociobiological claim that women's greater involvement in child-rearing follows naturally from their greater "parental investment"—the fact that they can produce fewer children than men can during a reproductive lifetime, and consequently need to expend extra effort to ensure the survival of the children they do produce. Whatever the validity of this sociobiological inference, there can be no doubt that women are the ones who invest nine months in the gestation of each child, and a further period for lactation. The male investment, though equal from a genetic standpoint, is minuscule by comparison when it comes to the investment of time and physical resources. This difference in reproductive roles is the paramount biological distinction between men and women.

In mammalian species, it is clear that the differences in reproductive functions are closely linked with the greater female role in nurturing the young. Although there is considerable variation among the different species of nonhuman primates with respect to how actively males participate in interaction with infants, the bulk of caretaking is done by females.[5] The greater female responsiveness to infants begins before females are old enough to breed: juvenile females show a great interest in the infants born within a troop, while young males show little or none.[6]

Hormonal priming. As we saw in Chapter 5, there is some evidence (from research with nonhuman mammals) that the female hormones present at the time of parturition help to "prime" maternal behavior. But even without the aid of these hormones, virgin females will display maternal behavior—retrieving young who stray from the nest, crouching over them to keep them warm, and so on—merely in response to the presence of infant animals of their own species. These responses are stronger in females who have not given birth than they are in males, suggesting that females have some predispositions for caretaking that do not depend on the hormones of pregnancy and delivery, and that are not shared by males.

Lactation. Female lactation is a function that requires an enormous output of calories and requires the mobilization of extra capacity from heart, kidneys, and liver. Breast-feeding creates a biologically based link between a mother and her offspring. Not only does the infant need the mother's milk, but the mother needs to nurse; at least until the infant has been weaned, missed feedings can be a source of considerable discomfort to nursing mothers, and a feeding provides physical satisfaction to both participants. In addition, of course, breast-feeding provides the opportunity for intimate social interaction: touching and holding, mutual gazing, the exchange of vocalizations. There is evidence that breast-feeding does help to get mother-infant interaction off to a good start.[7] Breast-feeding, then, can be counted as a bond-supporting factor that is available only to mothers, not to fathers.

Responsiveness to infants' cries. What about other predisposing conditions eliciting parenting behavior? An infant's cry is a powerful stimulus: adults of both sexes find it distressing. Do men and women respond to it differently? In some early laboratory work, Frodi and colleagues (1978) enrolled adults (all of whom had young infants of their own) in a study in which they listened to tape recordings of the cries of unfamiliar infants. The subjects' levels of emotional arousal were monitored (via measures of heart rate and galvanic skin responses). The researchers found that both mothers and fathers responded with increased emotional arousal to the infants' cries, and equally so. Similarly, when the physiological responses of children and adolescents (aged 8 or 14) to infants' cries were monitored, boys and girls responded as had the adults (Frodi and Lamb, 1978). But when these children and adolescents were left briefly in a waiting room where there was an infant in a playpen, the girls were more interested in the infant, and more responsive to it, than were the boys (Feldman, Nash, and Cutrona, 1977, reported the same thing). The authors concluded that parents of the two sexes are equally primed physiologically to respond to infant signals, but that women, more than men, are socially conditioned to respond to their own arousal with nurturant behavior. Thus they attributed the similarity between men and women in affective arousal to "nature," and the difference in behavioral responsiveness to "nurture."[8] However, there is no reason why "nature" could not have primed women to respond more strongly than men with infant-directed behavior, whether or not they are equally aroused physiologically when an infant cries. In other words, the degree of arousal is only one possible mediator of sex difference in responsiveness to infants, and there may be others. The issue remains an open one.

The elements discussed above, taken together, mean that mothers, on average, may have somewhat stronger parental "instincts" when it comes to responding to young infants. Certainly, many women experience a strong upsurge of maternal feelings when they first see and hold their newborn infants. But many women do not report such feelings, and many men—especially those who have been present at the birth—do experience a flood of strong loving and protective feelings when they first hold their newborn child. The research is not definitive when it comes to comparing the strength of maternal and paternal instincts, but even if women's nurturant responses have stronger physiological underpinnings, it is likely that men, too, have some biologically based predispositions to respond nurturantly to infants and young children. These "instincts," however, like all instincts, require the presence of specific eliciting conditions for their manifestation. In the case of parenting instincts, the necessary eliciting condition is the close, continuing presence of a needy infant. All human cultures put mothers in close contact with their infants from the time of birth onward. Cultures vary enormously with respect to the amount of contact fathers have with infants, but usually it is much less than for mothers, so that whatever readiness fathers have for infant care is less often activated.

Culture and Social Influences

In Chapters 6 and 7, I discussed how cultural practices—via direct socialization pressures and widely held cultural beliefs—affect the development of the major gendered phenomena of childhood. But I did not consider there the kind of social shaping processes that might be preparing young people for their future responsibilities as parents. As far as the cognitive component is concerned, it is clear that it would be impossible for a child to grow up without acquiring some understanding of whatever scripts that child's society specifies for the roles of the two sexes in parenting. As we have seen, women take the primary role in child care in all known cultures and subcultures. Girls therefore grow up with the expectation that they will take on the major responsibility for the day-to-day care of children when they are adult, and boys grow up with the expectation that they will become the family's major breadwinner. There is considerable variation among cultures and subcultures with respect to the involvement of men in the care of children, but there is relatively little variation in the predominant role of women. It is as though cultures respond to the universal biological role of women in child-bearing and lactation by setting up universal cultural arrangements that place women and children together, not only in infancy but beyond. Thus cultures augment women's primary biological role in childbirth and early nurturance with a heavy overlay of cultural expectations and demands.

At the same time, cultures place demands upon men to "provision" women and children—to provide economic support for them. As Lamb and colleagues say, "In almost all cultures, direct paternal involvement is a discretionary activity, whereas provisioning is mandatory" (Lamb, Pleck, Charnov, and Levine, 1987). Griswold, in his book *Fatherhood in America* (1993), traces the role of fathers through the nineteenth and twentieth centuries, showing what a central place bread-winning has occupied in men's family roles. He claims that considerable reorganization and confusion in men's fathering role has resulted from women's rapidly increasing participation in bread-winning during the past several decades.

It is not possible to document all the myriad ways in which societies shape children of the two sexes toward divergent parenting roles, but a few can be pointed out as illustrations. Foremost is the modeling provided by parents and other adults whom children have an opportunity to observe. There is direct "training," too, for gender-specific future roles: Little girls are given dolls to play with far more frequently than boys, and adults often discourage a boy from playing with dolls when he shows signs of wanting to. In middle childhood and early adolescence, girls are far more likely to be assigned as baby-sitters and mothers' helpers. Although the requirements placed upon boys as preparation for fatherhood are somewhat less clear, their training as apprentices for income-producing jobs can be seen in this light.

Social pressures continue into adulthood and emanate from many sources other than an individual's family of origin. Fathers who do take a primary role in child care while their wives work run the risk of scornful or contemptuous reactions from other men (Russell and Russell, 1982; Huang, Elden, and Fransson, 1984), and may find that they are not readily accepted into informal groups of mothers who talk to each other in public places, such as parks, where they have taken their children to play.

The legal system embodies traditional beliefs about differential parental roles: When couples with children divorce, it is a common assumption made by both parents (as well as by many attorneys and mediators) that the children will remain in the primary custody of their mothers. Despite recent modifications of custody law toward greater gender neutrality, fathers probably need to have an especially strong claim (or mothers an especially weak one) if a father is to gain custody in most jurisdictions (Maccoby and Mnookin, 1992). At the same time, noncustodial fathers are far more often ordered to pay child support to their ex-spouses than are noncustodial mothers. Although this primarily reflects differences in the ability of the two parents to pay, it probably also reflects some cultural assumptions about which parent is more responsible for providing economic support.[9]

The Economics of Family Support

I noted above that even when young couples plan to share child-care duties equally, they find that in practice it is difficult to do so. The practicalities of optimizing family income during the period when young children are present in the home seem to press many families toward a differentiation of maternal and paternal roles. If one parent is to reduce out-of-home work time to care for children, it is clearly desirable, from the standpoint of family income, for it to be the parent who earns less, and this is the wife in a large majority of families. To make up for her lost income, the husband not infrequently works longer hours, which increases the discrepancy in their time with the children.

It would take us too far afield to examine the multiple reasons why women's incomes are so much lower than men's, but in the context of couples embarking on child-rearing, it is pertinent that husbands are usually several years older than their wives, and have therefore usually accumulated greater job experience and become qualified for higher earnings. In addition, husbands on the average have at least a few years' more education than their wives. Some of this additional education contributes to job skills and job eligibility. These factors together imply a greater investment in work on the part of the husband in many—perhaps most—working couples.

Childbirth necessitates a period away from work for mothers, not for fathers. Even for women who go back to work as soon as possible, a brief period is required for recovery from childbirth, and if there are complications during the pregnancy, work must sometimes be interrupted even before the child is born. Add to this the inconvenience of returning to work while breast-feeding, and it is evident that the intrusions of childbearing upon work are much greater for women than for men.

Men, on the average, hold jobs that are less compatible with the demands of child care than are women's jobs. Many women have chosen schoolteaching as a career because it is easier to coordinate the time schedules of schoolteaching than those of other jobs with the requirements for being at home with children (for instance, summer vacations would coincide).[10] It has been noted that women tend to "discount" their jobs so as to permit juggling work and child-rearing, taking jobs that are closer to home, that don't involve unexpected overtime work or out-of-town travel, that permit taking time off for care of the sick (Joshi, 1984; Funder, 1986). We can see a circular process here: working mothers choose jobs that are compatible with child-rearing; then these jobs become labeled "women's work," and women drift into them whether or not they have children. Then, once they are in these jobs and have children, they become more likely to carry out a larger share of the child-rearing responsibilities because their jobs permit them to do so more easily than do their husbands' jobs.

There's another kind of circular process at work here: The fact that women more than men reduce their working time, and interrupt their career trajectories, when children are born (because the husbands earn more, or because the mother wants to breast-feed, or for whatever other reason) produces further discrepancies between the mother and father with respect to their viability in the workforce—their career progression and their earning power. These further discrepancies add to the likelihood that the mothers will be the ones who continue to perform most of the child-care duties as the children grow older.

To summarize: biological factors, social and cultural pressures, and the requirements for economic support of families all press parents in the same direction: toward greater involvement of mothers than fathers in the day-to-day care of children, particularly when children are young. Clearly, this role differentiation is multiply determined, even overdetermined.

Mothers' and Fathers' Parenting Styles

To what extent do men and women bring different skills, different styles, to their interaction with children? Over and above the question of how much time they spend with their children, do mothers and fathers perform different parental functions or carry out their parental roles in different ways? If so, do any such differences appear to be related to the experiences men and women have had at an earlier time in the same-sex groups of childhood?

Some years ago, Parsons and Bales (1955) wrote about leadership in small task-oriented groups, and claimed that two different leaders often emerged, one who carried out the "instrumental" leadership of the group and one who specialized in dealing with the affective or "expressive" issues that arose during the group process.[11] Parsons (1955) analyzed the family in terms of this theorizing about small groups, claiming that fathers usually carry out the instrumental leadership functions, mothers the expressive ones. In the light of what we know today about family functioning, this analysis fails badly. Mothers do, of course, provide nurturance and comfort, and express a great deal of affection to their children. But they also carry out many management functions for the family. They are usually the ones who establish the timetable for children's meals, baths, and bedtimes, assign household chores, arrange for out-of-home child care, and organize the family's recreational activities. When fathers are at home, they may play with the children, but they usually leave to mothers the job of directing the children through the routines of the day. Mothers, then, assume both "instrumental" and "expressive" leadership where the children are concerned, and fathers are at least as "expressive" as mothers, being not only playful, but at least as warm and affectionate toward the children as mothers are (Collins and Russell, 1991; see also Bronstein, 1988, for a summary of some cross-cultural evidence). There are, however, some differences in the styles mothers and fathers employ when interacting with their children, and as we will see, these differences do indeed seem to be related to the social history that persons of the two sexes bring to the parenting process.

Roughness of Play

Even with infants, fathers are more "physical" in their interactive style (see Park and Tinsley, 1981, and Bronstein, 1988, for reviews). This does not mean merely that they are more likely to toss an infant in the air, although fathers do occasionally do so. More often it means that fathers' "games" with babies are likely to involve such activities as moving their limbs ("bicycling" their legs, for instance) in ways that are arousing to the child. Yogman (1981), observing a small group of parents interacting with their infants in a laboratory, reported that this kind of arousal was involved in 70 percent of the father-infant games, and only 4 percent of the mother-infant games. Fathers have also been observed to do more bouncing and lifting of the baby. Mothers' games are usually more "distal": they involve exchanges of smiles, glances, and vocalizations, mutual imitation, or demonstrations of toys by the mother. As the infant grows older, the mother is more likely than the father to use toys as a way to initiate interaction, while the father's style moves more in the direction of the rough-and-tumble play young boys often indulge in.

As children grow into the preschool years, these stylistic differences between the parents are maintained. An example from Jacklin's and my research (Maccoby and Jacklin, 1983) will illustrate the point. When the children in one of our longitudinal cohorts had reached the age of 45 months, we visited the families' homes, bringing along a box of toys. The toys were spread out on the floor, and each parent in turn played with the child for 15 minutes (while the other parent was being interviewed in another room). The parent and child were free to select and use the toys in any way they chose. Some of the play that occurred could be described as rough-and-tumble—chasing, rolling, tickling, play-boxing, or play-wrestling. Both parents were more likely to engage in this kind of play with sons than with daughters; but, more pertinent to the present topic, fathers were considerably more likely than mothers to engage in such play, and this was true whether the father was playing with a son or a daughter. Each parent was rated on how "arousing" the play session seemed to be overall, and father-child play was rated as considerably more arousing than mother-child play.

Both boys and girls seemed to enjoy this kind of play with their fathers very much. In one study (Ross and Taylor, 1989), mothers and fathers experimentally adopted either a "maternal" or a "paternal" (physical and active) playstyle with their three-year-old sons. The young boys reacted especially positively to the physical, active playstyle, whether it was offered by the father or the mother. (The study did show, though, that it was easier for fathers than mothers to display this style.) Unfortunately, this study did not include little girls, so we don't know how they would have reacted to the different parental styles.

Not surprisingly, children usually do not seem to react to their fathers as though their greater size and strength made them in any way threatening. We may infer that most fathers have learned to calibrate the vigor of their play appropriately to what the child can tolerate. Fagot and Hagan (1991) made an interesting observation concerning the play of parents with five-year-olds: these researchers observed 172 five-year-olds at home when both parents were present, and one aspect of parent-child interaction they recorded was "large motor activity." They found that fathers were more likely than mothers to respond positively to such activity in a child, whether the child was a boy or a girl. Thus fathers not only initiate such play; they respond positively to an invitation from a child for such play.

Sensitivity to the Child's Signals and Emotional States

Are mothers in some sense more "tuned in" to their children's needs, moods, ways of thinking? Can they read a child's signals more accurately? There is evidence that, on average, they can. During the first two years of a child's life, communication between parent and child is accomplished largely through nonverbal, affective channels. Infants respond to tones of voice, facial expressions, and bodily contact. Gradually, joint routines are developed between child and caretaker so that holding and touching are replaced by more distal interchanges. Most of the observations of this kind of development have been done with mother-child pairs, so there is little information to go on to tell us whether the father-child interchanges generally develop in the same ways. What little evidence there is suggests that fathers are less likely to hold infants close to their bodies, and less likely to hold them face-to-face for exchanges of looks, smiles, and vocalizations (Field, 1978; Hwang, 1986; Lamb, Frodi, Frodi, and Huang, 1982). Infants, for their part, may be more "tuned in" to mothers' than to fathers' voices, although the evidence is meager.[12]

When the two parents are observed at home interacting with a young child, any differences in their responsiveness to the child are likely to be a function of the tacit agreement between the parents as to which of them is responsible for caretaking at any given time. This, of course, is most often the mother (even when the father is at home), and consequently if she is the one who gets up and goes to an infant when the child fusses, this does not necessarily imply a difference in interactive style. More insight as to styles can probably be obtained in situations in which only one parent at a time is present to interact with the child. A study by Power (1985) illustrates what is revealed in this sort of comparison: Power videotaped short sessions of play between a mother and child alone, and the father and child alone. The children in this case were infants who were either 7, 10, or 13 months old. Earlier work (Schaffer and Crook, 1980) had shown that a mother was more successful in getting an infant to engage an object in a desired way if the mother carefully monitored the infant's attentional state, and timed her efforts to engage the infant according to where the infant was looking and what the infant was doing at the time of the maternal intervention. Power (1985) wanted to see whether mothers and fathers differed with respect to this kind of sensitivity. He reports his findings as follows: "When attempting to influence their infant's behavior, mothers were more likely to follow up on their infant's natural curiosity . . . while fathers . . . often disregarded the infant's cues of interest and attention and often directly interfered with ongoing infant behavior" (p. 1522). In short, the mothers in this study were more likely than fathers to take an infant's attentional state into account and coordinate their own actions to suit it; perhaps in consequence, mothers were more successful with the 13-month-old infants in influencing the child's behavior in the desired direction.[13]

Communication with a young child gradually shifts toward the verbal level as the child acquires language, although the microscopic level of communication illustrated in the Power study never disappears from the coordinated behavior of intimate pairs. Both mothers and fathers adapt their speech so that it is more understandable to children: speak more slowly, with simpler constructions, and use more tonal variations. There is some evidence, however, that mothers may fine-tune their utterances more closely than fathers to the needs of an individual child. Gleason (1987) reports that the mother's mean length of utterance is more closely related to that of the child she is addressing than is the father's, and that fathers used more unfamiliar, difficult, or specialized words.

The child's first words may only roughly approximate adult forms, and some children develop their own idiosyncratic words for certain objects or actions before they have fully graduated into the lexicon of older speakers. In addition, syntax and enunciation at this early stage can be rudimentary in the extreme. The consequence is that a young child's early language can be difficult to understand. I remember giving my 24-month-old granddaughter her lunch, and being puzzled when she said, "Mo ahpadoo eehee Numy." My daughter, overhearing from a neighboring room, interpreted: "She wants more apple juice in her cup." Gleason (1987) summarizes data from several studies of the verbal interactions of young children with their parents, and reports that mothers are considerably more able than fathers to understand the early utterances of young children (see also Weist and Stebbins, 1972). Of course, this difference surely reflects, at least in part, the fact that most mothers have spent more time with their toddlers.

Fathers' mini-"conversations" with young children are shorter than mothers'. When a father and a young child are talking together, there are fewer "conversational turns" than is the case between a mother and her child. As Mannle and Tomasello (1987) have shown, this happens in part because fathers are less likely to maintain a joint focus of attention with a child, and because mothers' replies to a child are more contingent—more directly related to what the child has just said or done. The result is that mother-child conversations become more reciprocal and extended (see Mannle and Tomasello, 1987, for a summary of studies).

Reciprocity versus Power-Assertion

As children grow older, this reciprocal quality in the exchanges between mothers and children takes new forms. One form is thematic play, in which mother and child take reciprocal imaginary roles, such as customer and sales clerk in playing "store." Role-integrated thematic play has been found to be more common in mother-child pairs than father-child pairs (Maccoby and Jacklin, 1983).

Sometimes mother-child reciprocity takes on the quality of bargaining or negotiation when the mother wants the child to do something and the child resists. An example (from Perlman, 1984, reported in Gleason, 1987):

Mother: Now I'm going to cut your roast beef, honey.
Boy: I don't want to eat it.
Mother: Well, I thought you liked roast beef!
Boy: I'm not going to eat it.
Mother: Why not?
Boy: I'm too full.
Mother: . ... Okay, if you don't eat this roast beef you have no more twinkies. You understand that?
Boy: I'll eat one.
Mother: No, you'll eat half of it. I'll cut this much off.
Father: You just take it.

Clearly, the mother's responses to the child conveyed a willingness to have a discussion with him about what she was demanding and how much compliance was really expected, although she did eventually insist on a modified demand. The father intervened with an imperative without doing any prior bargaining with the child.

There is now extensive evidence that fathers use more imperatives and other forms of power-assertion in talking to children.[14] In Gleason's (1987) observations, fathers used unqualified imperatives twice as often as mothers, saying such things as "Do it! Now!" "Come here," or "Put that down." Mothers, by contrast, were more likely to soften their demands by making them more polite (saying please), using endearments, or putting them in the form of a question ("Would you take your plate off the table, sweetie?"). Fathers' power-assertive style is further illustrated by the fact that they interrupt their children more frequently than mothers do (Greif, 1980).

Gleason also reports that fathers at home are more likely to use disparaging remarks and name-calling with their children: one of the fathers in his study called his son a "dingaling"; another called a child a "nutcake," and still another, during a laboratory session, called his son a "wise guy." Threats and pejorative names of this sort were more likely to be directed by fathers to sons than to daughters.

Which parental style is more effective? When it comes to getting the child to do what is wanted, the father's may be, at least in the short term, though the evidence is mixed. Hetherington, Cox, and Cox (1982), observing both intact and divorced families, found that on the average four-year-old children complied more readily to a father's demand than a mother's. Lytton (1979), observing a large sample of boys aged 2½ years at home with their parents, also found greater immediate compliance to fathers' than mothers' demands and directions. We should be aware, however, that there is more than one way to get compliance from young children. Parpal and Maccoby (1985) found that if preschoolers and their mothers first played a game in which the mother followed the child's lead, the child's subsequent compliance to maternal demands was enhanced. Thus mothers' more responsive or "tuned-in" style can be seen as a mode of supporting a child's willingness to enter into a relationship of reciprocal cooperation—something that is associated with a child's complying with parental standards, perhaps especially when the parent is out of sight. More recent work by Kochanska (1995) has underscored this point. Of course, most parents—both mothers and fathers—use both forms of control, depending on the situation. It is only that the balance between the two forms is tipped more in favor of power-assertion among fathers.

As children grow beyond the preschool years, the interactions between mothers and children continue to have a more intimate, more give-and-take quality. Russell and Russell (1987), observing a group of Australian six-year-olds and their parents in their homes, indicated that the interactions of mother and child had a greater element of mutuality or two-way exchange than the interactions between father and child. Mothers gave more information and directives, but they were more likely than fathers to consult the children's point of view before deciding on a directive (see also Bronstein, Duncan, Frankowski, and D'Ari, 1992). Reciprocally, the children expressed their feelings more openly to their mothers, bargained more about their directives, and made more independent decisions when dealing with their mothers than their fathers.

The give-and-take quality of mother-child exchanges is manifested in a readier understanding of each other's meanings. This was shown in the longitudinal study I did with Jacklin when the children had reached the age of six.[15] Each child engaged in a referential communication task (Dickson, 1979) with each parent. The task was designed to assess how accurately a "sender" could convey a message to a "receiver." In some trials, the parent was the sender, with the child as a receiver; in other trials, the roles were reversed. In each trial, the sender's task was to describe one of four ambiguous, hard-to-describe pictures, and the receiver was to choose the intended picture from a matching set. In the case of an incorrect guess by the receiver, the sender could provide more clues, the receiver could ask questions, and the receiver then made another guess. When an error was made, it could be due to lack of clarity in the sender's message, lack of attention or understanding on the part of the receiver, or some combination of these factors. The error score is thus a joint score that reflects the communicative competence of the parent-child pair. The mother-child pairs were more successful, on the average, than the father-child pairs in understanding each other. Furthermore, there were fewer communication errors between parents and daughters than between parents and sons. The upshot of these two factors was that the mother-daughter pairs were the most successful, the father-son pairs the least.

The work reported above suggests that when mothers are interacting one-on-one with children of early school age, the interaction is, on the average, more reciprocal, more integrated with the child's ongoing stream of activities, than is the case for father-child interaction. A picture emerges from these studies of mothers being more likely than fathers to chat informally with their children, and listen to them. In the process they glean information about the children's friends, whereabouts, preferences, and problems. It is not surprising, then, that when children have reached adolescence, they report that their mothers know them better than their fathers do (Youniss and Smollar, 1985). A parent's intimate knowledge about a child has consequences: it permits the parent to supervise and monitor the child's activities more effectively, and to be aware of early warnings of impending trouble.

In a study of divorced parents and their children I conducted with Robert Mnookin, we found that custodial fathers reported somewhat more difficulty than custodial mothers in supervising their children's health habits (nutrition, cleanliness). These fathers also found it somewhat more difficult to keep track of their children's whereabouts, friends, and activities (Maccoby and Mnookin, 1992, p. 207). The adolescent children of these divorced parents also reported that custodial fathers were less likely to "really know" what the young people were doing in their out-of-school hours than was the case for custodial mothers. And weak monitoring by the custodial parent was linked to various forms of problem behavior (Buchanan, Maccoby, and Dornbusch, 1992).

We should be aware, however, that the average differences between mothers and fathers are not large; and the mother's reciprocal style is not the only avenue to intimacy with a child. A father's history of playful interaction may be an alternative pathway. A number of writers (for instance, Kochanska et al., 1997) have stressed the importance of shared positive affect in the growth of intimacy between the members of a pair.

Confrontation and Discipline

The parental role calls for supportive caretaking, responsiveness to children's needs, teaching that is geared to the child's capacities, and the maintenance of positive moods through play and humor. But it also calls for being firmly directive, and for imposing discipline and restrictions when occasion demands. Do mothers and fathers differ in their readiness to take up the "tougher" aspect of the parental role? It might be expected that fathers would be more comfortable confronting their children when necessary, given their interactive style. Yet following up on demands and imposing restrictions may be seen as integral parts of the managerial functions that are more commonly carried out by mothers, especially when children are young. The fact is that mothers are the ones who more often impose discipline, partly because they are the ones who are most often present when the need arises, but also because they are considered to be the responsible parent even when both parents are home. The fabled threat "Wait till your father comes home! *He'll* deal with you" is apparently quite rare, although his support of the mother's authority is no doubt implicitly present much of the time. Still, imposing discipline may be subjectively more difficult for one parent than the other.

When the children in Jacklin's and my longitudinal study were six years old, parents were interviewed about their usual relationships with the children at home. They were asked about how they felt about making demands and enforcing discipline. Specifically, the questions were: "Does it bother you at all to enforce discipline with (child's name)?" And: "Suppose you want (child's name) to do something, and you know in advance that he/she is not going to want to do it. Do you think it's best to go ahead with it, or wait till you will have a better chance of getting cooperation?"

Most mothers and fathers fell toward the midpoint of our 5-point scale on the wisdom of pressing a demand in the face of possible opposition. They were likely to say their decision depended on such factors as whether the child was tired, how important the demand was, and so forth. But mothers were somewhat more likely than fathers to hesitate to enforce discipline, and to refrain from making a demand in order to avoid a confrontation. One mother said, talking about her daughter, "Well, if what I am going to do could be put off to a better time I would probably put it off, because everybody would enjoy it rather than have an argument." Her husband, however, answering the same question, said, "I would say that, knowing the way we conduct our lives—pretty busy—probably we would go ahead and do it anyway whether she liked it or not." Speaking about her son, another mother said, "I think he and I have a pretty good relationship. There is a certain power struggle that goes on periodically, but nothing really difficult. So when times are rough I just kind of ride it out and don't put pressure on him. There is no point in provoking a battle of the wills with a six-year-old. It puts me at a disadvantage, and I don't like to be at a disadvantage with my own child."[16]

Parents of both sexes recognized the costs to the parent of exacting compliance from an unwilling child. Fathers occasionally said they were tired when they came home from their day's work, and would let the children get away with undesirable behavior rather than muster the energy to confront them. One mother said about her son: "He's stubborn. If he says he wants something and he can't have it, he'll give me a bad time. He'll keep screwing the screws in tighter and making me suffer." This is an example of the coercive process so well described by Patterson (1980, 1982), who found that mothers are much more often the victims of children's coercive attacks than are fathers. We do not know whether the fact that children are more willing to counter-argue with a mother, and put up resistance to her demands, leads mothers to be more hesitant about imposing demands, or whether the mothers' hesitance about confronting their children leads the children to be more willing to put up resistance. Probably it works in both directions. In any case, mothers appear to be more likely than fathers to feel that their patience is sorely tried by the children. In Mnookin's and my study of divorcing families, custodial mothers, more often than custodial fathers, reported difficulty remaining calm and patient with their children. They also found it more difficult to enforce discipline (Maccoby and Mnookin, 1992, pp. 206–207).

Given that fathers are more willing to confront their children and enforce discipline, it is not surprising that children see them as having more authority. (Men's larger size and louder, deeper voices may contribute to this perception too.) Andersen (1978), working with a group of children aged 4 to 7 years, assessed their perceptions of their parents via play sessions in which the children were asked to enact family scenes with puppets representing mother, father, and child. She also observed the children in real-life interaction with their parents. She found that in their puppet play, the children depicted fathers as issuing many more imperatives than mothers, to both their spouses and their children. Puppet mothers were depicted as being more likely merely to hint at what they wanted done by other family members, including the puppet fathers. Clearly, then, the children had assimilated the difference in parental styles noted above, and saw them as characterizing not only the ways parents spoke to children but also the ways in which parents spoke to each other. These perceptions were associated with the behavior of the children toward their two parents when interacting with them in an observation room: the children issued three times as many simple imperatives to their mothers as to their fathers. The children addressed their fathers more deferentially, using questions and polite forms such as "Would you button me?" rather than the more direct demands they issued to mothers, such as "Gimme daddy's flashlight." Andersen noted that the children seemed to adopt a more familiar tone with their mothers than with their fathers.[17] The greater respect accorded fathers is further underscored by Cowan, Drinkard, and MacGavin (1984), who studied the strategies that children in the sixth, ninth, and twelfth grade use to influence other people with whom they interact. They found that these young people used weaker, more indirect strategies with their fathers than with their mothers and their friends.

Teaching

In socializing their children, parents must teach them a myriad things. When the children are young, the teaching is largely focused on small routines and skills: how to tie shoes, use table utensils, brush teeth, and to put things where they belong. There are also many "don'ts": not to sneeze or cough in other people's faces; not to pull hair or run recklessly into other people; not to make too much noise; not to damage household objects; not to tamper with other people's belongings. Mothers do more of the day-to-day training in routine do's and don'ts, because they are more often the responsible parent on the scene. But fathers do a good deal of it too when they are present, and there are other kinds of teaching which begin to predominate as children grow older. Parents help with school-work; teach skills in operating household gadgets and sports equipment, in accomplishing household maintenance, and in performing chores; and convey information and opinions about a wide range of practical matters, public events, and moral issues. Fathers participate actively in teaching, explaining, and giving information (Bronstein, 1988), and there is some evidence that they especially value and support their children's intellectual development—perhaps more than mothers do (Coleman, Ganong, Clark, and Madsen, 1989).

If fathers do in fact value intellectual achievement and interests more than mothers, it might be expected that fathers would be more involved in teaching their children, putting pressure on them to achieve, and en-gaging in intellectual discussion with them. In fact, however, there appears to be little difference between mothers and fathers in these kinds of involvement with children.[18] Indeed, there is some evidence that the *mother* may be the more active parent when it comes to giving support for achievement—at least, for academic achievement. A time-budget compari-son of mothers and fathers in 12 countries (Stone, 1972) showed that mothers spent considerably more time than fathers working with children on homework. This was especially true if the mothers were not employed, but even in households where both parents worked, mothers spent be-tween 9 percent and 20 percent more time on children's homework, depending on the number of children in the family.[19] More recently, Russell and Russell (1987), in their studies of Australian children and their parents, similarly found mothers to be more involved than fathers in helping with homework.

Relationships with Adolescents

When children have grown into adolescence, the relationships that mothers and fathers have with them are in a sense the end product of all the years of childhood in which the foundations of these relationships have been laid. But there are changes, too, stemming in part from the children's increasing demands for autonomy. How do mother-child and father-child relationships compare at this late period of the children's development? Youniss and Smollar (1985) studied the relationships between each parent and his or her children in several large samples of adolescents, and they summarized what they found as follows:

> The modal relation with fathers appears to be an extension of the structure of unilateral constraint that was in place at the end of childhood . . . Fathers seem to have a narrow view toward their sons and daughters, thinking of them as potential adults and caring most about their progress toward productive adulthood. As a result, fathers share only a small part of adolescents' here and now interests . . . Mothers, no less than fathers, hold adolescents to performance standards that refer ultimately to impending adulthood . . . But this aspect of the relationship is only one aspect of its full character, and it is communicated in a different style than is common in the paternal relationship . . . Mothers maintain regular contact with their sons and daughters . . . Mothers engage themselves in adolescents' interests, whatever they might be. Mothers closely monitor their sons and daughters . . . Mothers do not solely take the role as authorities, but serve as confidantes who share experiences—with the end result being empathy. Mutuality enters the relationship . . . The mark of the mother-adolescent relationship is conversation for its own sake—the kind of conversation in which ideas and feelings are exchanged, not instructional episodes that are designed to influence or persuade. (Youniss and Smollar, 1985, pp. 89–91)

Fathers As the Agents of Sex-Typing

Although in many respects parents treat children of the two sexes much alike, they do offer different toys to boys and girls, and they do discourage boys from behaving in ways, such as playing with dolls, that appear feminine to parents. Here we must consider once again an issue that was raised earlier, in Chapter 6: whether fathers are more likely than mothers to treat boys and girls differently. As the studies reported there indicated, it appears that there is a moderate but consistent tendency for fathers to differentiate more in their treatment of children of the two sexes. Mothers, on the whole, are remarkably even-handed as between sons and daughters. Fathers, by contrast, are more controlling toward sons than daughters, and more likely to reprimand or discipline them (see also Bronstein, 1984). In Jacklin's and my observations of parents with their 45-month-old children at home, fathers were more likely to use "soft" approaches with daughters—suggesting or making offers—than to use imperative demands (Maccoby and Jacklin, 1983). Siegal reported that fathers' interaction with sons was also more "physical" than it was with daughters. In particular, fathers react negatively to behaviors in their sons that could be considered feminine.[20] On the positive side, many fathers appear to take a special interest in their young sons even in the first few years, and the father-son relationship reflects a growing communality of interests as boys grow older: fathers do more projects and activities with boys than with girls.[21] Furthermore, fathers may be more willing to listen to their sons than to their daughters.[22]

Fathers treat girls more gently, one might even say more chivalrously: witness the fact that fathers are more likely to carry a toddler girl than a toddler boy in a public place (Birns, 1976). Furthermore, fathers often express approval of the femininity of a little girl—they comment on her pretty clothes or long hair, or speak of her as "a little flirt" (Goodenough, 1957). By contrast, some fathers express very strong negative reactions to femininity in a boy. Goodenough asked a father if he would be disturbed by signs of femininity in his son, and the father replied: "Yes I would be. Very, very much. Terrifically disturbed. Couldn't tell you the extent of my disturbance. I can't *bear* female characteristics in a man." Although the reactions of most fathers may not be as strong as this, clearly there are elements in fathers' attitudes that reflect the homophobia found in boys' and men's groups earlier in the life course.

We see, then, that fathers tend to treat sons to some extent in the same way they have treated other males, and to treat their daughters as they have traditionally treated females. To mothers, the more important thing about young children is their childishness—their needs stemming from immaturity. Since these are much the same for children of the two sexes, her response tends to be impartial as to gender.

When children reach adolescence, fathers tend to withdraw from intimacy with their daughters but not their sons (Steinberg, 1987), whereas mothers maintain equal levels of intimacy with children of the two sexes throughout childhood and adolescence.

The Co-Parental Enterprise

In most cases, parenting is not something that is done alone. Whatever experiences the two parents may bring from their early histories, if they are to raise children jointly, they must first of all work out some division of labor, so that each knows what each is responsible for doing. In addition, they must adapt to each other's parenting styles, discuss differences, and find common ground. Especially with a first child, they are frequently confronted with situations that neither has experienced before. They usually feel the need to work out a joint strategy for how to proceed. There are reports that parents talk to each other about their children more than they talk about anything else. For each parent, there are subtle questions concerning whether and how to get involved when the other parent is dealing with the child: certain actions could be perceived by the other parent as interference when they were meant as backup. In the best case, the two parents gradually become effective teammates who understand each other's intentions and rely on each other's coordinated actions.

Of course, not all couples are equally successful in achieving a coordinated teamship. A group of researchers at Pennsylvania State University, headed by Jay Belsky, have studied the parental alliance in 69 two-parent families with toddler sons (aged 15 to 21 months). They provide examples of supportive and unsupportive co-parenting.[23] Here are some supportive episodes:

1. Mother to child: "Get out of there!" Father to child: "Listen to your mother, you're gonna get hurt, come over here!"

2. Mother is feeding child, saying pleasantly: "Bite, bite." The child stops eating, and begins to bang two toy tractors together. Mother says: "Hey, I'm gonna take the tractor if you keep doing that." Dad

says sternly: "Hey, I'm not going to let you play with them if you keep crashing them together." The child stops crashing them.

3. Child walks toward the kitchen. Mother says: "Oh, I bet he wants a drink. Would you help him out?" Dad complies to mother's request, gets up and goes into kitchen behind the child.

Examples of unsupportive episodes are:

4. Mother to father: "Peter wants some Pepsi." Father to child: "Drink your milk." Mother gets up from table, carries her glass of Pepsi closer to Peter. She holds the glass while she allows Peter to drink some of the Pepsi.

5. Child goes to a cupboard in the room. In a very stern tone mother says: "No, you can't get in there." Boy does not comply. He opens the door of the cupboard and the father jokingly says: "He just did." Mother says firmly: "No he didn't." Father: "But he opened the door." Father's tone is still one of joking with the mother, but she is tense.

6. Child has hurt himself. Mother says: "Come here honey, I'll kiss it better." Father to child: "Oh, toughen up; quit your belly-aching!"

7. Mother to child at table: "You want that heated up, don't you?" Father to child: "No, you just want it cool, huh?"

8. Child leaves kitchen, walks down hall toward bedroom, carrying a frying pan. He accidentally bangs the pan against the wall. Father calls impatiently to Mother from the bedroom: "Hey, he's knocking holes in the wall!" Mother leaves kitchen, goes down the hall and stops the child. She goes to the bedroom door and says quietly but firmly: "Then you can entertain him." Father says: "I don't want to." Child remains in bedroom with Father while Mother returns to kitchen.

In two-hour observations, the number of supportive episodes averaged over 20, while unsupportive events were much less frequent (6.6 when the child was aged 15 months, 4.4 at age 21 months). Furthermore, fathers gave support to the mothers almost twice as often as mothers supported fathers, while the two parents were equivalent in the frequency of undermining.[24] Probably, the greater frequency of support by fathers reflects the fact that there are more occasions for them to give support, in view of the mother's greater activity and initiative in dealing with the child. Some spouses were consistently supportive of each other's parenting, while others were consistently more likely to undermine each other's efforts.

As children grow older and become more self-regulating, the frequency of episodes in which one or both parents attempt to control or respond to the child declines. And the nature of the issues that arise and the parents' reactions also change. But occasions for joint parental activity continue to occur. Here is an episode with a six-year-old girl:

9. Child exuberantly runs out the back door, bumping into the screen door and knocking it off its track. Father gets up to reset the screen, saying irritably: "Janie, that's the *third* time you've knocked that door off."
  Child: "I didn't do it."
  Father: "Yes you did!"
  Child: "No I didn't."
  Father leaves the door, goes to child, holds her shoulders firmly, looks directly into her face, and says loudly: "Don't tell me you didn't do it. I *saw* you. You didn't mean to, but you *did* do it!"
  Child wails and goes to mother. Mother puts her arm around daughter, rubs her back, says: "It's all right, honey. You didn't mean to. But you have to be more careful, so Daddy won't always have to be fixing the screen door."[25]

This and the other vignettes presented above offer some clues as to the roles played by the two spouses in the co-parenting endeavor:

Parents combine forces. The mother and father form a united front. This takes the form of the father's adding the weight of his (greater?) authority to the mother's (Episodes 1 and 2).

Father as helper. We see some spin-offs from the overall arrangement in which mother is the general manager of the household and the children; father is then cast in the role of helper. Mother tries to recruit him into her action plan, and he does or doesn't agree (Episodes 3 and 8).

Father seeks to assert dominance over mother. In Episode 8, he tries to use her as his "executive" in controlling the child; in Episode 5, he laughs at her when she fails to get compliance from the child; in Episodes 4 and 7 he overtly countermands her perception of what the child wants.

Mother covertly undermines father's directive to child (Episode 4).

Mother mediates between child and father. Mother shields the child somewhat from the impact of father's direct power-assertion while not undermining his socialization objective (Episode 9).

Parents have different socialization objectives. In Episode 6, earlier reported in Chapter 6, mother reacts to child's short-term need for soothing, father acts in terms of the longer-term goal of "toughening" his son. We see here a source of strain in the parental alliance, stemming from the fact that fathers make more distinctions than mothers do in their treatment of sons and daughters, so that fathers have objectives with sons which mothers may not share.

The usual relationship of affection, friendship, and good will between the parents implies a readiness to help each other in the co-parental arena. Although the father is more often seen as a helper by both parents, his helping need not be a matter of contention: his help can be expected by the mother, cheerfully given by the father. But, clearly, issues of dominance between husband and wife do come into play in some families. Is the father so much the mother's "helper" that it is understood that she may direct his familial behavior as well as the children's? Or in contrast, is the mother the father's "executive," so that her authority is dependent on his and subject to his agreement with what she is doing? Is either parent free to countermand the other's directives, and if so, how directly or indirectly can it be done?

To think about these questions is to see the potential for role conflict for both fathers and mothers. As we have seen, many parents see child-rearing and child care as part of the female role. A father's male spousal role, then, calls for withdrawing and letting his wife deal with the children. His parental role, though, calls for nurturing, teaching, and directing the children. When he is interacting with the children in his wife's absence, he can assume the parental role with little conflict. When she is present, however, he must balance his own level of involvement with the functions he feels should properly belong to the children's mother.

Gjerde (1986) observed the way fathers interacted with young teenagers when the child's mother was or was not present. He found that when their wives were present, fathers were less responsive and supportive toward sons—less cooperative with them, more critical—and that a father would put less pressure on a son to engage in interaction with him when the mother was present than when she was absent. (It is notable that the mother's presence or absence made much less difference in the way fathers interacted with their daughters.) In general, however, the fathers were more relaxed (including being more humorous) in interaction with a child of either sex when the mother was not present.

Though fathers may experience conflict in whether or when to take an active part in dealing with children, there is little conflict for them in terms of the content or style of what they do. Men are accustomed, in the other contexts of their lives, to hierarchical relationships. Their paternal role calls for them to assume authority with children, and most men have a ready set of scripts with which to do so.

A mother's situation in attempting to integrate the female and maternal roles is somewhat different. As a mother, she must be firm and directive as well as nurturant. As a feminine person, she is expected to be compliant, accommodating, "sweet," or "nice." And as a wife, she must (traditionally) defer to her husband to some degree, or at least appear to do so (see Johnson, 1988). There may be some difficulty in being both parental and wifely (or feminine) at the same time. In many families, when the husband is present, he often assumes (or is given by his wife) the role of head of the household. As a familiar example, he is more often the one who drives the car on family outings, even though all family members know that the mother is an equally skilled driver. And as we have seen, men more often give directions in an imperative mode to their wives, while women's influence attempts are more indirect. Children observe these things, and do seem to conclude that their fathers are the primary authority in the family. In consequence, mothers in many families appear to need authority backup from their husbands more than vice versa. This may be especially true when mothers are dealing with sons. Gjerde found, for example, that mothers interacted more frequently and effectively with their teenaged sons when the father was present than when he was not, while his presence did not affect the mother's interaction with her daughter.[26]

Most of the evidence I have drawn upon so far comes from Western, industrialized countries. In societies with much greater sex-role differentiation, a woman's authority with children must be largely derived or delegated. Especially with sons, who come to expect deference from their mothers and sisters, fathers may have to take a more active and direct socialization role as children grow older. Also, in such societies, one might expect father-son and mother-daughter coalitions to be strong, although it is also true that mothers derive power from the loyalty of their grown sons in male-dominated societies.

Summary and Comment

There are some unmistakable parallels between parenting styles and the social-interactional styles that characterized the two sexes at earlier points in their lives. The arousing, physical quality of fathers' play with children echoes the rough-and-tumble style of the fathers' own childhood play. Their imperative speech style to children strongly resembles the way boys talk to each other in male playgroups. Fathers' greater willingness to confront children, and their use of derogatory comments and simple power-assertion, mirror the direct style employed by boys in the dominance encounters of childhood.

The fact that fathers treat sons and daughters differently, taking special interest in their sons and encouraging their "masculinity," while mothers treat children of the two sexes very similarly, is also reminiscent of what happened in childhood: that boys, more than girls, were oriented toward others of their own sex, more responsive to them and more concerned with being "masculine" than girls were with being "feminine."

Mothers' styles with children bear a strong resemblance to the dual-agenda nature of the social relationships they experienced in girls' groups in childhood: mothers are concerned with being directive and trying to achieve desired goals, while at the same time trying to preserve group cohesion and interpersonal harmony. Both as young girls and later as mothers they tend to do this by avoiding confrontation, using indirect and polite ways of influencing others, offering emotional support, and responding to a partner's initiatives. Mothers' greater intimacy with children—more frequent chatting, reciprocal exchange of ideas and feelings, willingness to listen to the child's point of view and arrive at a compromise—also echoes the interaction styles among girls in middle childhood and adolescence. When one considers the social histories of the two sexes, it is not at all surprising that mothers have more difficulty enforcing discipline, and more often complain that the children are "running all over them"; nor is it surprising that fathers more often lack the day-to-day knowledge of children's activities and interests that underlies successful monitoring.

I am suggesting that the modes of interaction acquired earlier in life in same-sex peer groups are carried over to a considerable degree into the parental role.

Having noted the continuities, I must also point out that they are attenuated. Many factors influence how an individual functions as a parent, over and above the distinctive interaction styles acquired in peer groups at an earlier time. There are temperamental qualities in both parent and child which mean that some parent-child combinations are fraught with difficulties while others run a smooth course. Then, too, both parents bring to the parenting process certain assumptions, knowledge, and beliefs derived from having observed their own parents. Either parent may be determined to create a family climate that is different from the one he or she experienced as a child, or may wish to do things in much the same way his or her own parents did, but the influences are there, whether positive or negative. And the quality of parental functioning also reflects a variety of current circumstances: employment and income, the safety of the neighborhood, and so forth. Most important, in two-parent families each parent must adapt to the quality of parenting brought to the family by the other parent. There is an infinite variety of ways in which these and other factors can combine, with the result that modes of parenting are highly individual. There is great variation among mothers, and among fathers, in the way parenting processes are carried out.

These variations mean that the average difference between groups of mothers and groups of fathers tends to shrink. So far I have been contrasting mothers and fathers in terms of their average characteristics. But the fact is that the average differences are greater on some dimensions of parenting than others, and in some respects the differences are quite small. There are many fathers who chat with their children, listen to them, and are well "tuned in" to a child's moods and states of readiness, even though the majority of fathers may show these characteristics to a lesser degree than the average mother. Similarly, there are many mothers who are perfectly willing and able to confront their children when the situation requires it, although most mothers might avoid doing so.

We do not know much about the origins of these variations. Is it the men and women who were most closely integrated into a same-sex peer group in childhood who are most likely to take up a sex-typical style of parenting? Are mothers who were "tomboy" girls and liked to play with boys more likely to roughhouse with their own children and confront them when disciplinary issues arise? What kind of male peer-group experiences foster a man's becoming an empathic, sensitive father, or one who supports his wife's parenting? This last question reminds us that peer groups are not monolithic. As we have seen, male peer groups vary greatly in their values and activities, particularly in adolescence, and some groups may offer experiences which can be constructively utilized in the parental role at a later time, while others do not.

The roles of the two sexes in parenting go beyond the question of what kind of parents individual men and women will become. They also affect decisions about child-bearing. In the long history of humankind, people had little choice about whether to become parents once they became sexually active adults. In the modern world, they do have a choice about whether to have children, and how many to have. It becomes especially important, then, to understand the conditions that determine whether men and women are ready and willing to take on the responsibilities of parenthood. In this chapter we have seen that there are continuing issues between husbands and wives concerning the division of child-care duties. The very low birthrates in many modern societies point to the likelihood that many couples are resolving these issues by deciding to have fewer—or no—children. Collectively, these decisions add up to trends that are of the greatest importance to society as a whole.

Overview

A primary message of this book is that gender matters greatly in childhood as well as at later phases of the life cycle. Although this may seem so obvious as to be hardly worth stating, it is different from the way some researchers, including me, saw things a number of years ago, when comparisons of boys and girls on a large variety of measured attributes revealed few consistent sex differences. As it turns out, we learn very little about the powerful gender phenomena of childhood from studies in which researchers simply compare the average characteristics of boys and girls without regard to social context. What this book shows is that a child's sex matters greatly if we consider simultaneously the child's own sex and that of the child or children with whom the child is interacting. Another way of putting this is to say that gender distinctions arise mainly in the context of pairs or groups, with all-male and all-female groups being demonstrably different from each other and from mixed-sex social configurations.

There is a powerful tendency for children to seek out, and play more actively with, playmates of their own sex, and to avoid children of the other sex. This segregating impulse becomes apparent quite early. The beginnings of the tendency to separate may be seen in the third year of life, among children who are brought together in daycare centers or playgroups. At this early age there is still a good deal of play in mixed-sex groups, and some children form devoted cross-sex friendships. But the tendency to prefer same-sex playmates—or avoid children of the other sex—becomes progressively stronger through the preschool years, until by grade school age it is powerful indeed. Same-sex playmate preferences are stronger on the playgrounds of traditional schools than they are at "progressive" schools, but same-sex social groupings are seen nevertheless in all the settings so far studied.

By around the age of six, the large majority of children seem to be drawn into same-sex peer groups and same-sex best friendships without regard to how sex-typed they are as individuals and without regard to the variations in socialization experiences they have had in their families of origin. Children's playgroups are segregated by gender in many different cultures—in villages in the Third World as well as in modern industrialized countries. And it is clear that gender segregation in play occurs whether or not there is a marked degree of such segregation in the adult society in which the children are growing up. In short, there does not seem to be much room for individual differences among children of a given sex in whether they will have mainly same-sex playmates in middle childhood. There is plenty of room for individual differences, however, in terms of *which* same-sex group a child will enter, what role a given child will play within a same-sex group, and how much investment a child will make in such groups compared with how much time the child will spend alone, with family members, or in mixed-sex contexts, such as classrooms or after-school activities that have been structured by adults.

All-male and all-female peer groups differ from each other in a number of respects: in their size and the locus of their play; in the nature of their activities; and in their typical interaction styles. Although some of these differences are large and quite consistent across settings and population groups, the differences are probably not so robust as is segregation itself.

This point is difficult to pin down because of limitations in the evidence. Much of the work on children's groups is ethnographic, and is based on samples of convenience—on groups to which the ethnographer happens to have access. In studies of discourse processes, the researchers seldom have any information on how much variation there is from one group to another, or on how representative the studied groups might be. There is a persuasive degree of consistency among the groups that have been studied so far, showing differences between all-male and all-female groups; for example, girls are more likely than boys to use conflict-mitigating strategies when negotiating with their same-sex friends. But we do not know whether there are some all-girl groups in which these strategies are seldom used, or whether they predominate among certain groups of boys as well. In the absence of information about group variability, it is difficult to be sure how robust the differences between male and female playgroups are.

What we can say at present is that existing studies do point to differences in the way children interact with each other in the two kinds of playgroups. Boys in their groups, more commonly than girls in theirs, engage in "grandstanding," risk-taking, rough play, direct mutual confrontation, and striving for dominance; boys are also more reluctant to reveal weaknesses to each other. Among girls there is more self-disclosure (including disclosure of weakness), more reciprocal and sustained discourse, and more explicit attention given to maintaining positive social relations, along with avoidance of open conflict. Among girls, the expression of hostility toward others tends to be indirect.

Girls in their groups also have more open communication with adults. It is a fairly consistent feature of childhood that boys' groups, more than girls' groups, separate themselves strongly from adults, actively test the limits and power of adult rules, exert pressure on their members not to tattle to adults, exclude and ignore children of the other sex, and vigilantly monitor the boundaries between the sexes. In short, boys in their groups achieve more autonomy than girls do in theirs, and probably achieve more group cohesion as well, despite the higher levels of conflict within boys' groups.

Though living their social lives in largely separate spheres, boys and girls are intensely conscious of each other as future romantic and sexual partners. Boys in their groups engage in sexy talk about female bodies, while girls talk among themselves about boys in more romantic terms. Children tease each other for showing signs of "liking" or "loving" a child of the other sex, and presumably this teasing cuts off approaches that might otherwise be made to an other-sex child. Children of the two sexes are able to work together with little discomfort when adults have assigned them to mixed-sex working groups. In such adult-structured situations, children are protected from any appearance of having chosen an opposite-sex child on their own initiative—protected, that is, from teasing by their peers.

The Origins of Gender Divergence in Childhood

Playstyles

Initially, an important factor in same-sex playmate choices appears to be that children find the playstyles of same-sex others to be more compatible with their own. Boys' rough, vigorous playstyle is attractive to many or most other boys, while many girls are wary of male rough play and tend to withdraw from it. Probably, they are more wary of boys *in groups* than of individual boys encountered one at a time. Though boys and girls do often employ different toys as "props" for their play, enacting somewhat different themes, the two sexes tend to separate in preschool even when their play involves sex-neutral activities, such as climbing on a jungle gym. Thus there is something about the way children of a given sex interact with age-mates that is a primary element in segregation, with the specific play themes and props being manifestations of this primary element.

Exactly what it is about male play that attracts other boys and provokes wariness in girls is an elusive matter. I have used the descriptive phrase "rough-and-tumble play" as a proxy for whatever this male quality is, but rough play is probably only one element in the larger process of boys' proving their toughness to male peers and establishing a place in the male dominance hierarchy. Given that the male playstyle is one of the major factors underlying the initiation of gender segregation, the obvious questions become: Why are males more likely to display this particular style, and why do other males like it while females usually don't? A similar set of questions may be asked concerning girls' playstyles: What is it that girls do that is attractive to other girls, but not to boys? This female quality is harder to describe, and is much less well understood, than male-type play. What attracts girls to girls undoubtedly has something to do with affectively positive social approaches, and perhaps also with a less impulsive, more self-regulated mode of behaving. Yet these qualities alone would presumably be attractive to children of both sexes. Avoidance of girls by young boys is hard to understand in terms of female playstyles, and perhaps is better understood as a male response to girls' lack of interest in the kind of play boys seek.

Biological Factors

The gender-differentiated phenomena of childhood documented in the early chapters of this book fit quite well with an evolutionary perspective. There are striking similarities between human children and their nonhuman primate cousins with respect to differentiated playstyles and gender segregation.[1] It is plausible that the distinctive agendas enacted in male playgroups—in particular, the formation of dominance hierarchies—serve to regulate male in-group aggression and socialize boys for cooperative endeavors with other males, as some evolutionary theorists have suggested.

And there are some possible ways in which segregation of the sexes in childhood might serve to minimize inbreeding. Certainly the greater involvement of adult females in child care is consistent with the sociobiological claims concerning the reproductive strategies that best serve the inclusive fitness interests of adult females as compared with adult males. But it is also important to note how much variability there is, among species and subspecies, in the amount of investment in parenting made by males. It would seem that biology has left males flexible in this regard, permitting them to adapt to the variable social conditions that determine whether or not male investment is needed to permit offspring to grow safely to maturity.

A plausible evolutionary rationale could be devised for almost any sex-differentiated pattern that emerges from the relevant research. Such rationales, then, are best used as hypotheses, to guide us as to where to look for more proximal causes. If members of the two sexes have indeed evolved to be genetically predisposed to certain distinctive behaviors, these predispositions can become manifest only through physiological processes, which in turn interact with environmental factors for their elicitation. Some physiological processes have been identified. For example, experimental studies in which androgens have been administered prenatally to genetically female monkeys have changed their postnatal playstyles: these young females engage in more rough-and-tumble play than untreated females. Among human children, girls who receive excess androgens prenatally tend to display tomboy tendencies.

So far, no evidence has been found for an effect of *female* hormones on playstyles. We can say, then, that it is primarily the presence of large amounts of androgens during specific periods of gestation that predispose children—usually genetically male children—to male-style play.

Perinatal androgens may also be implicated in the tendency for males to separate themselves more strongly from adults than females typically do. In one study, the administration of an androgen-antagonist to newborn male monkeys delayed their move away from adults and into a male peer group. We see then a modest bit of evidence that the asymmetry between boys' and girls' groups—the greater independence and stronger boundaries of male groups—is influenced by hormones present at or near the time of birth.

There may be other aspects of physiological development that bear on female playstyles. If, as is currently being claimed, productive language and self-regulatory capacities do mature more rapidly in toddler girls than in toddler boys, such differences could partially account for the more reciprocal aspects of female play. However, we do not yet know how differential maturation rates might intersect with differential socialization in the development of female playstyles.

I suggested in Part II that binary phenomena call for binary explanations. To the extent that all children of one sex show a given characteristic, and all children of the other sex show a different characteristic, we need to look for causes that would affect all male children in one way, all female children in another. To the extent that children of a given sex differ among themselves, we need to look for causes that would lead to within-sex differentiation. It is clear that at least by the time children reach middle childhood, gender segregation is a phenomenon that is more of the first kind than the second: There is a strong tendency for boys to be alike in their preference for congregating with other boys, with individual differences among boys in this respect being of relatively minor scope. And girls, similarly, are quite homogeneous in being attracted to other girls as friends and playmates. Biological factors are good candidates for helping to explain segregation, then, in that whatever biological forces are powerful enough to have created the distinct, biological categories of male and female could, by implication, also be powerful enough to create binary distinctions with respect to certain forms of behavior.

Having said this, I should emphasize that biological predispositions never manifest themselves without the appropriate environmental conditions being present to activate them. I suspect that the major activating condition for male-style play in a boy is the presence of other young male peers. Similarly, the nurturant predispositions of children of both sexes are activated (perhaps to different degrees in boys and girls) by the presence of vulnerable young creatures or their surrogates (dolls). Biological and environmental factors are inextricably linked.

In sum, genetic predispositions probably are involved, to some degree, in childhood gender segregation. But the case is weaker for the influence of such factors on the distinctive interaction styles that emerge in same-sex groups. For one thing, the styles are not as distinctive as playmate choices themselves. And although some aspects of the sex-distinctive interaction styles probably differ little across cultures, other aspects—such as the content of the play themes that children enact in their same-sex groups— do differ considerably with time and place and cultural gender roles.

Cognitive Factors

What children know about gender undoubtedly affects childhood gender differentiation, but some aspects of gender cognition matter more than others. Simply being aware of gender stereotypes—which sex wears certain clothes, prefers certain toys or activities, and so on—does not seem to be related to the tendency to segregate, at least not at the outset. But knowledge of one's own gender identity and that of others probably is. Children are able to distinguish persons of the two sexes very early in life—by the end of the first year; and by the age of three, most are able to use gender labels to classify themselves and others. Most studies do not show that becoming able to use gender labels accurately is either a necessary or a sufficient condition for children to begin associating primarily with others of their own sex. Perhaps only the most primitive form of gender cognition—perceptual discrimination—is all that is necessary to initiate the process. But of course knowing that one is a member of a gender category does reinforce any tendencies to segregate that already exist. A sense of belonging to an own-sex in-group develops, and the things that usually go along with in-group membership come into play: own-group attraction and favoritism, out-group stereotyping.

Gender identity, like biological sex, is almost completely binary. Hermaphrodites do exist, and for them the assignment of a gender category is not straightforward. And some transsexual people believe that their gender is not the same as their biological sex. Some cultures give social recognition to a third sex, or intersex: witness the berdache in certain American Indian tribes. For the overwhelming majority of people, however, their own gender, and that of other people, falls into one of two categories: male or female. While the basis for being labeled at birth as a male or female is of course biological, the labeling itself is social. Adults of a society decide which sex category an infant belongs to, and from then on the child is named appropriately for this category, dressed appropriately, referred to by whatever binary linguistic labels (he, she; his, hers) the culture provides. That a child should come to understand his or her own gender identity at an early age—as well as the gender identities of others—is no surprise. It is an overdetermined matter. And it forms a strong element, acting together with the biological sex differentiation on which it was based, to bring about binary behavioral distinctions. In particular, knowledge of their own gender identity is what enables children to take advantage of their accumulating knowledge concerning the behaviors their society deems appropriate for people of their sex, and to adapt themselves accordingly. Although simply knowing about cultural stereotypes may not have much to do with childhood gender segregation itself, there can be no doubt that as the cultural messages, the social assumptions, and the scripts concerning gender are absorbed by children, they have a powerful impact on the way children construct their identity as male or female individuals.

Socialization

When we say that boys have been "socialized" to behave in one way, girls in another, we could be referring to a variety of sources of sex-typing pressure: from parents, from teachers, from athletic coaches, from peers. But considering that gender differentiation starts quite early, when children are spending most of their time in the parental home, it has been widely assumed that parents must be the people most involved in shaping young children's gendered characteristics. However, the family home in which most children grow up is not a setting in which the sexes separate. There is usually an adult male-female couple, and children's siblings may be of either sex.[2] It is true that same-sex siblings are more likely than opposite-sex siblings to share a room, but at least during the preschool years, children play frequently with whichever sibling is closest to themselves in age, regardless of gender. Gender segregation, then, is usually only a very limited part of children's experience in their family homes. I have argued that for this reason the family home is unlikely to be the point of origin of children's tendency to segregate. Rather, this tendency is primarily a property of peer-group formation.

If we think about what happens in simpler societies than our own, it would seem obvious that children must congregate with others of their own sex mainly because adults manage children's daily lives in ways that separate boys and girls. In some societies, boys are sent out away from the household to help with the herding of animals, while the girls are kept close to the household and involved in domestic enterprises, such as caring for toddlers, helping with cooking, or fetching water from a village well or tap. It follows naturally that children in such a society encounter mainly children of their own sex during major portions of the day while they are doing their chores. In some societies, only the boys are sent to school; in other cultures, children go to separate, single-sex schools. In either case, it is obvious that their opportunities to associate with the other sex are limited. Less stringent forms of adult-managed segregation may be seen when there are separate playgrounds for the two sexes at coeducational schools, or when teachers seat boys and girls separately in classrooms or have them line up separately when moving from place to place.

It is clear, however, that such adult-managed separation is by no means the whole story. In societies where parents send their children to mixed-sex schools or daycare centers, the children separate nonetheless.[3] The separation occurs in preschools even when the teachers are making conscious efforts to treat children of the two sexes equally.

Perhaps children have been influenced somehow at home in ways that make them think that playing with others of their own sex is the right and expected thing to do. My review of the socialization literature has indicated that such pressures from parents, if they exist, are minimal. At least this is true in modern, Western societies. Most parents in these societies appear to be comfortable about having their children play with neighborhood children, or friends' children, of either sex. Of course, if a boy of grade school age were to choose to play only with girls, parents might become concerned that he was effeminate. But barring unusual cases of this kind, children segregate even when parents (and teachers) exert very little direct pressure on them to do so. I have argued that children do not seek same-sex companionship primarily because they believe such choices are what their parents or teachers want and expect of them.

Children do experience social pressure to segregate, but this pressure comes mainly from their peers rather than from adults. Gender segregation, then, is something pertaining distinctively to childhood culture. If it is passed on from one cohort of children to the next (rather than being reinvented by each new cohort), what we are seeing is the transmission of a cultural pattern from older children to younger ones, not from adults to children. So far, then, we cannot see segregation as an outcome of direct socialization pressures from the adult generation.

There is, however, another possible avenue for parental influence. I have nominated differential playstyles as a leading candidate among the factors that initially influence children to seek same-sex playmates and to avoid playmates of the other sex. It might be that within-family socialization has its effect through its influence on playstyles. Are boys and girls trained by their parents to adopt the playstyles that then become the basis for initiating segregation?

We know that parents of both sexes play more roughly with little boys than little girls, and fathers in particular roughhouse with their young sons. It would seem plausible that fathers are activating an interest in rough play in their young sons—a preference that the boys then bring to the peer-group setting. The problem is that the meager information available so far does not indicate that, for individual children, being played with roughly by parents in early life is related to a child's adopting a rough playstyle with peers at a later time. The degree of a boy's involvement in rough-and-tumble play with other boys does not seem to depend on how much, or whether, his parents played roughly with him when he was a toddler. If what parents do with individual boys in their homes makes a difference, it appears that individual parent-child effects are somehow translated into *aggregate* effects on groups of boys, with the contributions of the home socialization received by individual boys being lost in the translation.

There is another important way in which parents treat young sons and young daughters differently. They talk more about feelings with girls than with boys. Starting when the children are toddlers, and continuing into their preschool years, parents talk more often to little girls about how the child is feeling now, was feeling earlier, or might feel if certain things happened. They more often discuss with daughters how a child's actions make other people feel. How do these differences come about? Partly they may stem from girls' faster progress with language acquisition, so that parents can talk to them in ways that go beyond simple two- or three-word utterances. Or they may reflect girls' greater willingness to listen to, and participate in, talk about emotions. Or it may be that talk about feelings seems somehow too "soft" in dealing with a boy—not entirely compatible with parental stereotypes about male toughness. Indeed, we know that parents, especially fathers, put pressure on boys not to cry, not to show fear or weakness. Whatever the reason, the fact is that talk about feelings does occur more frequently between parents and daughters. And such talk facilitates children's ability to adopt the perspective of other people at a later time. It may very well contribute to girls' capacity for being more open than boys to listening to their play partners, cooperating with them, and avoiding confrontation with them.

We see, then, that in-home socialization probably has a greater effect on the interaction styles that emerge in single-sex playgroups than it does on the separation into these groups in the first place.

Clearly, whatever effect parents have on their children's playstyles is magnified by the formation of same-sex groupings; there is a feedback loop. Here is a plausible scenario: Individual boys, each prenatally sensitized (or primed by parents) to respond positively to overtures for rough, arousing play, will choose each other as playmates, and when they engage in play, will build up a dyadic or group process that is more distinct from female-type play than their individual tendencies would dictate. And girls, individually sensitized by their parents to others' feelings, or in a state of greater readiness to receive socialization inputs of this kind from their parents, will use these developed attributes to build a new and distinctively female type of interaction with their playmates.

I am arguing that the whole is greater than the sum of its parts—that the merging of individual children, with their individual socialization histories, into a group, will produce a new form of interaction that is different from what they have experienced with their parents. Once the male group process is set in motion, its very existence increases the likelihood that boys will preferentially choose (or be chosen) to participate in it, and that girls will avoid it. In a similar way, girls who originally select other girls on the basis of individual playstyle compatibility or because they share a gender category, will construct forms of reciprocal interaction that can only occur in female dyads or groups once these are formed. Participating in these forms of interaction will make girls more likely to seek out other girls with whom they have experienced satisfying forms of female-typical interaction. And by virtue of the same-sex group interaction that occurs, a group identity, a group esprit, is built up, distinctive to all-girl or all-boy groups.

So far, I have focused mainly on in-home socialization practices as a possible source of children's gender divergence, and have shown that there are indeed some respects in which parents treat children of the two sexes differently. Such differential treatment is, however, modest in degree and scope, and may not have a great deal of weight in bringing about the powerful patterns of gender separation and distinctive interaction styles that I have sought to explain. But parents are only one element in the larger socialization picture. Whole societies socialize children. Cultural practices have a powerful impact, whether or not parents are the conduit through which these practices are brought to bear on children's lives. For example, we saw in Chapter 6 that in societies with the greatest status discrepancies between the sexes—with males having more prestige and power—boys are more likely to distance themselves as early as possible not only from female playmates but from adult females, including their mothers, as well. Thus culture-wide status distinctions can serve to weaken the influence on boys of a major in-family socialization agent. And the sex-differentiated cultural practices surrounding marriage, childbirth, and child-rearing surely create powerfully different socialization milieus for children of the two sexes. Sociologists and anthropologists have long been concerned with how this culture-wide socialization takes place. It is a topic beyond the scope of this book. But considering that gender is expressed in childhood largely in the context of groups, it is obvious that we need to think more deeply about the role that children's groups may play in transmitting cultural practices across generations.

Transitions to Adulthood

Echoes of Childhood

As I have examined the way the two sexes function as adults—as lovers, as coworkers, as parents—I have called attention to echoes or carry-overs from childhood. These fall into three main categories.

Gender segregation. The forces impelling the two sexes to occupy separate social spheres do not cease operating in adolescence and adulthood. Despite the powerful pull of heterosexual attraction in adolescence and adulthood, people continue to maintain same-sex friendship networks throughout the time when they are engaged in finding heterosexual partners. And gender-based separation is strongly present in the workplace. When mated couples are established, they are sometimes drawn into a mainly mixed-sex social milieu, but not in all cultures. Cultures range all the way from those practicing seclusion of women (purdah in India, for instance) in which married adults continue to spend much of their social time with others of their own sex, to modern industrialized societies in which many adult couples go out together and spend their social time with mixed-sex groups made up mainly of other couples and relatives of both sexes. But even in these more modern societies, things change when children are born. The gender-based division of labor that usually occurs within households, with women taking the major responsibility for child-rearing, brings about some degree of resegregation. When women are raising young children, they tend to rely on female social networks, and husbands and wives often lead more separate lives than they did before they became parents.

Interaction styles. It is tempting to speak about the similarities between childhood and adult patterns of interaction as though different patterns learned early in life had become embedded in men's and women's personalities, so as to be almost automatically expressed in a variety of adult contexts. But interactive styles are not carried over intact from childhood. True, experiences in same-sex playgroups add somewhat different elements to boys' and girls' interactive repertoires, but adult contexts differ in terms of how much and whether these repertoires are called upon. Recall, for example, Carli's work showing that women use "tentative speech" more when interacting with men than with other women; we see here that adult cross-sex contexts call for different behaviors than do the same-sex ones, just as they did in childhood. However, there is reason to believe that women are less "tentative" in talking with their husbands than with men they do not know well. And there are situations in which a childhood repertoire may actually need to be inhibited. A major case in point is male "stonewalling" in conflicts with wives. I have suggested that men find, when dealing with spousal conflict, that they cannot successfully use the direct confrontational style they developed as children in conflicts with male peers. So men find that they must set aside a well-learned repertoire, though this requires effort and generates tensions that must then be dealt with in their own right.

The balance of power. For children, life within the nuclear family is lived within a strongly hierarchical structure. Especially when children are young, the discrepancy is enormous between themselves and their parents in terms of size, strength, and competence of all sorts. Parents can and do arrange the circumstances of their children's lives; they set the agendas and the standards the children must live by. I have argued that the sex of the child matters only minimally in this situation where power is concerned, and that any differential status of male and female children is dwarfed by the subordination of children to adults.[4]

In middle childhood, the subordination to adults continues in many settings (school classrooms, for example), and in such settings the child's sex once again fades into the background, as far as power is concerned. But in situations where adult hierarchical constraints are absent or distant, children separate along gender lines, and spend most of their free social time with others of their own sex. Issues of dominance emerge strongly within all-male groups, but are of much less importance among groups of girls. The question of who is dominant as between male and female children seldom arises by virtue of the fact that they usually interact in situations where adult power constraints are present. Nevertheless, the evidence shows that boys tend to ignore suggestions made by girls, while girls respond more equally to influence attempts coming from peers of either sex.

Let us now consider how these three themes—the tendency to separate, divergence in interaction styles, and the balance of power—work themselves out in each of the three adult interaction contexts described in this book (Chapters 8–10).

Heterosexual Pairs

Considering how separated the free-time lives of boys and girls are in childhood, it might be thought that when they become romantically attracted to each other, their initial contacts would be clumsy and fraught with difficulties. It is true that their distinct interaction styles tend to carry over from childhood, with young women using conflict-mitigating styles and making more efforts to sustain positive moods, and young men using forms of ego display, when the two sexes begin to interact with each other. These styles do not always mesh well. And there can be awkwardness in the effort to find common interests, as well as intense concerns over how to make oneself attractive to specific persons of the other sex. Still, both sexes find the uncharted territory of the other sex's qualities intriguing and exciting. The process of adapting to a new kind of partner, occurring in concert with the growth of romantic love and sexual bonding, can be infinitely satisfying.

Is it more satisfying to one sex than the other? It might be expected that men, being accustomed to functioning in dominance hierarchies in their male groups, would automatically employ their power-assertive style to establish dominance in their relationships with women. And women would then of necessity do more of the adapting, allowing themselves to be influenced more, and subordinating their true selves in the interests of attracting a man into a committed relationship. It would be understandable if young women did not negotiate the transition into heterosexuality as comfortably as men under these conditions.

I have argued that the scenarios emerging in courting couples are more varied and more complex than this. Young women's resources for exerting influence over the men who are interested in them are considerable. While some women do adopt a self-abnegating posture toward men—and perhaps in consequence become depressed—many do not.

As stable couples are formed, the hierarchical relation of the members of a male-female pair depends greatly on the culture of which they are a part. Certain religious doctrines and related cultural traditions decree that men are to be regarded as the heads of households, and traditional societies have erected legal structures that award men more civic, economic, and domestic rights than women. Even in such societies, however, women can have considerable authority. Female autonomy can emerge, as it did in childhood, by virtue of separation. The sexual division of labor that attends strongly sex-differentiated adult roles in traditional societies implies that each sex exercises considerable hegemony in its own sphere. In more egalitarian modern societies, the "spheres of influence" of the two sexes are much less distinct. In such a setting the balance of power between the members of a heterosexual couple varies greatly, and in many cases it becomes very difficult to identify which member of the couple has more influence over the other. Granted that men are stronger and more capable of physically coercing their wives than vice versa, many (probably most) men inhibit physical aggression, or even verbal power-assertion, toward their wives. I have argued that, as couples continue to live together and jointly pursue shared goals, issues of dominance become less relevant to their relationships.

Issues of dominance aside, there are risks for both sexes in their entry into the heterosexual marketplace. The risks are considerably greater for women, however, at least in modern societies, where marriage is delayed and premarital sexual activity widely condoned. Not only do women bear the primary risks of pregnancy and its consequences, but they must cope with a continuing double standard such that sexual indiscretions carry a much greater risk of damaged reputation and loss of future opportunities for women than for men. I suspect that these issues are fully as serious for large numbers of young women as the problems of self-subordination that have been so widely emphasized.

Workplace Relationships

The forces that operate in the workplace reflect both old themes and new ones. Two prior cultures provide established gender scripts: the childhood culture, where gender was expressed mainly by separation, and the dating culture, where heterosexual attraction was the primary context for cross-sex interaction. Although some people have experience, before they enter the workplace, in cooperative mixed-sex activities where issues of sexual attraction are subordinated, many do not, and they lack scripts for how to interact with people of the other sex in whom they are not romantically or sexually interested. Tendencies toward both gender separation and heterosexual attraction continue to be evident, often in ways that are dysfunctional when people of the two sexes need to cooperate in carrying out workplace tasks.

Of course, when men and women work in situations where they seldom encounter each other during their day-to-day working life, they do not have to negotiate issues of power between them on an ongoing basis. Power relations in a segregated workplace are embedded in the organizational structure. But when women seek to gain entry to predominantly male work situations, they must negotiate with men; furthermore, they must negotiate with them *as a group,* rather than dealing with one man at a time as they do in forming intimate relationships. I have argued that male groups tend to be stronger in a number of respects than female groups, and the power differential between the sexes is greater when males have formed cohesive groups, as they usually do in the workplace. Male working groups typically resist the entry of women into their all-male cultures. There are strong echoes here of the way in which male childhood groups actively monitored the activities of their members so as to maintain the boundaries between themselves and females, and resisted or ignored influence attempts from females.

In the work settings where men and women do work together, vertical segregation frequently prevails, such that men occupy the higher-status jobs and women the lower-level ones. In such situations, the formal structure of the organization functions to legitimize male authority. When sexual attraction emerges in these settings, it can easily take on overtones of harassment or exploitation of subordinate women by men in positions of power. As is well known, women have encountered many difficulties in gaining promotion in these male-dominated structures; what may not be so well known is that when they do achieve supervisory positions, they have proved able to exercise supervisory authority with as much confidence and competence as men in similar positions.

Men and Women As Parents

When adult couples become parents, the modes of interaction they employ with their children show some clear parallels with the interaction styles they had developed in the segregated peer groups of their own childhood. Mothers develop more reciprocal, more intimate relationships with their children, and tend to avoid confrontations with them, just as they did when interacting with their girl friends when they were much younger. Fathers deal with their children in a more imperative mode, but also play roughly with them and engage them in light-hearted banter and teasing—modes of relating which also bear the stamp of the interaction styles characteristic of the male peer groups of childhood. At the same time, there are some distinctly new elements in fathers' relations with children: their intense love for them, and their self-sacrificing commitment to the children's welfare, involving often-stressful struggles to provide economic support.

Issues of power become more complex when the two parents together exercise authority over their children. In some families and some cultures, issues of power between the parents in dealing with the children recede into the background by virtue of division of labor: Mothers are understood by both husband and wife to be the ones who are to take responsibility for management of the children's lives, including responsibility for standard-setting and discipline. In such households, the father then becomes a playmate to the children, occasionally backing up the mother's authority when needed. The mother in turn protects his autonomy and his working schedule from intrusions by the children or by family-management concerns.

A quite different pattern involves the father's assuming—or being granted by his wife—authority over the mother in her child-rearing functions. In the extreme case, both parents see the mother as the father's "executive" where child-rearing is concerned, and the father is understood by both to have the right to veto the wife's decisions, or to make the final decisions in important matters concerning the children. This level of paternal authority is, of course, more common in traditional societies. And, historically, some of these societies have taken boys away from their mothers and sent them to all-male institutions such as boarding schools, where they are socialized into male culture by male authority figures.

In modern Western societies, many couples work together as a co-parental team, exercising decision-making authority jointly. In such families, children who ask one parent for permission to engage in some desired activity are likely to hear: "We'll see. I'll talk to your mother (father) about it." As far as possible, a united front is presented to the children and parental disagreements are discussed behind closed doors.

In studies of families, researchers find an infinite variety of modifications and combinations of these patterns. Indeed, in a substantial number of families, the balance of parental authority is continually negotiated and can be the locus of considerable conflict, with significant changes taking place as the children grow older. I believe that the great range of variation in co-parental authority indicates clearly that this is an aspect of male-female relations that is not inherent in our biology in any deep sense, but like other aspects of the relationships between heterosexual couples, is a matter to be negotiated between the members of a pair of parents. Of course, such negotiations may be taken out of the couple's hands by strong cultural practices that brook little deviation. Such cultural practices, however, are themselves subject to change from one generation to the next.

The ways in which the interaction styles and power relationships developed in childhood playgroups are carried over, or *not* carried over, into adult contexts are just beginning to be explored. At present I can only point out the parallels that do exist. I think it is likely that the interactive repertoires learned in same-sex peer groups are used for interaction with same-sex others throughout life. Cross-sex interactions among adults, however, clearly call for modifications of repertoires learned in early life. The nature of the modifications depends, at least in part, on whether the adults are interacting as lovers, as co-parents, or as coworkers. And certainly the modifications must depend on the nature of the cultures in which adult lives are being lived, and how rapidly these cultures are changing.

Leverage Points for Social Change

We have seen that there are points in the life course when the two sexes diverge, others when they converge. Relationships between males and females change accordingly, but certain patterns in male-female relationships, and in same-sex relationships, show some continuity over time. I have said that these patterns make sense from an evolutionary standpoint, and have cited evidence pointing to physiological processes that have evolved in our bisexual species such that male and female persons are, to a modest extent, predisposed to build different relationships with people of their own sex and people of the other sex.

Does this mean that what males and females are or can become is pretty much determined by biology? Of course not. Human beings have developed cultures infinitely more complex than those that existed at the time when our species characteristics evolved. Obviously our evolved characteristics play themselves out in relation to the changing physical and social milieus in which any given generation lives, and this applies to gender relations as well as to all the other aspects of social interaction. Our capacity for learning and adapting to new circumstances probably exceeds that of any other species. Vast social change is not only possible but typical for human beings.

When it comes to the social roles of the two sexes, and the relations between the sexes, social change has been especially rapid in the twentieth century, more rapid in some parts of the world than in others but significant everywhere. Wars and migrations and economic change have uprooted families from their traditional way of life. Technology has changed the nature of the work to be done, and education has prepared both men and women for working and living in ways that are greatly different from the ways in which their forebears lived only a few generations earlier. The technology that allows people to control their fertility has profoundly affected the lives of both men and women, but in particular has greatly modified the forces that once kept women tied to the domestic sphere.

So, biology is not destiny. Societal gender roles are flexible. Still, certain sex-differentiating patterns of social behavior that emerge in childhood appear to have some biological roots, and have consequences for the kinds of social interactions that occur between men and women in their adult years. These childhood patterns can be seen as exercising a kind of inertial counterweight against changes in gender roles and gender relations. Is it desirable to try to change them, and if so, can we achieve social consensus on what kinds of interventions to undertake?

Preventing or Modifying Childhood Segregation

I have pointed to children's single-sex groups—in particular, *boys'* groups—as a source of some tendencies and practices that many view as sexist in adult contexts. Should those of us who are strongly committed to gender equity then try in some way to break up these childhood single-sex groups, or prevent them from forming? To do so would probably mean that adults would have to impose some fairly stringent structures on children's leisure time. How, for example, could we see to it that children did not informally allocate certain tables in the school lunchroom as "boys' tables" or "girls' tables"? Probably only by having adults give children preassigned seats in the lunchroom. How could playground space be allocated to prevent girls from taking over a certain area for jump-rope or four-square, and boys from preempting a space (usually a *larger* space) for their games of keep-away or chase and play-wrestling? Perhaps it could be done by having adult monitors insist that boys participate in jump-rope, and having the monitors either stop the boys from chase-and-wrestle games or somehow entice the girls to join in with the boys' rough play while also persuading the boys to accept the girls' participation.

If we imagine such efforts on the part of adults, we realize that they go against the grain of some widely held values. Most of us believe that children need to be given some time for spontaneous self-expression, free from adult coercion. Furthermore, we might not succeed in efforts to prevent the formation of same-sex groups—at least not without the expenditure of more adult effort than seems feasible. But even if we did expend the effort, and did succeed, there might be unintended consequences. Children's same-sex groups provide a variety of useful socialization experiences, though somewhat different ones for the two sexes. In their male peer groups boys learn a good deal about the management of aggression and competition, and gain experience in fitting into a group structure and coordinating their activities with those of peers to achieve group goals. For girls, same-sex friendships are an important locus of social support. For children of both sexes, same-sex peer groups are the venue for the construction of norms for social behavior which, on balance, support children's adjustment. To what extent should these be sacrificed in the interests of gender equality? It would be difficult indeed to make the case that the benefits of freeing children from same-sex groups would outweigh the benefits children derive from their same-sex associations or the costs of preventing those associations, particularly since different segments of society might evaluate the benefits and costs differently.

Encouraging Cross-Sex Cooperation

A second strategy is to make the most of opportunities within existing structures for adults to guide children into more cooperative cross-sex partnerships and forms of interaction. In the discussion of cross-sex tensions in the workplace, we saw that at the time they enter the job market many people lack experience with mixed-sex cooperative enterprises in a nonsexualized context. It seems likely that more prior experience with such enterprises would facilitate gender integration in the workplace. Such experience would presumably also facilitate the formation of egalitarian pair bonds between mated couples, particularly since over time the importance of sexual passion diminishes and the working teamship side of a couple's relationship grows in importance.

Our public schools provide multiple opportunities for mixed-sex cooperative experience. I suspect that the very fact that our public schools are coeducational has contributed to the movement toward gender equality in this century. It is customary to blame schools for discrimination against girls: witness the allegations that teachers pay more attention to boys in the classroom, or that school counsellors steer girls away from careers in math and science.[5] However true these allegations may be, the more pervasive fact is that boys and girls are present together in the same classrooms, are given the same assignments and the same tests, held to much the same standards, and for the most part are accorded the same "rights" and "duties" of school citizenship. David Tyack and Elisabeth Hansot, in their book on the history of coeducation in America (1990), point out that our public schools may indeed be the least sexist institutions in our society.

Thorne (1986) has noted instances in which gender loses its salience in the classroom or even on the playground, with boys and girls joining together readily. This happens when the children are engaged in an absorbing group task or when their joint membership in a non–gender-defined group becomes important. However, it is well known that merely bringing disparate groups together in the same social setting or similar classroom activities does not necessarily breed good, cooperative relationships. Racial desegregation of the schools has sometimes improved interracial harmony, sometimes worsened it. As far as gender relations are concerned, elements of cross-gender teasing and same-sex coalitions are brought into coeducational classrooms by the children themselves, apart from any gender differentiation the teachers may contribute. Clearly, children in mixed groups do not always learn the gender-minimizing lessons that adults have in mind. In mixed-sex work groups, it happens not infrequently that boys dominate the interaction that occurs, and teachers must exercise considerable ingenuity (by setting up formal rotation of leadership roles, for example) to bring about egalitarian cross-sex cooperation in such groups. Nevertheless, in modern times many girls of grade school age—perhaps most—have the self-confidence, and the solid subject-matter competence, to hold their own in interaction with boys when working on joint projects, particularly when adults are exercising supervisory authority.

Schools, of course, are not the only setting in which attempts have been made to bring about gender integration. In many communities, mixed-sex groups of youth have been mobilized—or have mobilized themselves—for community service projects. And indeed mixed-sex youth service organizations have been formed on a national level—the Peace Corps and Americorps. We assume that such enterprises offer opportunities for young men and women to join together in cooperative work toward joint goals. Yet we do not know to what extent the young men and women who are involved in community service enterprises actually do gain experience in equal-status, cooperative work. Nor do we know whether those who have participated in youth service projects have made gains in their ability to work comfortably in mixed-sex work groups at subsequent points in their careers. These are important matters for a research agenda.

Promoting the Development of the Two Sexes Separately

There is a very different point of view about the high road to gender equality: rather than seeking to increase the amount of cross-sex interaction among children, or trying to make such interaction less sexualized and more equal in status, some advocates for women urge that we should concentrate on empowering girls and women so that they will be able to demand and achieve greater equality in their interactions with males. In her work with inner-city youth groups, McLaughlin (1996) makes some instructive observations concerning community centers that formerly served only boys and were then opened to youth of both sexes. She reports that girls who come to such centers sometimes form girls' gangs that emulate the boys' gangs in toughness and macho behavior. Alternatively, the girls tend to hang around at the fringes of the boys' groups (for example, watching them play pool). Genuine integration and cross-sex cooperation, she observes, are rare. McLaughlin urges that girls in these settings need some separate, all-girl activities (other than girl-gang activities) that will let them form female group ties and identities—something, she believes, that will put them on a firmer footing in dealing with the established male groups. We may suspect further that cross-sex cooperation will only come about in these settings by virtue of programs and facilities—beyond pool tables and basketball courts—that draw male and female youth into joint activities that are absorbing to both sexes.

Proponents of single-sex education advocate socializing and training the two sexes separately. In a sense, this strategy amounts to working with, rather than against, the children's own separatist tendencies. For advocates of gender equality, the assumptions are: (1) that girls will develop a greater range of competencies and become more self-confident and more self-reliant if educated in an atmosphere that is free from male dominance; (2) that girls will benefit from strengthening bonds with other girls; and (3) that in the adolescent years, heterosexual forces run counter to the long-run best interests of many girls—that girls need at least one context for continued development in which they can be free of the pressures of heterosexual concerns.

It would take me too far afield to try to review here the considerable body of research on single-sex education and its outcomes. Suffice it to say that there is evidence that girls and women who have attended single-sex schools and colleges do indeed appear to benefit in certain respects. In particular, they often reach higher levels of individual achievement (graduate and professional degrees; high earnings).[6] Little attention has been paid, however, to the outcomes of single-sex education for girls' and women's subsequent relations with men, in the workplace and in intimate relationships.

Single-sex education for boys has been less studied, and its effects are not well understood. It has been claimed that boys who are at risk for educational failure would fare better in all-boy classrooms taught by male teachers, but to my knowledge we do not have empirical tests of this claim. From the standpoint of promoting gender equality in adulthood, however, there is reason to be wary of all-male schools. In traditional settings, they have augmented the already-existing power differential between the sexes by strengthening male ties and male exclusionary attitudes toward women and girls, to say nothing of sexist attitudes toward women as sex objects.

But there is a contradiction here. If one believes that adults and social institutions should deal evenhandedly with children of the two sexes, it's difficult to justify being in favor of single-sex education for girls and against it for boys—to say nothing of the practical impossibility of implementing such a view. In our present state of knowledge (or ignorance!) it is very difficult to make a sensible choice between coeducation or single-sex schools for both sexes. It is quite possible that single-sex schools would be helpful for some kinds of children but not for others, at some ages but not at others. What we need is some cautious experimentation (indeed, some is already going on), with careful evaluation of the impact of single-sex education over time on diverse populations of children. In particular, we need much more information than we now have concerning the outcomes of coeducational versus single-sex education for subsequent relations between the sexes.

Increasing Male Participation in Child Care

Social change has been rapid when it comes to women's participation in the labor force, and quite rapid as well when it comes to their gaining entry to previously all-male jobs or moving up to higher levels of management. In modern societies, more and more women hold jobs even when their children are very young. These changes have of course raised new questions about who is to care for young children while the women who previously carried out this function are at work, and who should be responsible for child care when two working parents are both at home. Many have advocated that, in view of women's increasing role as breadwinners, men should take on a larger role in the care of children. But social change in this respect has been quite slow.

In traditional societies, women have done a large share of nondomestic work during their child-bearing years, and have relied on older girls and female relatives for help in caring for young children while the mothers worked. But in recent years, these resources have been shrinking: nowadays, grandmothers usually live separately from their grown children, and as families have become more geographically mobile, few relatives live nearby. In addition, female relatives who might otherwise have been available to help are now usually in the labor force themselves.

Hired servants—baby-sitters, nannies, au pairs—have helped to fill the gaps in in-home child care, but this option has always been more accessible to affluent families, and increasing numbers of families cannot afford to hire enough in-home help to cover parents' working hours. We might expect that fathers as well as mothers would reduce their working hours to have more time for being at home with the children, but in fact few fathers do this. Increasingly, families have relied on paid out-of-home care. In a small but increasing number of low-income families where child-care costs are especially difficult to meet, the two parents work different shifts so that there can always be one parent at home with the children. In such cases, however, it is usually the mother who works the night shift, and is at home to do the daytime care of house and children.

In families where both parents work, there has been some increase in the fathers' participation in domestic duties, including child care, during their nonworking hours. Still, mothers continue to be the parents who assume the major share of child-care duties, and the ones more likely to cut back on hours of work, or to take time off from work, to deal with family demands.

It is obvious that for many fathers in two-parent families, there is increasing pressure to take on a greater share of domestic work, including child care. But men do not always respond to these pressures by increasing their investment of time in their families; some join (or pressure) their wives in decisions to have fewer children. Still others withdraw from their commitment to both the marriage and the children. It all depends on how strongly each parent wants children, on how strongly committed each is to the marriage, and on how well they agree concerning what is an acceptable division of labor between them.

The gender discrepancy in parenting becomes even more marked when parents separate or divorce. Relatively few divorced couples have managed to maintain joint physical custody, and in the large majority of cases the children of divorced parents live with their mothers. So do children of never-married mothers.

It is not at all clear how a greater involvement of fathers could be brought about. All in all, the tilt toward mothers as the major agents of child care continues to be strong. There do not seem to be any firm leverage points for more rapid change, or even a strong social consensus as to what division of labor between parents is most desirable from the standpoint of producing well-functioning families.

A Personal Note

Recently, I gave a talk on the subject of this book to a university audience. Afterward a young man came up, looking distressed. He said, "Just tell me one thing: what's good about being male?" I was startled. I had not intended my message to be anti-male. I did not, and do not, *feel* anti-male; quite the contrary. But it is true that once the phenomena described in Chapters 1–3 and Chapters 8–10 have been laid out as objectively as possible, the trends described can be interpreted as meaning that it is mainly men who have stood in the way of achieving equality between the sexes. There is some truth to this interpretation, but it is not the whole truth. The deeper questions have to do with what kind of equality we want.

Many of us believe that we, as a society, should strive for greater equality between men and women in their intimate relationships, and greater opportunity for women to have a life beyond the domestic arena. Of course, men need to know how to adapt to other men and women to other women. But to most of us it is equally obvious that men and women need each other, and must adapt and accommodate to each other. It seems clear that in the past women have done more than their share of the adapting. But the flow of influence between partners *can* be fully bidirectional, and I would urge that it ought to be. Still it seems likely that what is good about being female and what is good about being male need not be exactly the same thing. I believe that the strengths of the two sexes can be brought into integration within a framework that involves some degree of differentiation of function while being at the same time equitable.

From the standpoint of achieving gender equity, the story that has been told in this book is sobering. It seems evident that we will not be able to make much progress toward gender equality simply by giving little boys dolls to play with or giving girls gender-neutral names and dressing them in blue jeans. I have argued that children would probably separate into same-sex groups during spontaneous play regardless of the efforts their parents and teachers might make to create a unisex environment, and further, that the separation of the sexes in childhood has consequences that cannot be ignored.

Still, there is a great deal that societies can do to create opportunities for equal-status interaction between boys and girls. I take it as an article of faith that doing so will have benefits for the quality of the interaction the two sexes will have at a later time in their adult contexts. Perhaps equally important, however, is the set of social rules and practices that children look forward to as the contexts in which they will lead their adult lives.

In my view, the vast changes that have taken place during this century in the rules and expectations concerning the roles of the two sexes have occurred in spite of, rather than because of, the way boys and girls are socialized by their parents. A generation of girls whose mothers were typically housewives nevertheless was able to take advantage of an ever-widening array of opportunities. Many parents have come to have wider aspirations for their daughters, too, but in recent years each new generation of girls has been somewhat ahead of its parents in terms of work-related aspirations and achievements. Both young men and young women have come to see women's participation in this broader sphere as natural, though men have not yet become as fully convinced that these changes are desirable. We surely have not reached the limits of social change when it comes to more equal participation of the two sexes in public life—in civic life as well as the world of work. I believe that the rapid social changes this century has seen are evidence in themselves of the enormous power of human cultures and social institutions: their power to override what many have seen as deep-seated "natural" differences between the sexes.

As we have seen, social change has been slow and uneven in the roles of the two sexes in the rearing of children. To many, especially to career-oriented women, the gender discrepancy in child-care roles seems patently unfair. Yet to date, there is very little agreement concerning what could or should be done to ease the disproportionate "second shift" stresses on working women. In the recent past, a suggestion was made that there should be two career tracks for working women: a "mommy" track for women who wanted to combine careers with motherhood—involving slower career advancement but flexible arrangements for time off for child-related duties and no requirements for travel—versus a full-speed-ahead career track that would make no concessions for any conflicts that non–work-related domestic duties might entail. There was a furor of outraged, angry reaction to this suggestion. The intensity of these reactions testifies to how deeply many people hold the belief that our social goal should be for working parents to share child care equally. It was strongly argued by those who rejected the mommy track that if we were going to create a career track that would accommodate the demands of child care, it should be a "parent track," and as many fathers as mothers should be included in it.

The issues concerning the proper roles of men and women in rearing children are thorny indeed. It is not only the interests of mothers and fathers that need to be considered, but the interests of children as well. Other things being equal, I believe it is optimal for children to be reared by two deeply committed parents *who are in a harmonious relationship with each other.* Within this framework, wide variation is possible, ranging from an exact division of child-care functions between the two parents, to a strong division of labor in which one parent does most of the child care and the other most of the out-of-home earning of economic support for the family. Our social institutions should be geared to this diversity, so as to permit maximum flexibility for families to arrive at the division of child-care responsibilities that best suits their individual circumstances.

There are many reasons to continue to press for greater male involvement with children, but the father role can involve different functions from the mother role while nevertheless being highly important in the lives of children. I believe that it is probably not realistic to set a fifty-fifty division of labor between mothers and fathers in the day-to-day care of children as the most desirable pattern toward which we should all strive as a social goal. We should consider the alternative view: that equity between the sexes does not have to mean exact equality in the sense of the two sexes having exactly the same life-styles and exactly the same allocation of time.

Most women give high priority to child-rearing, and many freely choose to stay home with young children even when this entails some financial sacrifice for the family. But most will want to return to work at some time as the children grow up. For those who remain in the labor force—by choice or necessity—their work commitments must often be scaled back while their children are young. There can be no doubt that women's child-rearing role has adversely affected their status vis-à-vis men in terms of their participation in the public sphere, their incomes and career development, and their access to leisure activities. If for whatever reason women are going to continue to be the ones who invest more heavily in child-rearing, then it would seem that our efforts ought to be directed to minimizing the penalties they have to pay for doing so. Most modern Western societies have already adopted a variety of policies aimed at enhancing the ability of working parents to care for children (parental leave; subsidized daycare; child-support payments from noncustodial parents). When properly implemented, these policies help redress the imbalance between mothers and fathers who differ in their investment in child care.[7] It seems to me axiomatic that public investment in such programs is eminently justified, on the grounds that anything that eases the pressures on parents and enables them to foster their children's healthy development will redound to the benefit of society as a whole. In the end, there is no reason to expect that men and women will want to make exactly the same choices about the way they invest their time. But there is every reason to work toward equity in power and resources, so as to make each sex's choices as free as possible.

Notes

References

Index

Notes

Introduction

1. See Chodorow (1978, chaps. 6 and 9) for a detailed account and critique of early psychoanalytic thinking about the personality organization of the two sexes. And see the critique by Maccoby and Jacklin (1974, part 2).

2. See Cherlin (1996, chap. 3) for a detailed account of this perspective.

3. A presentation of the classic top-down learning-theory account of socialization may be found in J. L. Gewirtz (1969). The social-learning theory position is presented by Albert Bandura (1969) and by Walter Mischel (1966).

4. Eagley (1995) argues that a number of differences, though small in an absolute sense, are nevertheless consistent and large enough to carry social consequences.

5. For a fuller account of these different meanings, see Maccoby (1987).

6. We will see (Chapter 7) that even in the first year, when children are too young to apply a verbal label, they can make perceptual distinctions between male and female voices or pictured faces. This implies that children of 33 months might notice the difference if first paired with a same-sex partner and then with a different-sex partner. In the work being described here, however, children were paired with only one partner and so did not have the benefit of contrast.

7. Maccoby and Jacklin (1974); Huston (1983, 1985); Crombie and Desjardins (1993). And see Chapter 4 above.

8. See also the comment by Archer (1996), who supports an interactive perspective for studying gender issues, noting that social behavior necessarily involves another person or persons, and recommends that the sex of an individual's interactive partner should always be taken into account when considering sex differences in the social domain. He concludes: "The main effects perspective . . . is no longer appropriate" (p. 153).

1. Gender Segregation in Childhood

1. Some of the children studied by Howes were in family daycare homes large enough to have other children of the same age as the target child; others were in daycare centers.

2. Such studies have usually used a procedure of behavioral time-sampling. Each child in a group or classroom of children is taken in turn as a target for observation for short time periods throughout a portion of the day. For a child engaged in social play during a targeted time interval, the observer records whether the child is playing with one or more same-sex partners, one or more other-sex partners, or in mixed-sex groups. Another research technique has been to record the identity of each child's nearest neighbor, to determine how often same-sex children, as distinct from other-sex children, are to be found within a child's "personal space."

3. For a summary of the results of a large group of studies of play-partner preferences, see Maccoby and Jacklin (1987).

4. See Whiting and Edwards (1988, p. 231, and tables 6.6 and 6.7).

5. For this section I have drawn primarily on the following sources: an earlier review by Maccoby and Jacklin (1987); reviews by Lockheed (1984, 1985) and Hartup (1983); books by Whiting and Whiting (1975) and Whiting and Edwards (1988); a chapter by Thorne (1986) and a paper by Thorne and Luria (1986); a book by Lloyd and Duveen (1992); and a paper by Eisenhart and Holland (1983).

6. Table 7.3 in Whiting and Edwards (1988, p. 257) shows that in six cultures, social acts are initiated by children aged 6 to 10 five times as often to same-sex as to opposite-sex peers.

7. Lloyd and Duveen (1992) reported much greater congregation into same-sex groups for peer-organized than for teacher-organized activities.

8. Observing fourth- and sixth-graders during recess and lunch hour, Crombie and Desjardins (1993) found that children were playing 64 percent of the time exclusively with same-sex others, 27 percent of the time in mixed-sex groups, and only 1 percent of the time exclusively with children of the other sex.

9. See also Lockheed et al. (1981).

10. See Strayer (1985) and Ladd and Price (1986).

11. Ellis, Rogoff, and Cromer (1981); Thorne (1986).

2. The Two Cultures of Childhood

1. Lever (1976); Crombie and Desjardins (1993); Thorne and Luria (1986); Benenson (1993); Lloyd and Duveen (1992).

2. Benenson (1994) notes that from age 4 to 6 the size of girls' play networks decreases, while boys' groups remain stable (and larger) in size.

3. This playroom was located in an RV which could be driven to a number of different preschool sites.

4. See DiPietro (1981) and Maccoby (1988).

5. The amount of jumping on the trampoline was nearly twice as great for girls as for boys.

6. See Omark, Omark, and Edelman (1973) and Whiting and Edwards (1988).

7. For example, Jacklin and Maccoby (1978) saw more tugs of war in boy-boy pairs than in girl-girl pairs of children at the age of 33 months; Fagot (1991) noted more aggressive, conflictual behavior on the part of boys in the sample of 100 toddlers she observed in play groups from the age of 18 months to 30 months. It is notable, however, that boys also showed more *positive reactions* to their peers.

8. See reviews by Maccoby and Jacklin (1980) and Parke and Slaby (1983).

9. Charlesworth and Dzur (1987); Pitcher and Schulz (1983).

10. The two sexes did not differ in the frequency of reported distress (for example, crying or whining) or in displays of anger. In interpreting the results of this study we must be aware of the possibility that mothers' reports of their infants' moods could be influenced by the mothers' stereotypes concerning the characteristics they expect children of the two sexes to have.

11. An early study showing the greater frequency of dominance behavior among young boys was Anderson's 1939 study of kindergarten children, and a number of studies have reported similar findings since that time, e.g., Omark, Omark, and Edelman (1973) and Whiting and Edwards in their cross-cultural work (1988).

12. See Lever (1976) and Whiting and Edwards (1988, p. 259).

13. DeRosier, Cillesen, Coie, and Dodge (1994).

14. Crick and Grotpeter (1995) use this term, and distinguish relational aggression from overt aggression (the type of aggression more common among boys).

15. Cairns et al. (1989).

16. In the Crick and Grotpeter work, the sex difference between the mean standardized scores for relational aggression was .82 standard deviation units, while that for overt aggression was 1.86 standard deviation units.

17. Dunn and Morgan (1987), for example, reporting their observations in an Irish "infant" school, noted that on one occasion the boys raided the girls' kitchen corner and unscrewed the faucet handles in the miniature sink, to use as toy guns. Sheldon and Rohleder (1995) introduced a same-sex triad of preschoolers into a playroom equipped with materials for domestic play (toy cooking utensils and food; infant-care equipment). Boys were six times more likely than girls to transform domestic objects into pretend objects for nondomestic use (e.g., a spoon was used as a flashlight for exploring a cave; beans became bullets).

18. See Sanders and Harper (1976, p. 1182) and McLoyd (1983, p. 626).

19. See Pitcher and Schultz (1983, pp. 62–64).

20. Huston (1983, 1985). See also Crombie and Desjardins (1993).

21. Maccoby and Jacklin (1974); Fishhein (1996); Eisenberg, Wolchik, Hernandez, and Pasternack (1985); Bussey and Bandura (1992).

22. For this summary, I have drawn upon the following studies: Sachs (1987); Sheldon (1990); Black and Hazen (1990); Weiss and Sachs (1991); Leaper (1991); Black (1992); Cook, Fritz, McCormack, and Visperas (1985); Killen and Naigles (1995).

23. For example, see Miller, Danaher, and Forbes (1986).

24. See Maccoby (1990); Eisenberg, Martin, and Fabes (1996); Miller, Danaher, and Forbes (1986); Leaper (1991, 1994); Goodwin (1990); McClosky and Coleman (1992).

25. Thorne and Luria describe a game played by fifth-grade boys in a Massachusetts public school. The game consisted of a paragraph (in this case, from a textbook on the U.S. Constitution) with key words deleted. Players took turns filling in the blanks. As Thorne and Luria say, "Making the paragraph absurd and violating rules to create excitement seemed to be the goal of the game. The boys clearly knew that their intentions were 'dirty': they requested the field observer not to watch the game. Instead the observer negotiated a post-game interrogation on the rules of the game. The boys had completed the sentence 'The _____ was ratified in _____ in 1788' with 'The shit was ratified in Cuntville in 1788.'"

26. Putallaz and Wasserman (1989).

27. See also the review paper by Putallaz and Sheppard (1992). Male "hosts" ignored

the newcomer 39 percent of the time, while a pair of girls did so 24 percent of the time (Borja-Alvarez, Zarbatany, and Pepper, 1991).

28. See Lamb and Roopnarine (1979); Fagot (1985, 1989, and a review paper, 1994); Langlois and Downs, as reported in Maccoby (1980, p. 241).

29. See Fagot (1985) for evidence that even as early as the toddler years, the male peer group is developing a shared understanding concerning what activities are "not male," and that such activities are to be avoided, while girls do not systematically avoid male-type activities.

30. Chung and Asher (1996) report that boys who express willingness to go to an adult for help in resolving a peer conflict are unpopular with peers. For a girl to turn to adults in such a situation is not associated with peer rejection.

31. There have been some informal observations suggesting that there may be more bonding in larger groups among girls from minority ethnic backgrounds, up to and including the formation of girls' "gangs." So far, this is an undocumented possibility.

32. See Thorne (1994, pp. 103–109).

3. Cross-Sex Encounters

1. See Mahony (1985); Wolpe (1977); Dunn and Morgan (1987); Thorne (1994).

2. Personal communication from Greeno (1988).

3. This is a speculative point, since researchers have paid surprisingly little attention to the question of how many children of each sex are present and looking on during a cross-sex interaction.

4. What Needs to Be Explained

1. Eagly (1995) claims that sex differences typically fall in the range from .2 to .5 standard deviations. Hyde and Plant (1995), in their commentary on Eagly's paper, place the modal effect size for gender between .11 and .35. See also comments on Eagly's 1995 paper in the *American Psychologist*, February 1996.

2. The one-week stability coefficient for other-sex play was .17 for the sexes combined ($N = 40$), and was equally low when computed separately for boys and girls.

3. The male interest in guns and swords probably develops somewhat later than the interest in transportation toys, occurring when male play takes up heroic themes (see Chapter 2).

4. See Fein et al. (1975); Jacklin, Maccoby, and Dick (1973); Fagot (1974, 1985); Blakemore, LaRue, and Olejnik (1979); Blakemore, Lloyd, and Smith (1985); Smith and Daglish (1977); O'Brien and Huston (1985); Roopnarine (1986).

5. Berenbaum and Snyder (1995), in studies of adreno-genital syndrome children and unaffected controls, also found no relation between toy-activity preferences and same- or other-gender playmate preferences.

6. As Serbin (1994) notes, longitudinal data are needed to see whether playstyles predict subsequent same-sex partner choice.

7. Suggestive evidence also comes from a study by Alexander and Hines (1994) in which preschoolers and young grade schoolers were offered a choice, from pictures, between two possible playmates who differed in gender and playstyle indicators.

Especially for boys, choices were based more upon playstyles than upon the gender of the putative playmate when the two conflicted.

5. The Biological Component

1. This metaphor is not original with me. It appears to have originated with Donald Hebb.

2. On the basis of data from twin studies, heritability of a binary characteristic such as possessing a penis would be zero, since only same-sex twin pairs are used in twin studies designed to estimate heritability, and there is no within-sex variability for either monozygotic or dizygotic twins. Adoption studies, too, are not designed to provide estimates of the genetic contribution to sex differences.

3. Daly and Wilson (1983). See especially their discussion on pp. 28–32.

4. Mason (1961); Miller, Caul, and Mirsky (1967); Mitchell (1972). See Meany, Stewart, and Beatty (1985) for an extended discussion and summary of evidence on the role of play-fighting in social adaptation. They argue that, for males but not for females, play-fighting is a means for establishing a place in the same-sex dominance hierarchy.

5. See Meany, Stewart, and Beatty (1985, pp. 35–38) for a summary of such studies.

6. Jane Collier and Shelly Risaldo describe four hunter-gatherer societies which have remained out of contact with modern societies until very recently, in their article "Politics and Gender in Simple Societies," in Ortner and Whitehead (1981).

7. The preschoolers in this study were interacting with either one or three puppets.

8. See also the review by Carter (1987).

9. It is interesting that young females show even less rough play when interacting only with other females than they do when young males are also present (Goldfoot and Wallen, 1978). This finding indicates that the lower levels of female rough play in mixed-sex troops do not result from suppression of this behavior by the presence of males.

10. See Lovejoy and Wallen (1988) and Goldfoot et al. (1984). In the study by Goldfoot and colleagues, some of the young animals were reared with only same-sex peers available for play, others in heterosexual playgroups.

11. The evidence is solid for monkeys and apes, much thinner for human children, partly because in most observational research children are studied in interaction with others of their own age. The cross-cultural evidence points to greater interest in infants and younger children on the part of girls, and this is supported by a few laboratory studies in our own society (see the summary of evidence in Maccoby, 1980, pp. 217–221). Girls' greater interest in dolls may reflect the same tendency.

12. Eaton and Enns (1986) report a small but significant tendency for infant boys to be more active than infant girls. But other work not included in their review does not consistently yield the same result. For example, Fagot and O'Brien, in their 1994 study of two cohorts of children aged 12 and 18 months, did not find a sex difference in activity level. In Jacklin's and my longitudinal work, we have both the mother's reports of the child's activity at home and scores derived from observations taken either at home or in our laboratory. Neither source of information has shown boys to be typically more active in the first two years.

13. See Maccoby and Jacklin (1974). More recently Eaton and Enns (1986) sum-

marized a number of studies, and reported a substantial sex difference in activity level among preschoolers (mean difference, .44 standard deviations) as well as among children of grade school age (.64 standard deviations).

14. Eaton and Enns (1986, table 3) report a sex difference in activity when children are playing alone, but show that the difference is greater when children are playing with peers.

15. See Eaton and Enns (1986).

16. The child's future adult stature was estimated on the basis of the heights of the child's two parents. Although boys and girls are very similar in height at ages 5–8, boys will be taller than girls in adulthood; hence, girls on average have attained a larger proportion of their adult height in middle childhood than have boys.

17. A mediation model was tested with a multiple regression analysis. Sex by itself accounted for 25 percent of the variance in activity level, but this figure dropped to 15 percent when maturity was included in the model.

18. See Maccoby and Jacklin (1983, pp. 86–88). Rothbaum and Weisz (1994) also report that "difficult" behavior seems to have a different meaning for parents, depending on whether it comes from a boy or a girl. At least, they react more strongly to difficult behavior from a boy.

19. Although Lundberg (1983) initially reported that levels of catecholamines were higher among male than female three-year-olds during ordinary activities in a daycare center, follow-up work by Lundberg and colleagues (1987) with larger samples of preschoolers did not reveal either sex differences in resting levels of catecholamines or a greater rise in in the level of catecholamines in males during challenging activities (running, chasing and catching, watching a funny movie, trying to solve Ravens Matrices). Nor did these researchers find that catecholamines or cortisol excretions rose more in young boys than in girls (three-year-olds) when they underwent the stress of entering the hospital (Lundberg, 1986). In Megan Gunnar's laboratory, sex differences have not been found in base levels of cortisol and catecholamines among newborns and older infants, nor have measures of these hormones reflected any tendency for males to be more aroused by the stress of physical exams (including being weighed and measured) or the mild pain of heel-pricks (Gunnar, personal communication, 1989).

20. See Eisenberg et al. (1994), Eisenberg et al. (1991), and a summary of these and other studies in Fabes (1994).

21. For example, Schachter and colleagues (1978) reported that in their sample of toddlers, girls had a higher mean length of utterance than boys. Fernald, McRoberts, and Herrera (in press) assessed the word knowledge of a substantial sample of toddlers aged 15 or 19 months, by recording whether they looked at the correct picture when one of the pictured objects was named, and found that girls performed better. Huttenlocher and colleagues (1991) traced the development of spoken vocabulary in 22 children during the second year of life, by listening in on verbal exchanges between the children and their mothers during repeated visits to the families' homes. They reported that girls' spoken vocabularies increased more rapidly than boys' during the first part of the second year of life, but that the sex differences in rate of acquisition diminished in the second part of the year. Although children's rate of vocabulary growth was closely related to the frequency with which their mothers talked to them, mothers in the Huttenlocher sample talked with equal frequency to sons and daughters,

so that maternal inputs were not responsible for the sex difference in rate of vocabulary acquisition.

22. Such strong differentiation in cerebral localization is not found when the infants are listening to music or when they are in a baseline condition with no experimental auditory stimulation.

23. Smith and Daglish (1977); Minton, Kagan, and Levine (1972); Snow, Jacklin, and Maccoby (1983). In the Stanford longitudinal study, parents were asked about the occurrence of a variety of mischievous actions when the children were 18 months old; in one cohort of children, boys were reported to be more mischievous than girls (effect size approximately one half standard deviation), though in a second cohort this difference was not found (Maccoby and Jacklin, unpublished data).

24. Weinberg (1992), observing three- and six-month-old infants interacting with their mothers, reported that the boys were emotionally more labile, and specifically that they expressed both more fussy and more joyful states, while the girls were calmer, less emotionally reactive. Cunningham and Shapiro (1984) also reported that the male infants they studied had more intense emotional reactions (both positive and negative) than did the girls.

25. This is not the only explanation, however: when girls move indoors, they are more likely to take up sedentary activities involving books or table play materials (clay; coloring materials), while boys are more likely to play indoors with blocks or transportation toys—toys that may evoke more body movement.

26. A recent review of research on sex differences in inhibition (Bjorklund and Kipp, 1996) reports somewhat greater inhibitory ability for females in the social domain, specifically in the control of emotions, and weaker but still significant advantages for females in behavioral inhibition, particularly early in life. It is interesting that there are some parallel findings in nonhuman primates. Sackett (1974) reviewed the literature on sex differences in the effects of social isolation on rhesus monkeys, and found males to be considerably more affected. Following isolation, young males showed more self-aggression than females, more fear, and greatly reduced exploratory activity—sex differences that were the reverse of those observed in animals reared normally. Sackett hypothesized that the greater male reaction to isolation was due to a "developmental failure of inhibitory response mechanisms" in males—that males could not inhibit certain competing emotional responses that were incompatible with normal development (reported in Gottman and Levinson, p. 194). With human children, one finding runs counter to the greater self-regulatory abilities of females: boys seem better able to inhibit crying, at least in the presence of their peers.

27. See Kopp (1989) for a review of the role of language acquisition in emotional self-regulation.

28. Eisenberg and colleagues cite a limited set of other studies showing that poor regulation of affect is associated with being unpopular with peers (Eisenberg et al., 1993, p. 1420).

29. There is a second surge of male testosterone production at about the third month of postnatal life (see Maccoby, 1980, p. 207, for a summary), but this was not known at the time the early work on prenatal androgens was done.

30. This early experimental work is summarized in Money and Ehrhardt (1972).

31. See Berenbaum (1990) for a review of studies on AGS children.

32. The original Money and Ehrhardt work is reported in their 1972 book *Man and*

Woman, Boy and Girl. In this work, the characteristics of AGS girls were sometimes compared with those of girls representing population-wide norms, and questions were raised concerning the selective factors for membership in the adreno-genital group that might invalidate such comparisons. Subsequent work by Ehrhardt and Baker (1974) used a more comparable control group (the AGS girls' normal sisters), and their results confirmed the tomboy characteristics of AGS girls.

33. Recent work by Hines and Kaufman (1994) has found that AGS girls show stronger preferences for male playmates than unaffected siblings or cousins; however, in their sample there was no elevation in rough-and-tumble play for the AGS girls. As Hines and Kaufman noted, the specific androgenic priming effects undoubtedly depend on the prenatal timing of the onset of the AGS condition.

6. The Socialization Component

1. In the studies in which adults were asked to rate characteristics of a videotaped infant labeled as either a boy or a girl, their ratings were affected by the gender label in only 7 percent of the ratings made. In the studies in which an adult interacted with a live infant, an effect of the gender label was found in 18 percent of the comparisons, and studies were not consistent in terms of what kind of effect was found. For example, four studies coded the amount of talk directed to the live infant. One reported that infants labeled girls were talked to more, but the other three studies found that the gender label did not affect the amount of talk directed to the infant.

2. Lytton and Romney (1991) carried out a meta-analysis of 172 studies (including but adding to the studies previously reviewed by Maccoby and Jacklin, 1974).

3. Not all the three cohorts were observed at each age, so the size of the sample varied. At the infant and toddler ages, most of the observations involved the mother only, but fathers as well as mothers were observed in interaction with their children at 12 months, 45 months, and 6 years of age. Not all the results summarized here have been previously reported in published papers, but when they have, the papers are cited.

4. Fathers when interacting with sons were the most active in initiating male-type play. This is consistent with the study by Fagot and Hagan (1991) of larger samples of children aged 12 months, 18 months, or 5 years. Few consistent differences in parents' reactions to sons and daughters were found in this work, but at age 18 months boys did receive more positive reactions from their parents for male-type play than did the girls at this age, and fathers showed relatively few positive reactions to their sons when they engaged in female-type play.

5. The correlation was not significant when boys and girls were combined. When the sexes were analyzed separately, the correlation was low and nonsignificant for boys and of borderline significance for girls.

6. Blakemore (1990) reported that girls were more nurturant toward an infant sibling than were boys, but detailed observations of the mother's teaching or guiding the child into nurturant behavior did not show that she was more active in this respect with daughters. Fling and Manosevitz (1972) found that although parents did discourage cross-sex activities in their preschoolers, the degree to which they did so was uncorrelated with the children's sex-typing. Weinraub et al. (1984) reported that measures of gender identity and sex-typed toy choices in a child's third year of life were unrelated to the mother's sex-role attitudes or behavior toward the child, although

there were weak correlations between the father's responses and a son's sex-typed toy choices (only 15 percent of the correlations for fathers were significant, and none of the mothers'). Thompson (1975) found no relation between the rate of acquisition of gender labels in the third year and the traditionality of parents' attitudes. Weisner (1994) found very little relation between the traditionality or nontraditionality of the parents' households and the children's sex-typing. Especially surprising is a study by Tauber (1979) in which the toy choices made by children of grade school age were unaffected by whether the mother—or the father—was present in the room. The choices of the children did not seem to be affected by expectations of approval or disapproval from their parents.

7. Smith and Daglish (1977); Smetana (1989); Falender and Haber (1975); Minton, Kagan, and Levine (1971); Snow, Jacklin, and Maccoby (1983); Fagot and Hagan (1991); Frankel and Robbins (1983).

8. Most of the communities included in the Whiting and Edwards report were not industrialized and had relatively low levels of literacy. In a number of these (though not all), women had relatively low status, and boys could already have come to feel, by the age of 4 or 5, that they belonged to the privileged sex and that they did not need to accord the kind of deference to women, even to their mothers, that they would accord to a man.

9. At the second observation, the teachers were no longer "reinforcing" children of the two sexes differentially for positive or negative forms of communication.

10. It is difficult to know how much weight to give to this piece of evidence. For one thing, it was teachers, not parents, whose reactions were being recorded. Samples were fairly small—13 boys and 16 girls—and the number of teachers supervising these children in their playgroups was presumably still smaller. If one or two teachers showed biased reactions depending on the sex of the child, this would be enough to affect results computed on the basis of the number of children. When other children of the same ages were observed at home with their mothers and fathers, it was found that boys received both more positive *and* more negative parental responses for positive communication attempts than did girls (Fagot and Hagen, 1991, table 4)—a reinforcement pattern that would not automatically lead to girls' becoming more communicative. Furthermore, in the study of teachers' responses, we do not know whether it was the very boys who most commonly received attention from teachers for negative attention-getting tactics who had taken up coercive modes of interacting a year later— no individual scores or correlations between Time 1 and Time 2 are available.

11. Power et al. (1994); Power (1985); Power and Parke (1986); Fagot (1974, 1978). We should recall, however, that girls in the toddler and preschool years are not generally subject to more restrictions than boys are (and see Hanson, 1975, for evidence that at ages 3, 5½, and 9½ boys and girls are given equal freedom to explore by their parents, and receive equal amounts of direct teaching from the parents).

12. See Maccoby, Snow, and Jacklin (1984) for evidence of mothers' backing off from difficult boys.

13. See Lewis, Allesandri, and Sullivan (1992).

14. The reader will recognize here the claim that "authoritative" parenting is more likely to lead to self-regulation of antisocial behavior in children than is "authoritarian" parenting.

15. Lytton and Romney used meta-analysis to summarize the results of ten studies in which parental reactions to sons' and daughters' aggression had been compared.

They found that parents were slightly more likely to discourage aggression in girls, but the effect size was only .13 of a standard deviation, not approaching statistical significance.

16. Radke-Yarrow and colleagues analyzed mothers' speech to children aged 25–36 months, and reported more use of emotion words with daughters (Radke-Yarrow, Belmont, Nottelman, and Bottomly, 1990). They did not find that mothers spoke more to one sex than the other about other topics, however.

17. See also Kuebil and Krieger (1991), who reported that mothers talk more about sadness with their preschool daughters than with their sons, and that fathers talk with daughters more about being scared.

18. In a review summarizing 16 studies that dealt specifically with sensitivity to the emotional states of others, Haviland and Malatesta (1981) found clear evidence of greater sensitivity among females. We should, however, be wary of assuming that this sensitivity translates into greater *sharing* of others' affective states (empathy), or greater helpfulness to others growing out of empathy, on the part of females. In their review of sex differences in altruism, Radke-Yarrow, Zahn-Waxler, and Chapman (1983) found no consistent sex difference in any aspect of altruism, including empathic responses to others' distress.

19. Dunn and colleagues (1991) found that the amount of the *child's* talk about emotions to the mother predicted subsequent sensitivity to the emotional states of others much more strongly than did the amount of the mother's emotion-talk to the child.

20. Haviland and Malatesta believe that this finding—along with the finding that mothers gave a wider range of emotional responses to daughters, including nonmatching responses—suggests "a greater sense of empathy between mother and daughter" (1982, p. 201), but clearly other interpretations are possible.

21. Research supporting this conclusion is reviewed by Zahn-Waxler, Cole, and Barrett, (1991, p. 255).

22. See also Gunnar and Donahue (1980) for evidence of greater social responsiveness in infant girls at 6 and 12 months. In a similar vein, Martin (1981) reported that girls were less insistent (more compliant) at both 10 and 22 months than were boys.

23. See the summary of these findings in Maccoby (1980, p. 240).

24. In 20 of the 39 studies, a difference was found in fathers' treatment of sons and daughters; such a difference was almost never found for mothers.

25. I am acquainted with a family in which the strongly homophobic father refused to change his sons' diapers, but was willing and able to carry out this chore with his daughter.

26. Personal communication from Herbert Leiderman (and see Levine et al., 1994).

7. The Cognitive Component

1. See Kohlberg (1966), Huston (1983), Martin (1994), Bem (1981), and Levy and Fivush (1993).

2. Of course, there were large social changes, such as the employment of women in wartime and the advances in contraception, that created a climate in which activist women could have a greater impact.

3. Tajfel told research subjects that they shared a preference for a certain style of

painting, or that they shared a tendency to be either "underestimators" or "overestimators" when judging the number of dots in an array.

4. It is true that in some Native American tribes, a "third gender" has been recognized—the berdache. Still, members of the cultures undoubtedly know that berdaches are people with male bodies despite their having assumed female identities.

5. See Maccoby (1988) for a more detailed exposition of the distinction between binary categories and those that are prototypical (i.e., fuzzy sets), and how this distinction is relevant to gender cognition.

6. There is evidence that infants as young as 2 months of age can make this distinction (Jusczyk, Mullinnex, and Pisoni, 1990).

7. Adult viewers can distinguish people of the two sexes who are moving about in a totally dark room, if small lights have been attached to joints that are important for bodily movement (Cutting, Proffitt, and Koslowski, 1978). No comparable studies have been done with children.

8. See Fagot and Leinbach (1991) for a summary of the evidence.

9. Fagot, Leinbach, and Hagan (1986). See also Leinbach (1983). Whether early, preverbal categorical distinctions are perceptual or conceptual is a matter of debate (see Spelke, 1988, and Markman and Carey, in press).

10. Questions such as "Are you a boy (girl)?" call for at least a rudimentary command of spoken language. Asking children to pick out their own picture from a set of several pictures calls for picture recognition, and we would need to know that a child had the necessary recognition skills for the method to be valid. Still, this procedure has the advantage that children can answer simply by pointing or picking up a picture, without having to use verbal labels. Similarly, asking children "Which is the boy?" when they are shown a pair of pictures (a boy and a girl) allows them to answer merely by pointing, but introduces the complication of what pictures should be presented for their choice (how stereotypically masculine or feminine should they be?). Also, when children must choose one of two objects, they would be correct half the time if they were merely guessing, so that a child can demonstrate gender knowledge only by responding consistently above chance levels; this raises the issue of what percentage of correct responses will be considered "success."

11. For this summary, I have drawn primarily on three sources: Thompson (1975), Weinraub et al. (1984), and Leinbach and Fagot (1986). Each of these studies includes a review of other studies, and a more recent review may be found in a monograph by Serbin, Powlishta, and Gulko (1993).

12. See Thompson (1975). Weinraub and colleagues (1984) reported that children could sort their own pictures accurately somewhat earlier than they could classify the pictures of other adults and children by sex. But surprisingly, they were able to apply gender labels accurately earlier than they could sort pictures accurately into boxes: at the age of 26 months, about three fourths of the children gave accurate verbal gender labels to their own and others' pictures.

13. Serbin, Poulin-Dubois, and Colburne (1995) worked with children aged 24 months. They first showed each child his or her own picture, displayed on a computer screen, saying, "Look! Here you are!" Then they displayed a pair of photos: one of a school-aged boy, one of a school-aged girl, saying, "Find one like you!" (There was also a control condition in which the children were simply told: "Look at the children.") These very young boys looked somewhat longer at the school-aged boy's picture when asked to find "one like you," but not in the control condition. The toddler girls showed

no tendency to focus on the girl's picture under the "like you" instructions. We do not know what accounts for this early sex difference, or whether it would appear with other methods of assessing the gender matching of self and others.

14. Montepare (1993) showed preschoolers an array of pictures of other children who varied in age and sex. The children were asked to choose the picture of the child "most like me." Boys were considerably more likely to choose on the basis of similarity in gender; for girls, age similarity was somewhat more salient than gender similarity.

15. See Slaby and Frey (1975); Smetana and Letourneau (1984); Ruble, Balaban, and Cooper (1981); Wehren and DiLisi (1983); and Bussey and Bandura (1984). And see Maccoby (1990) for a summary and discussion of this work.

16. This evidence is not definitive, since it is conceivable that playing with same-sex playmates contributes to gender labeling, rather than vice versa. Or it might be that both accurate gender labeling and same-sex playmate choice are affected by a third factor (such as verbal or self-regulatory maturity). Still, the studies by Fagot and colleagues add considerably to the plausibility of gender-identity formation as a contributor to same-sex playmate preference.

17. For example, Serbin, Powlishta, and Gulko (1993) reported that boys of early grade school age attributed negative traits to male and female classmates equally, while girls attributed negative traits to boys more often than to girls.

18. See Chapter 2 for references; and also see Leaper (1994, p. 73).

19. See Huston (1985) for a summary of evidence available up to the mid-eighties.

20. Serbin, Powlishta, and Gulko (1993). In this study, in addition to a standard measure of sex-role knowledge (the "Serli"), there was a measure of sex-role flexibility, involving children's beliefs of how many items *could* be used by both sexes, even though one sex might usually use a given item more often. By this measure, flexibility increased with age from kindergarten through third grade.

21. For a fuller account of script theory as it applies to gender, see Levy and Fivush (1993).

22. For a discussion of the developmental lag in attributing different personality characteristics or playstyles to peers of the two sexes, see Huston (1985, p. 7) and Martin (1994). There is some evidence, though, that although children may not see boys as rougher, they do believe that once angered, males (both boys and men) express anger more intensely than do females (Karbon, Fabes, Carlo, and Martin, 1992).

23. In this study, the same videotaped infant was labeled male for some viewers, female for others; so the choices of descriptive adjectives could not have been based on any real differential attributes.

24. The number of children involved in this study was small—only 16. Still the observations are consistent with other work done at that time.

25. See Hetherington, Cox, and Cox (1982). Power, McGrath, Hughes, and Manire (1994) found greater compliance to fathers among children aged 4 years and older, but not among two-year-olds. The greater compliance to fathers was more apparent among boys than girls.

26. See Damon (1977) and the discussion by Serbin et al. (1993, pp. 12–13).

27. See Signorella et al. (1993) for a summary of studies and a demonstration of how much difference the wording of questions makes in terms of whether an increase in "flexibility" with age is found. See also Katz and Ksansnak (1994) for a study of changes in the flexibility of gender attitudes from grade school through high school.

28. The correlation was .19, *p* less than .09.

29. Serbin and colleagues report a correlation of -.10 between their measure of stereotype flexibility and same-sex playmate preference. This correlation is significant at the .05 level but accounts for very little variance.

30. Some recent work by Serbin and colleagues with very young children has indicated that girls' preference for dolls, and boys' preference for cars and trucks, appears by age 18 months, but at this age the children did not appear to be aware that these toys might be associated with one sex more than the other (Serbin, Poulin-Dubois, Colbourne, and Stoll, 1994).

31. There was also a no-model control condition.

32. See the review in Ruble and Martin (1997).

8. Heterosexual Attraction and Relationships

1. Extensive help in drafting the section on marriage in this chapter was provided by Laura L. Carstensen.

2. See Chilman (1983) for a summary of research showing the progressive liberalization of sexual attitudes and behavior in the United States through the sixties, seventies, and early eighties.

3. See *Sex and America's Teenagers* (1994) by the Alan Guttmacher Institute. Brooks-Gunn and Furstenberg (1989) report that while in 1950 only 7 percent of American girls had had intercourse by the age of 16, in 1982, 44 percent had done so. These changes among American youth have been closely matched by comparable increases in sexual activity among adolescents in England, Europe, and Australia (see Moore and Rosenthal, 1993, p. 2).

4. For this summary of the work on loss of voice, I have drawn on a chapter by Harter, Waters, and Whitesell (in press) entitled "Lack of Voice As a Manifestation of False Self Behavior among Adolescents: The School Setting As a Stage upon Which the Drama of Authenticity Is Enacted."

5. Speech attributes that were scored as "high voice" included being talkative, being open, being argumentative, being assertive, speaking one's opinions, being truthful, saying how one feels, being one's self; attributes scored as "low voice" included being quiet, keeping thoughts to one's self, being closed off, being withdrawn, not being completely honest, not being one's self, saying what others want one to say.

6. See Leaper (1994) for a summary of his own and others' studies on this subject.

7. For this section, I have drawn on Catherine Chilman's book *Adolescent Sexuality in a Changing American Society* (1983); S. Moore and D. Rosenthal's book *Sexuality in Adolescence* (1993); and papers in K. McKinney and S. Sprecher, ed., *Sexuality in Close Relationships* (1991). Readers are referred to these sources for further documentation of some of the trends discussed in the text.

8. See Larson and Wood (1996) for a summary of studies.

9. Survey conducted by the American Health and Psychology Today Service (1990).

10. Survey conducted by the American Health and Psychology Today Service (1990).

11. Pahl (1984), in a study in southern England, found that the gendered division of household labor was most clear-cut and conservative in households which included children under the age of 5.

12. See Maccoby and Martin (1983) for a discussion of the decline of dominance issues in communal relationships.

13. Falbo and Peplau were studying the intimate relationships of a sample of college

students, most of whom were not married to their partners. We should note that among the more long-standing marriages studied by Gottman and colleagues, the use of "tentative speech" by wives was rare (Gottman, 1996).

14. There is recent evidence that in men, more than in women, subjective distress and physiological arousal are linked (Levenson, Carstensen, and Gottman, 1994).

15. In severe conflicts, both members of a couple contribute to a pattern of joint escalation.

9. The Two Sexes in the Workplace

1. For this chapter, I have drawn mainly from the following sources: *Sex Segregation in the Workplace* (Reskin, 1984); *Gender, Work, and Space* (Hanson and Pratt, 1995); *Gender Inequality at Work* (Jacobs, 1995); *Working with Men* (Milwid, 1990); *Gender and Power in Organizations* (Ragins and Sundstrom, 1989); "The Relative Attractiveness Theory of Occupational Segregation by Gender" by Strober and Catanzarite (1994); "Sex Segregation in the Labor Force" by Sayed and Tzannatos (1995); and a previous paper of my own, "Gender Segregation in the Workplace: Continuities and Discontinuities from Childhood to Adulthood," in Frankenhauser, Lundberg, and Chesney (1991). An important theoretical source has been the book *Gender and Power* (1987) by the Australian sociologist R. W. Connell. Connell discusses the relations of adult men and women to each other in a variety of settings, and describes "constraints" that he believes structure the practices that can occur, or can be considered permissible, in a given social setting. Where gender is concerned, he points to three constraints. One is *separation,* or division: a tendency for the sexes to function separately, in same-sex groups, with little interaction across gender lines. A second is *authority,* control and coercion: the hierarchical relations between the sexes, having to do with which sex is in a position to regulate and monitor the activities of the other. The third is *sexual object choice.* Here the basic phenomenon is sexual attraction. In the large majority of cases this is attraction to an individual of the other sex, and hence runs directly counter to the theme of separation. Connell notes that the three kinds of constraints can exist simultaneously within a "gender regime" such as a workplace. Indeed, they may come into conflict with each other.

2. The Duncan index computes for each occupation under consideration the difference between the proportion of people in the male labor force who work in that occupation and the proportion of the female labor force who work in it. These differences are then summed across all the occupations being considered. The index ranges from 1 to 100; a zero score means that the distribution of the two sexes in the workforce is equal, in terms of their proportion in the workforce, while a score of 100 means that all occupations are either all-male or all-female (Duncan and Duncan, 1955; see also Beller, 1984). There is reason to believe that the Duncan index, based as it is on occupations rather than jobs, systematically understates the degree of segregation (Tomaskovic-Devey, 1995).

3. See Marini and Brinton (1984); and O'Donnell's 1984 book, The *Basis of the Bargain.*

4. See the analysis by Jacobs and Lim (1995) of occupational gender segregation in 56 countries from 1960 to 1980. See also the 1993 edition of Rosabeth M. Kanter's influential book *Men and Women of the Corporation,* in which she discusses changes

in the corporate roles of men and women over the 20-year period from the early 1970s to the early 1990s.

5. Tyack and Strober (1981); Strober and Gallagher (1992).

6. See Strober and Catanzarite (1994) for additional documentation.

7. The increase was at least 9 percent during the 1970s.

8. See also Strober and Arnold (1987).

9. See Strober and Catanzarite (1994) for a summary of studies.

10. Men and Women As Parents

1. See Feldman and Nash, 1984; Cowan et al., 1985; LaRossa and LaRossa, 1981; and Ruble, Fleming, Hackel, and Stangor, 1988. A summary of studies may be found in Thompson and Walker (1989).

2. Cowan and colleagues (1985) provide an excellent summary of studies, and add data of their own, documenting that the arrival of a child increases role differentiation between husband and wife, associated with added strain between the two, and greater dissatisfaction on the part of the women than the men.

3. See also Allison Clarke-Stewart (1978) for similar observations.

4. In a study of divorced families (Maccoby and Mnookin, 1992), the small group of fathers who had physical custody of a child under the age of 2 were usually living with their mothers, and it may be inferred that it was the paternal grandmother who cared for the child while the father worked.

5. An excellent species-by-species summary of paternal involvement with infants in monkeys and apes is provided by Redican and Taub (1981). Using a comprehensive classification of animal species, these authors conclude that "male parental care is rare in mammals, invertebrates and reptiles, but common in fishes, amphibians and birds" (p. 243). With respect to nonhuman primates, they conclude that "as diverse as this [male] behavioral range is, the primary caretaker in most primate—and mammalian—systems remains the mother."

6. Meany, Stewart, and Beatty (1985, pp. 16 and 17) provide a brief summary of their own and other studies documenting the higher levels of nurturant activity toward infants by juvenile females than juvenile males among several primate species. Lovejoy and Wallen (1988) found that among one-year-old group-living rhesus monkeys (equivalent to about age 3–4 years on the human developmental time-scale), the young females approached infants about three times as often as did the young males. Chamove and colleagues (Chamove, Harlow, and Mitchell, 1967) found that juvenile rhesus females directed more than four times as much positive social behavior to one-month-old infants as did juvenile males, while the males outnumbered the females by a ratio of ten to one when it came to hostile behavior directed toward infants.

7. Katherine Barnard, in the NCAST Feeding Manual (1993), reports that during the first four postnatal months, breast-feeding mothers (compared with those who do not breast-feed) are more responsive to their infants' cues and that their infants are more responsive to the mothers.

8. Feldman and Nash (1984) made a similar interpretation of their findings concerning the effects of life stage on the responses of men and women to infants. They found that men and women were not consistently different in their responsiveness to an unfamiliar infant in a waiting room so long as they were not yet parents themselves,

but that among people who had infants of their own, responsiveness was considerably enhanced in the women—more so than in the men.

9. We should note that despite these cultural assumptions, the economic burden of child support does shift strongly toward mothers after divorce (Peters et al., 1993; Peters and Argys, 1990).

10. Of course, there are other reasons why schoolteaching became "women's work": the general societal assumption that working with children is more "natural" for women, or that they understand children better.

11. In subsequent work, this distinction failed to hold up: instrumental and expressive leadership functions turned out to be most often centered in the same individual (Verba, 1961).

12. Werker and McLeod (1989) found that infants of both sexes showed more positive affect when listening to a segment of infant-directed speech recorded in a woman's voice rather than a man's, but much larger samples of male and female voices would be needed to determine how general this preference is, and what it depends on (pitch of the voice? stress patterns?).

13. Mannle and Tomasello (1987), in a study of infants 12–18 months of age in the presence of their parents, also reported that fathers were less likely to follow a child's current focus of attention.

14. Bellinger and Gleason (1982); McLaughlin (1983); McLaughlin, Schutz, and White (1980); NS Hart et al. (1992); see Gleason (1987) for a summary.

15. These findings are taken from the Maccoby-Jacklin longitudinal study of gender differentiation in the first six years of life. They have not been previously published.

16. Over the sample as a whole, the parents' attitudes about these matters did not depend on whether they were dealing with a son or a daughter.

17. The differences in perceptions of parental authority are probably greater in traditional societies. Berndt and colleagues (1993) found that young people growing up in three diverse Chinese cultures retrospectively reported that their mothers had been less controlling than their fathers, and said they had been more afraid of their fathers than their mothers. To them, their fathers had been the primary locus of household authority.

18. Collins and Russell (1991) summarize an array of studies on the cognitive and achievement-oriented interactions of mothers and fathers with their children, and do not find a clear difference between the two parents.

19. It is notable that in 1972, when the time-budget comparisons were made, the least amounts of time on homework were spent by parents in the United States, while the most were spent by parents in Eastern European (former Warsaw Pact) countries.

20. Fagot (1978); Langlois and Downs (1980), as reported in Maccoby (1980).

21. For evidence on fathers with young children, see the review by Bronstein (1988); for a report of parental interactions with preadolescents, see Bronstein et al. (1992).

22. In Jacklin's and my observations of mothers and fathers interacting with their child aged 45 months, fathers complied more readily to a son's influence attempt than to a daughter's, while mothers complied impartially to children of both sexes.

23. In abbreviated form, these kinds of interactions were described in a paper by Gable, Belsky, and Crnic (1993).

24. Personal communication from Sara Gable, November 1993.

25. This is an episode I observed informally at a friend's house. It was previously reported in Maccoby and Mnookin (1992).

26. A study by Draper (1981) is relevant here. He reported that single mothers felt less in control with sons than did mothers in two-parent families. These effects were not found with daughters. Lytton (1979), observing families with much younger children (boys aged 2½), reported that these toddler boys complied more readily with their mothers' directives when the father was present. And Gjerde (1988), observing the interactions of mothers and fathers with their five-year-old children, found that the mother-son dyad functioned especially well when there was high concordance between the mother and the father on child-rearing values, while this concordance was not so important for the other dyads, suggesting that mothers benefit from spousal agreement or backup, especially when dealing with sons.

Overview

1. The question of how children of the two sexes relate to infants has not been a central concern of this book. Still, we should note the greater interest in infants shown by juvenile females of nonhuman primate species and the possible connection this has with human girls' interest in dolls and possibly in live infants as well.

2. I am aware of the prevalence of single-parent households, and of the fact that perhaps as many as half of the children growing up in America today may spend some time in such a household. At any given time, however, at least three quarters of American children under 18 live in a household headed by an adult male-female couple.

3. There are anecdotal reports that in Japanese preschools gender segregation is minimal. In these preschools, teachers divide the children into mixed-sex small groups whose members do projects together and are in a sense responsible for each other; these adult-imposed structures appear to bring about strong mixed-sex group formations that preempt some of the gender segregation that might otherwise occur.

4. At least, I have claimed that this is true in modern Western societies. In societies where male children are much more valued than female children, boys from an early age may receive considerable deference from their mothers and join the higher-status group of males at a relatively young age. Still, in early childhood it is inevitable that mothers as well as fathers exercise considerable control over children of both sexes.

5. A series of reports by the American Association of University Women allege that girls are systematically "shortchanged in the classroom." But a number of scholars in the field of education have challenged these allegations and the validity of the studies on which they are based. See a summary in *Education Week,* September 28, 1994.

6. The research on the effects of single-sex schooling is plagued by problems of self-selection: girls and women who attend women's colleges tend to come from more advantaged backgrounds than those who attend coeducational institutions, and it is not always possible to account fully for the initial differences in interpreting the findings.

7. Notably, the United States has lagged considerably behind other Western industrialized countries in implementing these policies.

References

Abelson, R. P. 1994. Have you heard what they did? Perceptions of the collective other. Invited address, Presidential Symposium of the American Psychological Society, Washington, D.C., July.

Alan Guttmacher Institute. 1994. *Sex and America's teenagers.* New York: The Alan Guttmacher Institute.

Alder, C. 1982. An exploration of self-reported sexual aggression. Ph.D. diss., Department of Sociology, University of Oregon, Eugene.

Alexander, G. M., and Hines, M. 1994. Gender labels and play styles: Their relative contribution to children's selection of playmates. *Child Development,* 65(3), 869–879.

Allesandri, S. M., Sullivan, M. W., and Lewis, M. 1990. Violations of expectancy and frustration in early infancy. *Developmental Psychology,* 26, 738–744.

Andersen, E. S. 1978. Will you don't snore, please? Directives in young children's role-play speech. *Papers and Reports on Child Language Development,* 15, 140–150.

Anderson, E. 1989. Sex codes and family life among inner-city youth. In W. J. Wilson, ed., *The ghetto underclass: Social science perspectives.* Annals of the American Academy of Political and Social Science, vol. 501. Newbury Park, Calif.: Sage Publications.

Anderson, H. H. 1939. Domination and integration in the behavior of kindergarten children in an experimental play situation. *Journal of Experimental Education,* 8, 123–131.

Archer, J. 1996. Comparing women and men: What is being compared and why? *American Psychologist,* 51(2), 153–154.

Bacon, M. K., and Ashmore, R. D. 1985. How mothers and fathers categorize descriptions of social behavior attributed to daughters and sons. *Social Cognition,* 3, 193–217.

Bandura, A. 1969. Social learning theory of identificatory processes. In D. A. Goslin, ed., *Handbook of Socialization Theory and Research.* Chicago: Rand McNally and Co.

———— 1973. *Aggression: A social learning analysis.* Englewood Cliffs, N.J.: Prentice-Hall.

———— 1992. Exercise of personal agency through the self-efficacy mechanism. In R. Schwarzer, ed., *Self-efficacy: Thought control of action*, pp. 3–38. Washington, D.C.: Hemisphere.

Bandura, A., and Walters, R. H. 1959. *Adolescent aggression*. New York: Ronald Press.

Barkley, A., Ullman, G., Otto, L., and Brecht, M. 1977. The effects of sex-typing and sex-appropriateness of modeled behavior on children's imitation. *Child Development*, 48, 721–725.

Barnard, K. 1993. *NCAST feeding manual*. Seattle: University of Washington Press.

Barnett, R. C., and Baruch, G. K. 1988. Correlates of father's participation in family work. In P. Bronstein and C. P. Cowan, ed., *Fatherhood today: Men's changing role in the family*. New York: Wiley.

Bayley, N. 1965. Comparisons of mental and motor test scores for ages 1–15 months by sex, birth order, race, geographical location, and education of parents. *Child Development*, 36, 380–411.

Beach, S. R. H., Jouriles, E. N., and O'Leary, K. D. 1985. Extramarital sex: Impact on depression and commitment in couples' marital therapy. *Journal of Sex and Marital Therapy*, 11, 99–108.

Beller, A. H. 1984. Trends in occupational segregation by sex and race, 1960–1981. In B. Reskin, ed., *Sex segregation in the workplace: Trends, explanations, remedies*. Washington, D.C.: National Academy Press.

Bellinger, D., and Gleason, J. B. 1982. Sex differences in parental directives to young children. *Sex Roles*, 8, 1123–1139.

Belsky, J., Gilstrap, B., and Rovine, M. 1984. The Pennsylvania infant and family development project, I: Stability and change in mother-infant and father-infant interaction in a family setting at one, three, and nine months. *Child Development*, 55(3), 692–705.

Bem, S. L. 1981. Gender schema theory: A cognitive account of sex-typing. *Psychological Review*, 88, 354–364.

———— 1989. Genital knowledge and gender constancy in preschool children. *Child Development*, 60, 649–662.

Benenson, J. F. 1993. Greater preference among females than males for dyadic interaction in early childhood. *Child Development*, 64, 544–555.

———— 1994. Ages four to six years: Changes in the structures of play networks of girls and boys. *Merrill Palmer Quarterly*, 40(4), 478–487.

Benenson, J. F., Apostoleris, N. H., and Parnass, J. 1997. Age and sex differences in dyadic and group interaction. *Developmental Psychology*, 33, 538–543.

Berenbaum, S. A. 1990. Congenital adrenal hyperplasia: Intellectual and psychosexual functioning. In C. Holmes, ed., *Psychoneuroendocrinology: Brain, behavior, and hormonal interactions*, pp. 227–260. New York: Springer-Verlag.

Berenbaum, S. A., and Snyder, E. 1995. Early hormonal influences on childhood sex-typed activity and playmate preferences: Implications for the development of sexual orientation. *Developmental Psychology*, 31(1), 31–42.

Berman, C. M., Rasmussen, K. L. R., and Suomi, S. J. 1994. Responses of free-ranging rhesus monkeys to a natural form of social separation. I. Parallels with mother-infant separation in captivity. *Child Development*, 65(4), 1029–1041.

Berndt, T. J., Cheung, P. C., Lau, S., Hau, K. T., and Lew, W. J. F. 1993. Perceptions of parenting in mainland China, Taiwan, and Hong Kong: Sex differences and societal differences. *Developmental Psychology*, 29(1), 156–164.

Bianchi, B. D., and Bakeman, R. 1983. Patterns of sex-typing in an open school. In M. B. Liss, ed., *Social and cognitive skills: Sex roles and children's play,* pp. 219–233. New York: Academic Press.

Birns, B. 1976. The emergence and socialization of sex differences in the earliest years. *Merrill Palmer Quarterly,* 22, 229–254.

Bjorklund, D. F., and Kipp, K. 1996. Parental investment theory and gender differences in the evolution of inhibition mechanisms. *Psychological Bulletin,* 126, 163–188.

Bjorkquist, K. 1994. Sex differences in physical, verbal, and indirect aggression. *Sex Roles,* 30, 177–188.

Black, B. 1992. Negotiating social pretend play: Communication differences related to social status and sex. *Merrill Palmer Quarterly,* 38, 212–232.

Black, B., and Hazen, N. L. 1990. Social status and patterns of communication in unacquainted preschool children. *Preschool Developmental Psychology,* 26, 379–387.

Blakemore, J. E. D. 1990. Children's nurturant interactions with their infant siblings: An exploration of gender differences and maternal socialization. *Sex Roles,* 22, 43–57.

Blakemore, J. E. D., LaRue, A. A., and Olejnik, A. B. 1979. Sex appropriate toy choice: Sex appropriate toy choices and the ability to conceptualize toys as sex-role related. *Developmental Psychology,* 15, 339–340.

Block, J. H. 1978. Another look at sex differentiation in the socialization behaviors of mothers and fathers. In J. Sherman and F. L. Denmark, ed., *The psychology of women: Future directions of research.* New York: Psychological Dimensions.

Blumstein, P., and Schwartz, P. 1983. *American couples: Money, work, sex.* New York: William Morrow.

Borja-Alvarez, T., Zarbatany, L., and Pepper, S. 1991. Contributions of male and female guests and hosts to peer group entry. *Child Development,* 62, 1079–1090.

Boston, M. B., and Levy, G. D. 1991. Changes and differences in preschoolers' understanding of gender scripts. *Cognitive Development,* 6, 417–432.

Brewer, M. B., and Harasty, A. S. 1994. Seeing groups as entities: The role of perceiver motivation. In R. Sorrentino and E. T. Higgins, ed., *Handbook of motivation and cognition,* vol. 3: *The interpersonal contest.* New York: Guilford.

Brooks-Gunn, J., and Furstenberg, F. F. 1989. Adolescent sexual behavior. *American Psychologist,* 44, 249–257.

Bronstein, P. 1984. Differences in mothers' and fathers' behavior toward children across cultures. *Developmental Psychology,* 20, 995–1003.

———— 1988. Father-child interaction: Implications for gender-role socialization. In P. Bronstein and C. P. Cowan, ed., *Fatherhood today: Men's changing role in the family.* New York: John Wiley.

———— 1994. Patterns of parent-child interaction in Mexican families: A cross-cultural perspective. *International Journal of Behavioral Development,* 17, 423–446.

Bronstein, P., Duncan, P., Frankowski, J. J., and D'Ari, A. 1992. Differences in mothers' and fathers' involvement and interactions with girls and boys. Paper presented at the biennial meeting of the Society for Research in Adolescence, Washington, D.C., March.

Brown, B. B. 1996. "You're going with who?" Peer influences on adolescent romantic relationships. Paper presented in a special interest group pre-session at the biennial meeting of the Society for Research in Adolescence, Boston, March.

Brown, M., and Auerback, A. 1981. Communication patterns in initiation of marital sex. *Medical Aspects of Human Sexuality,* 15, 105–117.

Brown, S. S., and Eisenberg, L., ed. 1995. *The best intentions: Unintended pregnancy and the well-being of children and families.* Washington, D.C.: National Academy Press.

Buchanan, C. M., Maccoby, E. E., and Dornbusch, S. M. 1992. Adolescents and their families after divorce: Three residential arrangements compared. *Journal of Research on Adolescence,* 2(3), 261–291.

Buck, R. 1975. Non-verbal communication of affect in children. *Journal of Personality and Social Pyschology,* 31, 644–653.

Bumiller, E. 1995. *The secrets of Mariko: A year in the life of a Japanese woman and her family.* New York: Times Books.

Buss, D. M. 1989. Sex differences in human mate preferences: Evolutionary hypotheses tested in thirty-seven cultures. *Behavioral and Brain Sciences,* 12, 1–14.

Bussey, K., and Bandura, A. 1984. Influence of gender constancy and social power on sex-linked modeling. *Journal of Personality and Social Psychology,* 47(6), 1292–1302.

———— 1992. Self-regulatory mechanisms governing gender development. *Child Development,* 63(5), 1236–1250.

Cairns, R. B., Cairns, B. D., Neckerman, H. J., Ferguson, L. L., and Gariepy, J. 1989. Growth and aggression: 1. Childhood to early adolescence. *Developmental Psychology,* 25, 320–333.

Caporael, L. R. 1995. Sociality: Coordinating bodies, minds, and groups. Psycoloquy.95.6.01.group-selection.1.caporael.

Carli, L. L. 1990. Gender, language, and influence. *Journal of Personality and Social Psychology,* 59, 941–951.

———— 1995. No: Biology does not create gender differences in personality. In M. R. Walsh, ed., *Women, men, and gender.* New Haven: Yale University Press.

Carns, D. 1973. Talking about sex: Notes on first coitus and the double standard. *Journal of Marriage and the Family,* 35, 677–687.

Carter, D. B. 1987. The role of peers in sex role socialization. In D. B. Carter, ed., *Current conceptions of sex roles and sex typing: Theory and research.* New York: Praeger.

Carter, D. B., and McClosky, L. A. 1984. Peers and the maintenance of sex-typed behavior: The development of children's conceptions of cross-gender behavior in their peers. *Social Cognition,* 2, 294–314.

Chamove, A., Harlow, H. F., and Mitchell, G. 1967. Sex differences in the infant-directed behavior of preadolescent rhesus monkeys. *Child Development,* 38, 329–336.

Charlesworth, W. R., and Dzur, C. 1987. Gender comparisons of preschoolers' behavior and resource utilization in group problem-solving. *Child Development,* 58, 191–200.

Charlesworth, W. R., and LaFreniere, P. 1983. Dominance, friendship utilization, and resource utilization in preschool children's groups. *Ethology and Sociobiology,* 4, 175–186.

Cherlin, A. J. 1996. *Public and private families: An introduction.* New York: McGraw-Hill.

Chilman, C. C. 1983. *Adolescent sexuality in a changing American society.* New York: Wiley Interscience.

Chodorow, N. 1978. *The reproduction of mothering: Psychoanalysis and the sociology of gender.* Berkeley: University of California Press.

Christiansen, A., and Heavey, C. L. 1990. Gender and social structure in the demand/withdraw pattern of marital conflict. *Journal of Personality and Social Psychology,* 59, 73–81.

Chung, T. Y., and Asher, S. R. 1996. Children's goals and strategies in peer conflict situations. *Merrill Palmer Quarterly,* 42(1), 125–147.

Chusmir, L. H., Koberg, C. S., and Mills, J. 1989. Male-female differences in the association of managerial style and personal values. *Journal of Social Psychology,* 129, 65–78.

Clark, M. S., and Mills, J. 1979. Interpersonal attraction in exchange and communal relationships. *Journal of Personality and Social Psychology,* 37, 12–24.

Clarke-Stewart, K. A., and Allison, K. 1978. And daddy makes three: The father's impact on mother and young child. *Child Development,* 49, 466–478.

Clarke-Stewart, K. A., and Hevey, C. M. 1981. Longitudinal relations in repeated observations of mother-child interaction from 1 to 1½ years. *Developmental Psychology,* 17(2), 127–145.

Coleman, M., Ganong, L. H., Clark, J. M., and Madsen, R. 1989. Parenting perceptions in rural and urban families: Is there a difference? *Journal of Marriage and the Family,* 51, 329–335.

Collier, J., and Risaldo, S. 1981. Politics and gender in simple societies. In S. B. Ortner and H. Whitehead, ed., *Sexual meanings.* New York: Cambridge University Press.

Collins, W. A., and Russell, G. 1991. Mother-child and father-child relationships in middle childhood and adolescence: A developmental analysis. *Developmental Review,* 11, 99–136.

Condry, J., and Condry, S. 1976. Sex differences: A study in the eye of the beholder. *Child Development,* 47, 812–819.

Connell, R. W. 1987. *Gender and Power.* Stanford: Stanford University Press.

Cook, A. S., Fritz, J. J., McCornack, B. L., and Visperas, C. 1985. Early gender differences in the functional usage of language. *Sex Roles,* 12, 909–915.

Corsaro, W. A., and Eder, D. 1990. Children's peer cultures. *Annual Review of Sociology,* 16, 197–220.

Cowan, C. P., Cowan, P. A., Heming, G., Garrett, E., Coysh, W. S., Curtis-Boles, H., and Boles III, A. J. 1985. Transitions to parenthood: His, hers, and theirs. *Journal of Family Issues,* 6, 451–481.

Cowan, G., Drinkard, J., and MacGavin, L. 1984. The effects of target, age, and gender on use of power strategies. *Journal of Personality and Social Psychology,* 47, 1391–1398.

Crick, N. R., and Grotpeter, J. K. 1995. Relational aggression, gender, and social-psychological adjustment. *Child Development,* 66, 710–722.

Crick, N. R., and Ladd, G. W. 1990. Children's perceptions of the outcomes of social strategies: Do the ends justify being mean? *Developmental Psychology,* 26, 612–626.

Crombie, G., and Desjardins, M. J. 1993. Predictors of gender: The relative importance of children's play, games and personality characteristics? Paper presented at the biennial meeting of the Society for Research in Child Development, New Orleans, March.

Cummings, E. M., Vogel, D., Cummings, J. S., and El-Sheikh, M. 1989. Children's responses to different forms of expression of anger between adults. *Child Development,* 60, 1392–1404.

Cupach, W. R., and Metts, S. 1991. In K. McKinney and S. Sprecher, ed., *Sexuality in close relationships.* Hillsdale, N.J.: Lawrence Erlbaum Associates.

Cutting, J. E., Proffitt, D. R., and Koslowski, L. T. 1978. A biomechanical invariant for gait perception. *Journal of Experimental Psychology: Human Perception and Performance,* 4, 357–372.

Daly, M., and Wilson, M. 1988. *Homicide.* Hawthorne, N.Y.: Aldine deGruyter.

Damico, S. B. 1975. Sexual differences in the responses of elementary pupils to their classroom. *Psychology in the Schools,* 12, 462–467.

Damon, W. 1977. *The social world of the child.* San Francisco: Jossey-Bass.

Davis, J. D. 1978. When boy meets girl: Sex roles and the negotiation of intimacy in an acquaintance exercise. *Journal of Personality and Social Psychology,* 36, 684–692.

DeRosier, M. E., Cillessen, A. H. N., Coie, J. D., and Dodge, K. A. 1994. Group social context and children's aggressive behavior. *Child Development,* 65(4), 1068–1079.

Diamond, A. 1985. Development of the ability to use recall to guide actions, as indicated by infants' performance on A$\overline{\text{B}}$. *Child Development,* 56, 868–883.

———— 1988. Abilities and neural mechanisms underlying A$\overline{\text{B}}$ performance. *Child Development,* 59, 523–527.

Diamond, J. M. 1992. *The third chimpanzee: The evolution and future of the human animal.* New York: HarperCollins.

Dickson, W. P. 1979. Referential communication performance from age 4 to 8: Effects of referent type, context, and target position. *Developmental Psychology,* 15, 470–471.

Dien, D. S. 1992. Gender and individuation: China and the West. *Psychoanalytic Review,* 79(1), 105–119.

DiPietro, J. 1981. Rough and tumble play: A function of gender. *Developmental Psychology,* 17, 50–58.

Dodge, K. 1980. Social cognition and children's aggressive behavior. *Child Development,* 51, 162–171.

Draper, T. W. 1981. Son induced changes in the perceived locus of control of single mothers. Paper presented at the biennial meeting of the Society for Research in Child Development, Boston, April.

Duncan, G. D., and Duncan, B. 1955. A methodological analysis of segregation indexes. *American Sociology Review,* 20, 217–219.

Dunn, J., and Kendrick, C. 1982. *Siblings: Love, envy, and understanding.* Cambridge, Mass.: Harvard University Press.

Dunn, J., Bretherton, I., and Munn, P. 1987. Conversations about feeling states between mothers and their young children. *Developmental Psychology,* 23, 132–139.

Dunn, J., Brown, J., and Beardsall, L. 1991. Family talk about feeling states and children's later understanding of others' emotions. *Developmental Psychology,* 27, 448–455.

Dunn, J., Brown, J., Slomkowski, C., Tesla, C., and Youngblade, L. 1991. Young children's understanding of other people's feelings and beliefs: Individual differences and their antecedents. *Child Development,* 62, 1352–1366.

Dunn, S., and Morgan, V. 1987. Nursery and infant school play patterns: Sex-related differences. *British Educational Research Journal,* 13(3), 271–281.

Eagley, A. H. 1995. The science and politics of comparing women and men. *American Psychologist*, 50, 145–158.

Eaton, W. O., and Enns, L. R. 1986. Sex differences in human motor activity level. *Psychological Bulletin*, 100, 19–28.

Eaton, W. O., and Yu, A. P. 1989. Are sex differences in child motor activity level a function of sex differences in maturational status? *Child Development*, 60, 1005–1011.

Eckert, P. In press. Vowels and nail polish: Their emergence of linguistic style in the preadolescent heterosexual marketplace. In L. Bilmes, M. Chen, M. Oliver, N. Warner, and S. Wertheim, ed., *Gender and belief systems*. Proceedings of the Fourth Berkeley Women and Language Conference. Berkeley, Calif.: Berkeley Women and Language Group.

Ehrhardt, A. A., and Baker, S. W. 1974. Fetal androgens, human CNS differentiation, and behavior sex differences. In R. C. Friedman, R. M. Richart, and R. L. Vande Wiele, ed., *Sex differences in behavior*, pp. 53–76. New York: John Wiley.

Eichorn, D. 1970. Physiological development. In P. H. Mussen ed., *Carmichael's manual of child psychology*, 3rd ed., vol. 1. New York: John Wiley.

Eisenberg, N., Martin, C. L., and Fabes, R. A. 1996. Gender development and gender effects. In D. C. Berliner and R. C. Calfee, ed., *The handbook of educational psychology*. New York: MacMillan.

Eisenberg, N., Wolchik, S. A., Hernandez, R., and Pasternak, J. 1985. Paternal socialization of young children's play: A short-term longitudinal study. *Child Development*, 56, 1506–1513.

Eisenberg, N., Fabes, R. A., Nyman, M., Bernzweig, J., and Pinneulas, A. 1994. The relations of emotionality and regulation to children's anger-related reactions. *Child Development*, 65, 109–128.

Eisenberg, N., Fabes, R. A., Schaller, M., Carlo, G., and Miller, P. 1991. The relations of parental characteristics and practices to children's vicarious emotional responding. *Child Development*, 62, 1393–1408.

Eisenberg, N., Fabes, R. A., Bernsweig, J., Karbon, M., Poulin, R., and Hanish, L. 1993. The relations of emotionality and regulation to preschoolers' social skills and sociometric status. *Child Development*, 64(5), 1418–1438.

Eisenhart, M. A., and Holland, D. C. 1983. Learning gender from peers: The role of peer groups in the cultural transmission of gender. *Human Organization*, 42(4), 321–332.

Ellis, S., Rogoff, B., and Cromer, C. C. 1981. Age segregation in children's social interactions. *Developmental Psychology*, 17(4), 399–407.

Erikson, E. 1951. Sex differences in the play configurations of pre-adolescents. *American Journal of Orthopsychiatry*, 21, 667–692.

Erwin, P. 1985. Similarity of attitudes and constructs in children's friendships. *Journal of Experimental Child Psychology*, 40, 470–485.

Fabes, R. A. 1994. Physiological, emotional, and behavioral correlates of gender segregation. In C. Leaper, ed., *Childhood gender segregation: Causes and consequences*. San Francisco: Jossey-Bass.

Fagan, J., and Browne, A. 1994. Violence between spouses and intimates: Physical aggression between women and men in intimate relationships. In A. J. Reiss, Jr., and J. A. Roth, ed., *Understanding and preventing violence*, vol. 3 of the *Report of* the National Research Council Panel on the Understanding and Control of Violent Behavior. Washington, D.C.: National Academy Press.

Fagot, B. I. 1974. Sex differences in toddlers' behavior and parental reaction. *Developmental Psychology*, 10, 554–558.

———— 1978. The influence of sex of child on parental reactions to toddler children. *Child Development*, 49, 459–465.

———— 1985. Beyond the reinforcement principle: Another step toward understanding sex-role development. *Developmental Psychology*, 21, 1097–1104.

———— 1989. Cross-gender behavior and its consequences for boys. *Italian Journal of Clinical and Cultural Psychology*, 1, 79–84.

———— 1991. Peer relations in boys and girls from two to seven. Paper presented at the biennial meeting of the Society for Research in Child Development, Seattle.

———— 1994. Peer relations and the development of competence in boys and girls. In C. Leaper, ed., *Childhood gender segregation*. San Francisco: Jossey-Bass.

Fagot, B. I., and Hagan, R. 1991. Observations of parents' reactions to sex-stereotyped behaviors: Age and sex differences. *Child Development*, 62(3), 617–628.

Fagot, B. I., and Leinbach, M. D. 1991. Gender-role development in young children: From discrimination to labeling. *Developmental Review*, 13, 205–224.

Fagot, B. I., Leinbach, M. D., and Hagan, R. 1986. Gender labeling and the adoption of sex-typed behaviors. *Developmental Psychology*, 22, 440–443.

Fagot, B. I., Hagan, R., Leinbach, M. D., and Kronsberg, S. 1985. Differential reactions to assertive and communicative acts of toddler boys and girls. *Child Development*, 56, 1499–1505.

Falbo, T., and Peplau, A. L. 1980. Power strategies in intimate relationships. *Journal of Personality and Social Psychology*, 38, 618–628.

Falender, C. A., and Haber, R. 1975. Mother-child interaction and participation in a longitudinal intervention program. *Developmental Psychology*, 11, 830–836.

Fein, G., Johnson, D., Kosson, N., Stork, L., and Wasserman, L. 1975. Sex stereotypes and preferences in toy choices of 20-month-old boys and girls. *Developmental Psychology*, 11, 527.

Feiring, C., and Lewis, M. 1987. The child's social network: Sex differences from three to six years. *Sex Roles*, 17, 621–636.

Feldman, E., and Dodge, K. A. 1987. Social information processing and sociometric status: Sex, age, and situational effects. *Journal of Abnormal Child Psychology*, 15, 211–227.

Feldman, S. S., and Nash, S. C. 1984. The transition from expectancy to parenthood: Impact of the firstborn child on men and women. *Sex Roles*, 11, 61–78.

Feldman, S. S., Araujo, K., and Winsler, A. 1994. The relationship context of sexual attitudes and behaviors: Gender and ethnic differences. Paper presented at the Sexuality Symposium at the biennial meeting of the Society for Research on Adolescence, San Diego, February.

Feldman, S. S., Brown, N. L., and Canning, R. D. 1995. Pathways to early sexual activity: A longitudinal study of the influence of peer status. *Journal of Research in Adolescence*, 5, 387–412.

Feldman, S. S., Nash, S. C., and Cutrona, C. 1977. The influence of age and sex on responsiveness to babies. *Developmental Psychology*, 13, 675–676.

Fernald, A., McRoberts, G. W., and Herrera, C. In press. Effects of prosody and word position on infants' ability to recognize words in fluent speech. *Journal of Experimental Psychology.*

Field, T. M. 1978. Interaction patterns of primary versus secondary caretaker fathers. *Developmental Psychology,* 14, 183–184.

Finkel, M. L., and Finkel, D. J. 1981. Sexual and contraceptive knowledge, attitudes, and behavior of male adolescents. In F. F. Furstenberg, R. Lincoln, and J. Menken, ed., *Teenage sexuality, pregnancy, and childbearing.* Philadelphia: University of Pennsylvania Press.

Fivush, Robyn. 1993. Emotional content of parent-child conversations about the past. In C. A. Nelson, ed., *Memory and Affect in Development.* Minnesota Symposium on Child Psychology, vol. 26, pp. 39–78. Minneapolis: University of Minnesota.

Flannery, K. A., and Watson, M. W. 1993. Are individual differences in fantasy play related to peer acceptance levels? *Journal of Genetic Psychology,* 154, 407–416.

Fling, S., and Manosevitz, M. 1972. Sex typing in nursery school children's play interests. *Developmental Psychology,* 7, 146–152.

Floge, L., and Merrill, D. M. 1985. Tokenism reconsidered: Male nurses and female physicians in a hospital setting. Paper presented at the Eightieth Meeting of the American Sociological Association, Washington, D.C., August.

Fox, N. A., ed. 1994. The development of emotion regulation: Biological and behavioral. *Monographs of the Society for Research in Child Development,* 59(2–3).

Frankel, M. T., and Robbins, Jr., H. A. 1983. Does mother know best? Mothers and fathers interacting with preschool sons and daughters. *Developmental Psychology,* 19, 694–702.

Frankenhaeuser, M. 1975. Experimental approaches to the study of catecholamines and emotion. In L. Levi, ed., *Emotions: Their parameters and measurement.* New York: Raven Press.

Frankenhaeuser, M., Lundberg, U., and Chesney, M. 1991. *Women, work, and health: Stress and opportunities.* New York: Plenum Press.

Frodi, A. M., and Lamb, M. E. 1978. Sex differences in responsiveness to infants: A developmental study of psychophysiological and behavioral responses. *Child Development,* 49(4), 1182–1188.

Frodi, A. M., Lamb, M. E., Levitt, L. A., and Donovan, W. L. 1978. Mothers' and fathers' responses to infant smiles and cries. *Infant Behavior and Development,* 1, 187–198.

Funder, K. 1986. Work and the marriage partnership. In P. McDonald, ed., *Settling up: Property and income distribution on divorce in Australia.* Australian Institute of Family Studies. Sydney: Prentice-Hall.

Gable, S. 1993. Personal communication.

Gable, S., Belsky, J., and Crnic, K. 1993. Coparenting in the child's second year: Stability and change from 15 to 21 months. Paper presented at the biennial meeting of the Society for Research in Child Development, New Orleans, March.

Game, A., and Pringle, R. 1983. *Gender at work.* Sydney: Allen and Unwin.

Gewirtz, J. L. 1969. Mechanisms of social learning: Some roles of stimulation and behavior in early human development. In D. A. Goslin, ed., *Handbook of socialization theory and research.* Chicago: Rand McNally.

Gilligan, C. 1982. *In a different voice.* Cambridge, Mass.: Harvard University Press.

——— 1993. Joining the resistance: Psychology, politics, girls, and women. In L. Weis and M. Fine, ed., *Beyond silenced voices.* Albany: State University of New York Press.

Gilligan, C., Lyons, N., and Hamner, T. J. 1989. *Making connections.* Cambridge, Mass.: Harvard University Press.

Gjerde, P. F. 1986. The interpersonal structure of family interaction settings: Parent adolescent relations in dyads and triads. *Developmental Psychology,* 22, 297–304.

———— 1988. Parental concordance on child-rearing and the interactive emphasis of parents: Sex-differentiated relationships during the pre-school years. *Developmental Psychology,* 24, 700–706.

Gleason, J. B. 1987. Language and psychological development. Keynote address, Stanford Child Language Forum, Stanford University, April.

Goldfoot, D. A., and Wallen, K. 1978. Development of gender role behaviors in heterosexual and isosexual groups of infant rhesus monkeys. In D. J. Chivers and J. Herbert, ed., *Recent advances in primatology,* vol. 1. London: Academic Press.

Goldfoot, D. A., Wallen, K., Neff, D. A., McBriar, M. C., and Goy, R. W. 1984. Social influences on the display of sexually dimorphic behavior in rhesus monkeys: Isosexual rearing. *Archives of Sexual Behavior,* 13(5), 395–412.

Goodenough, E. W. 1957. Interest in persons as an aspect of sex differences in the early years. *Genetic Psychology Monographs,* 55, 287–323.

Goodenough, F. L. 1931. *Anger in young children.* Minneapolis: University of Minnesota Press.

Goodnow, J. J. In press. From household practices to parents' ideas about work and interpersonal relationships. In S. Harkness, C. Super, and R. Niew, ed., *Parental ethnotheories.* New York: Guilford Press.

Goodwin, M. H. 1990. Tactical uses of stories: Participation frameworks within girls' and boys' disputes. *Discourse Processes,* 13, 33–71.

Goslin, D. A. 1969. Introduction. In D. A. Goslin, ed., *Handbook of socialization theory and research.* Chicago: Rand McNally.

Gottman, J. M. 1993. The roles of conflict engagement, escalation, and avoidance in marital interaction: A longitudinal view of five types of couples. *Journal of Consulting and Clinical Psychology,* 61, 6–15.

———— 1994a. *Why Marriages Succeed or Fail.* New York: Simon and Schuster.

———— 1994b. *What predicts divorce? The relationship between marital processes and marital outcomes.* Hillsdale, N.J.: Lawrence Erlbaum.

———— 1996. Toward a process model of men in marriages and families. Paper presented at a conference on men in families, Pennsylvania State University, State College, Penn., Fall.

Gottman, J. M., and Levenson, R. W. 1988. The social psycho-physiology of marriage. In P. Roller and M. A. Fitzpatrick, ed., *Perspectives on marital interaction.* New York: Taylor and Francis.

———— 1992. Marital processes predictive of later dissolution: Behavior, physiology, and health. *Journal of Personality and Social Psychology,* 63, 221–233.

Gottman, J. M., and Parker, J., ed. 1986. *Conversations of friends.* New York: Cambridge University Press.

Goy, R. W. 1970. Experimental control of psychosexuality. In G. W. Harris and R. G. Edwards, ed., *A discussion on the determination of sex,* pp. 149–162. London: Philosophical Transactions of the Royal Society, Series B., vol. 259.

——— 1973. Hormonally induced pseudohermaphroditism and behavior. In A. G. Motulsky and W. Lentz, ed., *International Congress Series no. 310, birth defects.* Proceedings of the Fourth International Conference, Vienna, Austria, Excerpta Medica, Amsterdam.

Goy, R. W., Bercovitch, F. B., and McBrair, M. C. 1988. Behavioral masculinization is independent of genital masculinization in prenatally androgenized female rhesus macaques. *Hormones and Behavior,* 22, 552–571.

Grant, L. 1985. Race-gender status, classroom interactions, and children's socialization in elementary school. In L. C. Wilkinson and C. B. Marrett, ed., *Gender influences in classroom interaction.* Orlando: Academic Press.

Gray, P., and Feldman, J. 1997. Patterns of age mixing and gender mixing among children and adolescents at an ungraded school. *Merrill Palmer Quarterly,* 42, 67–86.

Greeno, K. 1988. Personal communication.

——— 1989. Gender differences in children's proximity to adults. Ph.D. diss., Stanford University.

Greif, E. B. 1980. Sex differences in parent-child conversation. *Women's Studies International Quarterly,* 3, 253–258.

Griswold, R. L. 1993. *Fatherhood in America.* New York: Basic Books.

Gunnar, M. R. 1989. Personal communication.

Gunnar, M. R., and Donahue, M. 1980. Sex differences in social responsiveness between six months and twelve months. *Child Development,* 51(1), 262–265.

Halverson, C. F., and Waldrop, M. F. 1973. The relations of mechanically recorded activity level to varieties of preschool play behavior. *Child Development,* 44, 678–681.

Hanson, R. 1975. Consistency and stability of home environmental measures related to IQ. *Child Development,* 46(2), 470–479.

Hanson, S., and Pratt, G. 1995. *Gender, work, and space.* New York: Routledge.

Harlan, A., and Weiss, C. L. 1982. Sex differences in factors affecting managerial career advancement. In P. A. Wallace, ed., *Women in the workplace.* Boston: Auburn House.

Harris, J. 1995. Where is the child's environment? A group socialization theory of development. *Psychological Review,* 102, 458–489.

Hart, C. H., DeWolf, D. M., Wozniak, P., and Burts, D. C. 1992. Maternal and paternal disciplinary styles: Relations with preschoolers' playground behavioral orientation and peer status. *Child Development,* 63, 879–892.

Harter, S., Waters, P., and Whitsell, N. In press. Lack of voice as a manifestation of false self behavior among adolescents: The school setting as a stage upon which the drama of authenticity is enacted. *Educational Psychologist.*

Hartup, W. W. 1983. Peer relations. In E. M. Hetherington, ed., *Socialization, personality, and social development,* vol. 4 of the *Mussen Handbook of Child Psychology.* New York: John Wiley.

Hartup, W. W., French, D. C., Laursen, B., Johnston, M. K., and Ogawa, J. R. 1993. Conflict and friendship relations in middle childhood: Behavior in a closed-field situation. *Child Development,* 64(2), 445–454.

Hatfield, E. 1988. Passionate and companionate love. In R. J. Sternberg and M. Barnes, ed., *The psychology of love,* pp. 191–217. New Haven: Yale University Press.

Haviland, J. J., and Malatesta, C. Z. 1981. The development of sex differences in nonverbal signals: Fallacies, facts, and fantasies. In C. Mayo and N. M. Henley, ed., *Gender and non-verbal behavior.* New York: Springer-Verlag.

Heath, S. B. 1991. "It's about winning!" The language of knowledge in baseball. In L. Resnick, J. M. Levine, and S. D. Teasley, ed., *Perspectives on socially shared cognition,* pp. 101–124. Washington, D.C.: American Psychological Association.

Heiss, J. S. 1962. Degree of intimacy and male-female interaction. *Sociometry,* 25, 197–208.

Hetherington, E. M. 1967. The effects of familial variables on sex-typing, on parent-child similarity, and on imitation in children. In J. P. Hill, ed., *Minnesota symposium on child psychology,* vol. 1. Minneapolis: University of Minnesota Press.

Hetherington, E. M., Cox, M., and Cox, R. 1982. Effects of divorce on parents and children. In M. E. Lamb, ed., *Nontraditional families.* Hillsdale, N.J.: Lawrence Erlbaum.

Hines, M., and Kaufman, F. R. 1994. Androgen and the development of human sex-typical behavior: Rough-and-tumble play and sex of preferred playmates in children with congenital adrenal hyperplasia (CAH). *Child Development,* 65(4), 1042–1053.

Hochschile, A. 1989. *The second shift.* New York: Viking.

Hort, B. E., Leinbach, M. D., and Fagot, B. I. 1992. An investigation of the conceptual parameters underlying the metaphorical constructs of gender. Paper presented at the Southwest Conference for Research on Human Development, Tempe, April.

Howes, C. 1988a. Peer interaction of young children. *Monographs of the Society for Research in Child Development,* serial no. 217, 53(1).

———— 1988b. Same- and cross-sex friends: Implications for interaction and social skills. *Early Childhood Research Quarterly,* 3, 21–37.

Howes, C., and Phillipsen, L. 1992. Gender and friendship: Relationships within peer groups of young children. *Social Development,* 1(3), 230–242.

Huang, C. P. 1986. Behavior of Swedish primary and secondary caretaking fathers in relation to mother's presence. *Developmental Psychology,* 22, 749–751.

Huang, C. P., Eldén, G., and Fransson, C. 1984. *Arbetsgivares och arbetskamraters attityder till pappaledighet.* Göteborg, Sweden: Psykologiska Institutionen, Göteborg Universitet.

Huston, A. C. 1983. Sex typing. In P. H. Mussen (series ed.) and E. M. Hetherington (vol. ed.), *Handbook of child psychology,* vol. 4, *Socialization, personality, and social development,* 4th ed., pp. 387–467. New York: John Wiley.

———— 1985. The development of sex-typing: Themes from recent research. *Developmental Review,* 5, 1–17.

Huston, T. L., and Ashmore, R. D. 1986. Women and men in personal relationships. In R. D. Ashmore and R. K. DelBoca, ed., *The social psychology of male-female relations.* New York: Academic Press.

Hutchins, E. 1991. The social organization of distributed cognition. In L. Resnick, J. M. Levine, and S. D. Teasley, ed., *Perspectives on socially shared cognition,* pp. 283–307. Washington, D.C.: American Psychological Association.

Huttonlocher, J., Haight, W., Bryk, A., Seltzer, M., and Lyons, T. 1991. Early vocabulary growth: Relation to language input and gender. *Developmental Psychology,* 27, 236–248.

Hyde, S., and Plant, A. E. 1995. Magnitude of psychological gender differences: Another side to the story. *American Psychologist,* 50, 159–161.

Jacklin, C. N., and Maccoby, E. E. 1978. Social behavior at 33 months in same-sex and mixed-sex dyads. *Child Development,* 49, 557–569.

Jacklin, C. N., DiPietro, J. A., and Maccoby, E. E. 1984. Sex-typing behavior and sex-typing pressure in child/parent interaction. *Archives of Sexual Behavior,* 13(5), 413–425.

Jacklin, C. N., Maccoby, E. E., and Dick, A. E. 1973. Barrier behavior and toy preference: Sex differences (and their absence) in the year-old child. *Child Development,* 44(1), 196–200.

Jacklin, C. N., Maccoby, E. E., and Doering, C. H. 1983. Neonatal sex-steroid hormones and timidity in 6- to 18-month-old boys and girls. *Developmental Psychobiology,* 16, 163–168.

Jacklin, C. N., Snow, M. E., Gahart, M., and Maccoby, E. E. 1980. Sleep pattern development from 6 through 33 months. *Journal of Pediatric Psychology,* 5, 295–303.

Jacobs, J. A. 1989. *Revolving doors: Sex segregation and women's careers.* Stanford: Stanford University Press.

Jacobs, J. A., ed. 1995. *Gender inequality at work.* Thousand Oaks, Calif.: Sage Publications.

Jacobs, J. A., and Lim, S. T. 1995. Trends in occupational and industrial sex segregation in 56 countries, 1960–1980. In J. A. Jacobs ed., *Gender inequality at work.* Thousand Oaks, Calif.: Sage Publications.

Johnson, M. M. 1988. *Strong mothers, weak wives.* Berkeley: University of California Press.

Joshi, H. 1984. *Women's participation in paid work: Further analysis of the women and employment survey.* Research paper no. 45, Department of Employment, United Kingdom. London: HMSO.

Jusczyk, P., Mullinex, J., and Pisoni, D. B. 1992. Some consequences of stimulus variability on speech processing by 2-month-old infants. *Cognition,* 43(3), 253–291.

Kagan, J., and Moss, H. 1962. *Birth to maturity.* New York: John Wiley.

Kanin, E. J. 1985. Date rapists: Differential sexual socialization and relative deprivation. *Archives of Sexual Behavior,* 14, 219–231.

Kanter, R. 1977. *Men and women of the corporation.* New York: Basic Books.

—— 1993. *Men and women of the corporation,* 2nd ed. New York: Basic Books.

Karbon, M., Fabes, R. A., Carlo, G., and Martin, C. L. 1992. Preschoolers' beliefs about sex and age differences in emotionality. *Sex Roles,* 27, 377–390.

Katz, P. A., and Ksansnak, K. R. 1994. Developmental aspects of gender role flexibility and traditionality in middle childhood and adolescence. *Developmental Psychology,* 30(2), 272–282.

Killen, M., and Naigles, L. R. 1995. Preschool children pay attention to their addressees: Effects of gender composition on peer disputes. *Discourse Processes,* 19(3), 329–346.

Kinsbourne, M., and Hiscock, M. 1983. The normal and deviant development of functional lateralization of the brain. In P. H. Mussen, ed., *Handbook of child psychology,* 4th ed., vol. 2, *Infancy and developmental psychobiology.* New York: John Wiley.

Kochanska, G. 1997. Mutually responsive orientation between mothers and their young children: Implications for early socialization. *Child Development,* 68, 94–112.

Kochanska, G., Aksan, N., and Koenig, A. L. 1995. A longitudinal study of the roots of preschoolers' conscience: Committed compliance and emerging internalization. *Child Development,* 66(6), 1752–1769.

Kochanska, G., Murray, K., Jacques, T. Y., Koenig, A. L., and Vandegeest, K. A. 1996. Inhibitory control in young children and its role in emerging internalization. *Child Development,* 67, 490–507.

Kohlberg, L. 1966. A cognitive developmental analysis of children's sex role concepts and attitudes. In E. E. Maccoby, ed., *The development of sex differences,* pp. 82–172. Stanford: Stanford University Press.

Kopp, C. B. 1989. Regulation of distress and negative emotions: A developmental view. *Developmental Psychology,* 25(3), 343–354.

Koss, M. P., Gidycz, C. A., and Wisniewski, N. 1987. The scope of rape: Incidence and prevalence of sexual aggression and victimization in a national sample of higher education students. *Journal of Consulting and Clinical Psychology,* 55, 162–170.

Krauss, R. M., and Fussell, S. R. 1991. Constructing shared communicative environments. In L. Resnick, J. M. Levine, and S. D. Teasley, ed., *Perspectives on socially shared cognition,* pp. 172–200. Washington, D.C.: American Psychological Association.

Kuebil, J., and Krieger, E. 1991. Emotion and gender in parent-child conversations about the past. Paper presented at the biennial meeting of the Society for Research in Child Development, Seattle.

Ladd, G. W., and Price, J. M. 1986. Preschoolers' behavioral orientations and play patterns: Relationship to peer status in the classroom. Paper presented at a meeting of the American Educational Research Association, San Francisco.

LaFreniere, P., Strayer, F. F., and Gauthier, R. 1984. The emergence of same-sex affiliative preferences among preschool peers: A developmental/ethological perspective. *Child Development,* 55, 1958–1965.

Lamb, M. E., and Roopnarine, J. L. 1979. Peer influence on sex role development in preschoolers. *Child Development,* 50, 1219–1222.

Lamb, M. E., Frodi, A. M., Frodi, M., and Huang, C. P. 1982. Characteristics of maternal and paternal behavior in traditional and non-traditional Swedish families. *International Journal of Behavioral Development,* 5, 131–141.

Lamb, M. E., Pleck, J. H., Charnov, E. L., and Levine, J. A. 1987. A biosocial perspective on paternal behavior and involvement. In J. B. Lancaster, J. Altman, A. S. Rossi, and L. R. Sherrod, ed., *Parenting across the lifespan.* New York: Aldine de Gruyter.

Langlois, J. H., and Downs, A. C. 1980. Mothers, fathers, and peers as socialization agents of sex-typed play behaviors in young children. *Child Development,* 51, 1217–1247.

LaRossa, R., and LaRossa, M. M. 1981. *Transition to parenthood: How infants change families.* Beverly Hills: Sage Publications.

Larson, R., and Richards, M. H. 1991. Daily companionship in late childhood and early adolescence: Changing developmental contexts. *Child Development,* 62(2), 284–300.

———— 1994. *Divergent realities: The emotional lives of mothers, fathers, and adolescents.* New York: Basic Books.

Larson, R., and Wood, G. 1996. The emotion of romantic relationships: Do they wreak havoc on adolescents? In W. Furman and B. B. Brown ed., *Romantic relationships in adolescence.* New York: Cambridge University Press.

Leaper, C. 1991. Influence and involvement in children's discourse: Age, gender, and partner effects. *Child Development*, 62, 797–811.

———— ed. 1994. Exploring the consequences of gender segregation on social relationships. In C. Leaper, ed., *Childhood gender segregation: Causes and consequences.* San Francisco: Jossey-Bass.

Leaper, C., and Gleason, J. B. 1996. The relationship of play activity and gender to parent and child sex-typed communication. *International Journal of Behavioral Development*, 19, 689–703.

Leaper, C., Anderson, K. J., and Sanders, P. In press. Moderators of gender effects on parents' talk to their children: A meta-analysis. *Developmental Psychology.*

Leaper, C., Hirsch, T., and Kremen, A. 1989. Parent-child sequences and the socialization of gender in preschool children. Paper presented at the biennial meeting of the Society for Research in Child Development, Kansas City, April.

Leaper, C., Leve, L., Strasser, T., and Schwartz, R. 1995. Mother-child communication sequences: Play activity, child gender, and marital status effects. *Merrill Palmer Quarterly*, 41(3), 307–327.

Lees, S. 1986. *Losing out: Sexuality and adolescent girls.* London: Hutchinson Education.

Legault, F., and Strayer, F. F. 1990. The emergence of gender-segregation in preschool peer groups. In F. F. Strayer, ed., *Social interaction and behavioral development during early childhood.* Annual research report, Laboratoire d'Ethologie Humaine, Département de Psychologie, Université de Québec à Montréal.

Leigh, B. C. 1989. Reasons for having sex: Gender, sexual orientation, and relationship to sexual behavior. *Journal of Sex Research*, 26, 199–209.

Leik, R. K. 1963. Instrumentality and emotionality in family interaction. *Sociometry*, 26, 131–145.

Leinbach, M. D. 1983. Gender discrimination in toddlers: Identifying pictures of male and female children and adults. Paper presented at the biennial meeting of the Society for Research in Child Development, Detroit, April.

———— 1993. Which one is the daddy? Children's use of conventionally and metaphorically gendered features to assign gender to animal figures. Poster presented at the biennial meeting of the Society for Research in Child Development, New Orleans, March.

Leinbach, M. D., and Fagot, B. I. 1986. Acquisition of gender labels: A test for toddlers. *Sex Roles*, 15, 655–666.

Levenson, R. W., Carstensen, L. L., and Gottman, J. M. 1994. The influence of age and gender on affect, physiology, and their interrelations. *Journal of Personality and Social Psychology*, 67, 56–68.

Lever, J. 1976. Sex differences in the games children play. *Social Problems*, 23, 478–487.

Levine, R., Dixon, S., Levine, S., Richman, A., Leiderman, P. H., Keefer, C. H., and Brazelton, T. B. 1994. *Child care and culture: Lessons from Africa.* New York: Cambridge University Press.

Levy, G. D., and Fivush, R. 1993. Scripts and gender: A new approach for examining gender role development. *Developmental Review*, 13, 126–146.

Lewis, C. E., and Lewis, M. A. 1984. Peer pressure and risk-taking behaviors in children. *American Journal of Public Health*, 74, 580–584.

Lewis, M., Allesandri, S. M., and Sullivan, M. W. 1992. Differences in shame and pride as a function of children's gender and task difficulty. *Child Development*, 63, 630–638.

Lloyd, B., and Duveen, G. 1992. *Gender identities and education: The impact of starting school.* New York: St. Martin's Press.

Lloyd, B., and Smith, C. 1986. The effects of age and gender on social behaviour in very young children. *British Journal of Social Psychology,* 25, 33–41.

Lockheed, M. E. 1984. Sex segregation and male preeminence in elementary classrooms. In E. Fennema and M. J. Ayer, ed., *Women and education: Equity or equality?* Berkeley: McCutchan.

———— 1985. Some determinants and consequences of sex segregation in the classroom. In L. C. Wilkinson and C. B. Marrett, ed., *Gender influences in classroom interaction.* Orlando: Academic Press.

Lockheed, M. E., and Hall, K. 1976. Conceptualizing sex as a status characteristic: Application to leadership training strategies. *Journal of Social Issues,* 32, 111–124.

Lockheed, M. E., and Harris, A. M. 1984. Cross-sex collaborative learning in elementary classrooms. *American Educational Research Journal,* 21(2), 275–294.

Lockheed, M. E., Amarel, M., Finkelstein, K. J., Harris, A. M., Flores, V., Holland, P., McDonald, F., Nemceff, W., and Stone, M. 1981. *Year one report: Classroom interaction, student cooperation, and leadership.* Princeton: Educational Testing Service.

Lovejoy, J., and Wallen, K. 1988. Sexually dimorphic behavior in group-housed rhesus monkeys *(Macaca mulatta)* at 1 year of age. *Psychobiology,* 16(4), 348–356.

Lundberg, U. 1983. Sex differences in behavior pattern and catecholamine and cortisol excretion in 3–6 year old day-care children. *Biological Psychology,* 16, 109–117.

———— 1986. Stress and Type A behavior in children. *Journal of the American Academy of Child Psychiatry,* 25(6), 771–778.

Lundberg, U., Westermark, O., and Rasch, B. 1987. *Type A behavior and physiological stress responses in preschool children: Sex differences at the ages of three and four.* Report from the Department of Psychology, University of Stockholm, no. 664.

Lytton, H. 1979. Disciplinary encounters between young boys and their mothers and fathers: Is there a contingency system? *Developmental Psychology,* 15, 256–268.

Lytton, H., and Romney, D. M. 1991. Parents' differential socialization of boys and girls: A meta-analysis. *Psychological Bulletin,* 109(2), 267–296.

Maccoby, E. E. 1966. *The development of sex differences.* Stanford: Stanford University Press.

———— 1980a. *Social development: Psychological growth and the parent-child relationship.* New York: Harcourt, Brace, Jovanovich.

———— 1980b. Commentary and reply on G. R. Patterson's monograph, *Mothers: The unacknowledged victims. Society for Research in Child Development Monographs,* 45, 56–64.

———— 1987. The varied meanings of "masculine" and "feminine." In J. M. Reinish, L. A. Rosenblum, and S. A. Sanders, ed., *Masculinity/femininity: Basic perspectives.* New York: Oxford University Press.

———— 1988. Gender as a social category. *Developmental Psychology,* 24, 755–765.

———— 1990. Gender and relationships: A developmental account. *American Psychologist,* 45, 513–520.

———— 1995. Divorce and custody: The rights, needs, and obligations of mothers, fathers, and children. In G. B. Melton, ed., *The individual, the family, and social good: Personal fulfillment in times of change,* pp. 135–172. Lincoln: University of Nebraska Press.

Maccoby, E. E., and Jacklin, C. N. 1974a. Myth, reality, and shades of gray: What we know and don't know about sex differences. *Psychology Today,* 8(7), 109–112.

——— 1974b. *The psychology of sex differences.* Stanford: Stanford University Press.

——— 1980. Sex differences in aggression: A rejoiner and reprise. *Child Development,* 51, 964–980.

——— 1983. The "person" characteristics of children and the family as environment. In D. Magnussen and V. Allen, ed., *Human development: An interactional perspective.* New York: Academic Press.

——— 1987. Gender segregation in childhood. In H. Reese, ed., *Advances in child behavior and development.* New York: Academic Press.

Maccoby, E. E., and Martin, J. A. 1983. Socialization in the context of the family: Parent-child interaction. In P. H. Mussen (general ed.) and E. M. Hetherington (series ed.), *Manual of child psychology,* vol. 4, *Social development.* New York: John Wiley.

Maccoby, E. E., and Mnookin, R. H. 1992. *Dividing the child: The social and legal dilemmas of custody.* Cambridge, Mass.: Harvard University Press.

Maccoby, E. E., Snow, M. E., and Jacklin, C. N. 1984. Children's dispositions and mother-child interaction at 12 and 18 months: A short-term longitudinal study. *Developmental Psychology,* 20, 459–472.

Maccoby, E. E., Buchanan, C. M., Mnookin, R. H., and Dornbusch, S. M. 1993. Postdivorce roles of mothers and fathers in the lives of their children. *Journal of Family Psychology,* 7(6), 24–38.

Maltz, D. N., and Borker, R. A. 1982. A cultural approach to male-female miscommunication. In J. J. Gumperz, ed., *Language and social identity,* pp. 195–216.

Mannle, S., and Tomasello, M. 1987. Fathers, siblings, and the bridge hypothesis. In K. A. Nelson and A. van Kleek, ed., *Children's language.* Hillsdale, N.J.: Lawrence Erlbaum.

Marcus, J., Maccoby, E. E., and Jacklin, C. N. 1985. Individual differences in mood in early childhood: Their relation to gender and neonatal sex steroids. *Developmental Psychobiology,* 18, 327–340.

Marini, M. M., and Brinton, M. C. 1984. Sex typing in occupational socialization. In B. F. Reskin, ed., *Sex segregation in the workplace.* Washington, D.C.: National Academy Press.

Markman, H. J. 1992. Marital and family psychology: Burning issues. *Journal of Family Psychology,* 5, 256–275.

Markman, E. M., and Carey, S. In press. Cognitive development. To appear in D. Rumelhart and B. Martin, ed., cognitive science volume of the *Handbook of cognition and perception.*

Markman, H. J., Renick, M. J., Floyd, F. J., Stanley, S. M. 1993. Preventing marital distress through communication and conflict management training: A 4- and 5-year follow-up. *Journal of Consulting and Clinical Psychology,* 61, 70–77.

Martin, B. 1975. Parent-child relations. In F. D. Horowitz, ed., *Review of Child Development Research.* Chicago: University of Chicago Press.

Martin, C. L. 1989. Children's use of gender-related information in making social judgments. *Developmental Psychology,* 25, 80–88.

——— 1993. New directions for investigating children's gender knowledge. *Developmental Review,* 13, 184–204.

———— 1994. Cognitive influences on the development and maintenance of gender segregation. In C. Leaper, ed., *Childhood gender segregation: Causes and consequences.* San Francisco: Jossey-Bass.

Martin, C. L., Eisenbud, L., and Rose, H. 1993. Children's gender-based reasoning about toys. *Child Development,* 66, 1453–1471.

Martin, J. A. 1981. A longitudinal study of the consequences of early mother-infant interaction: A microanalytic approach. *Monographs of the Society for Research in Child Development,* serial no. 190, 46(3).

Martin, J. A., King, D. R., Maccoby, E. E., and Jacklin, C. N. 1984. Secular trends and individual differences in toilet training progress. *Journal of Pediatric Psychology,* 9, 457–467.

Mason, W. A. 1961. The effects of social restriction on the behavior of rhesus monkeys: III dominance tests. *Journal of Comparative Physiological Psychology,* 54, 694–699.

Matthews, W. S. 1977. Sex role perception, portrayal, and preference in the fantasy play of young children. Paper presented at the biennial meeting of the Society for Research in Child Development, New Orleans, March.

McCabe, M. P., and Collins, J. K. 1990. *Dating, relating, and sex.* Sydney: Horowitz Grahame.

McClosky, L. A., and Coleman, L. M. 1992. Difference with dominance: Children's talk in mixed- and same-sex dyads. *Sex Roles,* 27, 241–257.

McKinney, K., and Sprecher, S., ed. 1991. *Sexuality in close relationships.* Hillsdale, N.J.: Lawrence Erlbaum.

McLaughlin, B. 1983. Child compliance to parental control techniques. *Developmental Psychology,* 19, 667–673.

McLaughlin, B., Schultz, C., and White, D. 1980. Parental speech to 5-year-old children in a game-playing situation. *Child Development,* 51, 580–582.

McLaughlin, M., Irby, M., and Langman, J. 1994. *Urban sanctuaries.* San Francisco: Jossey-Bass.

McLoyd, V. C. 1983. The effects of the structure of play objects on the pretend play of low-income preschool children. *Child Development,* 54(3), 626–635.

Meaney, M. J., Stewart, J., and Beatty, W. W. 1985. Sex differences in social play: The socialization of sex roles. In J. S. Rosenblatt, C. Beer, C. M. Busnell, and P. Stater, ed., *Advances in the study of behavior,* vol. 15, pp. 1–58. New York: Academic Press.

Miller, C. L. 1983. Developmental changes in male/female voice classification by infants. *Infant Behavior and Development,* 6, 313–330.

Miller, P. M., Danaher, D. L., and Forbes, D. 1986. Sex-related strategies for coping with interpersonal conflict in children aged five and seven. *Developmental Psychology,* 22(4), 543–548.

Miller, R. E., Caul, W. F., and Mirsky, I. A. 1967. Communication of affects between feral and socially isolated monkeys. *Journal of Personality and Social Psychology,* 7, 231–239.

Milwid, B. 1990. *Working with men: Professional women talk about power, sexuality, and ethics.* Hillboro, Ore.: Beyond Words Publishing.

Minton, C., Kagan, J., and Levine, J. A. 1971. Maternal control and obedience in the two-year-old. *Child Development,* 42, 1873–1894.

Mischel, W. 1966. A social-learning view of sex differences in behavior. In E. E. Maccoby, ed., *The development of sex differences.* Stanford: Stanford University Press.

Mitchell, G. 1972. Looking behavior in the rhesus monkey. *Journal of Phenomological Psychology,* 3, 53–67.

Money, J., and Ehrhardt, A. A. 1972. *Man and woman, boy and girl: The differentiation and dimorphism of gender identity from conception to maturity.* Baltimore: The Johns Hopkins University Press.

Montepare, J. M. 1993. Young children's age- and gender-based self-perceptions and perceptions of others. Paper presented at the biennial meeting of the Society for Research in Child Development, New Orleans.

Moore, S., and Rosenthal, D. 1993. *Sexuality in adolescence.* London: Routledge.

Moskowitz, D. S., Suh, E. J., and Desaulniers, J. 1993. Situational influences on gender differences in agency and communion. Paper presented at the annual meeting of the Canadian Psychological Association, Montreal, May.

Muelenhard, C. L., and Cook, S. W. 1988. Men's self-report on unwanted sexual activity. *Journal of Sex Research,* 24, 58–72.

Newson, J., and Newson, E. 1968. *Four years old in an urban community.* Harmondsworth, Eng.: Penguin Books.

Nicolopoulou, A. 1997. Worldmaking and identity formation in children's narrative play-acting. In B. Cox and C. Lightfoot, ed., *Sociogenic perspectives in internalization,* pp. 157–187. Hillsdale, N.J.: Lawrence Erlbaum.

Nicolopoulou, A., Scales, B., and Weintraub, J. 1994. Gender differences and symbolic imagination in the stories of four-year-olds. In A. H. Dyson and C. Geneshi, ed., *The need for story: Cultural diversity in classroom and community,* pp. 102–123. Urbana: National Council of Teachers of English.

O'Brien, M., and Huston, A. C. 1985. Development of sex-typed play behavior in toddlers. *Developmental Psychology,* 21, 866–871.

O'Donnell, C. 1984. *The basis of the bargain.* Sydney: Allen and Unwin.

Omark, D. R., Omark, M., and Edelman, M. 1973. Formation of dominance hierarchies in young children. In T. R. Williams, ed., *Psychological anthropology.* The Hague: Mouton.

Pahl, R. E. 1984. *Divisions of labor.* Oxford: Basil Blackwell.

Parke, R. D. 1967. Nurturance, nurturance withdrawal, and resistance to deviation. *Child Development,* 38, 1101–1110.

Parke, R. D., and Slaby, R. G. 1983. The development of aggression. In P. Mussen, ed., and E. M. Hetherington (vol. ed.), *Handbook of child psychology,* vol. 4, *Socialization, personality, and social development,* pp. 547–641. New York: John Wiley.

Parke, R. D., and Tinsley, B. R. 1981. The father's role in infancy: Determinants of involvement in caregiving and play. In M. E. Lamb, ed., *The role of the father in child development.* New York: John Wiley.

Parpal, M., and Maccoby, E. E. 1985. Maternal responsiveness and subsequent child compliance. *Child Development,* 56, 1326–1334.

Parsons, A. 1964. Is the Oedipus complex universal? The Jones-Malinowski debate revisited, and a south Italian "nuclear complex." *The Psychoanalytic Study of Society,* 3, 278–326.

Parsons, T. 1955. Family structure and the socialization of the child. In T. Parsons and R. F. Bales, ed., *Family, socialization, and interaction process,* pp. 35–131. Glencoe, Ill.: The Free Press.

Parsons, T., and Bales, R. F. 1955. *Family, socialization, and interaction process.* Glencoe, Ill.: The Free Press.

Patterson, G. R. 1980. Mothers: The unacknowledged victims. *Monographs of the Society for Research in Child Development,* 45(5).

———— 1982. *A social learning approach,* vol. 3, *Coercive family process.* Eugene, Ore.: Castalia.

Patterson, G. R., Reid, J. B., and Dishion, T. J. 1992. *A social learning approach,* vol. 4, *Antisocial boys.* Eugene, Ore.: Castalia.

Peplau, A. 1979. Power in dating relationships. In J. Freeman, ed., *Women: A feminist perspective.* Palo Alto, Calif.: Mayfield.

Perlmann, R. Y. 1984. Variations in socialization styles: Family talk at the dinner table. Ph.D. diss., Boston University.

Perret-Clermont, A. N., Perret, J. F., and Bell, N. 1991. The social construction of meaning and cognitive activity in elementary school children. In L. Resnick, J. M. Levine, and S. D. Teasley, ed., *Perspectives on socially shared cognition,* pp. 41–62. Washington, D.C.: American Psychological Association.

Perry, D. G., and Bussey, K. 1979. The social learning theory of sex differences: Initiation is alive and well. *Journal of Personality and Social Psychology,* 37, 1699–1712.

Perry, D. G., Perry, L. C., and Weiss, R. J. 1989. Sex differences in the consequences that children anticipate for aggression. *Developmental Psychology,* 25, 312–319.

Perry, D. G., White, A. J., and Perry, L. C. 1984. Does early sex typing result from children's attempts to match their behavior to sex role stereotypes? *Child Development,* 55, 2114–2121.

Peters, H. E., and Argys, L. M. 1990. *Economic consequences of divorce.* Mimeograph, University of Colorado, Boulder.

Peters, H. E., Argys, L. M., Maccoby, E. E., and Mnookin, R. H. 1993. Enforcing divorce settlements: Evidence from child support compliance and award modifications. *Demography,* 30(4), 719–735.

Petit, G. S., Bakshi, A., Dodge, K. A., and Coie, J. D. 1990. The emergence of social dominance in young boys' play groups: Developmental differences and behavioral correlates. *Developmental Psychology,* 26, 1017–1025.

Phoenix, C. H., Goy, R. W., and Young, W. C. 1967. Sexual behavior: General aspects. In L. Martini and W. F. Ganong, ed., *Neuroendocrinology,* vol. 2. New York: Academic Press.

Pipher, M. 1994. *Reviving Ophelia: Saving the selves of adolescent girls.* New York: Ballantine Books.

Pitcher, E. G., and Schultz, L. H. 1983. *Boys and girls at play: The development of sex roles.* South Hadley, Mass.: Bergin and Garvey.

Poulin-Dubois, D., Serbin, L. A., Kenyon, B., and Derbyshire, A. 1991. Intermodal gender concepts in 12-month-old infants. Paper presented at the biennial meeting of the Society for Research in Child Development, Seattle, April.

Powell, G. N. 1990. One more time: Do female and male managers differ? *The Academy of Management Executives,* 4(3), 68–75.

Power, T. G. 1985. Mother- and father-infant play: A developmental analysis. *Child Development,* 56, 1514–1524.

Power, T. G., and Parke, R. D. 1986. Patterns of early socialization: Mother- and father-infant interaction in the home. *International Journal of Behavioral Development,* 9, 331–341.

Power, T. G., McGrath, M. P., Hughes, S. O., and Manire, S. H. 1994. Compliance and self-assertion: Young children's responses to mothers versus fathers. *Developmental Psychology*, 30(6), 980–988.

Powlishta, K. K. 1995. Intergroup processes in childhood: Social categorization and sex-role development. *Developmental Psychology*, 3(5), 781–788.

Powlishta, K. K., and Maccoby, E. E. 1990. Resource utilization in mixed-sex dyads: The influence of adult presence and task type. *Sex Roles*, 23, 223–240.

Presser, H. B. 1989. Can we make time for children? The economy, work schedules, and child care. *Demography*, 26(4), 523–543.

Putallaz, M., and Sheppard, B. H. 1992. Conflict management and social competence. In C. U. Shantz and W. W. Hartup ed., *Conflict in child and adolescent development*. New York: Cambridge University Press.

Putallaz, M., and Wasserman, A. 1989. Children's naturalistic entry behavior and sociometric status: A developmental perspective. *Developmental Psychology*, 25(2), 297–305.

Radin, N. 1988. Primary care-giving fathers of long duration. In P. Bronstein and C. P. Cowan, ed., *Fatherhood today: Men's changing role in the family*. New York: John Wiley.

Radke-Yarrow, M., Zahn-Waxler, C., and Chapman, M. 1983. Children's prosocial dispositions and behavior. In P. H. Mussen, ed., *Handbook of child psychology*, 4th ed., vol. 4, *Socialization, personality, and social development*. New York: John Wiley.

Radke-Yarrow, M., Belmont, B., Nottelman, E., and Bottomly, L. 1990. Young children's self-conceptions: Origins in the natural discourse of depressed and normal mothers and their children. In D. Cicchetti and M. Beeghly, ed., *The self in transition: Infancy to childhood*. Chicago: University of Chicago Press.

Ragins, B. R., and Sundstrom, E. 1989. Gender and power in organizations: A longitudinal perspective. *Psychological Bulletin*, 105(1), 51–88.

Redican, W. K., and Taub, D. 1981. Male parental care in monkeys and apes. In M. Lamb, ed., *The role of the father in child development*. New York: John Wiley.

Reskin, B. F. 1993. Sex segregation in the workplace. *Annual Review of Sociology*, 19, 241–270.

Reskin, B. F., and Roos, P. 1990. *Job queues and gender queues: Explaining women's inroads into male occupations*. Philadelphia: Temple University Press.

Richards, M. H., and Larson, R. 1993. Pubertal development and the daily subjective states of young adolescents. *Journal of Research on Adolescence*, 3, 145–169.

Roopnarine, J. L. 1986. Mothers' and fathers' behaviors toward the toy play of their infant sons and daughters. *Sex Roles*, 14, 59–68.

Roscoe, B., Diana, M. S., and Brooks, R. H., 1987. Early, middle, and late adolescents' views on dating and factors influencing partner selection. *Adolescence*, 22, 59–68.

Ross, H., and Taylor, H. 1989. Do boys prefer daddy or his physical style of play? *Sex Roles*, 20, 23–33.

Rothbart, M. K., and Bates, J. E. 1997. Temperament. In W. Damon and N. Eisenberg, ed., *Handbook of child psychology*, vol. 3, *Social, emotional, and personality development*, 5th ed. New York: John Wiley.

Rothbart, M. K., Posner, M. I., and Rosicky, J. 1994. Orienting in normal and pathological development. *Development and Psychopathology*, 6, 635–652.

Rubin, J. Z., Provenzano, F. J., and Luria, Z. 1974. The eye of the beholder: Parents' view on sex of newborns. *American Journal of Orthopsychiatry*, 44, 512–519.

Ruble, D. N., and Martin, C. L. 1997. Gender development. In W. Damon and N. Eisenberg, ed., *Handbook of child psychology,* vol. 3, *Social, emotional, and personality development.*

Ruble, D. N., Balaban, T., and Cooper, J. 1981. Gender constancy and the effects of sex-typed televised toy commercials. *Child Development,* 52, 667–673.

Ruble, D. N., Fleming, A. S., Hackel, L. S., and Stangor, C. 1988. Changes in the marital relationship during the transition to first-time motherhood: Effects of violated expectations concerning division of household labor. *Journal of Personality and Social Psychology,* 55, 78–87.

Russell, G. 1982. Shared care-giving families: An Australian study. In M. E. Lamb, ed., *Nontraditional families: Parenting and child development.* Hillsdale, N.J.: Lawrence Erlbaum.

Russell, G., and Russell, A. 1987. Mother-child and father-child relationships in middle childhood. *Child Development,* 58, 1573–1585.

Sachs, J. 1987. Preschool boys' and girls' language use in pretend play. In S. U. Phillips, S. Steele, and C. Tanz, ed., *Language, gender, and sex in comparative perspective,* pp. 178–188. Cambridge: Cambridge University Press.

Sackett, G. P. 1974. Sex differences in rhesus monkeys following varied rearing experiences. In R. C. Friedman, R. M. Richart, and R. L. Van de Wiele, ed., *Sex differences in behavior,* pp. 99–112. New York: John Wiley.

Sanders, K. M., and Harper, L. V. 1976. Free-play fantasy behavior in preschool children: Relations among gender, age, season, and location. *Child Development,* 47(4), 1182–1185.

Sayed, H., and Tzannatos, Z. 1995. Sex segregation in the labor force. Washington, D.C.: World Bank.

Schachter, F. F., Shore, E., Hoddapp, R., Chaflin, S., and Bundy, C. 1978. Do girls talk earlier?: Mean length of utterance in toddlers. *Developmental Psychology,* 14, 388–392.

Schaffer, H. R., and Crook, C. K. 1980. Child compliance and maternal control techniques. *Developmental Psychology,* 16, 54–61.

Schelling, T. C. 1971. Dynamic models of segregation. *Journal of Mathematical Sociology,* 1–2, 143–186.

Schofield, V. W. 1981. Complimentary and conflicting identities: Images of interaction in an interracial school. In S. A. Asher and J. M. Gottman, ed., *The development of children's friendships.* New York: Cambridge University Press.

Selman, R. L., and Yeates, K. O. 1987. Childhood social regulation of intimacy and autonomy in early adolescence. In W. M. Kurtines and J. L. Gewirtz, ed., *Moral development through social interaction,* pp. 44–101. New York: John Wiley.

Serbin, L. A., Poulin-Dubois, D., and Colburne, K. 1995. Self-categorization by gender in the second year of life. Poster presented at the biennial meeting of the Society for Research in Child Development, Indianapolis, March.

Serbin, L. A., Powlishta, K. K., and Gulko, J. 1993. The development of sex typing in middle childhood. *Monographs of the Society for Research in Child Development,* 58(2), 1–74.

Serbin, L. A., Tronick, I. J., and Sternglanz, S. H. 1977. Shaping cooperative cross-sex play. *Child Development,* 48, 924–929.

Serbin, L. A., Sprafkin, C., Elman, M., and Doyle, A. B. 1984. The early development of sex differentiated patterns of social influence. *Canadian Journal of Social Science,* 14(4), 350–363.

Serbin, L. A., Moller, L. C., Gulko, J., Powlishta, K. K., Colburne, K. A. 1994. The emergence of gender segregation in toddler playgroups. In C. Leaper, ed., *Childhood gender segregation: Causes and consequences.* San Francisco: Jossey-Bass.

Shaw, M. E., and Sadler, O. W. 1965. Interaction patterns in heterosexual dyads varying in degree of intimacy. *Journal of Social Psychology,* 66, 345–351.

Sheldon, A. 1990. Pickle fights: Gendered talk in preschool disputes. *Discourse Processes,* 13, 5–31.

———— 1992. Preschool girls' discourse competence: Managing conflict and negotiating power. In M. Bucholtz, K. Hall, and B. Moonwomon, ed., *Locating power,* vol. 2 of the *Proceedings of the 1992 Berkeley Women and Language Conference,* pp. 528–539. Berkeley: Berkeley Linguistic Society.

Sheldon, A., and Rohleder, L. 1995. Sharing the same world, telling different stories: Gender differences in co-constructed pretend narratives. In D. Slobin, J. Gerhardt, A. Kyratzis, and G. Jiansheng, ed., *Social interaction, social context, and language.* New York: Lawrence Erlbaum.

Shucard, D. W., Shucard, J. L., and Thomas, D. G. 1987. Sex differences in the patterns of scalp-recorded electrophysiological activity in infancy: Possible implications for language development. In S. U. Phillips, S. Steele, and C. Tanz, ed., *Language, gender, and sex in comparative perspective.* New York: Cambridge University Press.

Siegel, M. 1987. Are sons and daughters treated more differently by fathers than mothers? *Developmental Review,* 7, 183–209.

Signorella, M. L., Bigler, R. S., and Liben, L. S. 1993. Developmental differences in children's gender schemata about others: A meta-analytic review. *Developmental Review,* 13, 147–183.

Slaby, R. G. 1990. The gender concept development legacy. In D. Schrader, ed., *The legacy of Lawrence Kohlberg,* pp. 21–30. San Francisco: Jossey-Bass.

Slaby, R. G., and Frey, K. S. 1975. Development of gender constancy and selective attention to same-sex models. *Child Development,* 46, 840–856.

Smetana, J. G. 1989. Toddlers' social interactions in the context of moral and conventional transgressions in the home. *Developmental Psychology,* 25, 499–509.

Smetena, J. G., and Letourneau, K. J. 1984. Development of gender constancy and children's sex-typed free play behavior. *Developmental Psychology,* 20, 691–696.

Smith, P. K., and Boulton, M. 1990. Rough and tumble play, aggression, and dominance: Perception and behavior in children's encounters. *Human Development,* 33(4–5), 271–282.

Smith, P. K., and Daglish, L. 1977. Sex differences in parent and infant behavior in the home. *Child Development,* 48, 1250–1254.

Snow, M. E., Jacklin, C. N., and Maccoby, E. E. 1983. Sex-of-child differences in father-child interaction at one year of age. *Child Development,* 54, 227–232.

Snyder, J. J., and Patterson, G. R. 1995. Individual differences in social aggression: A test of a reinforcement model of socialization in the natural environment. *Behavior Therapy,* 26, 371–391.

Spelke, E. S. 1988. Where perceiving ends and thinking begins: The apprehension of objects in infancy. In A. Yonas, ed., *Perceptual development in infancy.* Minnesota Symposium on child psychology, vol. 20. Hillsdale, N.J.: Lawrence Erlbaum.

Sroufe, L. A., Bennett, C., Englund, M., Urban, J., and Shulman, S. 1993. The significance of gender boundaries in preadolescence: Contemporary correlates and antecedents of boundary violation and maintenance. *Child Development*, 64(2), 455–466.

Steinberg, L. 1987. Recent research on the family at adolescence: The extent and nature of sex differences. *Journal of Youth and Adolescence*, 16, 191–197.

Stern, J. M. 1989. Maternal behavior: Sensory, hormonal, and neural determinants. In F. R. Brush and S. Levine, ed., *Psychoendocrinology*. San Diego: Academic Press.

Stern, M., and Karraker, K. H. 1989. Sex stereotyping of infants: A review of gender labeling studies. *Sex Roles*, 20, 501–522.

Stoddard, T., and Turiel, E. 1985. Children's concepts of cross-gender activities. *Child Development*, 56, 1241–1252.

Stone, P. J. 1972. Child care in twelve countries. In A. Szalai, ed., *The use of time: Daily activities of urban and suburban populations in twelve countries*. The Hague: Mouton.

Straus, M. A., and Gelles, R. J. 1986. Societal change in family violence from 1975 to 1985 as revealed by two national surveys. *Journal of Marriage and the Family*, 48, 465–479.

Strayer, F. F. 1977. Peer attachment and affiliative subgroups. In F. F. Strayer, ed., *Ethological perspectives on preschool social organization*. Memo de Recherche 5, Département de Psychologie, Université de Québec.

——— 1980a. Child ethology and the study of preschool social relations. In H. C. Foot, A. J. Chapman, and J. R. Smith, ed., *Friendship and social relations in children*. New York: John Wiley.

——— 1980b. Social ecology of the preschool peer group. In W. A. Collins, ed., *Development of cognition, affect, and social relations*. Minnesota Symposium on Child Psychology, vol. 13. Hillsdale, N.J.: Lawrence Erlbaum.

——— 1985. The origins of sexually based peer discriminations. Paper presented at the biennial meeting of the Society for Research in Child Development, Toronto.

Strayer, F. F., and Strayer, J. 1976. An ethological analysis of social agonism and dominance relations among preschool children. *Child Development*, 47(4), 980–989.

Strober, M. H., and Arnold, C. L. 1987. Integrated circuits/segregated labor: Women in computer-related occupations in high-tech industries. In H. Hartman, ed., *Computer chips and paper clips: Technology and women's employment*. Washington, D.C.: National Academy Press.

Strober, M. H., and Catanzarite, L. M. 1994. The relative attractiveness theory of occupational segregation by gender. In P. Beckmann and G. Englebrech, ed., *Arbeitsmarkt für Frauen 200: Ein Schritt vor oder ein Schritt zurück?* Nuremberg: Institut für Arbeitsmarkt-und Berufsforschung der Bundesanstalt für Arbeit.

Strober, M. H., and Gallagher, T. 1992. Abandoned tracks: Gender and clerical work in the railroad industry, 1930–1987. Unpublished manuscript.

Tajfel, H. 1982. Social psychology of intergroup relations. *Annual Review of Psychology*, 33, 1–39.

Tannen, D. 1990. *You just don't understand: Women and men in conversation*. New York: William Morrow.

——— 1994. *Talking from Nine to Five*. New York: William Morrow.

Tanner, J. M. 1970. Physical growth. In P. Mussen, ed., *Carmichael's manual of child psychology,* 3rd ed. New York: John Wiley.

Tauber, M. A. 1979. Sex differences in parent-child interaction styles during a free-play session. *Child Development,* 50, 981–988.

Taylor, M. G. 1995. Relations between children's gender-role flexibility and beliefs about the development of gender differences. Poster presented at the biennial meeting of the Society for Research in Child Development, Indianapolis, March.

Theokas, C., Ramsey, P. G., Sweeney, B. 1993. The effects of classroom interventions on young children's cross-sex contacts and perceptions. Paper presented at the biennial meeting of the Society for Research in Child Development, New Orleans, March.

Thompson, L., and Walker, A. J. 1989. Gender in families: Women and men in marriage, work, and parenthood. *Journal of Marriage and the Family,* 51, 845–871.

Thompson, S. K. 1975. Gender labels and early sex role development. *Child Development,* 46, 339–347.

Thompson, S. K., and Bentler, P. M. 1971. The priority of cues in sex discrimination by children and adults. *Developmental Psychology,* 5, 181–185.

Thorne, B. 1986. Girls and boys together, but mostly apart: Gender arrangements in elementary schools. In W. W. Hartup and Z. Rubin, ed., *Relationships and development.* Hillsdale, N.J.: Lawrence Erlbaum.

———— 1994. *Gender play: Girls and boys in school.* New Brunswick, N.J.: Rutgers University Press.

Thorne, B., and Luria, Z. 1986. Sexuality and gender in children's daily worlds. *Social Problems,* 33, 176–190.

Tomaskovic-Devey, D. 1995. Sex composition and gendered earnings inequality: A comparison of job and occupational models. In J. A. Jacobs, ed., *Gender inequality at work.* Thousand Oaks, Calif.: Sage Publications.

Tronick, E. Z., and Cohn, J. F. 1989. Infant-mother face to face interaction: Age and gender differences in coordination and the occurrence of miscoordination. *Child Development,* 60, 85–92.

Turner, P. J., and Gervai, J. 1995. A multidimensional study of gender typing in preschool children and their parents: Personality, attitudes, preferences, behavior, and cultural differences. *Developmental Psychology,* 31(5), 759–779.

Turner, P. J., Gervai, J., and Hinde, R. A. 1993. Gender-typing in young children: Preferences, behaviour, and cultural differences. *British Journal of Developmental Psychology,* 11, 323–342.

Tyack, D., and Hansot, E. 1990. *Learning together: A history of coeducation in American schools.* New Haven: Yale University Press.

Tyack, D., and Strober, M. H. 1981. Jobs and gender: A history of the structuring of educational employment by sex. In P. Schmuck and W. W. Charters, ed., *Educational policy and management: Sex differentials.* New York: Academic Press.

U.S. Bureau of the Census. 1992. Current population reports. In *Marriage, divorce, and remarriage in the 1990's,* pp. 23–180. Washington, D.C.: U.S. Government Printing Office.

Van Leishout, C. F. M. 1975. Young children's reactions to barriers placed by their mothers. *Child Development,* 46, 879–886.

Verba, S. 1961. *Small groups and political behavior.* Princeton: Princeton University Press.

Wallen, K., Maestripieri, D., and Mann, D. R. 1995. Effects of neonatal testicular suppression with GnRH antagonist on social behavior in group-living juvenile rhesus monkeys. *Hormones and Behavior*, 29, 322–337.

Wasserman, G. A., and Stern, D. N. 1978. An early manifestation of differential behavior toward children of the same and opposite sex. *The Journal of Genetic Psychology*, 133, 129–137.

Wehren, A., and DiLisi, R. 1983. The development of gender understanding: Judgments and explanations. *Child Development*, 54, 1568–1578.

Weinberg, K. 1992. Boys and girls: Sex differences in emotional expressivity and self-regulation during early infancy. Paper presented in the symposium conducted at the International Conference on Infant Studies (ICIS), Miami, May.

Weinraub, M., Clemens, L. P., Sockloff, A., Etheridge, R., Gracely, E., and Myers, B. 1984. The development of sex role stereotypes in the third year: Relationships to gender labeling, gender identity, sex-typed toy preferences, and family characteristics. *Child Development*, 55, 1493–1503.

Weisner, T. S. 1994. Domestic tasks, gender egalitarian values, and children's gender typing in conventional and nonconventional families. *Sex Roles*, 30(1–2), 23–54.

Weiss, D., and Sachs, J. 1991. Persuasive strategies used by preschool children. *Discourse Processes*, 14, 55–72.

Werker, J. F., and McLeod, P. J. 1989. Infant preference for both male and female infant-directed talk: A developmental study of attentional and affective responsiveness. *Canadian Journal of Psychology*, 43(2), 230–246.

Whiting, B. B., and Edwards, C. P. 1988. *Children of different worlds: The formation of social behavior*. Cambridge, Mass.: Harvard University Press.

Whiting, B. B., and Whiting, J. W. M. 1975. *Children of six cultures*. Cambridge, Mass.: Harvard University Press.

Williams, C. L. 1989. *Gender differences at work: Women and men in nontraditional occupations*. Berkeley: University of California Press.

——— 1995. *Still a man's world: Men who do women's work*. Berkeley: University of California Press.

Wolf, A. 1995. *Sexual attraction and childhood association: A Chinese brief for Edward Westermarck*. Stanford: Stanford University Press.

Wolpe, A. M. 1988. *Within school walls: The role of discipline, sexuality, and the curriculum*. London: Routledge.

Wortman, C., Biernat, M., and Land, E. 1991. Coping with role overload. In M. Frankenhaeuser, U. Lundberg, and M. Chesney, ed., *Women, work, and health: Stress and opportunities*. New York: Plenum.

Wright, R., and Jacobs, J. A. 1995. Male flight from computer work: A new look at occupational resegregation and ghettoization. In J. A. Jacobs, ed., *Gender inequality at work*. Thousand Oaks, Calif.: Sage Publications.

Yogman, M. W. 1981. Development of the father-infant relationship. In H. Fitzgerald, B. Lester, and M. W. Yogman, ed., *Theory and research in behavioral pediatrics*, vol. 1. New York: Plenum.

Youniss, J., and Smollar, J. 1985. *Adolescent relations with mothers, fathers, and friends*. Chicago: University of Chicago Press.

Zahn-Waxler, C., Cole, P., and Barrett, K. C. 1991. Guilt and empathy: Sex differences and implications for the development of depression. In J. Garber and K. Dodge, ed., *The development of emotion regulation and dysregulation*. New York: Cambridge University Press.

Index

Abelson, R. P., 163
Abuse, 219, 223
Activation, state of, 99–105
Active vs. passive trait, 2, 87, 144
Activity: and adreno-genital syndrome, 112;
   and boys, 55, 100–103, 110, 213, 226; and
   boy vs. girl, 44–46, 85–86, 110, 115, 124,
   125, 126, 185; and friendship, 55, 226; and
   gender segregation, 110–111; and language, 125; level of, 100–103, 110; and maturity, 102; and metabolism rate, 115;
   nature of, 102; and parental treatment,
   124, 125, 126; and partner compatibility,
   84; preference in, 84, 85–86; and same-sex
   preference, 290; and sex-typing, 144, 172;
   sharing, 213, 226; and stereotypes, 165, 171
Adolescence, 1, 229; and child care, 263; and
   cross-sex interaction, 69–70, 191–215; and
   discourse, 196–197; and father vs. mother,
   276, 279; and gender segregation, 224;
   influence of childhood on, 192, 195, 197;
   and single-sex education, 309; and teasing,
   69–70
Adornment, 42, 85. *See also* Attractiveness
Adrenaline, 103, 104
Adreno-genital syndrome, 112, 114, 117,
   320n5, 323n32
ADS. *See* Attention deficit syndrome
Adults, 191–286; and arousability, 103–104;
   and boys, 52–53, 65, 77, 94–95, 96, 116–
   117, 147, 164, 252, 289, 297–298, 320n30;
   and child's interest, 232; culture of, 144,
   149, 151; and gender labeling, 293; and
   gender segregation, 28, 288; and girls, 63,

73, 94, 289, 320n30; and group care, 20;
   influence of childhood on (*see* Influence);
   knowledge of gender, 144; as models, 177–
   178; separation from, 52–53, 77, 94–95,
   98, 99, 114, 116–117, 147, 164, 289, 291,
   297–298; and socialization, 3–5; and structure, 20, 25, 26–27, 28, 30, 73, 229, 289,
   295, 305–306, 312. *See also* Parents
Adultery, 94
Adventure, 178, 209, 242, 243–244. *See also*
   Heroism
Affection, 124, 125, 144
Affiliative behavior. *See* Same-sex preferences
Africa, 20, 21, 149–150, 193
African Americans, 207–208
Age: and aggression, 35; and child care, 257;
   discrepancy of in couples, 213; and exclusion, 240; and socialization, 129; and Stanford longitudinal study, 124; and
   stereotypes, 169–170
Agentic action, 249
Aggression: and age, 35; and boys, 34–37, 39,
   40, 41, 57, 80, 130, 131–132, 133, 306; and
   boy vs. girl, 130, 133; and deviance, 37;
   and dominance, 38, 93; and evolution,
   290; and family, 131; and fantasy themes,
   43, 44; and fourth year, 35; and girls, 35,
   36, 40, 41, 57, 80, 130, 133–134; and hierarchy, 38, 93; and individual, 36, 37; and
   nurturance, 114; and parent, 130, 134–
   135; and personality, 36, 37; physical, 40–
   41; and primates, 93, 99; and sex, 210; and
   sex difference, 98; and socialization, 130;
   and third year, 35–36; and toddlers, 36